Letters to W.B. Yeats and Ezra Pound from Iseult Gonne

*Other publications by A. Norman Jeffares*:

Trinity College, Dublin: Drawings and Descriptions
W.B. Yeats: Man and Poet
Oliver Goldsmith
The Poetry of W.B. Yeats
George Moore
The Circus Animals: Essays on W.B. Yeats
A Commentary on the Collected Poems of W.B. Yeats
A Commentary on the Collected Plays of W.B. Yeats (with A.S. Knowland)
Jonathan Swift
A History of Anglo-Irish Literature
Brought up in Dublin (poems)
Brought up to Leave (poems)
A New Commentary on the Poems of W.B. Yeats
A Pocket History of Irish Literature
W.B. Yeats: A New Biography
Images of Imagination: Essays on Irish Writing
The Irish Literary Movement

*Edited works include*:
Poems of W.B. Yeats
Selected Poems of W.B. Yeats
Selected Prose of W.B. Yeats
Selected Plays of W.B. Yeats
Selected Criticism of W.B. Yeats
Cowper: Selected Poems and Letters
W.B. Yeats: The Critical Heritage
Whitman: Selected Poems and Prose
Restoration Drama (4 vols)
Yeats, Sligo and Ireland
Poems of W.B. Yeats: A New Selection
Yeats's Poems
Yeats the European
W.B. Yeats: A Vision and Related Writings
The Gonne–Yeats Letters: Always Your Friend (with Anna MacBride White)
Swift: The Selected Poems
Victorian Love Poems
Irish Love Poems
Irish Childhoods (with Antony Kamm)
W.B. Yeats: The Love Poems
Ireland's Women: Writings Past and Present (with Katie Donovan and Brendan
    Kennelly)
James Joyce: The Poems in Verse and Prose (with Brendan Kennelly)
The Love Poems of Ireland: Wonder and a Wild Desire
Oliver St John Gogarty: Poems and Plays

# Letters to W.B. Yeats and Ezra Pound from Iseult Gonne

## A girl that knew all Dante once

Edited by

A. Norman Jeffares

Anna MacBride White

and

Christina Bridgwater

First published 2004 by
PALGRAVE MACMILLAN
Houndmills, Basingstoke, Hampshire RG21 6XS and
175 Fifth Avenue, New York, N.Y. 10010
Companies and representatives throughout the world

PALGRAVE MACMILLAN is the global academic imprint of the Palgrave Macmillan division of St. Martin's Press, LLC and of Palgrave Macmillan Ltd. Macmillan® is a registered trademark in the United States, United Kingdom and other countries. Palgrave is a registered trademark in the European Union and other countries.

ISBN 1–4039–2134–2 hardback

This book is printed on paper suitable for recycling and made from fully managed and sustained forest sources.

A catalogue record for this book is available from the British Library.

Library of Congress Cataloging-in-Publication Data
Gonne, Iseult, 1894–
    [Correspondence. Selections] Letters to W.B. Yeats and Ezra Pound from Iseult Gonne, a girl that knew all Dante once edited by A. Norman Jeffares, Anna MacBride White, and Christina Bridgwater.
        p.  cm.
    Includes bibliographical references and index.
    ISBN 1–4039–2134–2
    1. Yeats, W.B. (William Butler), 1865–1939—Correspondence.  2. Yeats, W.B. (William Butler), 1865–1939—Relations with women.  3. Pound, Ezra, 1885–1972—Relations with women.  4. Poets, American—20th century—Correspondence.  5. Poets, Irish—20th century—Correspondence.  6. Gonne, Iseult, 1894—Relations with men.  7. Pound, Ezra, 1885–1972—Correspondence.  8. Gonne, Iseult, 1894—Correspondence.  9. Women—Ireland—Correspondence.  I. Yeats, W.B. (William Butler), 1865–1939.  II. Pound, Ezra, 1885–1972.  III. Jeffares, A. Norman (Alexander Norman), 1920–  IV. White, Anna MacBride.  V. Bridgwater, Christina.  VI. Title

PR5906.A44 2003
821'.8—dc22                                                2003056398
[B]

10  9  8  7  6  5  4  3  2  1
13  12  11  10  09  08  07  06  05  04

Printed and bound in Great Britain by
Antony Rowe Ltd, Chippenham and Eastbourne

52575617

*To Jeanne, Kay and Thora*

# Contents

# List of Illustrations

# Foreword

As a granddaughter of Iseult Gonne, I am delighted that the opportunity is now here for her voice to be properly heard. It is undoubtedly a valuable voice within the context of her friendship with Yeats and Pound, but also very interesting for the intrinsic worth of her thoughts and activities, these revealing her to be a very different character from her mother, Maud.

My own mother, Kay Bridgwater, spent many years researching and exploring Iseult's life, aiming to publish an edited volume of her correspondence with Yeats and Pound and I would like to acknowledge here the enormous amount of work Kay did towards that end. She was very attached to her mother and was anxious that justice should be done to her as a person and to her various intellectual interests and friendships. Her very nearness to Iseult made this work difficult, and the Bridgwater family are very grateful to Anna MacBride White and Derry Jeffares for stepping in after Kay's death to take on the task of producing this edition. Anna and Kay partly grew up together in the Gonne household, so Anna is in a position to pass on a sense of the flow of Iseult's life as understood within the family.

There is, for us all, very much a sense of gladness, and indeed relief, that others will now be able to hear Iseult speak for herself through these letters.

CHRISTINA BRIDGWATER

# Editors' Note

Iseult wrote her letters on various notepapers; the dates are often not precise. In editing them we have regularised the position of address and date at the top right of the letter. Where we have estimated the place, month and year we give these in square brackets. We also use square brackets where we supply letters or words omitted or, rarely, for a word in error. Uncertain words or readings are preceded by a question mark in square brackets. Where the script occasionally presents particular difficulty we have inserted '[indecipherable]'. Passages or words underlined once are in italics, but where Iseult underlined her signature or address we have retained the underlining in the text (see pp. 81, 82, 85, 104, 109–12, 115–19, 121, 122, 124, 127 and 128). Any words in capitals are printed thus.

Iseult misspelt some English words and we have retained these misspellings if only to remind us that she regarded English as her second language. We have given the titles of books, poems or articles as she wrote them. We have also retained her punctuation and syntax.

Our notes attempt to identify individuals and subjects mentioned in the text, although in some few cases identification of minor characters has proved impossible. The linking passages and notes offer some guidance to public events where these seem germane, and to the details of lives which impinged on the Gonne family. Abbreviated source references are included in the Notes. A chronology of Iseult's life is also provided, as is a select general bibliography.

# Acknowledgements

Editing these letters was begun by the late Mrs Bridgwater, Iseult's daughter, Kay. After her death her daughter, Christina Bridgwater, invited Anna MacBride White, Maud Gonne's granddaughter, and A. Norman Jeffares to collaborate with her in this collection of Iseult Gonne's letters to W.B. Yeats and Ezra Pound.

We wish to thank the following who have been most helpful in providing suggestions about the identification of people, places and various obscure references and who have assisted in many other different ways: Professor Michael Alexander, Dr Caoimhghin S. Breathnach, Professor Davis Coakley, Mary de Raschewiltz, David Forrester, Professor Roy Foster, Professor Warwick Gould, Bernard Hanratty, Professor John Kelly, Professors Janis and Richard Londraville, Professor Jack (J.B.) Lyons, Sinead McCool, Daphne Maxwell, Dr Wim Van Mierlo, Emer NiCheallaigh, Mary O'Doherty, Professor Daithi O hOgain, Dr Margaret O hOgartaigh, Colonel Eoghan O'Neill, Deirdre Toomey, Professor Colin Smythe and Declan White. Jeanne Jeffares has translated Iseult's French. Anna MacBride White's daughters, Iseult and Fiona, and her son, Conleth, have helped with the ordering and processing of material in Dublin as has Anna Rush in Fife Ness, and for this aid we are very grateful indeed. We also owe a great deal to Dr Hana Sanbrook for compiling the index.

A. NORMAN JEFFARES
ANNA MACBRIDE WHITE
CHRISTINA BRIDGWATER

# Chronology

1894  Iseult Germaine Lucille Gonne born 4 August, at 51 Rue de la Tour, Passy, the child of Lucien Millevoye and Maud Gonne (MG).

1895  Millevoye regains his seat in the Chamber of Deputies and becomes political editor of *La Patrie*. MG moves to larger apartment, 7 Avenue d'Eylau, Paris. MG rents house in the Rue de Barbeau, Samois-sur-Seine. The households, there and in Paris, in the charge of Madame de Bourbonne.

1898–9  MG tells Yeats of her affair with Millevoye and of Iseult's existence, and says she has not had relations with Millevoye since Iseult's birth. They enter into a mystic marriage.

1899  Yeats (WBY) visits Paris, proposes to MG (the first of his many proposals was made in 1891). MG in Mayo where tenants are being evicted.

1900  MG starts for second lecture tour in USA, January. Iseult has influenza; her lung is affected, March. MG is with her at Samois-sur-Seine May–June. Iseult meets her aunt Mrs Kathleen Pilcher and her cousins on holiday at Port Aven, Brittany and her lifelong friendship with her cousin Thora begins, August. MG breaks with Millevoye. Iseult starts school in autumn. Major MacBride arrives in Paris, November.

1901  MG joins John MacBride on lecture tour in USA (her third, previously there in 1897 and 1900). He proposes to her, February–May. Madame Dangien acts as Iseult's governess, is a member of the household until 1911. MG brings Iseult to Salvan where she collapses with high fever, meningitis feared at first and a lung affected, July. Iseult stays from time to time at the convent at Laval run by Madame Foccart.

1902  MG rents 26 Coulson Avenue, Rathgar, Dublin, spring. She tells her sister she intends to marry John MacBride, June. Iseult baptised at Laval, Madame Foccart her godmother, July. She has a summer holiday with MG's friend Madame de Grandfort, who suggests MG should buy Les Mouettes, Colleville, which she does in 1903. Mrs Meredith ('Bowie'), former nurse of MG and Kathleen, dies at Farnborough where she had been looking after the 16-year-old Eileen Wilson (otherwise Daphne Robbins), the illegitimate half-sister of MG and Kathleen, who now joins the household in France. She and Iseult stay at Laval, autumn. Iseult contracts diphtheria, November.

1903 MG received into Catholic Church at Laval, February; marries John MacBride 21 February. May Bertie-Clay named as Iseult's guardian in MG's will at time of the marriage. MG gets Les Mouettes ready for occupation and explores Normandy with MacBride before honeymoon in Spain. Summer spent there. The plot of MG and MacBride to assassinate Edward VII in Gibraltar fails through MacBride's drunkenness. Household settles in 13 Rue de Passy, rented by Maud, October.

1904 Jean Seaghan (later known as Sean) born at 13 Rue de Passy, 26 January 1904, baptised in Dublin, Terenure Parish Church, 1 May, MG and the children staying in Coulson Avenue. Eileen Wilson marries MacBride's brother Joseph, 3 August, in St Ethelred's Church, Ely Place, London; they then live in Mayo. MG returns from Dublin to Paris, October, summoned by Madame Avril de Sainte-Croix as household disturbed by MacBride's behaviour. Iseult terrified by him. MG goes to London, tries but fails to arrange a peaceful settlement, December.

1905 MG begins divorce proceedings, in Paris, January; these continue intermittently until January 1908. She leaves politics (temporarily) and studies painting. MacBride allowed an hourly visit once a week to see Sean. MG draws Iseult (reproduced in Joseph Hone, *W.B. Yeats 1865–1939* (1942), p. 239 and in Nancy Cardozo, *Maud Gonne. Lucky Eyes and a High Heart* (1979), p. 148).

1906 MacBride's libel action against the *Irish Independent* fixes his domicile in Ireland, June. He asks the court for custody of Sean, July. Because he proves Irish nationality and domicile, separation, not divorce, granted to MG in August; custody of Sean given to Maud. Iseult ill with fever, September. MG hissed by audience in Abbey Theatre, Dublin, October. Iseult attends the Lycée.

1907 Ella Young visits Paris. Iseult begins to translate some of her Celtic tales. (*The Coming of Lug* (1909) and *Celtic Wonder Tales* (1910) were illustrated by MG.) Iseult makes her first communion in Notre Dame de Paris, 18 April. The summer spent at Les Mouettes, Colleville.

1908 MG fails to get a divorce in her appeal, though she can get it in French courts in three years if she wishes, January. She fears MacBride may steal Sean. She and children at Les Mouettes, April. Iseult writes to thank Yeats for his gift of Andrew Lang, *Tales of Troy and Greece* (1907). MG and WBY renew their mystic or spiritual marriage in Paris in June. WBY meets Iseult for first time since June 1899 and is surprised by her declaring the *Iliad* her favourite book. The Pilcher family at Les Mouettes, summer. Iseult flirts with Toby Pilcher there. Iseult back at Lycée, October. WBY in Paris. He and MG may have slept together, December.

1909   Iseult and MG begin to try to learn Irish. Madame Avril de Sainte Croix very ill, nursed by MG, February. Family at Les Mouettes, Colleville for Easter, April, and at Evian-Les-Bains in the Haute Savoie, then at Bernex, June; the children stay there while MG goes to Aix-Les-Bains with her cousin May for three weeks then returns to Bernex. MG and children at Les Mouettes, Colleville, August. WBY visits MG in Paris, July. The incident of the moving picture seen by Iseult, then by MG, May and Ella Young. WBY sends fan to Iseult.

1910   Iseult at Laval for the New Year and the rest of her holidays. Owing to floods in Paris Madame Dangien takes Iseult and Sean to Les Mouettes, they stay until March, visiting Bayeux in Holy week, Iseult and MG at Laval, April; Iseult at Tours with Madame Foccart, latter part of April. WBY's first visit to Les Mouettes, May. Iseult proposes to him, is refused as too much Mars in her horoscope. Family at Les Mouettes in July. MG takes Iseult, Sean and Madame Dangien to Ireland; they visit Mayo in August. MG begins to work on the need for school meals in Ireland.

1911   Iseult writes to WBY giving reasons why he should join the family in Italy, where they go, April and May, Mary Barry O'Delaney accompanying them. They have an audience with the Pope and receive Communion from him. Iseult begins her *Journal* in French recording *inter alia* her pleasure that her aunt Kathleen's family are also in Italy; she enjoys Thora's company. She stays with MG's cousin May Bertie-Clay in London, and with her aunt, Kathleen Pilcher, resuming her flirtatious relationship with Toby Pilcher (begun in 1908). Jean Malyé becomes a visitor in Paris. The family at Les Mouettes, June to late September. Visitors there include Helen Laird, Michael Gonne and Joseph Granié. Madame Dangien leaves the household.

1912   The family move from 13 Rue de Passy to 17 Rue de l'Annonciation, January. Sean has operation for appendicitis, January. Iseult stays with May Bertie-Clay at her Villa Castiglione, Via Montughi, Florence. Family at Les Mouettes June to September, visitors include Jean Malyé and M. Pelletier. WBY writes some of his Introduction to Tagore's *Gitanjali* there in summer. Iseult and Sean stay for three months with May Bertie-Clay in Florence, arriving in November. Iseult flirts with Toby there in December. John Quinn buys Granié's pencil drawing of Iseult's head, a study for the Angel of Annunciation.

1913   Iseult and MG see Isadora Duncan dancing, March. Iseult returns from Italy, 15 May. Family then go to Les Mouettes. Iseult in London, staying with May Bertie-Clay at 39 Alexandra Court then with Kathleen Pilcher at 12 Milner Street. Meets several of WBY's friends,

T. Sturge Moore, Arthur Symons, Ezra Pound, W.T. Horton and Lady Cunard, also Rabindranath Tagore whose nephew (and translator) Devabrata Mukerjee she had met in Paris. He begins to teach Iseult and Christiane Cherfils Bengali, August. Family at Arrens in the Pyrenees, September; they attend the Irish National Pilgrimage at Lourdes. Iseult helps MG in Dublin with aid for school meals for poor children, November. Kathleen and her family go to Paris for New Year.

1914 MG begins to write frequently to WBY about getting Tagore's permission for Iseult and Christiane Cherfils to translate *The Gardener* or *The Crescent Moon* into French. Iseult's invented mystery of Mukerjee's departure. MG, Iseult and Sean at May Bertie-Clay's Villa Castiglione, Florence, Easter. Iseult fractures her foot in three places, June. She is told by doctor, who says she has a weak heart, to give up smoking, eat meat and keep her windows open, none of which she does. Mukerjee comes to Arrens with the family, July. They go to Eucharistic Congress at Lourdes. He and Iseult fall in love. Iseult sends translations of Tagore to WBY. MG and Iseult given rank of lieutenant, and nurse wounded soldiers in the hospital at Argelès-Gazost, September. Mukerjee leaves for India, September/October. MG and Iseult return to Paris, December.

1915 Tom Pilcher killed in battle at La Bassie, March. Iseult helps Kathleen nursing in a hospital near Etaples, May. Kathleen, May, Iseult and MG work in the Infirmière Hôpital Militaire 72 at Paris Plage, Pas de Calais, summer. They return to Paris, end of September. Millevoye's son killed in battle, September. Iseult becomes Secretary to an Aviation Society in Paris, October. She gives up hospital work, December.

1916 Family at Les Mouettes for a month, April. Iseult writes essays on d'Annunzio and Huysmans there. Easter Rising in Dublin begins on Easter Monday 24 April. John MacBride executed on 5 May. Iseult and May Bertie-Clay go to London, where WBY introduces Iseult to Shaw and she meets the Pounds at Woburn Buildings. She meets other friends of WBY, and he accompanies her back to Paris in June, staying at Les Mouettes for the summer. There he proposes to Maud and later to Iseult. She translates the Catholic poets for him; he writes 'Easter 1916' there and dictates some of the second volume of his *Autobiographies*. Iseult negotiates with Madame Péguy. MG told family could go to London but not to Ireland, December.

1917 Iseult reading Steiner, January. Family at Les Mouettes for Easter, stay till 17 April. WBY buys Ballylee Castle, County Galway for £35. He goes to Les Mouettes, August, accompanies family to London, gives Iseult ultimatum. She refuses him. MG rents a flat in 265 Kings Road,

Chelsea. She and Iseult forbidden to go to Ireland. WBY marries
Georgie Hyde Lees 20 October. Iseult works in the School of Oriental
Studies, University of London, October, is friendly with Arthur Symons.

1918  MG gets to Dublin in disguise. Joséphine Pillon stays with Iseult and
Iris Barry joins them, January. MG buys 73 St Stephen's Green,
Dublin, March. Iseult sees Arthur Symons and Ezra Pound, studies
Sanskrit, February. Pound suggests Iseult should work for the *Little
Review*, March. Their affair begins. Iseult, Joséphine Pillon and Iris
Barry move to 54 Beaufort Mansions, Chelsea, March. Lucien
Millevoye dies, 25 March. Mary Barry O'Delaney follows the family
to Ireland, (collecting the parrot and the monkey from Iseult in
London en route). MG arrested in Dublin 15 May, sent to Holloway
Prison. Iseult leaves School of Oriental Studies, begins work for Ezra
Pound, late June/early July. WBY and his wife move Iseult to Woburn
Buildings, August. They rent MG's house, 73 St Stephen's Green,
Dublin. MG released from prison, end of October, goes to London
nursing home, then to Woburn Buildings, November. End of First
World War, 11 November. MG again in disguise goes to Dublin, late
November. WBY and MG quarrel when he refuses to have her at 73
St Stephen's Green. MG, Iseult and Joséphine Pillon stay with various
friends in Dublin until the Yeatses leave 73 St Stephen's Green,
11 December. Lloyd George calls General Election 14–28 December.
Sinn Fein standing on an abstentionist platform secures 73 of Ireland's
105 seats.

1919  The War of Independence begins in Ireland and turns into guerrilla
warfare. Kathleen Pilcher dies in Switzerland. Sinn Fein MPs form Dail
Eireann, an abstentionist government, January. Anne Butler Yeats
born in Dublin, 28 February. MG buys Baravore in Glenmalure, County
Wicklow. WBY gives up tenancy of Woburn Buildings, June. Iseult
tells WBY of meeting Harry Francis Stuart, in letter of 17 November;
she tells him she thinks of getting married the following Easter,
December.

1920  Black & Tans (former British troops) arrive and warfare intensifies,
March. Stuart becomes a Catholic, 30 January (receiving his first
Communion on 15 March). He and Iseult go to London; they marry
in Dublin, 6 April. The marriage runs into difficulties. They stay at
Baravore for three weeks, then at 5 Ely Place, Dublin, June. Stuart
falls behind with rent of flat, goes to London to sell Iseult's necklace
and falls in love with Tamara Karsavina there. Iseult rents flat in
67 Fitzwilliam Square. She is with MG in Glenmalure when WBY arrives
to help, 30 July. He arranges that Iseult, who is pregnant, should
consult Dr Bethel Solomons and go to a nursing home. WBY visits

MG, Sean and Cecil Salkeld in Glenmalure, September. His tonsils removed by Dr Oliver St John Gogarty, October.

1921 The Stuarts go to Bournemouth, then stay in Sussex with Thora, who had married William Forrester in 1919. Furniture removed from Fitzwilliam Square flat, though rent was paid, but is returned to 73 St Stephen's Green. Iseult's daughter Dolores born 6 March. Stuarts give up Dublin flat, stay with his mother Lily Clements at bungalow in Bettystown, County Meath, April. Dolores dies of spinal meningitis at St Ultan's Hospital, Dublin, 24 July. Truce agreed, July. Anglo-Irish Treaty signed, December.

1922 Dail Eireann approves the Treaty, January. MG brings Stuarts for continental holiday, Sean, buying arms for the IRA, with them as far as Brussels. They visit Munich. Stuart takes Iseult on holiday from holiday, to Prague (where Karsavina was dancing), then to Vienna. WBY decides to live in Merrion Square, Dublin, March. The Four Courts, occupied by IRA, shelled by Irish Free State forces, Sean taken prisoner, April. MG turns St Stephen's Green house into hospital. Stuart in Belgium arranging arms shipment for IRA; he takes part in fighting in Dublin, Cork and Wexford. Arrested in Dublin, 9 August, he is held in Maryborough Prison. MG and Mrs Despard move to Roebuck House, Clonskeagh, County Dublin (which they bought in August). WBY becomes Senator of Irish Free State, December.

1923 MG arrested January, released from Kilmainham Gaol after 20 days' hunger strike. MG's house raided by Free State soldiers, all her papers and Iseult's (including most of their letters from WBY) lost. Stuart moved to Curragh Internment Camp, County Kildare, February. Iseult arrested in general sweep of arrests, May, released through pressure from WBY. Ceasefire agreed in Civil War, 24 May. Sean escapes when being moved from Mountjoy to Kilmainham Gaol, October. Stuart wins prize in Poetry; advance copy of his poems *We Have Kept the Faith* (1924) sent to WBY, December. WBY awarded Nobel Prize in Stockholm, December.

1924 The Stuarts move into Ballycoyle, a cottage outside Enniskerry, in the Glencree Valley, County Wicklow, spring. Stuart gives lecture on 'Nationality and Culture', March. The two numbers of *Tomorrow* published from Roebuck House; it includes Iseult's 'The Poplar Road'. Iseult in Holles Street Hospital for operation, May. Stuart's *We Have Kept the Faith* wins Royal Irish Academy Award at Tailtearn Games, Dublin, 9 August.

1925 Stuart buys a racehorse for 40 guineas at bloodstock sales, Ballsbridge, Dublin; the horse is trained in Cork.

1926   Sean MacBride marries Catalina Bulfin, January. WBY writes 'The Death of the Hare', 3 January. The Stuarts spend some days with the Yeatses in 82 Merrion Square. Their son Ian born in Dublin nursing home, 5 October. Lily Clements now lives with the Stuarts for long periods.

1927   Stuart's horse Sunnymore, comes second in race at Phoenix Park, Dublin. The Stuarts move to Laragh Castle, County Wicklow.

1929   WBY and George are driven to the Royal Hotel, Glendalough, County Wicklow by Lennox Robinson; they visit Laragh Castle, July.

1930   Hilda Burnett appointed assistant in poultry farm at Laragh Castle. Lily Clements now lives permanently with the Stuarts. Iseult goes to Dax with MG then on to Lourdes with Stuart.

1931   Katherine (known as Kay) Stuart born in Dublin, 21 May. Stuart in Paris. He rents flat in Dublin and learns to fly. He stays with Liam O'Flaherty on various visits to London.

1932   Stuart's novel *Pigeon Irish* published February. WBY writes 'Stream and Sun at Glendalough', 23 June. WBY stays at Royal Hotel, Glendalough, County Wicklow from 7 July; he finds Stuart 'rather flat', on his own as Iseult was at Roebuck house assisting MG. She did return for the weekend.

1933   Stuart's play *Men Crowd Me Round* staged in Abbey Theatre, Dublin.

1935   WBY tells Iseult he and George have become alienated.

1936   Stuart investigates possibility of having marriage annulled, falls in love with Honor Henderson, then with a chorus girl, Margery Binner, who acts in his play *Glory* in Arts Theatre Club production, London. He gives her £10 to buy an engagement ring.

1937   Stuart's *Racing for Pleasure and Profit* published.

1938   MG's autobiographical *A Servant of the Queen* published by Gollanz.

1939   WBY dies in Hotel Idéal Séjour, Menton, 28 January, buried in Roquebrune. Stuart lectures in various German cities, offered lectureship at University of Berlin late May/early June. He returns to Ireland, late July. Confirms acceptance of lectureship, 21 September.

1940   Stuart arrives in Berlin via Switzerland, meets Herman Goertz, who is dropped by parachute into County Meath. He walks to Laragh Castle. Iseult buys clothes for him in Dublin and he goes to Stephen Held's house outside Terenure, escaping police and going on the run for 19 months before being captured. Iseult questioned for two days at Garda station, Bray, 23 May, then interrogated at Collins Barracks,

Dublin, charged under Emergency Powers Act and imprisoned in Mountjoy Prison, tried in camera, 1 July, found not guilty and released. Nora O'Mara, formerly Goertz's secretary, becomes Stuart's mistress, and secretary, until September, in Drahtlose Dienst where Stuart was translating news bulletins. He becomes involved with a Kashubian student, Gertrud Meissner who acts as his secretary in the Redaktion, the radio station in the Rundfunkhaus, Charlottenberg, where his broadcasts were transmitted until August 1943.

1941   Gertrud Meissner, now called Madeleine, begins to live with Stuart, April. He is now also teaching at the Berlin Technical College.

1942   Stuart begins broadcasts to Ireland, August.

1944   Stuart and Madeleine transferred to Luxembourg, September. They move to an area near Lake Constance, then to Dornbirn in Austria.

1945   Stuart goes to Paris, August. Iseult tries to get money to him there, but Irish ambassador tells him to return to Dornbirn. Iseult tells him he should return to Ireland, autumn. She sells possessions to finance him. Stuart and Madeleine arrested by French intelligence officers, November, then imprisoned and moved to Freiburg six months later.

1946   Stuart and Madeleine under house arrest until July. Stuart arrested, October, released, November.

1947   Stuart writes to Iseult to say their marriage is impossible, spring. Herman Goertz commits suicide.

1948   Ethel Mannin calls on Stuart and Madeleine, June. Stuart allowed to leave Freiburg, October.

1949   Iseult suffering from anaemia, March. Ian visits Stuart in Freiburg; he is at 2 Schwartzwelt Street, March. Ian and Kay visit Stuart and Madeleine, mid-June. Stuart gets passports, goes to Paris, July, gets post for Madeleine there as domestic servant, August.

1950   Iseult in hospital suffering from angina. Madeleine in hospital for appendectomy. Iseult has a heart attack in July but Dr Moriarty is pleased with her progress; she enjoys the views over Dublin Bay from St Michael's Nursing Home. Lily Clements has a stroke. Kay writes her car off in a collision, December. Iseult has various tests at Mater Hospital, Dublin. Dr Moore tells her that her backache is unpleasant and incurable but not dangerous.

1951   Stuart flies to Ireland, 7 March, stays briefly at Laragh Castle where his mother has had a stroke. His first meeting with Iseult for 11 years. Ethel Mannin arranges Madeleine's entry to England as her domestic servant, 16 June. Stuart tries to get £500 from his mother's trust;

executors refuse this, October. Iseult tells Sean no money must be raised for Stuart on the house his aunt Janet Montgomery had left Ian and Kay. Stuart argues he should have half of Laragh Castle. Ian and Imogen marry, August.

1952    Iseult tells Stuart of her illness and the injections she was getting. She gets fits of unconsciousness and wonders if this is an effect of the drugs she is taking. Her oedema improves, she can walk to the garden but complains that she is either in pain or half drugged, August. Kay gets First Class Honours in German, second in Spanish. Sean brings Iseult to Roebuck House where MG's health is declining fast. Iseult has congestion of the liver, March 5.

1953    In March Kay writes letters for Iseult. MG dies 27 April and Iseult regrets Stuart does not write to her. She tells him her health is deteriorating, May. She has oedema. Finds dromoran, prescribed by Dr O'Shaughnessy, helps her to sleep.

1954    Iseult's last letter to Stuart, 15 March, telling him 'Whatsoever we did or said or refrained from, from the best in us we recognised and these the times when we were closest to each other.' Iseult dies in her sleep, 22 March.

# 1
# Prologue

*Anna MacBride White*

## Early childhood 1894–1902

Iseult Gonne was born on 4 August 1894 in Paris at 57 Rue de la Tour, Passy. Her other names were Lucille Germaine. Her parents were Maud Gonne and Lucien Millevoye. Her older brother, Georges, born in January 1889, died 18 months later in August 1891. These bald facts hide a highly emotional and unconventional story.

Maud Gonne, daughter of an English mother, Edith Frith Cook, and Colonel Tommy Gonne, of Irish extraction serving in the British army, was brought up, in part, in Ireland when her father served there. Her mother died when she was four; thereafter she and her younger sister Kathleen were brought up by their devoted nurse, Mary Ann Meredith, whom they called Bowie or Biddy the Bounce Bounce, who was helped by a nursemaid. Their education was attended to by a succession of governesses. Their father, serving long periods abroad in India, or as military attaché in the courts of the Austrian Emperor and the Russian Tsar, wrote long chatty letters to his daughters while he was away on duty, sending them little presents and showing constant concern for their welfare, and, when on leave, taking them travelling around Europe. He was a cosmopolitan man speaking many languages and his daughters became familiar with European and especially Parisian society, speaking fluent French.

Maud was presented at court in Dublin on the occasion of the visit of the Prince of Wales to Ireland in 1885. Very beautiful and clever, she succeeded in achieving her ambition in becoming the Belle of the Season. Her father endeavoured to protect her from being affected by the appalling conditions of the poor in Ireland and the fearful unrest about which he himself was concerned, yet she had seen people die by the roadside after their houses had been destroyed by the authorities.

Tommy Gonne died suddenly of typhoid fever in the second year of Maud's gay social life in Dublin. Sometime before he died he told her that he intended to retire from the army and enter politics, supporting the

1

Home Rule cause for Ireland. Maud, overcome with grief for her adored father and moved to London by her wealthy relations, was determined by all the means in her power to break free from her family and, buoyed by her father's political decision, to work for the poor, and, in her own words, to 'free Ireland'. After her father's death, but before she came of age, while travelling in France with her great aunt, the Comtesse de Sizeranne, she met and fell in love with a Frenchman, Lucien Millevoye, a married man in his mid-thirties who came from a wealthy family, his grandfather being a well-known French poet. He himself was a lawyer, a political journalist, a considerable orator and one of General Boulanger's most able lieutenants. General Boulanger was a colourful and popular character in whom great hopes had been placed by a disparate collection of people who hoped to form a government under his presidency. Though in love, Maud, with her single-track determination, was not going to give up her political pre-occupations, but was enticed by this worldly man with a promise of a political alliance against their common enemy – England.

So when she came of age and found herself comfortably well off she set out on an independent life to 'free Ireland', a part of which was her combined affair of the heart and political alliance with Millevoye. Both activities were way outside what was respectable in conventional society. She returned to Ireland and with her unhaltable determination, beauty and charm intro-duced herself to nationalist and literary Dublin at a time when the Irish Literary Renaissance, of which she was to become a part, was about to be born. She made many lifelong friends at this time. Given an introduction by her Irish mentor, John O'Leary, she visited the Yeats family in London in January 1889. The young aspiring poet Willie Yeats fell instantly in love with her. After a few days in London seeing Yeats and finding many things in common with him she moved on and by April she was in Paris with Millevoye and became pregnant by him. She was now in her twenty-second year. Her son Georges was born in January 1890. She adored this child and with her passionate and romantic nature was convinced he had special qualities. Passing him off as a young relative whom she had adopted, she brought him to see her sister and cousins in London and to Ireland, includ-ing Donegal where she was observing the evictions and helping the evicted. In the summer of 1891 she came alone to Dublin and her friend and devoted admirer Yeats was horrified at her appearance, finding her very depressed. Torn with pity and love for her, he, a penniless poet, proposed to her, and she refused him. Years later Yeats learned the full story of her secret life. It would appear that her affair with Millevoye was not going well. He had promised to divorce his wife and marry her and this promise was not fulfilled; also at some stage he had asked her to have an affair with another man for his political advantage. This, to the idealistic Maud, was betrayal.

At this time political difficulties were very pressing and upsetting for both of them. Parnell, the leader of the Irish Party in the House of Commons, the hope of Ireland, was fighting for his political life, having been named as co-respondent in the O'Shea divorce case, with his party and the country split over the affair. In France, Boulanger had failed in his great promise of leading his party to government.

Shortly after Yeats's proposal in the summer of 1891 Maud returned to Paris where Georges died after a brief illness. Maud's grief was unbounded and in deep mourning she built a tomb for him in the new municipal grave-yard in Samois, outside Paris near Fontainbleu, presumably a place where she and Millevoye had been happy with the little boy. In spite of the extrava-gant burial, the 18-month-old boy's death certificate stated that his parents were unknown. He was an illegitimate child whose origins, for social reasons, were to remain in oblivion. For Millevoye, married and a well-known polit-ical and social figure, it would not have been convenient for it to be known he had an illegitimate son. For Maud in her single state the stigma would have been worse, near ostracization.

Shortly after the burial Maud, draped in mourning, returned to Dublin, on the same boat that carried Parnell's body. Yeats, overpowered by her grief, but not understanding the full implication of it, did all he could to help her. He introduced her to his occult friends and urged her to join the Golden Dawn, the occult group lead by MacGregor Mathers. Shortly after this General Boulanger committed suicide on his mistress's grave. Both Maud's and Millevoye's hopes were shattered, not only by Georges's death but also by the death of their political hopes.

Before Georges's death in 1891, ill with tuberculosis after overworking with the evicted in Donegal in the November wind and rains in 1890, Maud was advised to rest in the south of France. While there, presumably with the help and advice of Millevoye, she wrote an article on Ireland, which appeared in a well-known French magazine in May 1891. This was the start of her successful career. She always considered the worst year of her life was the year of 1891. But she buried herself in her work and again travelling between Dublin and Paris, she suddenly hit the headlines in January 1892 with a speech she made to a French society devoted to friendship between nations, which attracted much attention. She was interviewed by the prestigious *Figaro*, taken up by the university students, and was asked to speak on evictions and poverty in Ireland and the treatment of Irish polit-ical prisoners in English prisons all over France, and in Belgium and Hol-land. She became a highly effective publicist for her cause in France.

Millevoye's career was not doing so well. The Boulangist party had fallen apart, and, having been unwittingly involved in a political scandal, he had lost his seat in the Chamber of Deputies. For a proud ambitious man who had aimed to be prime minister under a Boulanger presidency this was complete failure. He became very depressed. Both were still mourning their son when Maud remembered the answer her occult friends had given to her question as to how a child could be reborn. So, following the occult ritual they described, she and Millevoye made love in the vault where Georges's coffin lay in Samois.

Maud became pregnant and her last public appearance was in March 1894. Over four months later, in August, her daughter was born. Whether she thought the infant was a reincarnation of Georges at that time is not known. She named her Iseult. Being a lover of old legends and Wagner's operas she must have seen many symbols in that name and the story of Tristram's two tragic loves – Iseult of Ireland and Iseult of Brittany. No one in Ireland knew any of this, but in 1898 she told Yeats when, by then, Iseult was truly loved for herself and there was no further mention of reincarnation. At the time Maud revealed these secrets of her life to Yeats, she also told him that after the birth of Iseult she had left Millevoye, though they remained political friends. She later persuaded him to take up the post of political editor of the failing *La Patrie*, which became an important Paris paper. He also regained his seat in the Chamber of Deputies.

After the birth Maud stayed out of public life for over four months before she took up her speaking engagements again for the amnesty associations working for the political prisoners, becoming their unofficial leader. Being a woman she was not eligible to join any of the political organizations in Ireland, though the men of these associations and of the Parliamentary Party were prepared to work alongside her.

Maud returned to her political life at the end of 1894. In the following year she moved to a large apartment on the newly built Avenue d'Eylau in Passy where there was room for the baby, her nurse and nursemaid, and for the many soirées Maud was to hold in the coming years. She also rented a house with a large garden on the Rue de Barbeau in Samois. The village of Samois is only a short drive from Fontainbleau, reached by train from Paris, and there, in the summer, Iseult could play in the garden away from the heat of the city. An elderly gentlewoman, Madame de Bourbonne, was engaged to look after her with the help of a nursemaid. There is no record of Iseult's early life. Maud continued with her political activities, providing for her daughter as her father had done for her and Kathleen; when at home, remembering her own mother and 'the morning glory' of joining her in her bed, she filled the child's life with her loving presence, returning from absences abroad in Ireland, England or America with gifts, and, as she and Kathleen had had in their childhood so now the house was full of pets – singing birds, dogs, cats and sometimes more exotic creatures.

Yet Maud did not fully realize the difference between her childhood and what she provided for Iseult. Maud had the stability of Bowie all her childhood, whose worth her father Tommy had truly assessed through his wife's long illness. She also had the constant companionship of her younger sister Kathleen, and the intermittent companionship of her cousins, all of whom remained her companions for the rest of their lives. All this was backed by the solidity of her aunts and uncles, some of whom she later rebelled against and some of whom supported her. Iseult in her early years had none of this; her childhood was much more solitary. Both Maud and Iseult adored their frequently absent, but charming and loving only parents to a degree beyond normal.

At the end of 1898 Maud was going through a time of great emotional stress seemingly due to overwork, failure of some of her political plans, and perhaps trouble in her relationship with Millevoye. On her arrival in Dublin Yeats was once more shocked by her appearance, which moved him to intense emotional concern for her. He followed her to Paris, proposing to her once again. It was during this highly charged period that she told him the full story of her life in France and of the existence of Iseult. She refused his proposal but it is from this time that Iseult comes out of obscurity and appears in Maud's letters to him; he hears of her progress, her illnesses, the pleasure her mother finds in joining her in Samois, and of playing with her in the large garden. At this time she was called Bellotte. Some in Samois remembered playing in the garden with her, the farm where they got their milk, having a *gouté* or snack, and Maud telling the little playfellows that the English soldiers were not good and they should not marry them. This last was during the Boer War when Maud was conducting an intense anti-enlistment campaign in Ireland as a means of helping the Boers. Besides

**Fig. 1** 'At this time she was called Bellotte' © Anna MacBride White

Maud's household in Paris and the freer life in Samois, where not only the people but all the animals adjourned, there were two other reliable constants in Iseult's life. Ghenia de Ste Croix, who was Maud's closest friend in Paris, a journalist, was a reformist feminist whom Iseult adored and who frequently acted as surrogate mother when Maud was away. The other was Mary Barry O'Delany whom Iseult later referred to in her *Journal* as Delany. She was Irish, a mediocre journalist, who had emigrated to Paris. She became Maud's devoted admirer long before Iseult was born, and became indispensable as a researcher and in a secretarial capacity. She had a happy ability to relate to young children: happier, perhaps, than Madame de Bourbonne, who is said to be the one who threatened to shut Iseult up in the cellar with the rats.

From 1900 the pattern established in Iseult's first six years started to change. Probably the first big event was when she was taken with her nursemaid to Port Aven, a pretty village in Brittany favoured by the Impressionist painters, to spend a holiday with her Aunt Kathleen Pilcher, who loved to paint, while Maud was having a rheumatism cure in Aix-les-Bains. There also was Maud's and Kathleen's cousin, May Gonne. Three of Iseult's cousins were there. Toby, the eldest and four years older than Iseult, ate with the grown-ups at a table nearby. Then there was Thora, two years older than Iseult, and Tommy, who, though younger, was a tease and bullied his sister. 'Baba' the baby brother was not there. The children sat at a separate table with their two nursemaids Berthe and Eugenie. Thora tells the story. The two nursemaids became great pals, met two boyfriends Grand Claud and Petit Claud and so found the children 'rather a nuisance'. Thora remembered how their nursemaid used to line the three younger ones up and made them 'bend over while she gave us a hit over our bottoms. I remember Isolda (she was called Isolda then) being very indignant that we obeyed. Isolda and I took to each other like a house on fire. She was the beautiful little girl that Aunt Maud had adopted and although two years younger than me was the same size and rather cleverer. She always stood up for me if I got scolded or punished.' One time Thora had denied stealing a sweet from her mother's room and on being told to open her mouth 'revealed the evidence' of her lie. The punishment was to have no dessert, but later at their meal Berthe gave her some and said 'Eat quickly'. Iseult said, 'Yes do, it is very good.' Guiltily she did and was caught in the act later being given a long lecture by her godmother, Aunt May, with Iseult standing by 'saying all the time "she did not want to do it. I made her. It is all my fault, let me be scolded or punished not her." My heart swelled up with such love for them both. I saw the truth of what Maycat [Aunt May] said and as for Isolda, what nobility of character! Isolda was always like that, she always tried to exalt me. She would give a higher motive than I had intended and put more in what I said than I had thought up.' Perhaps it was at this time that May began calling them gutter-cats.

It was probably after this holiday that Madame de Bourbonne left and Iseult started day school with a governess to supervise her lessons and care for her, providing continuity when Maud was away. Madame Dangien, or Dan as she came to be called, stayed with the family until the end of 1911. Where Maud was concerned she was a sensible reliable woman who had reared her own family, but Iseult was in frequent rebellion against her. Maud has written that about this time she had broken finally whatever friendship she had with Millevoye so the pattern of his visits probably changed. At the end of that school year Iseult became very ill. Her mother had been away for three months on her third lecture tour of America and had been ill herself on her return. A month or so later she wrote to Yeats:

> The heat in Paris tired little Iseult very much – without seeming to work hard she passed first in nearly every subject at her school, this may have been too much for her – she was looking very ill so I took her up to the top of a Swiss mountain to live the life of a little savage. Three days after her arrival she was taken very ill indeed, intense fever and one lung affected, for a day or two we feared meningitis, luckily a French doctor was taking his holidays & he was very good & helped me nurse her & now she is well again but he says she is frightfully delicate & for the future will be a great anxiety. She is much too tall & much too clever for her age.

This anxiety about Iseult's health did not persist, although Maud, having lost one child, subsequently reacted with great fear and anxiety when any child was ill.

By now Iseult was probably aware that her father was not welcome in her mother's home, that another strange red-haired Irishman with poor French was a frequent visitor and that her mother had a new friend, Suzanne Foccart, the Reverend Mother of an enclosed Carmelite convent in Laval in Mayenne. This latter friendship came about through an old Boulangist friend, Canon Dissard, now secretary to the Bishop of Laval, who enlisted Maud's help for the nuns. With the new laws of 1901 concerning religious orders, some contemplative religious left the country. Others, in order to remain, secularized by having a *raison sociale* and earning their living. Being beautiful embroiderers the nuns decided to earn their living by selling their work. Maud helped them on their first visit to Paris. Also they had to open part of the convent to the public, employ lay people and receive government officials, wear ordinary dress and appear on the streets of Laval. They later changed their names to Les Dames de Ste Thérèse. Maud, on her visits, stayed in the public part of the convent and loved their garden: she wrote 'it is such a wonderful quiet restful place with an immense garden with huge cedar trees & fountains & all a tangle of roses and lilies.'

Early in 1902 Maud's beloved old nurse Bowie died. One morning Delany found Maud in tears over the letter that brought the news of her death.

Many years before Maud and her sister Kathleen had come to the rescue of Mrs Wilson, their father's mistress, whose child had been born some time before his death in November 1866, when the two girls were under age. In those days a woman with a child found it virtually impossible to earn a living. About six years later when Maud was living in Paris an old Russian friend, Zakrefsky, asked Maud's advice about a governess. Maud recommended Mrs Wilson, who took the post. This was made possible by Maud and Kathleen asking their old, much loved and now retired nurse, Mrs Meredith, who had reared them since infancy, to care for the child. Bowie, who had always stood by Colonel Tommy Gonne in his widowhood, now took his child, Eileen, to rear in her retirement in Farnborough. Maud and Kathleen gave her financial support and stayed in close contact. Bowie, a little round woman in a lace cap, and Eileen had already visited Paris. Now Eileen was sixteen, and, concerned about her future, Maud brought her to Paris to live until her mother would decide her future. Eileen was paid to mind Iseult, lived with the family and was to learn French. It would appear that in this way she might later be able to earn her living as a governess.

A few months later Maud wrote to Yeats that she was in Laval for the past week because Iseult was being baptised a Catholic and that she felt inclined to be also. All Maud said about the matter was that Iseult looked lovely in a white veil and wreath of white roses, and that she was going to the seaside. Maud's old friend, Mme de Grandfort, had suggested Iseult should stay with her by the sea in Normandy while Maud was away. When Maud collected her, Iseult had rosy cheeks and recited Victor Hugo. Madame de Grandfort, who reminded Maud of her own great-aunt, the Comtesse de Sizeranne, persuaded Maud to buy an empty house nearby going cheap, much to the delight of Iseult.

In the summer of that year Maud wrote to Kathleen from her little rented house in Rathgar, Dublin about her intended marriage to John MacBride, the red-haired soldierly Irishman who had organised the Irish Brigade, which had fought for the Boers, and with whom she had gone on her last lecture tour of the United States. He was the hero of the Irish Nationalists, having taken up arms against their enemy, England. Now in her late thirties Maud wrote to her sister, 'I am getting old and oh so tired', but Kathleen did not think the marriage suitable, pointing out their social differences, for which Maud did not care a whit. More importantly, the couple's mutual friends warned them about their incompatibility and differences in character. How much Iseult was aware of the distancing of her father and the growing prominence of John MacBride is not known. The reasons for this ill-suited marriage are difficult to understand. Maud was very depressed and, added to that, she was someone who took hasty and impatient measures when unhappy. According to Maud, John MacBride was also depressed; having lived a hard life as a surveyor in the mines of South Africa, then fighting in the war out on the open veld, and now, extolled as a hero, he was living on a pittance in Paris on the edge of Maud's busy political and social life, homesick but unable to return to Ireland, where he could be tried for treason for having fought against the British. One reason for the marriage Maud gave was that they planned to assassinate Edward VII when he visited Gibraltar in 1903. Maud, in a stalemate in her work, desperate for action of some kind, was involved in the planning of the assignation and was convinced it was an adventure in which they would lose their lives. So she made plans accordingly, to give up her apartment, make a will leaving Iseult in the care of her cousin May and in the meantime leave her in a secure and safe place – the convent of Laval with Eileen, thereby also helping the nuns qualify for secular status. Maud gave another reason for the marriage to Yeats when she passed through London on the way to Dublin about three months after the wedding, 'looking worn out' according to Yeats. She told him she had married 'on an impulse of anger'. She had found that Millevoye had brought his current mistress to see Iseult. 'I resolved to get someone to keep him out & and to make a final breach.'

It is not the depth of her depression nor the complex reasons for her marriage which are as important here as how the marriage may have affected Iseult. Iseult adored her mother, who was her whole life. Unable to express the relationship by calling her 'mother' she called her 'Amour', love. Then, self-conscious as how this might sound in public, she transposed the A to the end of the word making 'Moura'; this was the name she called her mother all her life, the relationship in public being 'cousin' or later 'adopted daughter'. Whatever her relationship with her father had been before he was now no longer welcomed by her mother: there was another man instead. As well there was Eileen's relationship, one of family rather than employee. Both were people with whom she might have to share her mother's affection, and so their advent created a huge, unwelcome and anxious change in her life. At nine years old this could only have been an undefined fearful anxiety and dislike.

## Maud's marriage and divorce, 1903–08

Iseult had been in Laval in November 1902, and then got diphtheria before Christmas. An exhausted Maud wrote to Yeats, 'I had a fearfully anxious time & could think of nothing but nursing her', but mentioned nothing of her proposed marriage until just before the announcement was in the papers in February 1903. Writing from Laval in February, in answer to his three distraught letters, she added that she would be in Laval for a while, 'a lovely peaceful place where I can play with Iseult & forget for a little the worries of life.' Iseult had cried when Maud told her she was getting married. Now Maud was baptised in Laval. Iseult's childish signature appears on the certificate along with those of Maud's friends Canon Dissard and Madame Foccart, and the signatures of John MacBride's friend Victor Collins as godfather and Mrs Collins as proxy godmother in place of John's mother, both strangers to Iseult. Then Maud left for Paris. Again Iseult cried as she was leaving, Canon Dissard promising her he would hold a banquet on Maud's return. 'She only cried the louder and clung to me, and Sister Catherine had to drag her away.'

The marriage was a strange affair: Maud, wanting a quiet one, invited no friends, but Victor Collins seems to have taken it over with all his family taking part in the ceremonies. Iseult and Eileen remained in Laval all spring. Iseult hated being there and hated the Reverend Mother who disturbed the imaginative child by dressing her up as a doll and dressing herself as well in all sorts of strange clothes while parading in front of mirrors, a memory which lingered through the child's life to adulthood. Indeed there was much talk about Madame Foccart in Laval. Having to appear on the streets in secular clothes she was frequently seen walking with the bishop and gossip said they were having an affair. Much later, after a dispute with the same bishop, she had to leave Laval and died in poverty in Brittany in 1921. She had a son who worked for General de Gaulle.

Iseult also disliked Eileen. Eileen's feelings for Iseult were probably reciprocal. Eileen would most likely have been more aware of their invidious situation as illegitimate daughters, but Iseult, at least, had her mother, whereas Eileen had lost the nearest she knew to a mother in Bowie – except for letters and presents from her real mother in Russia whom she was never to see again. At some stage Iseult developed a furious temper. The earliest recorded account of it is when she rubbed butter into Eileen's hair. But Eileen loved Laval and got on well there, learning French and exquisite embroidery. Did the nuns hope they might have a postulant in young Eileen? But she was to fall in love with John MacBride's oldest brother Joseph, who was then in his early forties.

There was, however, a nameless nun whom Iseult loved and respected, and remembered; and there was Canon Dissard, whose photograph she kept. He probably looked after her spiritual education. His own story was all an imaginative child could wish. There was an affinity between him and her mother from their youth when he, as a young priest, wondered why she was not of the same religion as most of the people of Ireland. To this she had replied that it was because she believed in reincarnation and was sure some of the people she knew she had met in another life. Dissard had answered that 'the soul comes from God and returns to God when purified, when all things become clear, and who can tell the stages of that purification.' He also said that memories could be ancestral, transmitted in the blood. His own name Dissard came from 'Dis', the name of the god worshipped in the Auvergne and 'ard' meaning high. It was the name of the chief druid whose burial mound was on a little hill on the land his family had lived on for generations and which they guarded well. Both he and his mother had always known he would be a priest, not because of reincarnation but because of ancestral influence. Many years later the druids' hill was excavated and the treasure removed to a museum. When he was able he went to the Auvergne and saw the great scars of the excavation. His foot struck a piece of curved metal; he picked it up and when polished he discovered it to be a gold sickle – the sickle of the High Druid used for cutting the sacred mistletoe. Canon Dissard believed his ancestor had saved it for him and he kept it in a glass case in his house.

While the girls were in Laval, Maud and her husband went first to Normandy where Madame de Grandfort had bought the house she had mentioned and which Maud had not yet seen. She intended it for Iseult and paid for it with money she had inherited from her great aunt Augusta, as the money she inherited from her father was entailed. This was probably part of the final break with Millevoye and Samois which she had shared with him. She now hoped John, brought up by the sea, would like it. They stayed in St Laurent, a little fishing town not far from the village of Colleville where, nearby, the house stood on the edge of the sea. They spent some time exploring Normandy with its lovely old towns such as Bayeux and Caen, where, in the markets, Maud enjoyed collecting local items for the house, all for very little – brass milk cans, a carved Normandy cupboard and other quaint furniture. Then they went south through France and Spain, shadowed by British police – ducking the shadowers was an entertaining game for them. But in that chapter, of the few she wrote of her second unpublished autobiography, it is clear the incompatibilities were already showing. They became tragically blaring on arrival at their destination. Maud was to act as decoy while John was to go to meet his friends and do the deed. He arrived back late and drunk, the deed undone.

Next morning Maud, angry and desperately upset, packed her bags, saying she was returning to Paris and he could come if he wished. From Paris she went to Dublin to work on a publicity campaign against the proposed visit of the monarch who had so luckily escaped in Gibraltar. Publicity was work in which Maud was always successful. It is a measure of her state of mind at her marriage that she should have contemplated something like the Gibraltar affair. While in Dublin she realised she was pregnant and that for John and the child's sake she should return to her marriage. So with a heavy heart she went back to France to live the rest of her life.

That summer was spent on the coast of Normandy in the house Maud had bought, Les Mouettes – the Villa of the Seagulls – near the village of Colleville. Maud wrote it was

> ... an amazing Moorish looking house with blue tiles and terraces, whose tamarisk sheltered garden stretched down to the shingle on the beach ... clouds of yellow butterflies hovered over the flowers and blue sea. At night the sea was sometimes phosphorescent. The crest of the wavelets shone like jewels, if you splashed the water it made fountains of white

light. Even the marks of our footprints on the wet sand would shine like silver.... Every morning we had only to run out of our bedrooms for our morning dip in the sea,... some times surrounded by the yellow butterflies.

The sandy soil was very fertile where vegetables and flowers grew easily, though much of it was under water in the winter. Albertine, who cooked for many of the varied and ornate villas along the coast provided beautiful meals for them. Her husband, Havard, tended their gardens, providing them with ample vegetables, and acted as their caretaker. Fresh produce such as eggs, butter and cheese were bought from the local farmers. The family quickly learned how to put out lines at low tide and provide themselves with ample fish. It was an idyllic place for children, playing in the garden or, when the tide was out, on the long stretches of beach – except that they were forbidden to swim on their own because of shifting sands.

There were many guests that summer who came to enjoy the free life of Les Mouettes. Perhaps it was at this time that the relationship between Joseph and Eileen developed. Also among the visitors was Victor Collins. Maud did not like or trust him, suspecting him of being a spy, and of having undue influence over John, but above all she seemed to have a deep-seated fear of him. But as she was having her friends it was only fair that John should have his. This summer did not raise Collins in her estimation.

Among the first visitors to arrive were two of his younger children, 'a lonely little boy called Dan aged eight and a pale little girl of about 11' both of whom she discovered were also afraid of their father. The second morning they were there Iseult rushed into her mother 'with a white scared face',

**Fig. 2** Les Mouettes – 'an amazing Moorish looking house with blue tiles and terraces'
© Imogen Stuart

saying the little girl had fallen and 'she was dying in the garden'. The doctor when he arrived said she had had a bad fit of epilepsy. After a second fit Collins was asked to come and take her home as the doctor said the sea was bad for her. Both the doctor and Maud were amazed and Maud was also very upset at not being told of the child's condition.

Dan stayed on for the summer and Collins came to keep John company while Maud was away. The next incident happened when Maud had just left and the Avrils (Ghenia de Ste Croix and her new husband), coming to take her place, arrived a little late. On their arrival they found a half-drowned Iseult being taken out of the water by the coastguard who had seen the children being swept out to sea. Dan, more terrified by the beating he was going to get from his father than by his close escape, declared himself fine and Madame Avril did not realise he had also nearly drowned. For one who never used physical punishment, what horrified Maud more than anything else about the incident was that Collins would thrash his son for disobedience after such a frightening experience.

In a letter to Yeats in September Maud told him that her husband had been ill all summer and that 'Iseult is more beautiful & wild & fairy like than ever, she would fascinate you if you saw her by her wildness & originality, there is nothing banal about her.' On returning to Paris Maud found 'a queer charming little house in a rue de Passy' set back behind a high wall with a small garden and a tree; there the family settled and Maud awaited the arrival of her baby.

As her pregnancy advanced Maud was not well. There was considerable difficulty in the marriage and she appealed to Canon Dissard to ask John to be less demanding of his marriage rights, with little effect. Though she was unable to travel rumours reached her friends in Ireland. Violet Russell had a dream of her trying to hide and Yeats wrote to Lady Gregory that 'I have heard a painful rumour – Major MacBride is said to be drinking. It is the last touch of tragedy if it is true.' When the baby arrived on 26 January, 1904 there was great jubilation among nationalists; the boy, hailed as the child of heroes, had an heroic future forecast for him.

How the nine-year-old Iseult dealt with the highs and lows of these months is hard to say for there is no mention of her in letters, so it is not known whether the visits to Laval continued for some time (though they did become considerably less and peter out later) or what time they spent in Colleville. A new baby is an event of mixed emotions to the older sibling – fascination, interest, jealousy, anxiety – especially for an infant over which there was such a great fuss. As John could not follow her for fear of arrest Maud wrote that she went to Ireland a lot that year to escape the situation at home and to feel safe, taking the baby with her. Iseult went at least once. Eileen married Joseph MacBride in London that summer and went to live in Ireland. During school time Madame Dangien and school were probably the norm for Iseult with visits to see her father at the house of Ghenia de

Ste Croix, now Madame Avril. It is difficult to work out the logistics and sequence of some of Maud's domestic arrangements from the occasional remarks interspersed through her notebooks and letters.

They stayed in her little house in Coulson Avenue, Rathgar, next door to her friends Violet and George Russell, in the suburbs of Dublin. One of the occasions when they stayed nearly two months (while John MacBride was in America) was to have the baby, Sean, baptised. Iseult, walking into the little house, was surrounded by the wonder of fairies painted on the walls. They had been George Russell's wedding present to Maud, who wrote 'he said she looked like a fairy child needed to complete them and promptly bought a new canvas to paint her'. Maud's friend, Ella Young, describes Iseult at that time in the back garden of the house. 'Iseult sat on the top of the dividing-wall. Beside her sat Brian Russell, young as herself, and on the wall between them was a pile of snails in their brown shells.' The two were arguing vociferously, Iseult in her 'French voice', on the merits or demerits

**Fig. 3** 'She looked like a fairy child'. Portrait by George Russell, 1904 © Imogen Stuart

of the snails to agriculture which ended with Iseult giving him a whack as she jumped down from the wall. At that time Maud said that sometimes Iseult would stay with Madame Avril while she was away so as not to interrupt her school schedule. One day in the autumn of 1904 Maud got urgent messages from her concierge and Madame Avril to return home immediately, and on being met at the station by Madame Avril and Iseult a terrible tale was unfolded.

There are indications from what Maud has written here and there as well as what she wrote to Yeats the following year of how unhappy she was in this ill judged and incompatible marriage. John MacBride only wrote of it a little and later. Both their accounts show this incompatibility and lack of understanding. The upheaval that Maud met on her return is a measure of his acute unhappiness and sense of loss. According to Maud he had been drinking steadily and roistering with his visiting Irish friends, disturbing the quiet bourgeois Rue de Passy. Now while she was away he had what seemed like a drunken and sexual breakdown in which he had exposed himself and behaved in an unseemly manner to the women of the household, including the cook and Delany. Iseult had confided in Madame Avril that he had called her into his room to play and for some sweets and exposed himself to her.

By the time Maud had arrived in Paris John had left for London and Dublin. Maud was prepared to fight like a lioness for the safety of her children. First she went to London to Dr Anthony MacBride, John's brother, and another mutual friend, proposing a quiet, peaceful separation. Negotiations broke down on the custody of Sean. Always decisive and quick in her reactions and on the advice of her solicitor, Maud started legal proceedings. Early in 1905 it was decided that the case should be heard under French law as both parties were domiciled in France. Back in Paris to conduct his defence, John was allowed to see the child once a week under the supervision of someone appointed by Maud. She threw herself into working up her case and getting evidence from her servants and neighbours. Some evidence came up that John had 'tempted Eileen' before she had left to get married. For Maud, it was a dreadful time, but how much Iseult was aware of the situation is difficult to say; much would have been kept from her yet the atmosphere in the house could not have gone unnoticed even though school, lessons with Madame Dan and visits to Madame Avril to see her father continued. The two strangers who had entered her life for a few years were gone but the small and endearing baby was left.

Maud, having gone down the road of legal divorce, knew she could not return to live in Ireland until she was vindicated by a decision in her favour, but even then such action as she had taken was virtually unheard of in Catholic Ireland. The nationalists, though many sympathised with her, were worried about the effect her action would have on the cause, as she herself was. Having lived through the trauma of the Parnell divorce and split, Maud determined to stay in France and discourage anyone from taking sides. John MacBride's friends had no such compunction and worked hard to blacken her character and have her removed from the offices she held in the movement. Her own women's organisation stood by her, but she urged them not to engage in controversy. Having taken the decision to keep out of politics, feeling that perhaps her gifts were not needed any more, she purposefully turned her attention to following a long denied ambition of studying art and put into that all the drive and dedication she had put into her political causes, believing in hard work to drown her sorrows. So now, as well as supervising the conduct of her case, which continued intermittently for three years, she studied art intensely. This meant that though she was under the strain of her legal affairs, Maud was at home on a regular basis which gave a greater sense of security in the house, so life settled down to a new norm for Iseult, with the other constants of Dan, Delany and Madame Avril (whom she called Tatan) still there. Added to these was May Gonne, now Mrs Bertie-Clay, who was Maud's main confidante during

**Fig. 4**  Maud, Iseult and Bichon, 1904 © Anna MacBride White

the difficult period of the trial – Tante May to Iseult and the little boy Sean, to whom Iseult gave the name Bichon, curly-headed little puppy. Around him a great fear existed.

He was closely guarded lest he be kidnapped by his father or his father's friends to be brought up safely in Catholic Ireland, away from Maud, whom they considered highly immoral and therefore not a fit mother for him. At least one family in Dublin discussed the possibility of taking him in. The child was carefully minded and adored by his nurse, Margerite. He was highly nervous, crying hysterically if his mother was out of sight. To ensure his safety at all times Maud enlisted the help of Madame Dangien, showing her the evidence in the case, so that at all times either of them was in the house with him. Later Delany would take him to the park, accompanied by the big guard dog, Brutus. When he was two, if suddenly excited he would fall unconscious. If he was toddling after his mother and a door was banged by the wind she would find him unconsious behind it. She sometimes thought his life depended on her. Doctors could find nothing organically wrong and she thought it might be prenatal influence due to the terrible strain she had gone through before his birth. The doctors said he should grow out of it before he was seven.

The most difficult and worrying parts of the divorce proceedings were the evidence concerning Eileen and Iseult. The evidence about Eileen, known only as E, was used mainly in the hopes that John MacBride might settle the case to protect his sister-in-law, and that Eileen, quietly safe in the west of Ireland, might never be identified. This ruse failed and instead his lawyers called her as a witness and she and Joseph came to Paris, much to Maud's regret. As for the Iseult episode, it had been agreed by both sides before the judge that 'the affair would not be alluded to by either side'. Yet on the last day of the trial, in spite of protests, the story was gone into by Dr Anthony MacBride, which meant that Maud had to call Madame Avril and other witnesses to go into the matter. Wanting her to forget the incident Maud refused to call Iseult and have her 'dragged into the sea of mud'. 'She is a nervous child & was ill for days after from the terror of it & used to wake at night screaming that MacBride with his "eyes of an assassin" was running after her, even now she hardly likes going up stairs after dark alone because as she told me last week when I was laughing at her for being afraid she is always afraid MacBride may be hiding & run after her.'

The case dragged on intermittently until January 1908. Throughout this time Maud continued to have an active social life, entertaining her friends, mainly artists, writers and intellectuals, as well as many friends from Ireland. She worked hard at art, attending Humbert's Academy in the Place Blanche, and the anatomy classes at the Beaux Arts. She also worked with and learned from a great friend of hers, a graphic artist, Joseph Granié, who lived in Passy with his wife Marinette, also an artist. Maud worked long hours at the Gustav Moreau Museum, absorbed by the colour and mystery of his symbolist paintings. The century was young, cultural life was vibrant and interesting. The conversation among Maud's guests was probably wide ranging – about the latest Paris salon, or what was on in the theatre, or of magic and visions, ghosts and faeries, or Irish politics and the plight of the Irish poor, or of what Irish writers were doing, more especially Yeats, who sent her what he wrote.

Ella Young, a theosophist, Celtic scholar and Maud's friend, came to stay in 1907, when Iseult was twelve. Maud wrote to Yeats:

> Iseult is getting very big & very beautiful. She is translating some Irish legends that Ella Young has written that I am illustrating. She has done the translations so far wonderfully well & I hope to get it published here – I think she will write, she has great imagination & great taste.

Then later that year, hoping that Yeats might visit Paris she writes:

> ...I should have the pleasure of seeing you & showing you Iseult. She is the despair of her governess and of the school where she goes every day, because of her laziness & because she will not learn what doesn't interest her. She is extraordinarily clever but won't work.

That summer Maud wrote to Yeats for the first time from Colleville. The family may have stayed there in other summers after the divorce proceedings started. Colleville was to become a retreat at Easter and summer. Life was becoming more relaxed as by this time the legal proceedings were drawing to a close.

Early in 1908 Maud got the results of her appeal. The divorce had not been granted but she was given a legal separation with permission to try for divorce again in three years and was given full custody of her son. The decision against which Maud appealed was full of irony. The case in France was tried in camera but details were leaked and published abroad. Maud suspected Victor Collins, who was a newspaperman, and who had attended the trial with John MacBride, who sued the *Irish Independent* for libel in its reporting of the case. In the process he had to prove his domicile in Ireland. The final judgment given in Maud's case was that as his domicile was in Ireland the French court could not grant a divorce, which would not be recognised by the Irish courts, so could only give separation. Immorality was insufficiently proved but drunkenness was manifestly proven, which would have entitled Maud to divorce in France. The result of this was that she could not live with her family in Ireland without fear of having her son taken from her. On advice she had initiated the case in France because they both lived there. Perhaps, if she had been prepared to put Iseult on the witness stand, she might have got her divorce. Maud accepted the decision and never returned to the courts. Later she regretted her hasty and decisive legal action, writing to Yeats in the autumn of 1907 that though she had felt she should stay still and let fate work, perhaps she had not stayed still enough. She went on 'MacBride had to disappear from my life because fate

ordered it – I need not have troubled about helping fate by going to law.'
With a change of government in England John MacBride could and did
return home. Now Ireland was no longer a safe place for Maud to live.

## Thora and Iseult's first romance, 1908–10

Life in the little light-filled house in the Rue de Passy, with its mirrors and
singing birds, continued in a more settled way now that legal concerns
were out of the way. Maud worked hard at her art, on her illustrations for
Ella Young's books, starting to exhibit in the salons and gradually taking
commissions. As well as her other interests in Paris she had a sympathetic
interest with Indian nationalist exiles. She travelled to England and Ireland
and occasionally to Italy. Kathleen and her cousins May and Chotie came to
stay, especially if they were travelling on elsewhere. For a while she instituted
lessons in Irish for herself and the children. Suffering recurring homesick-
ness for Ireland she kept in close contact with what was happening there and
was glad to receive her Irish friends. One especially, Helena Molony, became
very close. She was the editor of the little women's paper run by Maud's
organisation, Inghínidhe na hÉireann. In April 1906 Kathleen and her
children passed through, staying for two days. Thora, who adored Maud,
wrote

> We arrived at Hotel de Passy and left our luggage there, crossed the road
> and there was 13 Rue de Passy opposite. There was an arched doorway
> cut out of a wooden fence in the street, through which one entered into
> a courtyard. By the doorway a large bob-tailed sheep-dog was chained,
> his name was Brutus. He was on guard in case John MacBride came to
> take away his son. Brutus was set loose in the courtyard at night and
> Aunt Maud had Séan in her bedroom and a revolver under her pillow.
> Opposite the entrance into the little courtyard Aunt Maud was there
> with open arms to greet us. Mama was to sleep at the house and the rest
> of us in the hotel and spend the day at No.13. On the ground floor of
> the house was the drawing room with sea-green walls and beautiful
> Persian rugs on a polished wood floor. Many lovely pictures and old
> brocades and a zither, and on the right the dining room, leading into a
> kitchen behind. From the dining room emerged the sound of twittering
> of many birds and there they were in a row of cages all along one side of
> the room.

Thora goes on to describe the animals, five in all including a little green
parrot who had the freedom of the house, 'one would sometimes find him
going up or downstairs' and Iseult's cat Grey Vermin 'for whom she wore
mourning when he died'. Iseult 'looked as if she had come straight from
fairyland'. Two years later they met again when the family was passing
through. By this time Iseult had made her First Communion in April 1907.

These visits continued in the following years and Thora, who in the general way of her life never met anyone quite like her, was captivated by her beauty and strangeness and wrote of Iseult at this time:

> She was Roman Catholic and had to go to confession. She used to invent sins she had never committed because she said life was very dull without embroidery. She said she often told lies to other people but she did not lie to herself and she would not lie to me, and I don't think she did. She spoke English with a slightly French accent and whatever she said was original and unique.

These rare visits of the Pilcher children were special events, and for Iseult, they were very far from the daily round of her Lycée, where she did not seem to have many friends. Apart from playing with her little brother, her passion in life was her interest in Greek myths. Maud wrote to Yeats in April 1908 that Iseult was 'mad on Greek Stories and knows the Illiad and the Odysée better than her prayer book.' Two months later Yeats came to visit for the first time since 1899 when he had seen Iseult as a toddler. May Bertie-Clay and Ella Young were also there. He stayed in the nearby hotel, was given his cultural tour and enjoyed the galleries. Iseult, beautiful and precocious, delighted him with her interest in the classics; he reported that she had almost set the house on fire by making a burnt offering to Athena. During this stay his friendship with the more relaxed Maud, busy with her children, guests and painting, entered a different phase which touched their spiritual marriage of earlier years. This new relationship developed over the next year with further visits from Yeats, reawakening in a different way their old friendship which led, it is thought, to a short physical affair, which Maud ended at the end of 1909. She had always claimed that physical love was only justified by children and now there was the extra bar of being a committed and devout Catholic and in the eyes of the Church still married. So the friendship returned to a new form of the old brotherly and sisterly relationship, the two sharing dreams and occult practices. During this time, the 14-year-old Iseult, perhaps sensing the love and affection in the air, proposed to him and confided to a diary that she was in love with him. She said he turned her down because there was too much Mars in her horoscope! It was at this time that Iseult wrote her first letter to him thanking him for his present of a fan, using in it May's old nickname for her.

Around Colleville as well as the long beach and sea were the woods, fields, and streams where Iseult wandered and could romanticise about the ancient Roman remains. Life in Les Mouettes was free and uncluttered with little routine. The guests could study and work or amuse themselves. On Sundays there was the walk to the village for those who wanted to go to mass in the ancient church with lunch to which the priest was often invited. The protracted Sunday meal could be boring for younger people. One Sunday

Bichon went missing and after a search was found asleep among the blankets in the old carved Normandy cupboard. The animals that came with the family on holidays were viewed with mixed feelings by the visitors. It was possibly the summer of 1908 that the whole Pilcher family came, Kathleen, Thora, Toby, and the youngest, Pat, with Miss Foster BA, Thora's governess, in the navy blue uniform with collar and tie, which she always wore. Mme Dan was there as well, and of course someone to do the cooking and cleaning. Thora remembered Iseult running barefoot, wild and free on the fringe of the sea, her long hair blown about by the wind. Iseult also took Thora to show her the secret cave where she had written the strange hieroglyphics of her secret script and painted antique figures on its walls. The same hieroglyphics and figures were part of her secret world of the imagination in her *Journal*.

That summer in Colleville Iseult, about 14, started a mild flirtation with her 18-year-old cousin Toby, with many stolen kisses and thought herself deeply in love. While taking it all very seriously she was yet delighted to have a serious sin to confess – 'Father, I accuse myself of having kissed a young man on the lips'. The romance with Toby lasted years.

Next door was a house owned by Tante Violette, a holiday house or a home for young prostitutes from Paris. Madame Avril worked hard to protect prostitutes and had a home for those who wished to reform, but many of them got bored and went back to their old life – Iseult called them repentant snakes. So between unrepentant and repentant snakes the girls had much thought-provoking material to discuss. Adjourning after lunch, perhaps when Toby had gone fishing with Havard, to the little garden behind the house they sat among the tall sunflowers and scarlet poppies, hoping for witch dreams by eating the poppy seeds from the dry seed heads. Here these matters were discussed. Iseult said she would rather die than sell her body for money.

Kathleen usually went abroad with Thora and her governess twice a year, winter and summer, the boys travelling out to meet them during their holidays from boarding school. This irregular life made it hard for Thora to make friends, and in this way she was like Iseult, who also seemed to have no friends. Then, in 1909 and 1910, Kathleen was not well and spent the winters in Davos, travelling through Paris with Thora, who went to finishing school in Lausanne. It was on these passing occasions that the girls had an opportunity to cement their friendship. Thora, while trying to be fair, found her mother somewhat cold and distant, so the visits to the Rue de Passy were an experience she never forgot:

It was almost too exciting to breathe, crossing that courtyard, past Brutus and entering the atmosphere, life odours, noises of all sorts, twittering of birds in their many cages, when one reached the house and Aunt Maud's outstretched arms with all the warmth and love in them embracing me,

I felt so full of joy. Every minute in that house was vibrant with intense life and every minute was important and not to be missed. We went to the Louvre and looked at Leonardo Da Vinci's pictures and other picture galleries of modern French artists. Iseult's original ideas never ceased to charm me and her beauty to delight me.

Maud's and Iseult's great height and beauty gave Thora

> ... the feeling they were not just ordinary mortals and when they were about, everything was transformed and got a quality of magic which cast a charm over their surroundings as well, and the people in their household, like Miss Barry O'Delany, that strange oddity, and Madam Dangien, tightly corsetted into the curve of the then fashionable Gibson Girl of fifty, unable to bend, were to me part of the enchanted scene and invested with caché. I think what I enjoyed most of all were the meals when we were all assembled together. Every one chattering happily together with the birds chiming in. If Iseult happened to be on good terms with Dan, Dan called her 'Mon petit Rat'.

Had this been a kindly conversion of Madame de Bourbonne's threat of locking her in the cellar with the rats? Iseult later signed her letters to her mother 'Rat' with a little squiggly rat drawn underneath.

There were, however, many times when Iseult was not on good terms with Madame Dangien, whom Thora said she disliked.

> Madame Dangien called her a perch for being tall and thin, and used to compare her to her own daughter at her age and always to Iseult's disadvantage. She used to say 'I swear on the head of my daughter' where other people might say 'I swear on the bible'. Iseult would say 'If only you knew the lies she swears on the head of her daughter'. Madam Dangien would say 'I would rather teach a devil than teach you', and Iseult would reply, 'I would rather be taught by a thousand devils than be taught by you'.

When Maud had visitors from Ireland she took them on a cultural tour of Paris. Iseult who knew all these places and people frequently went along. Ella Young, who visited regularly, describes Iseult and the visits they made, running one into another over the years. She tells of Yeats instructing Iseult how to chant his verse and of Iseult instructing a very young Bichon in art, poetry and literature, while she herself could hold her own in every conversation. Ella recounts their visit to Macgregor Mathers, self-styled Count of Glenstrae, the magician who had founded the occult Order of the Golden Dawn of which both Maud had been and Yeats remained members. A man of formidable gifts, Maud told her he had designed and drawn in one night the set of Tarot Cards used by the Order. Ella, herself a theosophist and interested in things Egyptian, was interested to meet him. 'Iseult', she wrote, 'had the most extravagant sagas about him – a righter of wrongs, a chastiser of evil doers, a champion of the oppressed'. The house was full of Egyptian treasures and a light burned on a small altar before the image of the god Toth. He himself was a large man and gave Ella the impression of power, efficiency and a certain ruthlessness.

After visiting the Louvre with Maud and Iseult she wrote:

> [they] want me to see in especial the pictures of Leonardo da Vinci. . . . for the rest, I devote myself to Egyptian sculpture, and the archaic Greek. The smile on those holds the attention of Iseult. She bids me remember that this archaic smile found hostel in the Cathedral at Chartres, innocent and subtle, before it captured Leonardo, subtlety triumphant and charged with the knowledge of a world not human.

By 1909 Iseult was being brought to the theatre and was reading Thomas Aquinas with her mother. Short visits to Laval and Madame Foccart became frequent for a while and she went to London to visit May. Before going to Colleville that summer Maud brought the family to Evian-les-Bains, a resort in Haute Savoie on the shores of Lake Geneva, for a cure for Iseult. There is no explanation as to why Iseult needed a cure. Immediately on arrival Sean started to run a fever and his anxious mother decided it had something to do with the place, so she moved the family higher up the mountain to a new and half-empty hotel at Bernex, which had beautiful views. They travelled the short distance to Evian for the cure. They stayed nearly two months in the Haute Savoie and did not get to Colleville until mid-August. A reference to Evian makes it clear she hated the place. Perhaps she felt cheated at not getting to Colleville earlier. Maud had left them there with Dan for a few weeks, partly to meet her old friend the Irish American layer, John Quinn, in Paris. She returned with two books with beautiful illustrations by Arthur Rackham. Beautifully illustrated books were frequent presents from Yeats and Quinn.

In Colleville later that summer strange things happened. When Ella Young and May were staying there Iseult suddenly saw the figure in a portrait of Maud move, the eyes open and shut, the lips move and the face become contorted, it was like Maud but different and she rushed to her mother, terrified, to tell her. Maud and her two friends watched the picture and saw it move over a number of days but they decided it could do no harm. Other strange things happened in the house, which Ella ascribed to Gilpin, her poltergeist, who had followed her to France. After all that Iseult went to stay with May in London in October.

Paris suffered severe floods at the start of 1910 and Maud worked on relief committees providing food and clothes for the homeless caused by the flooding. Before being sent away from the floods with Bichon to Colleville

Iseult wrote to her mother's Irish-American friend, John Quinn, to thank him for his annual Christmas present of books. 'They are simply heavenly... every evening while he [Bichon] is going to bed I have to translate to him one of the stories that are in it.... The flood is most interesting but I [think?] that we are too high up for it having any chance to come in our house; the idea of having to have a little black boat to walk about in the room is most exciting.' The following year Quinn was to buy a pencil sketch by Granié of Iseult, and in the years to come he continued to send them books and a barrel of American apples every Christmas, even through the war.

In April of that year Yeats paid his first visit to the family in Colleville, where May had also joined them. Before he arrived the family stayed in a convent in Bayeux for the Easter religious services, hoping young Sean's long curls would be sufficient disguise for the nuns to think him a girl. The religious event affected Iseult deeply.

After a sea and rail journey Yeats was met by Maud in a country cart, for she felt he would not manage changing trains with his poor French. They went to Mont St Michel, a place Iseult knew well by this time. It was Yeats's first experience of Colleville, where he was to spend many holidays.

Early in the summer, before they returned to Colleville, Maud brought the family to Ireland, including Madame Dan in the party. They visited Ballycastle, a village in a remote area of Mayo where Maud had worked during a famine 12 years before. She was given a great welcome, people in the cottages delighted to see her and inviting them into their homes. Madame Dan hated the primitive discomforts, disapproved of the priests wearing top hats and the continual rain. Young Sean, now seven, enjoyed riding donkeys and Iseult fell in love with the people and the remote, sparse scenery. Maud had plans to climb Nephin and go around to Belmullet by boat.

The previous year in the autumn of 1909 Maud had written to Yeats of Iseult, 'This is her last year of school grind, after this I shall let her take up what subjects she pleases – She is so intilectual [*sic*] she ought to do something interesting, but she declares energetically that she hates the thought of working hard at anything.' So at the end of the summer Iseult did not have to return to school.

## Young adulthood and Italy, 1911

By the beginning of 1911 Iseult's voice can be heard as she starts keeping a *Journal*, which she later transcribes into another hard-backed book. There is little that is average in the life of the 16- to 17-year-old girl. It is the first and most detailed picture of her and it is easy to see some of the child in the later woman, which helps to understand her and bears out Yeats's worry about her tendency to melancholia.

She starts by describing a sung requiem mass in the 'majestic Notre Dame'. She quotes the *De profundis* – 'Out of the depths I have cried to thee,

Oh Lord' thinking 'Oh how far we are from God in this terrible cathedral' and deciding it was God the Father who presided in its vastness as the choir boys sang the *Dies iræ* – the angry God, which ended with 'a long cry of distress through the vaulted ceiling'. As she left she thought 'will we ever reach God: he is so far from us.' At this time Iseult had been reading Huysmans with whom she identified and who seemed to influence her greatly as this entry shows. Her copy of *En Route* is heavily underlined, bringing up memories of childhood, especially the passage describing a convent garden which she identified with the nuns' garden in Laval which her mother loved so much – 'impregnated with the bitter salt scent of box, planted with trellises, whose green grapes never ripened...'.

The next entry is in Italy where the family joined Kathleen, Thora and May in Frascati outside Rome. She has resolved not to say ill of anyone in the *Journal* but the resolution was frequently broken as her dissatisfaction with her elders overflowed her best intentions. Instead of any ecstatic enthusiasm for all she saw, she suffered boredom and ennui, and a teenage disconnectedness with her family. As the trattoria in the square in Frascati where Kathleen was staying was full they booked into a convent pension nearby. The following day, having breakfast on the terrace overlooking the garden, the young priest who had said mass stopped to talk to them. On discovering that Sean had only recently made his first Communion, he asked had he seen the Pope 'who wants little children to come to Communion early'. A week later they had an invitation to mass in the Pope's own private chapel. This was a rare privilege and joy for Maud and Delany, who had followed them to Rome, as the saintly Pope's health had prevented him giving audiences. So, all in black wearing black veils, they went and the little boy was made much of. Their enthusiasm swamped Iseult. The 'bigotry of Delany and the fugitive piety of Amour' upset her. She wondered why one should feel more pious because of the Pope and why was Communion better from his hands. She came to the conclusion that she 'was decidedly pagan and would prefer to be strolling on the Palatine Hill.'

From Frascati they went regularly into Rome on a rattling little train. The only good things in this were being with Thora, the Forum and the remains of the grandeur of ancient Rome, going to the cinema and 'epic scenes with Delany, nearly as good as the cinema.' She disliked the 'ugly churches built on top of temples of gods destroyed by the first Christians and where, in the country of Scipio and Caesar, one should respect their gods and not openly take part in a religion which destroys the culture of these gods. All this won't stop me, when I get back to Paris, from kneeling under the roof of Notre Dame and to lower my head in front of the Christ when the brave notes of Tantum Ergo resound in that immense nave.'

Maud and Kathleen painted in the gardens of the large villas around Frascati, shaded by tall cypresses, with almond trees in flower, ornamental lakes, water falling from old fountains, olive groves, fields of violets and periwinkle, and the woods carpeted with wild cyclamen. Iseult wrote 'that Kathleen and even Amour, in spite of her habitual charm, spoilt the beauty of the landscape' and of her feeling 'that everything that one looks at is very ancient and that these great trees have seen centuries pass without really having noticed it and have seen more beautiful times.... All that I saw was unreal and not of our epoch, that the thinking behind these things did not accord with ours.' She tormented 'herself sometimes with the mad admiration which borders on adoration for all that is pagan, this devotion for the Iliad and the gods of antique Greece, yet a more profound sentiment will sometimes lead me to the foot of those enormous dark crucifixes full of piety placed in the corner of churches... to tell him how one is suffering.'

For the rest of the two months in Italy they visited Tivoli, Florence, Siena, Assisi, Perugia, Lugano and Venice. The girls managed to while away some of the boring hours by flirting with young Italian men, while assuring them that their mothers were dragons who had to be obeyed. The young men were adept at finding opportunities by climbing balconies or sending billets-doux addressed to 'Miss Beautiful Girl' by Bichon, the two girls and the little boy overcome with laughter at their own audacity, yet anxious their mothers would discover and scold them for their improper behaviour. While in Florence, staying in May's new villa, they went into town on the bus as their pocket money did not allow them to go on the *carroza* with their parents and so gathered a host of young Romeos on their way. Thora had copied two little black tulle hats with black grapes from one she had seen in an expensive Bond Street shop and was convinced that it was these which had done the work. 'But when a young man is handsome and smiles at you why not smile back?' Iseult wrote. She made a collection of their visiting cards, half of which she offered to Thora when they were parting.

It was only in Assisi that Iseult 'was almost happy'. The little town with its narrow and silent streets in the midday sun, with nothing modern to spoil it, became her ideal town of the Middle Ages. She loved the church of St Francis and the beauty of the frescos. As she wandered around, discovering the town's hidden beauties, to her joy she discovered a little temple to Minerva and she thought of the mysterious splendour of Greece and of Christianity and 'if one could unite the ideal pagan and ideal Christian then only would we have perfect beauty'. Because she had seen so much beauty in those days she felt herself more grown up and her melancholy 'resembled the calm sadness of summer nights'.

Apart from the girls' hidden flirtations there were only few other incidents recorded of interest. Kathleen always travelled with her canary and little dog. In Assisi the canary flew away and eventually came back to its open cage left out in the square for it. While they were in Frascati a minor earthquake occurred and all the town people seemed to gather in the square. It gradually subsided over three days. Delany seems to have stayed only while they were in Rome. Ending her account, Iseult, having talked with Thora through a moonlit night about the family, summarises her view of everyone, deciding she disliked everyone except her mother, who was never bored, and Thora, who suffered the same boredom as herself. But the others she found tiresome, and detailed their faults, then chastised herself for saying bad things about them proving 'that promising and keeping a promise are two different things'. First, Chotie is mentioned with 'her gentle saintliness', then 'insignificant' May with 'her infuriating mania of always wanting to have the last word even when she is wrong and her complete lack of justice'. She disliked Kathleen's egoism, though otherwise she considered her fairly charming with her lily-like complexion and her admiration for Greece. Bichon tells tales, otherwise she 'feels a little friendship' for him. But her godmother, Suzanne Foccart, comes out the worst, 'a stupid woman with very bad taste who let herself be stuffed into a convent when she had no vocation,... very greedy, with many self indulgences and sinking into the habit of petty nastiness'.

As opposed to Iseult's experience, Maud found great peace and spiritual fulfilment in Italy. One day, feeling very tired, she let the children go off to explore the Catacombs, while she sat down to rest and wait. There a deep sense of peace overcame her, and she had the sense that she was being told that love was all that was important. Later Thora described her in the rattling train singing a poem about love to her. When in Assisi, she became a devotee of St Francis and while there became a member of his Third Order. She held to this devotion all her life and was buried in the Order's habit.

They did not stay long in Paris on their return before going to Colleville for the summer, where they were joined by a stream of visitors including May, Helen Laird from Ireland, who was helping Maud on the school feeding project, and Joseph and Marinette Granié. Joseph was using Iseult as a model for a drawing of the Angel of the Annunciation. With their guests they visited the old Norman towns of Caen, Bayeux and Coutence, Iseult remembering her ecstatic experience at the Easter ceremonies in Bayeux two years before. Then she had found herself filled with joy and had spent days praying on her knees, and in a burst of love, cried her hatred of sin, for it seemed God was listening to her prayers and that the calm of her soul would never leave her. But now everything was different. Trying to get back to Christ she felt alone and abandoned with a vague unknown terror of something menacing her, so she stayed in the back of the church trying to say the *De profundis*.

There was great delight in learning to swim, experiencing the exquisite sensation that one feels in dreams where it is so easy to fly, swim, or walk on the water like ancient prophets. She wandered in the woods looking for fossils, sitting by the stream almost hidden by ferns, listening to its sound and the murmur of the summer insects while thinking sadly of Thora who had said 'I cannot understand people who are always admiring nature'. 'I, for my part', Iseult wrote 'think nothing is as beautiful as nature, it is a truth which has endlessly been repeated, repetition is a little banal, but who cares. When something is beautiful is it not better to repeat it a hundred times after everybody on earth has already said it than to disown it in order to follow modern time which always wishes one to sacrifice beauty for originality.'

She concluded that, like Pindar, she could never stick to the same subject, but unlike him poetry led her on in spite of herself because it was a proof of her mixed-up confused spirit. Through the three months of the summer she also read Plato and Chateaubriand, disagreeing with the latter when he said the literary beauty of the Bible was superior to pagan literature. Apart from the New Testament which she considered 'a marvel', comparing the literature of the old Jews to Homer seemed to her ridiculous.

While doing little herself she admired her mother 'who had not time to be bored' and who was painting a beautiful symbolic picture of the Sacred Heart, which should be in all the churches 'instead of the ugly productions of modern religious art'. She was also embroidering Celtic designs around a harp for a flag and enjoyed gardening with Dan and May. Bichon played with his 13-year-old cousin, Michael Gonne, May's nephew, who was later killed in the war in 1918.

Returning from Colleville near the end of September, Iseult and Maud only paused long enough to change their summer clothes, faded by the sun and sea, to something more respectable before going to London, where Iseult was to stay with May while Maud went on to Ireland to busy 'herself in her fine energetic way finding money to feed 500 school children for the winter.'

In London 'May was everything that was kind' and showered her with gifts, 'Kathleeen was charming' and everybody she met was 'agreeable' but she found London ugly and did not really like Kathleen and May. She was homesick, 'missing the melancholy solitude of our old ramshackle abode penetrated with humidity and in which the polished chairs break under the weight of Dan and the walls on which were scribbled the masterpieces of Bichon and me. I regretted all the things which were the despair of others.'

But she loved being with Thora again. They could discuss their boredom and frustrations and theorise about love – romantic love. Unless Iseult could have the pure love of Dante and Beatrice, she said 'let us take a lover but never a husband. Unless one got married in order to cheat the husband by enjoying the forbidden fruits of a lover, and then, fed up with the lover, come and sit in the Tuileries, pale faced, and think remorsefully of the enormity of the sin.' Later lying in bed imagining this she really thought she knew what this would feel like. Then they wondered whether, indeed, a lover was worth more than a husband and a marriage, which ended in a bourgeois friendship. Or was it not still better to be a nun and live the austere life of an ascetic like St Theresa? They both had a desire for liberty. Thora really shocked her when she had asked 'what do you call living' and Thora answered 'well living is loving' and added 'perhaps one day I will end up getting married to have a change'. Iseult felt deeply sad at the prospect of losing her to a man.

When in a less serious mode Iseult successfully shocked May by telling her that she had winked at a young man on the street. When in the house on their own they entertained themselves by making hoax calls, picking an unknown Mr Brown from the telephone book and asking 'Is that you duckey, have you forgotten our arrangement for this evening?' amid uncontrollable giggles.

She was back in Paris before her mother, whose 'beautiful energy' was raising money for school children. She wrote that 'between Dan and Delany I am as bored as ever and I have only one consolation, if it is one, to know that it is neither changing the occasion nor surroundings, nor habit which can change this state of boredom and I have decided by reading Marcus Aurelius, to accept my boredom without looking for the relish of forbidden joys, but to cure oneself in trying to cultivate a little more will and to acquire this peaceful solitude of which the Roman Emperor spoke.'

She went on to write of those around her who were so feeble and denigrated each other, were jealous and despised each other. As well as Dan and Delany she included Le Loup, as she called her father, and Tatan – Madame Avril. As for herself, she had deep down 'a beautiful disdain of other people' and had 'seen all the beautiful thoughts of my soul come like lightning and then go leaving space for my selfish and stupid boredom.' For her sleepless nights, when these thoughts circled, the doctor advised hot baths, but as the bath was broken that was useless, and anyway she thought little of doctors.

From the time they were children Thora was in awe of Iseult's intelligence. In earlier days Iseult would give Thora hard pinches and beat her with nettles to train her to be a stoic, as she thought herself to be, and called her Doucette. From then on Thora had also worried about Iseult's defeatist attitude, especially when she wrote, much to Thora's reluctant admiration:

Il y'a des animaux méchantes et nous sommes les pires
Hommes vous êtes fait pour souffrire et non pour jouire

Whatever Iseult understood of stoicism when young, apart from withstanding the pain of nettle stings, she now had a fuller appreciation of it with her increasing knowledge of philosophy and the thought of the ancient Greeks. Marcus Aurelius, the Roman Emperor of the second century A.D., had also studied the stoic philosophy of Zenon and Plato, and, wishing to achieve self-reliance and wisdom for himself and his people, wrote down his *Meditations* throughout his life.

From around 1905 Maud made frequent references to Iseult in her letters. She wrote of her growing beauty, her intelligence and of the contrasts in her character – childish and wise, tomboy and lazy, imaginative and wild, her interest in art and literature, her great taste and her gift of writing, for which her mother had growing hopes of her 'doing something interesting' yet over all was inertia and no motivation.

Iseult did write and made up a secret code for some her stories, illustrated by designs in pen and ink of weird animals and graceful Greek figures. Much of what she wrote has been lost. Her imagination was very different from the average. The philosophy and thought in her reading, as well as ancient literature, were mingled in a beautiful unrealistic web, stories pacing romantically and sadly through a formal life which could have stepped down from a Grecian frieze or an Etruscan urn, ordered sadness and tragedy once removed – an escape from the unpredictability and chaos of her immediate life. This escape into another world would stay with her always, changing scenes beyond antiquity as her reading expanded and fired her imagination.

Long before we first hear of her whipping Thora with nettles or burning an offering to Athena, her imagination probably had carried her away into another world whenever unpleasantness or loneliness distressed her. Maud's many long absences, Madame de Bourbonne's threatening her with rats in the cellar and perhaps other such horrors, Madame Foccart's ghoulish dressing up, the threat of Eileen and John MacBride to her fragile security, let alone his frightening behaviour, even if she was not fully aware of its implications, and then her mother's constant concern for her little brother, all these struggles of real life were abandoned for that of ordered and controllable imagination, where there could be great tragedy, and fantastic glorious things happening and beauty prevailing – 'the beautiful thoughts of her soul'. She needed, too, protection from the sadness of the anonymity of her birth, the reincarnation of someone else, no named father or mother, no one to whom she could say she wholly belonged, only niece or cousin to her mother, goddaughter instead of daughter to her father, and then the fear of all this being exposed. Lastly, did she need to protect herself from her shame and helplessness in contrast to her adoring mother's ability to occupy herself creatively and with purpose?

Though her mother was well known and respected among her friends, her situation was unconventional, an unmarried Irishwoman of means living in France, with her adopted 'cousin'. This in itself was difficult for a young child to explain to little friends. It was a problem her mother might never have met or understood herself. This was only the start of Iseult's problems. So when young though extremely intelligent and full of ideals, the contradictions in her life were beyond her immature ability to comprehend, yet that intelligence may have heightened her awareness of the wrongness of things, the sudden impatience when this awareness overflowed in frustration, the extravagances of her ideas and games an effort to shape her own norm. Later it would seem that the philosophical and spiritual reading she had undertaken and continued to undertake over the years was in a way her search to find some way through the maze of her unhappiness, a solution and a belief.

On her return from London, to shake herself out of her boredom, she used a device she probably employed frequently to shock people she despised or simply to relieve her frustration. She whiled away some of the time shocking Dan's Catholic sensibilities with outrageous comments, by which Dan was suitably shocked. She expounded the idea that, if her husband was of inferior intelligence she had not only the right but the duty to take a lover with an intelligence equal to hers, and if he were not handsome enough she would take another because one tires as quickly of a man as of a dress.

There were other entertaining moments. One evening she and Bichon were busy making a magic paste with ashes and eau de cologne. To get into the mood they had dressed in old rags, she with a blue veil which was 'as full of holes as the dining room chairs'. Malyé, a young Celtic scholar, came in and they all burst out laughing. The conversation turned to literature. Though Malyé was intelligent and educated she thought him too pedantic and he got on her nerves, especially when he compared Greek literature to seventeenth-century French literature. Then Dan appeared in her old dressing gown and it all became boring and she and Bichon longed to get back to their magic ash pie.

The only other event worthy of her comment that autumn was one she recorded with the great delight of excitement. 'Super, super, a new and remarkable thing is coming to trouble our gentle boredom.' The house had to be vacated as one of its gable walls was to be pulled down, so they 'were to have the joy of removal'. Her mother was passing 'charming days with lawyers', looking for compensation for the studio she had built in the garden, and Iseult was passing 'days no less ideal' looking for a new apartment and quite enjoying herself 'composing a different discourse for every concierge'.

Thora passed through, going to Switzerland with Kathleen and her brothers for the Christmas jollities in an hotel. Knowing that she would be utterly bored with such a holiday she wondered at Thora's taste – or was it really smart of her to be able to amuse herself with such good heart? As soon as they were alone Toby embraced her and she remembered the exquisite days three years before in Colleville when she thought herself completely enraptured by him, and remembered Dan, her nose glued to the window, while he kissed her in the dining room, and her satisfaction of having a sin worthwhile confessing.

## 17 Rue de l'Annonciation, 1912–13

In January they moved from the little house to an apartment on the Rue de l'Annonciation. Maud wrote to Yeats, 'This apartment is comfortable & modern & in a quiet street just opposite the Passy Church. It has electricity, central heating & a bathroom, lifts etc, but I miss my big studio – however I believe I shall get a small one on the top floor of this house soon'. Indeed now her visitors were able to rent a small apartment for themselves when they came to visit. Iseult's comment about leaving the little house was 'I don't regret it at all. I was too bored' she wrote. 'Another thing Dan has left, it was a little sad for a moment but now I have almost forgotten her.' She also gave up her class as it was too boring. This must have been something she took up when given the freedom to choose what she would like to study after leaving school. Life now was different for her and she was very free except she had 'to take the boy to school'. Also her mother sometimes invited some young people and some old ladies in the evenings. Among them were Marinette Granié, and the young scholars Pelletier and Malyé. Malyé talked boringly for hours on the Celtic question. Thora said that Maud, conscious of Iseult's illegitimate status, had taken pains to meet and invite to the house young men of a suitable kind.

With her new found freedom she entertained herself at first by practising the art of being a well brought up young lady and tried, 'like Thora nowadays', to lead a carefree and gay life, that of someone who only thinks of following the fashion. Hobble skirts were in fashion; Iseult who studied *Bon Ton* and other fashion books, loved to pose with a long cigarette holder, which may have started her smoking. So having spent half the day doing her nails and trying a new hair style, she paraded down the street in a costume with a very tight skirt in which she could hardly walk. A blouse and a big white jabot finished the ensemble. She felt she almost had the air of a mannequin in one of the big shops. Yet time refused to be killed for her so she took to reading books 'which perhaps make one blush'. For a while she found this better but then she began to think that there was more beauty and joy in vice, then realised that vice was not beautiful. Tired of dreaming of a real lover, either the one who ends by leaving or the one who bores, she returned to thinking of the platonic lover of her dreams, Celiste, of whom she spoke to nobody, as they would laugh at its impossibility. Then chastising herself for spending her nights with these stupid dreams, thinking if she tried to sleep instead she would be more reasonable and less of a child.

With May and Chotie she went to the theatre to see *Electra* in Greek and felt the actor had wonderfully understood the 'Hellenic grace' and it seemed to her as if she was watching the figures of an Etruscan vase actually moving. When there were no visitors she still sometimes went to the theatre, or the Louvre or Cluny, but mostly owing to lack of money she spent her time at home attempting to practise the austerities of Marcus Aurelius.

Feeling spring in the air she took long walks in the country. Yet after longing for spring she felt she was still sad. Thora came in March, Iseult wondering 'Why does she always talk of love? I had forgotten it while reading Marcus Aurelius and now I only think of love.' She also wrote stories, or rather her thoughts and dreams in the third person, stories of formalised people of another world, perhaps Greece of her imagining. Stories about the imminent beauty of nature or about love, 'trying to prove that it is love that causes discord between the body and spirit when actually she desired one thing and that was love.'

Early in January 1912 Maud had written to Yeats that her 'little Jean' was making charming progress at school, where he had apparently started that autumn, which reminded her of Iseult at about the same age when she nearly got meningitis. Iseult wrote in her *Journal* on 17 February that he was sick in bed and mentioned the fear of appendicitis. Many years later Maud wrote of this illness at length in a notebook. As always with her, her memory of the duration of time and date is unreliable but the detailed account shows how worried she was and her constant concern for her little boy, which, over the years, must undoubtedly have had an effect on Iseult.

The doctors said he would grow out of these illnesses and this seemed to be the case – they had all come back from Italy last year very well. It was then that Dan, who had been privy to all the worry concerning him, told her that when he had been having the fainting fits the doctors had said they thought he would not live to be seven. Obviously she thought he was safe now, as he was well and happy after the holiday and glad to be starting school. But now, regularly, he was brought home by a schoolmaster, unable to walk or stand from pain. For a few days or a week he would be all right and would want to return to school for it only to happen all over again. After a few months and a procession of doctors it was decided to operate for an appendix. Maud and one of the doctors thought it might be a return of the old symptoms but finally she let the operation go ahead. A judicial tip to the laboratory assistant and he gave her the appendix in a bottle with the remark 'there is not much wrong with it'. At the end of her account she wrote 'I had refused three operations for myself but had not the courage for my son'.

Operations for appendix were fashionable in Paris that year. Delany kept the bottle and the appendix as a souvenir of her 'glory boy'. Once Iseult told Thora that she was convinced Bichon could work up a temperature when his mother was going away. In one of her furies, upset at the injustice and his duplicity, she hid the thermometer. Maud watched and nursed the child until he was well enough for them all to go to Colleville in April, where Maud suffered a severe delayed reaction to Sean's illness. They stayed until September. Yeats came for two weeks in August when the weather was not good.

He worked very hard on a number of things including writing an introduction to *Gitanjali* by the Indian poet Tagore, whose work he greatly admired. He had recently met him and they had become friends. Iseult, too, grew interested in his poetry. Later, at her request, Yeats gave her a Bengali grammar and dictionary, so that she could read the poems for herself. It was this stay which inspired him to write two poems to Iseult: 'To a Child Dancing in the Wind', and 'Two Years Later'. Aware of her youth in contrast to his age and aware of her young vulnerability he thinks with sadness, tinged by bitterness, of the trouble and unhappiness that will come to her, as it came to him and to her mother.

The last few days of his visit and work were interrupted by an unexpected and, from his point of view, unwelcome visit from the rather adulatory Cousins and his wife from Dublin who had been staying some distance away confined by constant rain. Maud sent them an invitation to be 'drowned' with them rather than on their own. Maud, Yeats and Bichon met them at the nearby train station with a donkey cart. She took Mrs Cousins back to the house in the cart while Yeats and Cousins walked through the fields. Cousins describes Iseult, Madame's 'niece', who greeted him with 'much friendliness and natural freedom ... a tall, slender girl of great beauty of countenance and grace of form'. He describes all the very numerous animals, Yeats's totally absent-minded table manners and the conversation on astrology and mediumship after dinner around the open fire till after midnight. Next day, Sunday, all walked to mass, where Maud was to present a new embroidered altar cloth, except Yeats and Cousins who were left to 'work', Yeats in the drawing room and Cousins elsewhere. After some time Cousins heard 'a strange monotonous murmur'; following the sound through the house he finally located it in the kitchen, where Yeats was sitting on a chair facing close into a corner, and 'there was a constant repetition of the same sounds'. For three hours he went on. On her return Maud asked 'How did you get on, Willie?' He told her he had finished it. He had been composing a poem. Next day Maud, 'once the most virulent propagandist of anti-British sentiment in Ireland, who had cleared the English jails of Irish political prisoners', took them to Bayeux in a large Normandy farm cart with hooped canvas covering, 'through the leafy lanes of Normandy'. There were seven in all including Malyé and the driver. There she showed them the sights of the town and left them to see Yeats safely on to his train before they got theirs while she returned before dark, now carrying the newly arrived Pelletier with her.

After Yeats had left Maud wrote to him, 'I have still the house full of people and have to do Chaperone, it wastes a lot of time'. Malyé and Pelletier were still there. She hoped that Pelletier, who was Secretary to the Celtic League, would be able to turn it into a big movement. While staying with them he had written a remarkable essay as well as some rather good verses to Iseult. Maud wrote to Yeats, 'the thunderclap of Iseult's growing up has not come yet – she is at present enjoying herself wildly playing hide & seek with Bichon & young Micheal Gonne – '. Her mother probably had no idea of her secret imaginings or her stolen kisses with Toby, let alone whatever else she dreamed of.

With them all back in Paris for a short spell Maud writes of Iseult, 'she has been breaking several hearts lately! but I hope her own is quite untouched as yet.' Iseult writes nothing of these six months. One wonders if this is because she was relatively happy and occupied, so had no need to find release in her *Journal*. But in October the *Journal* again takes up, for she and

Bichon went to May in Florence for three months while Maud went to Belgium to study school feeding there and then to Ireland, meeting them in Florence for Christmas. Regretting that Yeats is unable to join them it is she who describes May's villa, writing from the Villa Castiglione, 'This is a wonderfully beautiful place – on a hill with olive groves all around & beautiful views of Florence & of the mountains. It is an old Italian house with marble floors & great high rooms such as you love – The weather is rather cold but very bright & sunny'. She added that both Bichon and Iseult were 'so well and happy'. Yeats sent Maud a copy of Tagore's poems for Christmas and an Indian book for Iseult.

Of course, Iseult's view was somewhat different. The only amusement was when Toby was there; he stayed for a month before joining the family at Adelboden in Switzerland.

To the great indignation of the family we spent our days together all alone in a large room upstairs and we really were an amusing spectacle. Each of us in a voluminous armchair beside the fire, him with his spectacles and his eternal pipe and always a big book of law [Toby later became a judge and was knighted] which he wasn't reading and I with my head enveloped in multi-coloured veils smoking innumerable cigarettes with Plutarch's *Lives* which I was reading or I wasn't reading. The state of things made for some famous family scenes, which amused me a lot, but I don't think Toby took them so cheerily. . . . there under the olive trees by a stream and a stone bench what a lot of poetry the unfortunate Toby had to submit to in the moonlight or in the setting sun, that moment which I always said was the most beautiful of the day, the moment when we are demi-gods and are almost becoming gods and fly far away into the golden clouds. Then like a swallow Toby went off to a distant country and I stayed alone in the respectable but not very amusing company of May and Chotie who accompanied me everywhere. Of course a young lady, it seems should not go out alone there.

Toby in the meantime went off to join the family, where the young Pilchers were skating, dancing and flirting. Though Thora was depressed and, at 20, felt life was over, she loved to flirt and arrayed in her new clothes she had 'many sweet bigles' – Iseult's word for boy friends. Though aloof and scornful, did Iseult secretly long for a taste of this life? Earlier that year Thora had been presented at court, resplendent in a feathered headdress and a yard's long train, and though Kathleen did not feel strong enough to entertain she ensured that Thora had a good time, escorted by Toby to dances, parties and weekends.

On returning from Florence Maud became very ill after nursing Bichon through measles. For a few days her life was at risk. Through all this she was terrified for the children, as she feared Bichon's father would claim him and the entailed money that went with him. For Iseult losing her adored mother would mean living with May. She had to write to Quinn in place of Maud to thank him for his Christmas gifts, saying 'I am writing for my cousin who is ill...' having to maintain the lie of her situation accentuates how alone she really could be.

She mentions nothing of Maud being so ill, in her by now rather sporadic *Journal*, nor that Kathleen and Thora spent April in Paris. Iseult was feeling the distance between them growing, though Thora assured her she was still a gutter cat. Thora describes this month. Though she did not find the apartment as charming and magical as the little house on the Rue de Passy Maud had made it attractive. She gave a soirée every Thursday. The *froteur* would come to polish the furniture, Iseult would arrange the flowers in many vases, one in each vase, then in their best dresses with fashionable blue ribbons in their hair they would meet the guests, writers, politicians and those interested in Ireland, who were served coffee and cakes. Bichon, now just ten, was full of fun. As well as going to the Jesuits around the corner, he was being tutored by the Abbé Combat from Passy Church opposite, who had taught him to say, 'God, how stupid women are.' Delany was bustling with importance. She told Iseult she almost liked Thora, except for her Protestant eyes. In spite of her serious Roman Catholicism and her self-importance Thora liked her because she was an integral part of the household which she loved.

Iseult took her to visit Granié whom Thora described as a little middle-aged man who sold his pictures to a shop. The apartment was downstairs in the same building, Marinette was in a hip bath as they passed through to the studio; unconcerned, she waved a welcome, sponge in hand. Granié said Thora was like a Florentine painting and wanted to draw her. He said they were both so beautiful but that they would be even more beautiful if they were in love. Women were never more beautiful as when they were in love. As he drew, Iseult stood by him helping and advising, 'it is not natural for her to have her mouth open' and so on. Thora was disappointed with the result; instead of a beautiful Florentine she saw her usual self, 'a tame pussy cat'. Kathleen had told Thora Iseult's story and she wanted to go with her the next time she was visiting her 'godfather', Le Loup as Iseult called him, which she did every month when he would give her a 'tip' of 50 francs. Escaping the house unnoticed they went to meet him in his office. He was very tall, slim and dark with polished manners and ready to flirt with Thora, saying she reminded him of Maud when she was young. Like many roués Thora found him charming, but a roué.

Thora slept in Iseult's room. As usual they told each other their secrets and desires and talked of their 'bigles'. Iseult said she could make any man love her, but she could do without a man, the essence of her soul was

**Fig. 5** Lucien Millevoye – 'Like many roués Thora found him charming' © Imogen Stuart

everything to her. Thora was good at singing and they quoted poetry and sang love songs. At another time, some hot summer that they slept on the roof, Iseult in a shirt uncle Yeats had left behind, they could see the lighted rooms of the other houses as people were going to bed.

Sometime after the Pilchers left Iseult went to Florence where May and Chotie continued to annoy her. As she was not yet well enough the doctor advised Maud not to go to the sea, so she sent Bichon off with Delany to Colleville, where Iseult remarked he was 'probably filling himself with filth of devotion and grand airs'.

In July Iseult travelled to London while Maud went to Dax for her rheumatism. Iseult and Thora had their usual heart-to-heart talks about life in Kathleen's attic bedroom. The chat was more mature but not any happier. Thora was 'very jolly at some moments, singing and telling me laughingly of all her little flirtations, then at other moments, so sad as not to know what to do with herself'. Iseult said with conviction 'one must marry a very rich man, with riches one does have a certain independence' and Thora asked 'is it any use to come out of the demi slavery of one's parents to fall into the same thing with a husband?' Toby was very busy and was shut in his office, and after tea he went to row at Putney until dinner but they 'managed to kiss each other a fair amount – may be a little more than was reasonable.' They discovered that natural love is not to be despised but not sufficient and really rather dangerous. Toby, she wrote, 'pleased her very much and he was very brave, incapable of a low mean trick and very companionable. But . . . ' and added 'alas, with nearly everything there is always a but.' There was another 'bigle', Augustus, whom she also saw. So her social life cannot

**Fig. 6** Toby Pilcher, Bichon and Iseult, c. 1912 – Toby 'was very brave, incapable of a low mean thing and very companionable' © Anna MacBride White

have been as bad as she thought. May took her to see her brother Charley and his son 'Pom Pom' (Vere Carol Melville Gonne, 1894–1961). The wife and mother Shelty was a suffragette. Their house could be seen from a distance because a large white and green flag flew from the roof top 'against the eternal grey of the English sky' and all the windows were obscured by posters demanding votes for women. Charley 'was charming with baroque ideas and an eternal optimism believing humanity would be good again when women had the same rights as men'. Iseult was not so sure of this outcome and was unmoved by his enthusiasm for women's freedom.

What she does not relate about this visit to London is that Yeats took her to meet Tagore. Maud had hoped that Yeats would come back with her to Paris and join them for a holiday in the Pyrenees in the company of Marinette and Joseph Granié. The place was suggested by the Abbé Combat, who had holidayed there.

Her August entry starts, 'What to say of the state of the Cafard' – this is the first time in her *Journal* that she names her state of mind using the slang French term for depression – 'of vague little dabbles with love, of removals where you lug along with you a trunk, dogs and parents and which one is conventionally expected to call voyages. It is in this unvarying theme I pursue my existence.' Maud wrote enthusiastically to Yeats saying the house they were staying in was at the edge of a torrent.

> The people remind me of our peasants at their best they are dignified & very courteous & hospitable & they have a real artistic sense. The women drape them selves in the most beautiful black cloaks on Sundays the folds make me quite envious, & their houses are beautiful in their comfortable simplicity & nearly all have wood carvings on their doors or interesting chiselled bronze knockers. We have two large white washed rooms with raftered ceilings a big chimney corner in a farm house. Life is quite beautiful & very inexpensive which is also a consideration for 4 francs a day one has everything one wants. We shall certainly return here next year.

Everyone's health had improved and they were all feeling well and were going to Lourdes, not very far away, to join the Irish national pilgrimage. Iseult loved the place; it was like Switzerland but wild, remote, untamed and without the Swiss.

In October, Maud took Iseult with her for about six weeks to help in Dublin where there was a strike and lockout in progress. They stayed with Ella Young in Temple Hill, on the road between Kimmage and Terenure, just beyond the end of the number 15 tram route, where Maud had found space for her furniture from Coulson Avenue and a room for herself. Also sharing the house with Ella Young was Miss Fox. It was a large, ramshackle house in its own grounds with a secret passage and 'a riotous ghost'. Maud sold her last remaining 'jewel', her diamond necklace, 'to keep up & increase the numbers of dinners for the children. Iseult is helping me in this.'

With dreadful poverty there was continual labour unrest in Dublin, which reached a climax when the Tramway men went on strike during Horse Show Week in August. At a proscribed meeting on 31 August in the city centre a huge crowd was baton-charged by the police, which resulted in 500 casualties and crowded hospitals. The Federated Employers locked out the strikers. All the prominent nationalists spoke out against the employers, including Yeats. George Russell wrote the most powerful condemnation in his 'Open Letter to the Masters of Dublin' in October.

A Citizen Army was formed by James Connolly and drilled by Captain White (the son of General White of Ladysmith) using broom handles and hurleys so that the strikers could defend themselves; this also helped to keep them occupied. A women's branch of the Citizen Army was formed. Maud had worked closely with James Connolly in the late 1890s, and now he encouraged many women to join his Citizen Army. Some of these were Maud's friends and had been members of her organisation Inghínidhe na hÉireann, which was now amalgamated with Constance de Markiewicz's Cumann mBan (Constance de Markiewicz had also formed and trained a boys' brigade, the Fianna). While in Dublin Iseult met many of these women working in the soup kitchen they set up in Liberty Hall for the starving strikers: she would have met Constance de Markiewicz peeling potatoes; Dr Kathleen Lynn, one of the first women to qualify in Ireland as a doctor, attending to the sick and the wounded; Helen Laird whom she already knew and Helena Molony who was to become her great friend.

Iseult relates none of this except to say that the strike and the political situation 'bothers poor Moura so much', more especially as there will be 'ten thousand poor idiots without work who will join the list of the starving who will end up emmigrating to America.' But she had to confess that she did not care and thought 'that life was a dirty trick, much more so for me than for them.' On her return to Paris she wrote a long philosophical dissertation, which ends by saying that she had set out to prove that all the religions since paganism, Christianity up to Atheism, have committed the same error of squashing man under his inferiority and his eternal dependency. 'The oak brakes, the willow bends but they both give way to the storm.'

All the same, she derived some amusement in Dublin. At one of George Russell's evenings she met a young man just returned from China who had read Huysmans and Anatole France and who pleased her in spite of the fact that he was small, that his complexion was brick coloured and his eyes like a lobster's. So she let him know that they 'received' at Temple Hill on Saturdays and that most days she read in the National Library. A few days later she was reading Stendhal when he turned up at the Library. But it only took a few meetings for her to find him out in his pretensions.

Back in Paris at the end of the year Maud wrote to Yeats 'Iseult was very proud at your idea of her wisdom – she is a strange mixture almost like two people, one the embodiment of youth and childhood almost, the other OLD Iseult disconcerts and alarms me though I have to admire her. She has intense imagination but lacks the energy & will to use it, and it often makes her sad and restless.' This is very true but her mother had no idea of the depth of her unhappiness, let alone understanding its multiple causes. She herself used activity to overcome unhappiness, either working constructively at her causes or working hard but creatively at her art, needlework and gardening. Her daughter's frozen inactivity which seemed like disinterest was beyond her comprehension. Even when young, Thora said, Iseult would dismiss political discussions.

Thora and Kathleen came for New Year on their way to Cairo. This was supposed to be a special treat for Thora now that she was 'out' and it made Iseult more aware of the distance growing between them. As it transpired it was not such a successful holiday because Kathleen was cut by the English people staying in the hotel since she was a divorcée and this naturally upset Thora very much, although everyone was very kind to her.

Some years before, on returning with Thora and her governess from a long holiday, Kathleen found the house full of pictures of her husband's mistress. This was the final straw in many years of unhappiness for Kathleen, who sued for divorce. On her honeymoon Kathleen had realised she had married the wrong one of her two particular suitors. David Pilcher was an ambitous soldier whose career she had thought she could help with the money she had inherited. It soon became apparent that his interests were not in marriage, but women, horses and gambling, and she was frequently expected to bail him out of debt. As the children grew she gradually led her own life, travelling abroad as much as she could, taking Thora and Miss Foster with her while the boys were at boarding school.

Her money, as was Maud's, was closely guarded by their trustees, who were members of the family and had the ethos of keeping money within it. In 1911 she was granted her uncontested divorce. Both Maud and Kathleen, constrained by their trustees, were careful with their money. Kathleen bought a London house at 12 Milner Street. Having had arguments with the trustees about decorating it, she managed to make it beautiful. Kathleen designed and made many of her own clothes. When travelling she would rent out the house for three months. Hotel life was peripatetic, different people, different hotels, different countries, so it was difficult for Thora to make lasting friendships. Because of this Iseult and she had more than the common bond of kinship in that they were lonely and lacking friends, but now that was changing for Thora, and Iseult felt she was being left more behind than before. On the return journey from Cairo Kathleen threw her heavy wedding ring into the sea.

## Devabrata Mukerjee and war, 1914–16

Early in 1913 some new people entered the life of the apartment on the Rue de l'Annonciation and were regular visitors over the next few years. One was Devabrata Mukerjee, a young Hindu scholar, a friend and admirer of Madame Cama, the Indian nationalist living in exile in Paris. He had translated Tagore's play *The Post Office*. Also there was the pianist Walter Rummel and his wife, friends of Ezra Pound who came with an introduction from Yeats, and Maud's old friends, James Stephens and his wife, who came from Dublin to live in Paris for a while. At some time Stephens was minding a cat for their friend, Stephen McKenna, and it had two kittens. One he kept for himself which he called Noiroo and the other he gave to the Gonnes, a little black persian who was to enter literary fame as Minoulouche.

Early in the spring of 1914, having given a few lectures in Paris on the poverty resulting from the strike in Dublin, Maud returned to Dublin with quantities of clothing she had been given as a result of her lectures. On her return, she was met by Iseult with the shocking news that Marinette Granié had been killed that morning in a road accident. Poor Joseph, lost without his wife, now spent much time with the Gonnes.

With the presence of the pleasant young Hindu, Mukerjee, Iseult started to learn Bengali with him as her teacher. Her friend Christiane Cherfils joined the lessons and they became interested in translating Tagore into French with his help. Maud, delighted at this development, wrote to Yeats at Mukerjee's request about the possibility of getting permission from Tagore to publish these translations.

Before Iseult, Maud and Sean left for Florence at Easter (where Sean contracted chicken pox) Mukerjee went away to London without saying anything. This turned into a little drama which continued on into July after he had returned and taken up the lessons again, but which, in the meantime, Maud puzzled over in letters to Yeats. She suspected that Malyé had some hand in the matter. He had proposed to Iseult, had been refused and was 'very jealous of her friendship with Mukerjee'. He was said to have reported that in London, where Mukerjee was applying for a professorship, he 'was drunk in public houses & all sorts of vague evil things'. Finally in July Maud wrote to Yeats on his return to London from a visit to Paris. 'Mukerjee arrived in Paris a day or so after your first letter – I sifted the mystery down – It was after all as you supposed when here, a literary invention of Iseult's, complicated by her having told it with wonderful amplifications to Christiane Cherfils who in her turn repeated it in half confidence & much excitement & it came round again to me, but I believe the whole thing originated with Iseult's imagination – & poor Mukerjee had never even heard of it'. This seemed to have been a complicated tissue of 'embroideries' Iseult had woven to obscure and evade a simple truth she wished to keep secret and which was never revealed. The matter-of-fact way her elders eventually decided it all originated from her shows that Maud probably had some previous experience of such behaviour.

The three were now working hard at Bengali and it was decided that Mukerjee and the Cherfils would all go with the Gonnes to Arrens to continue the work. So Maud's 'duties as chaperone' would be 'lightened'. But in the meantime, before Mukerjee returned, Kathleen and Thora had come to stay, probably on their return from Egypt and in June Iseult broke her foot, how is not recorded. An exasperated Maud wrote to Yeats after the Pilchers had left about her worry over Iseult, who

> ...has continued NOT to take care of her foot has been a great worry. In spite of her & of the Masseuse I got in another doctor, a specialist. He at once said what I had said from the first & which the first doctor denied that there was a fracture. We then had her foot radiographed which showed 3 *fractures*. The doctor was most urgent and told her that if she will not rest the foot *entirely* she will be lame for life. In spite of this she continues just as when you were here. I am worn out trying to persuade her to keep quiet. She is really a little mad. I hope now that Thora has left she will take to writing again, if she would it would fill her time & keep her quiet.

But Iseult's health continued to be a problem until they left for the Pyrenees.

> Iseult alarmed us very much by getting one or two faint fits last week – & several very severe nose bleedings. The Dr. is rather anxious about her, says her heart is weak. He orders her to give up smoking, to eat meat & keep her windows open – all of which she refuses to do. I think the country will do her good & she will find it harder to get the cigarettes she likes there.

This failure to look after her health is a recurring factor in Iseult's life, which may have stemmed from fear of her depression occasioning an unconscious self-destructiveness. Part of it, at this stage, is probably also a reaction to her mother's over concern. But it is obvious that she would seem to be also in a bad state of nerves, perhaps because of frustrations in her inner life and also because of the constant overseeing of her by her mother in the hot-house of a small apartment. This summer she would be 20 and in what way could she alter her life to make it more acceptable to her? Success with her translations maybe, but was her heart in the hard work for a vague possibility? In those days getting a job was not a real option for a girl, the only real option was marriage. Did she want that? She was in the same situation as Thora, who had wondered about leaving 'the demi-slavery of one's parents to fall into the same thing with a husband'. Iseult had not yet fallen sufficiently in love to consider such a situation. Her ideal was still the platonic love of Celiste of her imagining. She was, probably, still caught in her circling thoughts with no escape, except into her inner world of the imagination.

However, the Pyrenees were waiting and after an idyllic month her life was to change forever. Helen Molony, who had been ill, came to stay and to join them in the 'removal' to the remote village of Arrens in mid-July. Apart from Christiane, the Cherfils, unlike the Graniés, were not easy companions, finding the rather basic comforts not to their liking, and how long they stayed is not clear. For the rest all were happy though in the distance war clouds were gathering. The Bengali work continued and Maud wrote to Yeats urging him to write to Tagore, and adding that Iseult and Mukerjee were working hard at the translations. 'I can't tell you how glad I am to find Iseult really working & interested in the work.'

They spent their days in long walks and studying out of doors in the mountains, with Helen, now well and strong, practising voice production on the edge of a mountain torrent, all gathering for the main meal in the local inn. There was an idyllic sense of heightened companionship while the rest of Europe tumbled into the horrors of a dreadful war.

Maud heard the village church bell ring the tocsin that called the young men to come in from the harvest fields to go to war. She left the family to go to Paris in an effort to get permission to travel to Ireland; failing to get a passport she returned to Arrens and they stayed through August into September. Through Maud's scolding Iseult and Mukerjee eventually sent four specimens of their work to Yeats accompanied by a letter from Iseult on 16 August saying she hoped their work on the *Gardener* and *Crescent Moon* would be finished by the end of August.

Though unable, because of his poor French, to judge their quality himself Yeats wrote to Tagore about the translations in September asking him not to give the rights to anyone until he could find a suitable critic, and then send them, adding 'the girl has a delicate feeling for words despite her youth, and she has what may grow into a very great literary talent.' Maud reported that Iseult and Mukerjee 'had both got a spell of idleness on them. . . . Of course,' she added, 'Mukerjee has fallen in love with Iseult which has complicated things a bit'. They had moved into the nearby resort of Argelès by this time. Maud, by her unsympathetic annoyance with Iseult and Mukerjee, failed to understand the situation while Mukerjee was deciding whether to return to India, with difficulties in travel increasing. They consoled themselves for their last weeks together by reading Plato and Pater and talking metaphysics. They all went for two days to Lourdes for the Eucharistic Congress where the dignitaries of the Church from all over Europe gathered in their 'crimson and purple robes' with thousands of people of all classes to honour the little peasant girl and their belief in a spiritual life. Maud and Helen were deeply moved, as was Mukerjee, a Brahmin. Iseult's reaction is not recorded. Mukerjee left from there at the end of September to go to London on his way home to India. Thora said that they did not hear from him again. Eventually it was thought that he had died, perhaps had committed suicide. But in December 1916 Iseult wrote in her *Journal*:

> I opened to-day my Plato. It had remained closed since the days of Arrens; and between the leaves were still blades of grass and moss and the odour of the hay. Sad, sad, sweetness of memory! My little brother we spent too casually to-gether the gifts of the gods; I often think of it with remorse; a sinner to whom his sins have brought success is unrepentful; remorse you know comes with failure; that is why we have a right to remorse, you and I, my little brother. We have failed. Nostra Culpa, nostra maxima culpa.

The wounded were being brought from the front by train to the south, arriving in a dreadful state after the lengthy journey. The mayor of Argelès had come to the village of Arrens looking for help; all the hospitals were full and he was converting the casino into a hospital. The only two women most likely to be able to organise this were Maud and the pharmacist's wife in Argelès. It was for this reason that Maud had moved into the town. She wrote 'Every hospital is overcrowded & every public building throughout France is turned into a hospital. I have been taken on as a regular Red X nurse & Iseult and Helen Molony as helpers & even Bichon is employed as page'. Maud felt that though this might distract Iseult from her writing it would bring her into contact with 'real life' and, her basic philosophy coming to the fore, she added 'it is too awful to stand idly by & watch suffering.'

Helen was finally able to get home to Ireland and later to take part in her own war. The Gonnes stayed on working in Argelès for three months, getting back to wartime Paris by Christmas. Iseult is silent on this nursing experience. Unknown to his mother the ten-year-old 'page', Sean, had been wheeling body parts away from the operating theatre, but returned to school after Christmas.

During early 1915 Maud's obsessions, which must have affected Iseult considerably, were mainly concerned with the war and her desire and indecision about returning to Ireland where she might 'regain some of the careless peace' she used to have. As a compensation she urged Yeats to visit, as her cousins did, reassuring him that he was too well known to be mistaken for an anarchist; but by 1916 she was saying travel was very difficult. Her income was cut by half because of the war and she had to live quietly. She wrote that life was tragic, Paris was very sad, everyone seemed to be in mourning and the streets were full of maimed people, ruined houses, Zeppelin raids and falling bombs. She also worried about the uselessness of nursing men in order to send them back to the front as cannon fodder. She had been having strange psychic experiences, seeing those she knew dead on the battlefield, and then hearing of their death. Finally she gave up hope of getting Iseult to continue with Bengali. Captain White of the Citizen Army who was in Paris 'body snatching', rescuing the wounded from the field, had dinner with them and Stephens, so an attempt at normality continued.

At the outbreak of war Toby Pilcher had volunteered as a dispatch rider. Kathleen who had shut up her house, furnished an ambulance and hired a driver to bring the wounded to whatever hospital she was in, left Thora safe in London with friends and had gone to the front to nurse the wounded in Etaples so that she could be near her 'golden boy' Tommy if he should be wounded. He was killed at Neuve Chapelle in March. He was only 21. Maud and Iseult went to join Kathleen in Etaples. Iseult stayed on nursing on the wards with Kathleen while Maud returned to Paris and Bichon.

Later the three were working in Normandy in Paris Plage (near Etaples) in two French military hospitals within the sound of cannon fire and May joined them there. Sean was either with them for the holidays or boarding with the Jesuits, as he said later he did at times. Vera Brittain wrote of her experience of nursing in Etaples in 1917 where the wounded came in lorries direct from the dressing stations. She describes herself:

> ...gazing half-hypnotised at the dishevelled beds, the stretchers on the floor, the scattered boots and piles of muddy khaki, the brown blankets turned back from smashed limbs bound to splints by filthy blood-stained bandages. Beneath each stinking wad of sodden wool and gauze an obscene horror waited for me – and all the equipment I had for attacking it in this ex-medical ward was a pair of forceps standing in a potted-meat glass half-full of methylated spirit.
>
> *Testament of Youth* (1933), Ch. VIII

Maud wrote to John Quinn on 25 July 1915 that Iseult thought it 'an *abrutisement* life which leaves no room for the intellect', but added that she made a very good nurse all the same and 'the soldiers love her'. From intimations in her letters to Thora one can pick up this ability to make contact with her patients. But there was one searing episode, probably in her first days on the wards, which shocked her to the core, the memory above all others that lasted her whole life. She was caring for a man who had just had a trepanning operation and his wound started to bleed profusely. Not knowing what she should do, in a panic, she went looking for a qualified nurse, and ran down corridors looking for one. On finding her she explained breathlessly and to her utter shock she got a box on her ears for leaving her patient. Never having been scolded so forcibly or ever had her ears boxed, on top of her fright, this left a lasting sense of horror and injustice. But at another time when the doctors were on strike she had charge of the worst cases.

They stayed in Etaples for six gruelling months. Back in Paris at the end of August Maud had tea with Millevoye and his son; a few days later she saw

**Fig. 7** 'The soldiers love her'. Paris Plage, 1915 © Anna MacBride White

his son dead as she prayed in Passy Church, but told no one until she got a telegram from Millevoye saying his son had been killed. Some time later Iseult went to meet her father and found him weeping. She was full of pity for him over the loss of his only son, killed before his time, and spoke of this. To her shock and utter disillusion she discovered it was not for his son he wept but for his mistress who had left him.

Millevoye was chairman of the French army's committee on aviation and so was in a position to get Iseult a part-time job as secretary to an Aviation Society where she was to meet many engineers, politicians and aviators, very different to the academics, artists and writers to whom she was more accustomed. It earned her £100 a year, enough to enable her to buy her own clothes and to be somewhat independent. Later her mother reported that though the work enabled her to dress well, she was 'brought into contact with a nasty side of life & has had some nasty moral shocks – on the whole I think they have done her no harm, it has given me great confidence in her, for she has shown great moral dignity combined with tact & gracefulness – a really rare combination & quite surprising in anyone so young & in some ways such a child as Iseult.' She also nursed part time in a hospital in Passy set up in the Lycée Janson-de-Sally.

At some stage Millevoye displayed an interest in Iseult's future and suggested to her that she should become the mistress of a powerful man; he thought to be an Aspasia was a most influential and fulfilling life for a woman. Aspasia was the mistress of Pericles, (c. 493–29 B.C.). She was a beautiful and cultivated woman and their relationship was close and harmonious, but she came from a class of women, mostly slaves, called 'companions' or prostitutes, and there was a huge prejudice against her in Athenian society and much slander put abroad about her. Any child she might have was considered illegitimate. Iseult, even when young, sharing her secrets among the poppies and sunflowers, had sworn she would never sell herself – love was sacred. If one were to judge by Millevoye's attitude and values she herself was the result of such an alliance. He had hurt her in the same way he had hurt Maud when she was young by asking her, for his personal advantage, to sleep with another man, showing the value he put on both women.

At this time she went to a soothsayer, 'that stupid woman', who told her she would see Mukerjee again in years to come. 'Maybe then I will have learned the wisdom of strength' and she indulged in sad imaginings of both of them turning grey, meeting and greeting with open hands 'My little brother this is a good day and he replies "Indeed, a very good day, my sister".'

Yeats must have written to Iseult on her return from Paris Plage in September telling her of Tagore's letter of 31 August in which he had said that he remembered the beautiful girl he had met in Chelsea and would do all he could to help her in her Bengali studies and translations when he next met her. In answer to this Iseult said her knowledge of Bengali is 'misty' and she could not do the work now that Mukerjee was gone, for they could not correspond as the censor did not allow his letters through. Looking for advice and help in what direction she should now go she wrote 'you are the person in whose mind I trust and believe in most and I must apply to you.'

Maud also started working part time a few nights a week in the Hospital de Lycée Janson around the corner from where they lived. She was still having strange mystical experiences in the form of visions or dreams. She had been haunted by the rhythm of a dance she had heard in Ireland, a reel connected to the number 16. Then suddenly one day in church the music became wild and triumphant. She saw or felt herself amongst masses of the spirits of the dead killed in the war being drawn into this dance of freshness and joy, thousands of Irish soldiers being led back to their spiritual home, Ireland.

Thora and Kathleen passed through on their way to Switzerland as Kathleen's lungs were again troubling her, this causing Maud great worry. At that time 17 Rue de l'Annonciation was a sadder place as Joseph Granié had died while they were in Paris Plage. But Maud was very pleased with Iseult, writing to Yeats, 'Iseult has been writing some really VERY remarkable things lately. I am longing for you to see them.'

Her life was very difficult at this time with the constriction at home, her concern for her mother's distress over her visions and dreams, the ever present horror of war, and her loss of Mukerjee, coupled with her doubts about her own ability to love. Pater and Huysmans, whom she studied in detail, believed that the individual must be to himself the measure of things. For her to find her way and keep some form of balance in her life, let alone strive for her ideals, must have been beyond her ability, so she put too much strain on herself resulting in failures and consequent depression. But as she was now writing what Maud found so good it might seem that she was coming to some kind of resolution of her own. She also came to view her mother objectively. Thora thought that Maud was more casual in general in her attitude to Iseult than Kathleen was to her, and in particular keeping her protected and away from the horrors of the war. Iseult wrote a piece on Maud in a little blue notebook which greatly impressed Thora, and shows Iseult's ability to be objective.

> I look on Moura. I don't know why she makes me think of a live fountain springing from the soil, a spring of some healing water endowed with a primitive life-giving power. One could learn from her much courage and much charity, if those could be learned. They flow from her like the water from the spring, evenly, prodigally, blindly unaware of their power and of the meaning of such power. Who have I ever met with such richness of life, self-condensed, yet spreading all around. And with all that why does she not achieve a great reality? Why? Just through the lack of the knowledge of proportions and values.
>
> She is the boiling healing spring that scatters its waters over grey rocks in the hills and loses them among the boggy moors saying in its credulity 'Good is good for all and all is good for good'.
>
> And it is not so.

Good is only good for the living; and many that move around us, yes, perhaps those that move the most are not the living at all. They are as yet but the existing for which every thing which is not the daily food and bread of the body is not only useless but dangerous.

So long as she will judge people and things by their deeds and not by their possibilities she will make the wrong choice. Deeds are more often than not a lure. They are on the whole useful only for self-analysis, and there indeed of great use. If I were to symbolize my thoughts on this point I would say: 'Judge yourself by the fruit. Judge others by the blossom'.

And thus one is oneself alive and living among the living.

O torrent clair et limpid! Plus qu'aucun etre humain peut etre je t'aime. Ton instinct de vie est indentique au mien.

In a letter to Yeats in March Maud said Sean had got influenza and she had decided they should all go to Colleville for a month at Easter. Maud, being a great believer in self-sufficiency when needed, intended to supervise the sowing of the potato field and garden as a famine precaution.

According to Iseult, writing to Thora in March, May came to stay before they set out for Colleville and went with them. She also said that Bichon was always seedy and that Maud, fearing tuberculosis, was very worried about him. Like her manner of addressing Mukerjee Iseult opened her letter to 'My sweet brother Victor' and signed herself 'Maurice' (see note p. 80). This would seem part of her desire for the ideal brotherly love of Plato mixed with that of a noble and chivalric Christian ideal. Iseult was very depressed when writing this letter; it shows an unusual self-awareness in one so young and yet a hopelessness.

Have you got, darling, a blinding sense of failure that makes you feel occasionally that your life is as good as over?

That is the feeling I have now not occasionally but always. There is no poetry in it no bitterness or sadness even; just a dull knowledge that I will never achieve anything, that I will never be of any good either to myself or to others. I know now that I am not reliable to others nor even to myself. I don't think it is possible to realise anything more disheartening than that.

If you have a great secret that makes you unhappy, don't share it with me. I would probably keep it for a day or two, then suddenly I would make fun of it with the first fool who comes my way. I wouldn't do it out of wickedness or because I can't hold my tong [sic], but just because I would be in a light mood and feel everything was good for a joke. Then the next moment I would almost kill myself for having done [it] and feel an awful beast.

Of course I did that sort of thing in the old days only each time I thought it was quite an exception and that I would never do it again. I had faith in myself.

Now I know better.

Can you imagine anything more ghastly than to have at last realised that, just to make up to a fool, one is capable of betraying of turning into ridicule the dearest beings one knows? And not only them but one's own self.

Later Maud wrote from Colleville that the country was looking beautiful '& it is good to be away from the sadness of men among the songs of birds and the joy of life & the flowers.' Their peace, however, did not last long, for before she had finished the letter the French newspapers arrived with accounts of the Rising in Dublin, so in the same letter where she had written of the peaceful countryside she pleaded with him, 'of your charity, Willie, please send me some English papers'. And she described the horrible vision she had had at the start of the year.

She was worried and desperate for news of all her friends in Ireland, with good reason as the news that filtered through to France darkened day by day. The Rising started on Monday 24 April: British artillery cleared the streets and the city was bombarded from a gunboat on the river until the centre was in ruins. An agreed unconditional surrender was reached by 29 April. There was a huge round-up of prisoners, with subsequent courts martial and executions – 15 in all, the rest of the prisoners were marched onto boats and taken to prisons in England.

All Maud wanted to do was to get home, or at least go to London with Iseult, who had decided to go there with May. Eventually she did not leave Paris, staying with her son who had got enteritis and was very ill. His father was now a hero and Maud said he had left his son a name to be proud of. This was a huge emotional trauma for the 12-year-old boy. Whatever vague information he had been given about his father, he cannot have been unaware of the fear surrounding him. Now Maud said to him 'Your father has died for his country; he did not behave well to us – but now we can think of him with honour.' Going to school he had heard the roll read out of the honourable dead of the war, fathers of his fellow pupils; now his father's name was also read out. At last he had a father he could claim.

## Yeats, 1916

May and Iseult left for London in the middle of May. Shortly after her arrival Iseult had lunch with Yeats telling him she had come to find out where Helen Molony was, to see if she could get a passport for Maud and to ask him to return to Paris with her as Maud was sad and lonely and not sleeping well. Yeats decided Bernard Shaw was the best person to find where Helen was and he himself set about getting a passport for Paris, necessary now because of the war. Yeats wrote of Iseult to Lady Gregory:

**Fig. 8** Iseult c. 1918. 'She looks very distinguished & is now full of self possession'. (Photo also in *W.B. Yeats* by A. Norman Jeffares) © Christina Bridgwater

She looks very distinguished & is now full of self possession. She is beautifully dressed though very plainly. I said 'why are you so pale' & she said 'too much responsibility'.... She had had much difficulty with her passport & said 'you know that legally I have no name & that appears on the pass-port & that makes them suspicious.' I said 'do you mind having no name' & she said 'no I often think how much most girls would mind – I only mind when it is inconvenient'.

Yeats introduced her to several of his friends which he thought she enjoyed though she was still anxious about her mother. He reported to Lady Gregory that:

Rothenstein is to do her portrait & she is making a little stir. I have brought her to Rothensteins private view people have met her here. Lady Cunard came up to me in excitement 'oh who is she – never in my life have I seen such a complexion'. If she lived here she would be a reigning beauty in no time. Rothenstein said 'when she stood up she was superb', & so on. She seems to have suddenly grown up & has thrown off all her old anarchic ideas about life. She explained to me yesterday that because of her birth she must never be bohemian in any way.

She told him about her father trying to convince her that 'the life of an Aspasia was the most powerful & happy life for a woman', so now she was not speaking to him and said that it was 'no longer antiquity'.

There was still the possibility that Maud might join them. Yeats wrote discouraging her from travelling, saying that Dublin at the moment was not a place for someone who liked to speak out. In London people are arrested for doing so but in Dublin the 'whole Hotel would be arrested also'. Maud wrote saying she was pleased that Iseult was having a good time and that she herself had managed to get a passport to London but Bichon was still ill so she had decided not to travel for the moment. She thought that when Iseult and Yeats arrived they should all go to Colleville for the summer.

Now at 51 Yeats had a great urge to be married. A woman with whom he had been having an affair thought she was pregnant. This gave him a huge fright and great concern for a while, but fortunately for him it proved to be a false alarm. As a result Lady Gregory and his old friend Mrs Shakespear urged him to get married. He had more or less settled on asking Georgie Hyde Lees, but with the death of John MacBride, Maud was now free. Lady Gregory warned him that he should insist Maud give up politics if she married him.

At the end of June Iseult and Yeats travelled to Paris and on to Colleville where they all stayed until September. Yeats proposed once again to Maud. Concerned about her single-minded preoccupation with politics which he called the stone in her heart, yet moved by her quiet peacefulness, he asked her to give up politics for a life with him among writers and artists where she could still work for Ireland, but in a different way. Maud could be calm when activity was not possible. She was not prepared to compromise, so, as always, she refused him kindly, giving him many reasons. Later he asked her if he could propose to Iseult. She laughed and said he could but she doubted that she would accept.

This summer was to add a new and special aspect to Iseult's life. She thoroughly enjoyed flirting with her elderly admirer, father figure, and guru, each of these roles adding a much needed dimension to her introspective lonely life. He helped her self-confidence, worked with her to realise her own gifts, and lightened for a while, but alas did not dispel, her own self-imposed high standards of self-criticism. These later resulted in a total lack of confidence with frequent lapses into depression and apparent irrationality, all rendering her helpless.

By now Yeats was completely fascinated by Iseult. His letters to Lady Gregory were full of her. As they worked and studied together he was unsure of whether he was a father figure or a cautious and tentative elderly lover, but he hoped he was the 'resolute tutor and Father Confessor'. As usual the house was full of animals and birds, including a raucous parrot and Iseult's black Persian cat, Minoulouche. Yeats found Bichon very gentle, 'well bred and intelligent'.

**Fig. 9** Willie Yeats – 'resolute tutor and Father Confessor' © Christina Bridgwater

The servant at Colleville was Jospehine Pillon, a Normandy peasant, illegitimate and a good cook. Thora wrote of her 'she had been rather partial to drink and was known as a bit of a drunkard when she first applied for service to Aunt Maud at Colleville. Aunt Maud took her on condition she gave up the bottle. "Once drunk and you are out". It never came to that.'

Now Iseult had a companion on many of her long walks, someone who understood her ideas. He rationed her cigarettes, watched her run along the sea edge, her long straight hair flowing in the wind, or dance in the moonlight, Minoulouche, tail erect, dancing beside her. Iseult thought Yeats was somewhat like a swan, walking awkwardly on land but in his natural element in the water, swimming with great agility and power, able to stay under water for long distances. He adjusted their kite and got it to fly at great heights as he ran along the beach, much to the delight of Sean.

While trying to collect some of her writings for a little book, he came across a passage which he copied for Lady Gregory from Iseult's *Journal*. 'Oh Lord my God give me quiet and seclusion, the company of one or two dear friends, a wild and beautiful bit of the earth to live in I ask for no more' then comes this strange comment 'poor ambition' and yet 'ambition of the kind that through [sic] the angels from Heaven'. He did not record the end of that passage entitled 'Resignation':

To the eyes of the world that is but a poor ambition, and may be easily granted.
To thine, O my lord, it is an ambition of the kind that threw the rebell [sic] angels from heaven.
The world says:
'a little thatched house, a garden with a mulbberry [sic] tree and sunflowers that is a mild dream enough.'
Thou sayest:
'Such was Earthly Paradise that image of my own, but now my Seraph stands at the gate with a flaming spear.'
And only by the sweat of the brow can any paradise be gained anymore
I say:
'So be it. Let my life on the earth be dusty and mudy [sic] according to the weather; what matters in a town? And my death on the earth a long glory of dry bones or maybe a soul hovering regretfully over the joys that might have been.'
To thee that seems but a fair pay for the light of the sun; and to me . . . Oh what do I care!

Iseult told Yeats she did not wish that any of her original compositions should be published, explaining that she objected to the public display of her personal feelings. She felt that if one admitted 'spectators into the soul' one cannot be sincere with oneself. So he suggested a book on the Catholic poets, such as Péguy, Claudel and Jammes, which he thought would 'make her life in Dublin when she went there, fruitful & help civilise young Catholics'! He thought her too modest and 'not a happy child'. When they visited Bayeux he noticed that she prayed a good deal in the Cathedral and in the evening she explained to him why she had left the Catholic Church: 'Moura is happy there – she never suffers remorse. I could have accepted any dogma but how can I belong, considering my thoughts – loving nature as I do, loving each thing for itself & not for its creator.'

Because Yeats was interested in the writing of young contemporary Catholics in France, Iseult had been translating Péguy, Claudel and Jammes for him with the intention that he would give a lecture on them in the Abbey. He then thought that she should write a book on them, but towards the end of his stay it seems that they settled on her doing a book on Péguy only.

Meanwhile he thought her a wilful child, particularly in the matter of cigarettes, yet he thought she had 'indescribable gentleness' with 'moments of a beautiful gaiety' and had 'genius' with a 'very delicate gift for one of her age' and her work was 'an intense meditation'. She, however, had no confidence and was too modest about her own capacity. He feared the effect upon her spirits of the Dublin world. Concerned about her fragility he wrote 'in my heart – I hardly like to set the thought on paper – that she is like those who die young.'

Realising that for the first time in 20 years he was not in Coole with Lady Gregory for August Yeats wrote to her on the 19th of the month, 'I think you will forgive me now that you know that it was the wish, at first but half acknowledged to have an understanding with Iseult. She says she particularly admired in me that extreme vigour with which I put before her all the drawbacks in marrying an elderly man.'

Iseult wrote a long letter to Thora, her 'little brother Victor', from Colleville telling her of their work together and his proposal.

> . . . but that's quite between us, he has proposed to me!!.
>
> Thirty years difference is all the same a little too much, so of course I said *No* and it didn't seem to affect him much, he lost no appetite through this; so I came to the conviction that he had merely done it to follow a mad code of politeness which he has made for himself, he often told me: 'I think that a proposal is the myrrhe and the incense which every beautiful young woman has the right to expect from every man who comes near her'.
>
> I think Alas that the Myrrhe and the incense are not the compliments or the love that we receive but the love which we give. That alone would be happiness and a real homage to oneself. I wish I could fall in love! But I am almost afraid I never will.

The proposal only took a short space in a long revealing letter. Because it had been a long time since they had heard from one another she had felt 'as uncomfortable as if I had to write to some distant Aunt with whom one has to be a little ceremonious' or to whom she might write a 'nice polite letter such as I would to my godmother to wish her a good Xmas.'

> Yet when I am tired and lonely I go and lie down on my bed and tell myself stories, you know the kind; stories full of drama, of wild sick babes who want to escape the very dreary and sordid things of daily life. Well in those fairy tales you are always with me, I call it the land of Maia, and there we live together the most wonderful adventures and we always manage to do finer deeds than anybody else, and to be the object of everybody's admiration (Alas!!);

But she hoped they would see more of each other when they moved to Ireland. 'We are really old enough to make our families understand now quite gently that their difference of opinions, is not sufficient to make us live apart.' Then she moved on to their old subject of love, writing that lately 'in London and in Paris I have been behaving like a perfect genteel lady. Out of pride? I don't think so, but rather lack of interest, rather because of the growing feeling which I have that if one is not in love, playing with love is not much fun, and can even become a bore, a very great bore.' Yet she said she had not become 'a prude for all that – I still wish to win the heart of every man I meet, but I don't any longer wish to play with the hearts I have won.'

Vigorous in her dislike of jingoism, it would seem she might have suffered from an extra dose of it in London on account of wishing to see her revolutionary friend Helen who was then in jail, 'it was very painful and sad' and 'the family very sour'; feeling ran high against such people as Helen stabbing England in the back when at war.

> 'the most false and vulgar feeling which exists . . . a mixture of grotesque sentimentality and bloodthirstiness. War spirit is odious. Oh for the blessed Island, the Kingdom of Maia where we could seek refuge you and I and a few others maybe who have escaped the infection, and give our attention to the things that matter; individual affections, the beauty of this world, and the search after the other world . . . if there is an other world! Amen!

To Thora she conveyed the idea that she was taking Yeats's proposal fairly lightly, whatever her innermost feelings were. In September, when they had all left Colleville, he mentioned to many of his correspondents letters from her 'so full of tenderness that I am feeling very old. She would not dare to write such a letter to a young man.' Iseult's first existing letter to him after this summer was on 7th of September.

It was in December that she wrote in her *Journal* of her relationship with Devabrata Mukerjee:

> ...'the sad, sad sweetness of memory! My little brother we spent too casually together the gifts of the gods.'...The dream they might meet again when 'maybe then I will have learned the wisdom of strength'...is all rubbish.
>
> Two years have passed now. Of strength I know no more than I did then but I have learned the wisdom of weakness. I know why we failed and that doubtless if we were to be together now we should fail again.
>
> Deva, it is better we should not meet again. Oh! but these are hard words to write. Is it for ever really that you are gone?...We have passed each other by and said the wrong pass word – and now its all over. Well God bless you! May life be kind to you.
>
> In memory of you I write down here those passages of the 'Banquet' we had marked together.

The passages they had marked were mainly of love:

> It is not easy to find a better assistant than Love in seeking to communicate immortality to our human natures.

# 2
# The Letters to W.B. Yeats

*Iseult's letters to Yeats start when she is fifteen. Two other letters follow, one in 1914 when she was translating Tagore with Mukerjee, and one in 1915 after her return to Paris from nursing at the front asking his advice on her literary work. After the long summer of 1916 in Colleville, when Yeats and she spent so much time together, the correspondence increased.*

1
[Paris]
Dimanche 26 Décembre
1909

My dear Mr Yeats,

Thank you so much for having sent me such a beautiful fan and do thank also your sisters[1] for having painted it in such a lovely way. It is of a lovely colour and much too charming for a wild gutter[2] cat like I.

We are having quite a nice Christmas here with a heavenly warm sun shining over us.

Bichon[3] and I have done a lot of roller skating since 2 weeks it is awfully amusing.

I wish you a happy Christmas and it would be charming if you would come soon to Paris.[4]

I thank you again many times.

Yours always

Iseult

**2**
Arrens[1]
16 Aout 1914

My dear Willy,

I am enclosing four specimens, three from the "Gardener" no. 67.42.8. and one from the "Crescent Moon"[2] page 3. The translations[3] of both theese books will be finished by the end of August.

I hope you and Mr Tagore[4] will like them I am now in a great hurry to catch the post and will write a longer letter tonight.

Yours Affectionatly
Iseult


**3**
17 rue de l'Annociation
Paris (XVIème arr.)
25 8bre 15[August?]

My dear Willy,

You make me feel full of remorse and ungratefulness.

It is indeed too kind of you to take an interest in my work and to worry yourself as to weither I am going to waste sordidly my life in futility or to make a great task of it.

Alas! I am afraid not. I have'nt written to you because it felt hard to own the truth and to say that although I feel I ought to be doing something, yet I am not doing it through sheer weakness of mind.

For 6 months we have been nursing in the hospital at Paris Plage[1] and now we are back in Paris,[2] and Moura[3] is taking a rest cure but I still go on with hospital work. I am living just like a machine with no time or desire to wonder weither it's a pleasant way of living or not. I know physical work is no good for the mind, and I don't beleive in it, though once I did.

It gives one a dangerous feeling of activity and energy, but it's only an illusion for it requires no real effort of will.

Still I go on with[it], I really don't quite know why. But here in Paris I only go in the morning and in the afternoon I go to an aviation comity[4] of which I am secretary. Thats absolutly no good either.

I only meet dull practical people there, and write business letters; still earning ones life is a new impression though rather a minor one.

I should like to work indeed but practically speaking, how am I going to start? My knowledge of Bengali[5] is very misty, and even with the help of grammars and dictionaries I could'nt make a translation now that Mukerjea is gone;[6] we cannot even correspond for the censor does'nt let his letters through.

I am writing to you to ask for your advice as to what I am to do, and though my brain has got very rusty I shall really do my best to work on the line you will trace me.

I know it is very much to ask, and that you are busy with much greater things; still you are the only person who has encouraged me to work, in the real sense of the word; You are the person in whose mind I trust and beleive in most, and I must apply to you.

Forgive me for this childish confession and beleive me always

Your very affectionate

Iseult

**4**

Colleville[1]

7.9.16

My dear Willie,

I have just got a letter from Madame Peguy.[2] She says that her lack of knoledge of English makes it hard for her to make a quick decision as she has to inquire from others; she asks me also to give her more details as to my intentions.[3] I don't quite know what she means, but I suppose it is something to do with the publisher. I am writing to her that I shall be in Paris shortly and will go to see her. Meanwhile if it was'nt too much trouble, would you be so kind as to get me the sort of practical informations she might want about the publisher.

Do you think Mac Millan[4] would take the book? I am sorry to ask you such dull tiresome things; don't do it if its too much bother, because after all there is plenty of time yet.

Oh Willie I wish you could see the sea to day! It is so pleasingly untidy: blue in places green in others; black in the hollows of the waves and so white at their summits! Little streaks of foam all over, and such a sprightful wind! I am just come in from the shore, I never got such delight from running, so much that feeling of "wise delirium"![5] I think that even you, to day would have wanted to run for more than mere exercise's sake.

Moura, meanwhile, has gone for three days to make a retreat in a convent near Caen,[6] I think it will do her good, she always comes back happier from monastic seclusion.

I will get the last books you tell me of when I am in Paris, as there would be no time now to have them sent. Meanwhile I am reading Pater[7] and Landor.[8]

The two chapters in Marius[9] of Animula Vagula[10] and New cyrenaicism, has made me think over and shed a wonderful light and order on many of the things you used to discuss; I realize now with greater intensity how much I owe to you through that very clearness and precision I get bring [sic] into my thoughts.

But now I must leave you. I am going to pick blackberries in the fields

Yours also in all affection though stricken with lack of years

Maurice[11]

P.S. Yes your writing *is* . . . not exactly easy to read;[12] some more lessons in strokes might be quite a useful passetime; when I come to Dublin . . . But meanwhile don't bother for I can manage to read you.

5
17 rue de l'Annonciation (16ème)
2 Octobre 1916
Paris

My dear Willie,

Your letters are a great blessing to me in the dreary confused atmosphere we are living in just now. It is a stimulous and a solace to feel in communion with an other on the same line of thoughts yet so far beyond in realisation. You asked me if I was too young to know what a test of affection letters are. Maybe I am; for it seems to me that lyes hard to speak come easily; almost temptingly under the pen (I have just been writing a very sugary letter to Aunt Kathleen.[1]) But what I know, is that now when I am in great gloom and opressed by that old sense of sinking and failure, you are one of the very few whose thought brings me a life giving power – and that egotistical as it is, is a great test of friendship.

I was still at Colleville when your books arrived. Many, many thanks for them. I began reading Donne[2] then and was greatly charmed about some passages but then we went away and since I have had very little time to read. We were to start on the 5th, but the money settlement which was to be over by now is put off to the tenth, so we must wait here another fort-night; meanwhile we are proceeding to change of flat. The days are spent in moving furniture about hanging pictures and casseroles.

Bichon declares loudly that this is a real good life, but Moura and I insin-uate timidly that there can perhaps be too much of a good thing. I have written nothing lately. The state of filth and disorder,[3] and the stupid fatigue it brings is most dispiriting; nothing brings me more greyness of soul as a lack of material harmony, when there is no escape from it.

I regretted deeply during the last days in Colleville that you were gone. Theese days gave me much and no doubt would have given you more still. Automn was just beginning with its wonderful sweetness of light; the orchards and the shore took a new character of atmosphere closer full of a serious pathos yet of a light smiling joy. I was out all day, for I found every-thing on the way had a message to give. I read Marius,[4] and thought over many old things with the freshness of discovery, I made plans where those I love and myself were to be the happiest in the sweetest of worlds. I began to pray again, made a few renunciations[5] (yes laugh!) and even took resolu-tions. We had just entered the Dyonisac[6] months of the year that is the only way I can explain now this access of sacred delyrium.[7] I have great hope in the Order,[8] not that I wish for new ideals but rather for a unitive tradition and discipline to bring the old ones into life; without theese there can be but perpetual drifting and gradual sinking down. I had many thoughts for you at Colleville during those days I seemed to get a kind of insight into your soul and see into all your needs, and the kind of mental answers I got were full of good cheer and boyancy yet somewhat stern as the voice of a daimon[9] always is. I will tell it you all when we meet.

My date of birth is 6th of August 1894 at 3 in the morning. I have just heard from Madame Peguy,[10] she wants me to go and see her, which I will do on Monday. If Burns and Oats[11] does not accept, do you think there would be more chance with Methuen,[12] I am very grateful to you for helping me in this, frankly in my scattered condition it is the only kind of work I feel capable of.

Moura has just been making a very charming portrait of Madame Mielvarque[13] the pretty little lady who lives in the same house as we do. I find her a delightful compagnon, and when I have a moment free I go to her and she sings old tunes with a beautiful clear voice and is sweet to look at, nothing very impressive, but perfectly harmonious in every way. Tis a great rest. Cristiane Cherfels[14] I see but little, she is falling in an American set which is a little overpowering and makes one dream of provincial backwaters as paradise on earth.

Forgive this very silly letter. I will write you again a longer one when I feel better.

It will be good to see you again. I hate letters, they ring false, they make one feel apart in a way mere absence does not; words take fantastical shapes and make a ghost of a living thought or give to dreams too much consistency, so forgive me for not writing oftener. I wish we were both on the shore now outlining pentagrammes in the sand, counting on our fingers 1 2 3 4 5 (5 was the right number I think) seing some yellow come into the sky and our shadows lengthen and discussing with the greatest seriousness weither the sea could really be paler than the sky and what we should say when we came in late for dinner.

Yours in great affection
Iseult

P.S.   I am glad you like Claudel's[15] poems. I have been reading them again lately; read "Ténèbres" if you have'nt yet and especially the "Cathedral de Strasbourg". The book on Peguy[16] by Suarès is very fine indeed, I will bring it over for you; I have got something else for you and that is a bottle of miraculous water from the well of Sainte Claire on the road side of the valley.


6
15.10.6.
17 rue de l'Annonciation
Paris (16ème)

My dear Willie,

Our letters must have crossed. I had adressed mine to London, that may be the cause of the delay and yet, you ought to have had it by now. Also my cousin May[1] writes me that one must now sign ones name in full.

You guessed right. Sir Maurice[2] and I are both in prison, not in the jewelled bronzy hands of a Saladin;[3] but, alas, in the hard grubby claws of dame Necessity who keeps close watch on us. But when I get rampant and abuse her with most undignified words, Sir Maurice just smiles complacently and says that he on the contrary is very flattered that such a high lady should condescend to play the coquette with him though of course he is worthy of the favour of sweeter deities. This aspect of the situation does not touch me in the very least and I have even the bad taste to answer him: "Why did'nt she catch you only then, and leave me in peace?" Then Sir Maurice coughs and looks uneasy but finds nothing to retort and the discussion is closed.

To put this in a more Christian language, the Jew[4] who was to pay off on the 10th of October[5] says now that he will only do so on the 20th of November.

It is now the third time he puts it off and I don't see why he should'nt go on indefinitly; it may end even by a law suit. Of course we hope that it will come alright in the long run, but it may be longer than we think.

This is very dismal indeed.

I am very anxious just now too over Moura's health.[6] Her rheumatisms are so bad that she has to lean on me to walk in the street, and it has somehow affected her eyes also, she can hardly read even with spectacles. She will probably have to go to Dax; she would start almost immediatly to be back early in November. It isn't yet quite settled, but it is urgent that she should do something about it.

You tell me that you have had the coakrooch.[7] I am very sad to hear that for I know what it means: blankness of mind without repose, loneliness without solitude, and over every hope a withering doubt. But why it should come to you of all people I cannot understand. I am sure though that when you are in your castle[8] with nothing but peace and beauty around you, that feeling will go and you will find creative thoughts coming back to you in orderly abundance. Only the fool or the saint[9] can stand serene amid the discordance of modern civilization, for the first is part of it and the other stands above; but for the artist, it seems to me, it is more difficult; how can he transmute into a spiritual reality a material world already changed into a spiritual lye (among other things I think of this war and no, it isn't the denial, but the supreme achievement of our so called civilization not an outburst of wild madness but the crowning of mediocrity and all its sophismes) tis only in the country that things are pure and simple, for there they exist in their natural essence from which one is free to fashion truths or lyes ... or nothing at all. I love the description you make me of the place; it will be lovely to go and see you there.

Our "déménagement" is quite over by now thank heavens, and we are settled in the new flat.[10] In spite of its small size, it is much better than the other. There is at least some kind of seclusion here, and the surroundings seem more remote; and strange to say, in spite of the deception about our journey and some other troubles, I am beginning to feel an inner quiet. Many of the things we used to say last summer come back to me, and those three sayings of yours stand as living forces by me: to give a value to things or people make a sacrifice for them; only accept such thoughts and emotions as are seasonal; and before the inevitable, bow, and say: "Thy will be done".[11]

What need of 10 commandements with those three . . . if only one would follow them; and I, for my part, am far from it.

I have been reading the Equinox[12] a lot lately and have tried to work with symbols; but I have prejudice against doing anything which I do not understand quite. The book is full of names and quotations from the Kaballa;[13] I have tried to get a translation of the Kaballa but apparently it is very difficult to find. Do you know if there is at least a book on it, giving in clear terms an explanation of the principal names and grades?

I am sending you some fragments I have copied from a long poem of Péguy.[14] I think it will interest you if you have'nt yet read it; it is very beautiful of form, and here and there, very touching.

Your poem on the Easter week[15] has been the cause of great arguments in our household, as to the nature and value of sacrifice. Moura who cannot admit Art for art's sake would willingly admit sacrifice for sacrifices sake, and I have come to admit neither exactly, while poor old Delany[16] can only admit everything for God's sake and that's perhaps the wisest. I would remain happily talking with you longer but theres no more space.

Yours ever affectionately

Maurice

Iseult Gonne


Fragments from "Prière pour nous Autres Charnels"

I

Heureux ceux qui sont morts, car its sont retournés
Dans la premiere terre et l'argile plastique

----------

Heureux ceux qui sont morts, car ils sont retournés
Dans la première terre et dans la discipline
Ils sont redevenus la pauvre figuline
Ils sont redevenus des vases façonnés.

Heureux ceux qui sont morts, car ils sont retournees
Dans leur première forme et fidèle figure.
Ils sont redevenus ces objets de nature
Que le pouce d'un Dieu lui-méme a façonnes.

----------

Heureux ceux qui sont morts car ils sont revenus
Dans la demeure antique et la vieille maison.
Ils sont redescendus dans la jeune saison
D'ou Dieu les suscita misérables et nus.

----------

Mere voici vos fils qui se sont tant perdus
Qu'ils ne soient pas jugés sur une basse intrigue.
Qu'ils soient reintégrés comme l'enfant prodigue.
Qu'ils viennent s'ecrouler entre deux bras tendus.

----------

Qu'ils soient [?] comme de nobles fils.
Qu'ils soient réinstalés dans la noble maison.
Et dans les champs de blé et les champs de mais
Et qu'ils soient replacés dans la droite raison.


*Iseult wrote in her Journal in November*

*Here is a fragment from a letter I have just received from Willie 'Certainly
I think that only life matters. If by sacrifice we enrich the life (and that is enrich
the love) of the soul it is right; but if we sacrifice the love for an idea, we may
for all our sacrifice become no more spiritual than a gambler at Monte Carlo
who neglects his meals in his excitement. The strength and will is to be able
every day to give a little time to that mystic meditation that all the East practices with so perfect a regularity that it may win its reward and open the inner
pathway to God.*

*Dear, there is but one sacrifice; the winning of quiet. When one has found
it, one can, I think, be kind and thoughtful as easily as a bird can fly or
sing.'*

*Her comment was that 'quiet was a word of the soul. I know little of meditation,
though no doubt that is the higher form of life, I but know, outside of emotions, of
reasoning and action, therefore it is in the right management of action through
reasoning that I can fight for that winning of quiet.' Then she continued her
thoughts as in her answer written to Yeats on 9 November (p. 67).*

*In 1924 she published in* The Quest *a piece, 'Images of Quiet', in which she
extended her thinking on the subject.*

7
9 Novembre 1916
17 rue de l'Annonciation
Paris (16ème arr.)

My dear Willie,

I received two days ago only your letter dated 29th of October; the censor has evidently been pondering some while over it, and I did alike for it is a letter to read and to reread; for me it was like a strong shake hand and a kind greeting smile, now I want to write to you a long long letter because I feel I have a lot I want to share with you. I am in a talkative mood so I will probably speak a lot of pompous rubish, but you won't look too stern will you? You will only smile and pass your hand through your hair, and pinch the tip of your nose (remember not to do that too much by the way) and say: "Her Knighthood[1] wanders, but then knights always wander."

But first I must get through the tiresome dull things otherwise I would'nt say them at all; you ask me about Peguy, and I want to hide under the table or pretend to be asleep for I am deeply ashamed of myself; yet it is'nt altogether my fault. I went to see Madame Peguy[2] as I told you; she opened me the door and I took her for the cook, bad beginning; then we spoke of the translations, I had sent her some specimens but she had'nt been able to find any body talking English to give her an opinion. Then I told her about you and that you would write a preface, and that the editor[3] would probably be Mac Millan (what I thought at the moment). She is quite a peasant without the most elementary education and seems terrified of anything she does'nt know. She told me that she could'nt yet give me an answer for Yes or No, as there was a young man who had been a friend of her husband and who is now writing a life of Peguy in English and she does'nt know weither he does'nt mean also to do the translations. The young man, she says is now mobilised she does'nt exactly know where, but she is to let me know when she has heard from him. I had to be satisfied with that and leave her my address. Moura is coming back to morrow, so we shall all the same again go to see her with my [real?] offer, and I will tell you the result. It is really most aggravating, but what can be done?

I am glad to say that Moura writes that she is very much better, she will be with us to morrow. She had rather a pleasant time at Dax:[4] two portraits to make that have paid nearly all the expense of the journey, also she met old friends of Samois,[5] so it was'nt too dull and lonely. The money affair also is settled, the rogue has paid up the sum, so we shall probably be starting now in a very short while;[6] but regulations for journeys are made more and more tiresome, and though we are going abroad according to all probalitie's, I have I don't know why a strange feeling almost a certitude that we are *not* going. But as my presentiments are nearly always wrong that may be a good

omen. Still whatever happens, Willie you are wrong to say that I shall gradually forget that I am your pupil (and your teacher??)

You cannot think that; You know as well and better than I do that absence
means nothing or rather means a very great deal.

Tis in the presence of companionship that we take the rough block of
appearance and melt it in into the hot wax of thoughts and emotions and
give it plastic life. But t'is absence that selects and purifie's and finally fixes
and polishes the wax into imperishable shapes. Thus it is that now you are
nearer to me than when we were together, for, from all our common memory
I have kept but the best and I can shut myself up in a small but very dainty
treasure room and play with my gold like a miser. It's a good game, and the
best of it is that the gold goes on accumulating. Do you remember the
vision of the lake with the lilacs and the singing birds. In spite of the angels
advice, I dwell often there. I think sometimes that the only thing I can do is
to keep watch over those reflections in the water so that no wind should
disturb them.

I am reading Initiation by Steiner.[7] His philosophy seems to me very honest and healthy and his absence of paradox is very reposing. As time goes on
I want more and more subtlety in poetry and less and less in philosophy.
Theories should be very simple, because the realisation of any theory is so
very hard and intricate. Every evening before going to sleep, I say: "Tomorrow
with Gods help, I will be good." And goodness and God's help seem delightfully easy then, but to morrow comes and I find that God's help is to be
found no where, and goodness everywhere just like wickedness; and it all
seems altogether too complicated. Oh you are right to say that spiritual life
is both more simple and difficult than one can imagine!

You must be very happy now with a new creation in mind, I would love
to be with you and see you shaping it. It is very curious indeed that prophecy
of Horton.[8] "Your sins have found you out"...I do not quite understand;
and you say it is a version of what you have been going through. Now when
I think of last summer I see what I did not realise at the moment that you
must have gone through a terrible deal. While you were writing your
biography[9] I was merely interested in those evocations of the past, but little
did I think of the agony of it and of the courage it needs to settle memories
into a definite order. You did it to give them a lasting life in the soul, but
did you not at the same time have to give the last death stroke to many old
pathetic illusions? I read the other day: "All confession is a destruction."
And it is true and nothing hurts so much as to destroy. I don't understand
about your sins finding you out; but you have found out your delusions to
be sins; and that is a great suffering. Do not think to much of me Willie you
might find me out also; I want to see you again so that later on you can
think of me (I expected to say absurditie's, but I had'nt expected to talk like
a clergymans daughter! yet thats the way I feel for the present) Well anyway
I can think of you for I have found you out so many times that I know by
now that your memory survives it.

I don't know if it is because I am turning into a clergyman's daughter, but I have'nt had the coakrooch for a long time now. You speak of the winning of Quiet,[10] it is the key of simplicity and charity and the battle cry of all holy war in the spirit, isn't it. It is to be found in meditation and it is also to be found in action. I think the secret is this: make duty a game, and game a duty, bring fancy into work and seriousness into play; then both play and work seem good for they hold each other company and are no longer lonely in their tasks. A green lawn planted with trees where the sun and shade are equally divided on the grass in a trembling watery interwining, appears to me as the symbol of quiet such as we understand it, that is to say quiet in the heart of the contrasts of life, the only quiet that is really quiet because it leaves nothing out.

Mr Cherfils[11] discovered the other day on the quaies an anonymous book of English poems dated 1899. He took it for the binding, but when he had glanced through it he was very struck by it and lent it to me. I have copied for you the best. I admire it very much yet I feel a little shy in sending it to you; it is so easy to get caught by a pretty entanglement of words; and it may really be rather poor. Do tell me what you think of it. Did you read anything by Marcel Schwob?[12] He is most exquisitely perverse and puerile; quite as ?misled and precious as Jammes[13] but far more real. I will send you a book of his La Lampe de Psyché[14] you may like some of the rimes: the Prologue, [? Kismé], and the last one about Daphnis and Chloe. Le livre de Monelle is pleasing also. I am also sending you the poems of Samain.[15] I wonder how you will like them.

Who knows Willie, maybe this is the last letter I write to you for in a week we may be meeting; or... well I really don't know.

Now I must dress to go out for dinner. I think of the shore. And I am always your

very affectionate Maurice

Iseult Gonne

P.S. It seems such a waste to leave at bit of white paper at the end of a letter that I must really add something. Here are two thoughts of Heraclitus[16] that I am translating into English.

The harmony of the world comes back on itself like the lyre and the bow.

The Daimon of Man is his destiny.

Its an awful bore to have to go out to dinner.

(that last is'nt from Heraclitus.)

### The City of the Soul

In the salt terror of a stormy sea
There are high attitudes the wind forgets;
And undesired days are hunting nets
To share the souls that fly Eternity.
But we being gods will never bend the knee,
Though sad moons shadow every sun that sets,

And tears of sorrow be like rivulets
To feed the shallows of Humility.

Within my soul are some mean gardens found
Where drooped flowers are, and unsung melodies,
And all companioning of piteous things
But in the midst is one high terraced ground,
Where level lawns sweep through the stately trees
And the great peacocks walk like painted kings.

What shall we do, my soul, to please the King?
Seeing he hath no pleasure in the dance,
And hath condemned the honeyed utterance
Of silver flutes and mouths made round to sing
Along the wall red roses climb and cling,
And oh, my prince, lift up thy countenance,
For there be thought like roses that entrance
More than the langours of soft lute-playing.

Think how the hidden things that poets see
In amber eves or mornings crystalline,
Hide in the soul their constant quenchless light,
Till, called by some celestial Alchemy,
Out of forgotten depths, they rise and shine
like buried treasures on Midsummer night.

The fields of Phantasy are all too wide,
My soul runs through them like an untamed thing
It leaps the brooks like threads and skirts the ring
Where fairies danced and tenderer flowers hide.
The voice of music has become the bride
Of an emprisoned bird with broken wing.
What shall we do, my soul, to plese the King,
We that are free, with ample wings untied?

We cannot wander through the empty fields
Till beauty like a hunter hurl the lance.
There are no silver snares and springes set,
Nor any meadow where the plain ground yields.
O let us then with ordered utterance
Torge the gold chain and twine the silken net.

Each new hour's passage is the acolyte
Of inarticulate song and syllable,
And every passing moment is a bell,
To mourn the death of undiscerved delight.
Where is the sun that made the noon day bright,

And where the midnight moon? O let us tell,
In long carved line and painted parable,
How the white road curves down into the night.

Only to build one cystal barrier
Against this sea which beats upon our days;
To ransom one lost moment with a rhyme!
Or if fate cries and grudging gods demur,
To clutch Life's hair, and thrust one naked phrase
Like a lean knife between the ribs of Time.

8
Samedi 18–11–16
17 rue de L'Annonciation
Paris 16ème

My dear Willie,

This is a little note written in great gloom.

Moura wrote to you the other day saying that everything was settled and we were coming over. In fact we had our passeports alright. We went this morning to the controle office to get them vised. There was a great crowd; we just saw Major Lampton[1] a moment and he told us that he was to busy just then but to come back this afternoon and that he would viser them then. Moura asked him weither there would be any difficulty as she wanted to get the tickets immediatly and reserve bearths, and he assured her it would be alright. So she went and got the tickets for us three and the cook Josephine,[2] and this afternoon we went to the Controle office, and there they "vised" and stamped all our passeports alright; but when this was done Major Lampton said to Moura: "Now I must warn you Madame Gonne, that we have received instructions to tell you that you will be able to get to London, but you won't be allowed to go to Ireland." And we asked why, but he only said that he did'nt know the reasons. Then we asked weither at least we could come back to Paris from London. He said again he did'nt know, that he promised he would wire to ask that and we are to have the answer on Monday morning which would just give us the time to start on Monday evening if the answer is satisfactory. Otherwise of course it would be too unsafe to go. So this is how matters stand. And I don't know what is to be done about it.

I told you when I wrote to you last that I had an ominous feeling about that journey, and for once I was'nt wrong.

I have almost settled now with the editor of Madame Peguy[3] who I saw yesterday. He told me to see the english editor,[4] and make the final arrangements with him after.

But I feel so broken down to night I have'nt the heart to write anymore.[5]
Yours in deep sadness
Maurice
Iseult Gonne

*Preparatory to leaving for Ireland and to save money the family packed up and left their apartment, temporarily renting a small attic in the same building with a roof terrace from where they could see 'the chimney pots of all Paris & gorgeous clouds & sunsets'.*

9

Friday 1st of december
1916

17 rue de l'Annonciation

Paris (16ème)

My dear Willie,

Did you receive my last letters? It is a long time now I am without news of you. I fear you may be ill; I am rather anxious, or perhaps you are very busy, but do write me just a line.

There is a gloomy sense of forlorness and irony about life just now. The deceptions about that journey has been great to us, especially for Moura, she is very dispirited over it all.

Then she has been very ill; for a moment there was even danger of pneumonia, but now she seems better though still very weak.

The prospect of spending the winter in this tiny icy flat is certainly not cheering, we had made such beautiful plans, I was delighting in the thought of seing you and Helen[1] again, of taking life up again as a clean sheet of blank paper. And all thats' over. Its the moment to remember those words of resignation you have taught me: "Thy will be done." And in fact, I think I can repeat them now with all right humility.

Sterile revolt is vulgar as all useless outplay of energy. So I force myself to calm; I read a lot and write a little and am becoming more and more of a bear, and a somewhat uncouth one.

Did you read the poem[2] I sent you in a long letter written about three weeks ago? I have read all the others that were in the book, some of them are quite fine.

Tell me about yourself how you are and what you are doing
affectionately
Your old Maurice
Iseult Gonne

P.S.   I am sending you the letter for the editor[3] as I have now seen the French editor.

Do you think it will do?

10

17 rue de l'Annonciation
Paris (16ième arr.)
27.12.16

My dear Willie,

The censor seems indeed much interested in our correspondance. We were a long time without hearing at all from you and were feeling very anxious thinking you might be ill. At last some of your letters came all at least a fortnight old.

Lately I have been very lazy at letter writing. You must scold me sometimes, for I am getting into the comfortable sluggish way of picturing you and one or two dear friends alive with me and having beautiful imaginary conversations with you. Then I feel there is no more need for writing.

Yesterday there came a short note from you saying that letters must be short and readable to please the censor, but to day I want to write you a long scrible and hope to soften the censor's heart by telling him that I wear a blue and silver chineese dress and have put on my face a new kind of powder and have curled my hair all for his benefit, though he cannot see it, but feeling sure that he is a man of imagination.

Now for the long scrible! First of all, thankyou for that beautiful poem. I love its imagery and that quality of subdued and restrained sadness. Now, I suppose, you are to busy over Lanes pictures[1] and the theatre[2] to have much times for lyrics, but if you have writen any more do send me them. It is always a great joy.

The chances of our journey seem now very remote. Moura has received a few encouraging letters from Hugh Law,[3] Derfin[4] [DEVELYN deleted], Baily[5] and old William Field[6] who have taken the matter in hand, but I doubt that they will be able to do much against the big iron machine which is martial law. It is not possible for the war to last another five years as you say, but two years is quite likely. Meanwhile poor Moura is making herself ill with disappointment; in fact I think she is seriously ill. I wrote to you some time ago that we had all caught cold, but with her it turned into congestion of the lungs and since then she is always coughing and having chocking fits at night. The last two or three days however, she seems a little bit better, but we are always afraid of a relapse as she won't take care of herself and insists on going out in the cold.

As to me I am quite well and to day, in that talkative mood which used always to come on me at Colleville in the mornings when you had made me sit down at that dreadful table with two hours of work in front of me and three cigarettes doled out with a grudging hand.

Really there isn't much new, and if one was to search for the interest of life merely in external facts, life just now would seem terribly dull; So I feel thankful to be one of those old fashioned people who still enjoy slow time and the pleasant ease of back waters.

I see most of my friends here have the fear of rapidity and live so quickly that I cannot keep pace with them; but there are a few charming people who, though very busy, always look quiet and full of leisure. Among those are Rummel[7] the musician and his wife. You know them of course. They have become great friends of ours, and as we are quite neighbours we see a lot of each other; they are quite wraped in Steiner's philosophy[8] and have lent me some of his books. His style is unbearable, full of a heavy clumsy common sense and a perpetual appology and making up both to the scientific materialists and to the asectic mystics; for all that his comprehension of life is quite a revelation to me. Do you remember the great word that used always to come in our conversations. "*Transmute*". Well, that is the basis of his philosophy. It is word of life itself or rather of that part of life which is our share. Creation and destruction belong to God, but we can only be concerned with transmutation. Though he does not say it in so many words, I think he is striving to give the mind a fluidic impulse instead of the plastic one which has now given all it could, and can only repeat itself. I feel I am expressing myself badly, but it is very hard for me for I am talking of things which I understand yet but obscurely.

The whole system striked me as entirely new but *not modern*, and in a way, as both the reversal and the logical sequence of our ideas.

But I better stop with this for I am getting almost as diffuse as Ella Young[9] when she is expounding on the astral lights; by the way Moura got a letter from her the other day saying that Helen is still at Aylesbury[10] where life is very dismal for the rules are getting more and more strict, I do not like to annoy you with demands just now that you are so busy, but when you happen to see influencial people, it would be kind to remember to say a little word for her.

I love to hear about your castle.[11] It's such fun making plans for the arrangement of a house! Don't you keep awake sometimes at night thinking how a chair will look best in that corner or by the window or what patterns you will have on your curtains? I have been very busy lately with such thoughts for I had decided to turn my room into a kind of austere yet pagan little temple, and now I am almost pleased with the result. I have hung over my windows a kind of apricot coloured gauze so that the books and the gods and the old embroideries melt in a golden mist, there is a perpetual glow of sunset, and small thoughts and light silly little times appear very solemn and glorious.

But this is trying the censors patience and yours long enough.

I am always your affectionate

old Maurice,[12] Knight of the great Order of Nothingness known to the ordinary world as

Iseult Gonne

**11**
30–1–17
17 rue de l'Annonciation
Paris 16ème

My dear Willie,

I am writing to you in bed with 8 blankets over me, 2 woolen coats, a hot bottle on one side and Minoulouche[1] on the other. The frost makes on the windows a lovely arabesque pattern of palms and acanthus leaves and each breath one takes feels like a knife prick; A good weather to dream of a garden packed with flowers and grasshopers in some sunny corner of the south.

Oh I wish I could sleep all through the winter like a dormouse.

But you must wish it even more, for you seem to be having a most strenuous time, I do hope you will succeed in the end. Its a great work. The possession of art treasures[2] must ennoble a nation more than all the moral teachings of philantropists; but after, it would be a good rest for you to be with us here awhile, for when it is'nt too cold, our life here is as quiet and pleasant as it can be in a town.

Our friendship with the Rummels[3] has become very close

We see each other almost every day; one day we come to their house and the other they come to ours and we sit by the fire speaking of art and theosophy (not in Annie Besant's[4] sense you will be glad to hear!)

I love this atmosphere; there is something in it that reminds me of those transparent aquamarine mountain lakes; but I being more like a troubled unquiet little stream we are always mildly quarrelling.

This is the sort of discussion Rummel and I are always having; its aimless absurdity may make you laugh.

Rummel beginns for instance, to speak of bringing spiritual reality into Art

Then I say: "Beginn by bringing sensuous reality first; thats' more important". then he answers: "if you don't first bring spritual reality you will never get your sensuous reality"

I. – "Not all all, you must first shape the plastic world before you can give it the fluidic impulse of life"

R. – "This is altogether wrong. You must bring the spirit down into the matter, while the matter is yet shapeless and let it work through it. Think of Michel Angelo..."[5]

I. – "What about Leonardo da Vinci"...?[6]

R. – What about Villon?[7]

I. – What about Anacreon?[8]

R. – "What of Wagner?"[9]

Here he gets a mean advantage over me for I never dare to venture on musical grounds.

Yet to be quite honest I think he may be right, in fact I am almost sure that he is right, but that really matters little so long as there is plenty of wood to feed the fire and keep the cold out in a friendly company.

Oh I wish you were here too!

I have not been writing at all lately, for directly I try to think actively I feel my thoughts frozen and hard like blocks of ice; and expression becomes more and more difficult. I feel entirely in a receptive state of mind, so I read and study a good deal.

I have read more of Steiner;[10] it is really a deep and vast mind, curiously enough I was reading Nietzche[11] at the same time and they struck me as the two opposites not so much in their ideals as in their temperaments.

Nietzche is an aristocrate, an intense individualist; each verset for instance in Zarathoustra[12] is an entity connected with, but not depending on the other versets.

Steiner on the contrary is essentially a democrate. There, each thought is a link of the logical chain, each link is there to explain the preceding one and the next but is incomplete taken by itself, for in true democraty there can be no partial individuality, that is why it should be the doctrine of action or rather the canvas on which the aristocratic individuality can weave its coloured patterns.

To follow the road of Democraty with the smile and the demeanour of the aristocrate, that would be the dream.

I should so love to hear what you think about Steiner!

Initiation is really not the best book; you should read "Science Occulte"[13] I think it has also been translated into English.

I have been reading with exquisite pleasure Shelley and Keats[14] lately.

In spite of all its beauty there is something metaphorical and abstract in Shelley that I feel alien to, whereas Keats altogether delighted me.

Oh Willy I do need you badly, my thoughts are running wild and poor; our beautiful world, the sheltered aromatic garden of thoughts we had planted together is now far away, and the shadow of the abstract is over everything even an innocent tulip becomes an idea to me now before I have taken in its lovely shape.

May be this is an aspect of the Dark night of the Soul.[15]

Now I have no more room to write anymore. I will write you again shortly.

Affectionately
Maurice
Iseult Gonne


*In the following letter Iseult was not wrong in her presentiment, for the British Authorities had no intention of allowing Maud to enter Ireland. They considered they had enough trouble there as it was without Maud's well known ability to raise loud protest by meetings and publicity abroad. Once given permission to go to England she and the ports into Ireland were watched to prevent her unauthorised entry.*

**12**

17 Rue de l' Annonciation

Paris

[Feb 1917]

My dear Willie,

This is only a short scrible to tell you ... in fact nothing at all; there is a long time I have'nt heard from you. Are you lazy or too busy to write? (which really is the same thing.) Or is the bloccesˡ stopping letters coming?

I am fearfully lazy for my part, as I should have written you long ago to thank you for sending me the box and manuscript book; I haven't yet got it for I suppose they are keeping parcels waiting also. I say "Also" because we are equally prevented from starting. Moura had got some satisfactory answers from Mr Law² saying that the only difficulty rested now with the Home office and no longer with the War office, and that they really would raise no objections to our journey, and Moura was feeling very hopeful and beginning to talk of packing when the news of the Bloccos came; and now, I beleive there are no passenger boats going.

I almost wish we would'nt go at all now, at least for some time yet. Its an absurd feeling I can't explain even to myself, not exactly fear yet something like it. I don't mean on account of the submarines; that sort of danger which belongs to the witches and ogre type is rather sporting to face. No it's not that. I am afraid of wickedness. Of the cunning wickedness with a smile on its face that writes things down at a desk in a homely attitude. There might be a lot of that. I am afraid if we went over just now.

In a month Easter will come and we shall go to Colleville,³ and I will feel very sorry that you are not there to enjoy the lovely crispness and alertness of things in the spring with us.

Now already the weather is getting warmer; I felt near the river that peculiar odour of violets that is in the air at the approach of spring.

In our quiet little icy attic,⁴ the weather seems a very important person; even more than in the country; at meals Moura talks of the war, I of the cold weather, Bichon of his school and we all conclude "When will it ever end!" Each meaning their own complaint.

I have read a great lot of books lately, some interesting and some boring, but I am not in the mood to talk about them. I am trying to be very good, and it doesn't come off, but I am too lazy to be bad either.

Most thoughts end for me now by a point of interrogation and then a yawn; yet life is quiet bearable. I hope you are not in trouble now. write me a line when you feel like it; My dear Willie this is a very silly letter I have been writing, but then I felt I would like to chat with you aimlessly of slight things as if we were sitting round a table on a rainy day.

I am always your very affectionate
Maurice
<u>Iseult Gonne</u>

**13**
17 rue de l'Annonciation
Paris
4–3–17

My dear Willy,

I have received the writing box and the manuscript book; they are a great delight to me and a continual encouragement and reproach about my work.

I am so interested about what you tell me about your order.[1] There seems to me as far as I can make out to be two great currents in occidental occult-isme: one that takes its inspiration from the Kabbala[2] and the other from the Gospel of St John.

From what I have read, the Kabbala seems to me to work more from knowledge to power than from knowledge to love.

In some curious way I cannot help but associating it with the Hebraïc and Maçonic forces which may be at the root of this war; but this is only a vague intuition and perhaps quite wrong. I am still studying Steiner's theosophy;[3] it both repells and attracts me. The heavy pedantic form, the useless repetitions, the poor and farfetched comparaisons make one want to chuck the book for a soothing chapter of Pater;[4] and yet there is something that rings so true through it all that one goes on reading.

There is a little of the Godly eyesight in his vue of the universe; everything is of the upmost and equal importance because all things are connected from the growth of the tiny plant to the spiritual life of man and the evolution of plants, and all have vital need of each other. I feel there a patient far seing mind that never tempts one with the glare of immediate results nor by the emotional satisfaction of optimism or pessimism but by a quiet understanding of facts. No religious sentimentality but a great force of love.

I stop now, headache prevents me writing any more. I have just been hearing a long lecture on "Georges Dandin"[5] and "l'Etourde"[6] and had after that to sit through 8 acts of Mollière[7] which was altogether too much of a good thing.

Your affectionate
Maurice
Iseult Gonne

**14**
29th of March 1917
Colleville s. mer
par Vierville s. mer
Calvados

My dear Willie,

We left Paris a week ago and are now in Colleville; it is very different in this time of the year to what it was last summer, so different in fact that you would hardly know it for the same place.

The fields by the sea are under water, its all a long lake from the clifts to Vierville. The little hill behind is the strangest desolate sight; it has been all burnt to get rid of the dried grass and is now perfectly black, the shore itself is changed; do you remember that grey slippery stuff, the remnants of a prehistorical forest, that used to be only before St Laurent, it has been put bare here too and there are miles of it to the clifts. I am writing to you like a baby, but those are great events for me; You who know the all absorbing interest of country life, you will understand.

Oh what a comfort to be here! It seems like breathing again naturally after a long diseace, for town life is a dicease there is no other word for it. I love this place and I am a little ashamed of loving it so for its not either romantic or classical exactly nor beautiful nor spiritual but to me it personifies health and everything that is normal.

I am glad that you are at last quite secure about your castle;[1] that road of course is an annoyance but perhaps in time you will like it, if it is a real country and local road not infested with motorcars. It will be something like a clock and a company to you, you will know for instance that at 6 in the morning the baker and the milkcart pass; later on the herds of cows and sheep, and at some other time an old woman on a donkey and so on ...

And all these little events are pleasant by their regularity and become friendly and indispensable in the long run.

What you said on those little fragments I send you, has been very useful to me and I am trying to applie it in some things I am trying to write now. I think also that a kind of second rate archaïsme is a pretentious and sub-urban vice in style; but it is a great danger and temptation for people who have but a poor knowledge of a language as is my case with English but I will try in future to avoid it.

I have read the first half of Joyce's book.[2] It is a powerful but antipathetic book and I have admired it and disliked it intensely. I have not yet finished it because it needs a real effort for me to get over the repugnance it inspires [in] me and I can read but little of it at a time.

I do not write any more as it is bed time and my feet are cold after having padled in the pools.

Yours affectionately
Maurice
Iseult Gonne

**15**
16–4–17
Colleville

My dear Willy,

I am writing to you on the eve of our departure from here; it has been a quiet and happy time; you would have enjoyed it I think in spite of the cold; the solitude was perfect; not a soul to be seen anywhere, not even the bright dress of Madame Leroux[1] in the distance. When I came here I was very tired, but now for three weeks I have been leading my old Red Indian's life again among the rocks and the thorns; and I feel quite strong.

Your book has been welcomed with joy. I had read already Religio Medici but the Urn Burial[2] is new to me, and you are right in saying that it is even more beautiful. My dear Willy it is kind of you to offer to send me another manuscript book, but the first one is far from full yet. If you knew the difficulty I have to write and the little I can do at a time with the best will! It is very dispiriting. I am writing now a few little hymns in prose to the sea; I am very interested in the grouping of words, more than I used to be; but the old emotion has left me, and I write round a sentence and no more round a thought. I think this is because I am in a transitional period; something new has come into my spiritual life and it is'nt yet settled. I feel a chaos when I try to think deeply that frightens me and all I can do is to write light superficial things.

It is a wonderful thought you have about the meaning of the greec spirit and its influence on christianisme; but why do you made a difference between the Hebraïc and the Guabalastic[3] inspiration? The Guabalah seems to me the very essence of the jewish mind. talking about that I saw something very sad before leaving Paris.

I went to see MacGregor[4] to ask him for his translation of the Guabalah. I had'nt seen him for nearly a year and he was already very changed then; but now it is much worse.

You know those photographs of the Indian famine where men look like living skelettons. thats absolutly what poor MacGregor looks like. He speaks of the war like an enthusiastic old woman and makes cheap jokes with a harsh broken laughter that's painful to listen to.

What has happened to that clear mind? I fear something very dark has come over him. His wife[5] said to me at the door: "I am doing all I can, but I don't know that he can be saved." I am pained about what you say of Horton[6] and I can't help making some analogy; of course he is a much higher loving mind than Macgregor, but don't you think they are both a case of people that have gone too far into the astral without the right guide?

So you have really got your castle now for good. How happy you must feel! But you must find London very boring and be dying to start your arrangements. I should love to be with you when you are doing it to help you though perhaps its better not; we might quarell shockingly over the question of tradition and association's and you would end by wishing me to the devil.

You know I have decided Moura to have all the bedrooms here white-washed. This house is too ugly to bear any elaborate arrangements; it is pleasant for a certain wind swept and broad lighted feeling and best kept bare, and empty of small ornaments.

Moura is really quite recovered; she is happy with her garden and her birds, and has much about her now that feeling of Demeter[7] which you found last summer, and which means I hope that she is quieter, less home-sick and contented to pass a peaceful summer here.

How nice if you could really come over to Paris as you say, you would have the honour and joy of seing Minoulouche[8] again; she is more beautiful than ever, only I have kissed her ears so much that they are a little bald at the tip

She and I send you our greetings

Sir Maurice and

his cat

Iseult Gonne

for the censor

**16**

23–4–17

Paris

17 rue de l'Annonciation

(16ème arr.)

My dear Willy,

Thank you so much for the books of Morriss;[1] I kept them closed in Colleville; life was full and light enough there; but now I am reading them and they help me to pass those long hours of Paris. But the delightful family of Morriss[2] never invented anything so fairylike as that picture of your castle;[3] it is a perfect enchantement, and you can feel happy to have it your own. Did you say the old trees had been cut down? Still it may be even better in a bare desolate landscape.

This won't be a long letter. I have the coakrooch[4] to night. You see we are back in Paris; that's a sufficient explanation. It's hard to cope with town life.

I must tell you though of a curious experience I had this morning. I was lying in bed thinking there were things to be done and it was time to get up, but unable to do it or even to open my eyes through sheer depression; and I was thinking over those three weeks in Colleville, how pleasant they had been, how easy it was to work there and feel strong and loving minded, and how now all that had suddenly vanished and I wanted nothing but sleep and tabacco,[5] and those thoughts resumed themselves in my mind in one clear sentence "this is the hour of desolation" and I repeated that over several times because it seemed to sum everything up. A book of St Ignatius of Loyala[6] was on the table by me, and I took it up and opened it at Hazard. And on the top of the page I opened was written: "You must deal differently with the subject (meaning disciple) according to weither he is in the time of consolation or the time of desolation" and further on the same page: "Remind him to keep strong through the time of desolation".

This is I think the first convincing experience I have ever had of that kind, and I am grateful to St Ignatius though for a saint he seems a great ruffian; old Cherfils[7] lent him me. Cherfils himself is quite a delectable person: I met him this afternoon crossing the place du Trocadéro. He said to me: "Well Iseult you look well; it was pleasant in the country? Yes, I answered, but not pleasant to come back here." Then, He looked very deep and I knew at once he was going to say something cheery: "Life is very hard, my child, very hard, an oriental sage has said: the destiny of man is sad but the destiny of woman is detestable." So I laughed and said that for my part I found it bright enough; He looked reprovingly and nodded: "You are wrong; it's your duty to be sad; the destiny of woman is detestable." and with those hopeful words we parted.

I can never quite make him out; weither he means the things he says or weither its pure affectation but I like him because he always looks so deep over futilities and take serious things lightly; it's like country life; yet serious things are beginn to weigh heavily on me; I can't shake now the thought of the war; there is more and more darkness coming down and the feeling of still more to come. I wonder very much at those revelations from your spirits; I have heard of other predictions speaking of a long and fearful time overhead and I am more inclined to beleive in those; for horrible as things have been already the feeling of the climax has not yet come. If you have been in a mountain storm you know what I mean.

But maybe this is all emotional rubbish; anyhow I must stop now
Your affectionate but gloomy Maurice
Iseult Gonne for the censor


**17**
18–5–17
17 rue de l'Annonciation
Paris
(16ème arr.)

My dear Willie,

Those revelations[1] from your spirits are certainly very curious and interesting but...May I speak frankly? I can hardly attach much spiritual value to them.

I don't mean that I disbeleive their authenticity, only it seems to me hardly possible for mediumship of this kind to rise much beyond the astral no more than any other force of experimental psychich research.

Only the purifying fire of love can burn its way into the spiritual world. A Hard mystical training, a reshaping of self a constant work of transformation (though never of destruction) appears to me as the only way to get into communication with the spirits.

I have an instictive dislike and mistrust of "spiritism" or anything that gives a psychich result without inner effort.

The immediate, the easy, is never very high.

I only hope that these invisible beings you are speaking of don't come to you merely because they have need of you.

You must forgive me speaking in that way of things wich after all I know nothing about; and very likely I am quite wrong.

I have just received your letter with the plans of your castle; it sounds an ideal arrangement. The L shape[2] always makes a home very congenial and more secluded. May's Villa[3] in Florence had that shape also and it was the most lovely house I have ever staid in. What a joy also to have flowing water under your windows;[4] it is a sight one can never tire off.

I am sending you some little things I wrote by the sea as you ask me.

I did'nt do it sooner because I have got to hate them frankly and I dare'nt let you see that I can never do anything good at all. I get every day more dispirited over work; the only satisfactory thing is sleep and close that fit well.

These are very poor tastes for a knight,[5] but all knightly adventures safe the Holy Graâl seem insignificant, and the Holy Graâl is further and further away.

Did I tell you that Minoulouche's ears[6] were getting bald at the tip; it is very distressing Now I smear them with petrolium; he hates that and sits all the time on the top of the cupboard looking at me with a passive disdain that suits him even better than amiability. He looks on us all with utter dislike but sends you his greetings because you have never smeared his ears with petrolium.

How nice it will be to see you again next summer. I don't think either the submarine danger is very great for passenger boats. We shall have a lovely peaceful time in the country, and then, who knows we may be able to go over to Ireland together if the war is over but that is a very big if.

Yrs affectionatly

Maurice

Iseult Gonne

P.S. I am awfully sorry about those translations from Peguy.[7] I received the otherday a letter from the editor saying that to his great regret he could'nt come to settlement as Madame Péguy persisted in her desire not to have any other translations done now but the Pages Choisées which have been translated by a friend of her husband. I am going to make a last attempt by going to see her, but I have little hope of succeeding.

I am afraid all this has given you a lot of trouble for nothing[8] but I am very grateful to you.

**18**
6–6–17
17 rue de l'Annonciation
Paris
(16eme arr.)

My dear Willie,

Minoulouche and I are very grateful and honoured to have our names in your book.[1] He is a little familiar divinity and well at his place in an occult work, as for me I am wholly undeserving, but none the less proud.

I am very anxious to have that copy you promise me, all the more so that the last part of the Epilogue[2] puzled me extremely, where you write:[3] "Have not I too travelled through a like thought?" For nowhere before in your work or in your thoughts as I know them have I discerned a sense of collectivity as in Peguy;[4] I thought, on the contrary, that your mind moved more on the lines of the individual evolution, not quite as the "soul self-moving and self teaching" of Villiers de Lisle Adam,[5] but as the soul moving among, and sharing its gifts with the very few and the best like Huysmans[6] or Pater.[7]

Moura,[8] of course, was a little shocked about what you say of Catholic tradition in Irland; and I, though by the little I have seen of it over there think you must be right, still cannot help to feel a little pained. The dear old institution even though one has left it, still remains in ones thought as something venerable and somewhat sacred like a relic which should'nt be touched. But don't take that as a criticism; it is a matter of mere personal sentimentality, which you have'nt the same reasons as I to share.

I have just had an unpleasant dialogue with the Daimon;[9] he started moralising but I told him to mind his own business, which he did and went away, and now I feel even more dull and grumpy than usual. We have made friends with a man called Mowrier;[10] he is redactor of the Chicago Daily News, but there is nothing journalistic about him. He was great friends with Stephens[11] and writes charming poems curiously close to the earth in a curt descriptive way. He himself is concentrated and simple, I think you would like him.

Don't spend a long time over my little writings to find something kind to say. I know myself that they cannot be good as they are not sincere. I am now attempting to write other things which I would call: "Moods of inspiration" they may be better if I can only: "Hit the nail upon the head" to use the American expression.

Again with Minoulouche's[12] thanks added to mine
I am always yours affectionatly
Maurice
<u>Iseult Gonne</u> for censor

*Minoulouche, having interrupted their conversations on walks the previous summer
made an appearance with Iseult in Yeats's Prologue to his newly published work
Per Amica Silentia Lunae. It was a 'little philosophical book', a 'kind of prose
backing to his poetry' which their conversations had helped to clarify and he advised
her to read it when Minoulouche was asleep.*

**19**
Samedi [July ? 1917]
Villa Les Mouettes
Colleville s. mer
par Vierville s. mer
Calvados

My dear Willie,

I have been going through a disentagrating and restless time; you must
forgive me if I have'nt been writing you for so long; I was drifting.

We arrived here[1] three days ago; it seems comforting and full of solace
this healthy land; I go about walking with no purpose but to breathe deeply
and look at green things and water. It feels like a recovery.

O do come soon; this land will be good to you also; there's much and much
to tell and much to listen to; Bichon and I are repainting your room in
white; it's quite a hard work as we have to scratch off the wall paper before,
but it will be much improved.

I am most thankful to you for those criticisms you have made on my
scriblings.

Yes they *are* bad. I knew it all the while and I am glad of what you say about
truth and beauty. I will try and put it into practice; but just now I am still
too tired to work.

Moura all day weeds and digs at the Garden; it suits her, she looks strong
and contented. You will not know Bichon when you meet him again, he is
nearly as tall as we are, speaks with a man's voice and has at last acquired
some smoothness and grace of manner.

I have brought here a tronkful of books, and when I see them close packed,
all in a row they make me laugh, for when will they ever be read?

Write me what you are doing and how you are enjoying your castle[2]
Affectionately
Your old Maurice[3]
<u>Iseult Gonne</u> for censor

*On 27 May Iseult filled the last four pages of her Journal describing her sense of her hopelessness. Remembering the little shrine in the orchard in Colleville with the carving of a serpent biting its tail, symbolising eternity, made her think of her mind eternally running in a circle, biting its own tail, spellbound within its limits, a spell where she drops everything she tries to grasp. She saw philosophy, religion and love as ways to sanctity and beauty, but which were only useful provided one can walk in a straight line. But she could only walk round and round in the old circle, longing for the joy of flight going on and on into newness in a straight line.*

**20**
Colleville s/ mer
par Vierville s/ mer
Calvados
9 Juillet

My dear Willie,

I think Moura has already written you to say that it is likely that these good people who are with us now will be going sooner than they expected; there will be room earlier for you then and I hope that you will be able to come quick for we won't stay late in Colleville this year. Moura's rhumatismes is very bad. She will have to go to Dax[1] and then we mean to start for Ireland as soon as possible, I do hope that passports won't be refused us; I simply cannot bear the thought of another winter in Paris.

The good summer has given me back some life; and I am gradually getting strong again having giving up smoke altogether and having made myself a programme of mild discipline and keeping to regular hours.

I am indeed most anxious to read that essay of yours.[2] Religious thoughts and everything connected with the Gods are either mere illusions or the only things that count. There is no in between; and with me they have become an obssession because I cannot go deep enough into them.

Although last year you spoke to me of these things, kindly and simply, yet really I have not quite understood. I am looking forward to reading your essay immensely.

I have not much news to give from here. The people who are with us are tame and quite homely rather what is best in french "bourgeoisie". Their games are not mine, we are pleasant to each others at meals and for the rest leave each others in peace. You ask me about the circumstances of my life; truly they are not many at any time and the few there are dont count much. Imagine a beautiful woman you would be in love with. Her frowns would make you sad and when she smiled you would feel like smiling too, you would be keen on the sound of her voice yet hardly notice what she said, and you would love more the manner of her walk than where she went. Well that is the way I feel towards life. She moves me far more by her expression, by her manner than by what she says or does. No certainly I will never marry an American who would always be expecting me to bow down to the great importance of events. I suppose that's partly what gives them the "Eternal Youth" you speak of, for children also acknowledge nothing but events.

Talking about Americans an't you a little bit hard on poor Seeger?[3] Have you read his love sonnets among the last things he wrote? They seem to me to have a better and simpler kind of emotion than the rest. I have just heard something very poignant about him. It appears he killed himself. First he was wounded in the leg and the thigh during the attack, then probably forgotten among the lines like many others. When he was found, he was dead, shot through the temple with his revolver still in his hand.

Suicides pain me more than other tragedies; they are so restless, so unpacified! Still may be since his death he has by some act of resignation gained his peace. At least I hope so.

I cannot remember weither you said once that the Abbey theatre[4] was closed now for the duration of the war or not. I have just got a letter from Helen Molony;[5] she has no work just now and is pretty hard up. If the Abbey is still going on it would be most kind of you to think of her. Now by what I hear she has quite given up her old mania,[6] and intelligent and sensitive as she is I am sure she could do some good work.

Do not forget to send me the essay and to think of coming yourself soon
Your affectionate
old Maurice
Iseult Gonne
for the censor

*Yeats arrived in Colleville early in August 1917. His intention when there was to prepare a series of lectures he was to give in Paris and other work for the winter in London and Ireland. Unstated but understood by Lady Gregory was the hope that Iseult would finally accept his proposal. They had the same pleasant time working, talking, walking, and swimming as in the previous year.*

*But there was not, however, the same sense of pleasure and joy in his letters to Lady Gregory, and though life ran fairly smoothly worry crept in. There was one outbreak of protest from Maud when he suggested that London would be a better place for Iseult than Dublin, and the menagerie seemed to be irritating rather than amusing him.*

*They all returned to Paris early in September in the hopes of getting the ban on going to Ireland withdrawn. Iseult was in 'deep melancholy and apathy' on leaving the country, 'accusing herself of sins of omission'. Unspoken, but very present was the fact that Iseult faced a complete change in her life. Being French, the prospect of leaving France, which had been her home for the whole of her life, could have been very daunting. Maud, very frustrated and angry at the long hold-up of getting away, had lost that sense of quiet she had held for the past years and was according*

to Yeats, who hated her politics, 'in a joyous and self forgetting condition of political hate'. Iseult, 'something like a daughter' to him, Yeats thought now would not
marry him, but he was worried about her prospects and at the same time desperately needed to be settled in marriage. It was in these emotional states they started
for London, the permission to travel finally having come through, but only to
London. Josephine Pillon and some of the menagerie went, including Minoulouche,
the parrot Coco, the monkey, and maybe a dog and some singing birds.

At Le Havre, before embarking, Iseult went off by herself to cry, explaining to
Yeats that she felt 'selfish at not wanting to marry him and so lose his friendship'.
Confused as to where he stood and himself in a highly emotional state he arranged
with her that within a week of their arrival in London they would meet in a certain
ABC teashop, where she was to give him her definite answer. At Southampton
Maud and 'the harmless Iseult' were searched as spies and served with a notice
under the Defence of the Realm Act forbidding them to go to Ireland, and there
seemed to be doubt as to the possibility of their returning to Paris.

The Gonnes moved into a flat on the Kings Road and Iseult met Yeats in the
ABC as arranged. Yeats wrote to Lady Gregory that he was 'doing as Iseult
wishes'. Still in a confused state, he delayed going to propose to Georgie Hyde Lees
until he had talks with Iseult and Maud, having decided he was not in love with
Iseult but 'nearly mad with pity & it is difficult to distinguish between the two
emotions'. He promised Iseult that his marriage would not break their friendship
and to allay some of his worry about her, and to Maud's satisfaction, he undertook
a form of guardianship of Iseult. Then he went to propose to Georgie Hyde Lees, an
intelligent girl much the same age as Iseult, with many of the same interests.
He longed for order, and thought he would be content with a 'friendly serviceable
woman', and he thought her both 'serviceable & very able'. Maud and Iseult laughed
at his prosaic attitude but Iseult's comment was that he was 'tired of Romance
& the normal and ordinary is now to him the romantic'.

Having worked through much trepidation and anxiety for himself, Maud and
Iseult, Yeats thought he had persuaded Maud to study design 'instead of taking
up some wild political plans', and had himself recovered from Lady Gregory
saying something about him being married in the clothes he had 'bought to court
Iseult'. Yeats finally came to think his marriage had 'a great promise of happiness & tranquil work'. He was married on 20 October, with Ezra Pound as his
best man.

**21**
Tuesday evening
[Early October 1917]

My dear Willie,

I have forgotten the name of Geórgie[1] and have never known her address;
so am sending this on to you.

So sorry to have missed you to day. I was on the top of the buss and saw you in the street so I rushed down, but you had vanished from sight.

Moura tells me that you are going to be married on the 20th.[2] I wish you and Georgie great happiness and mutual understanding.

There is much in her of the quality of the sphinx, and she has awoken greatly not only my admiration but my curiosity; you must feel the same, and whenever there is curiosity and admiration together, there is romance.

She is (it seems to me) one of those minds who can give generously and, which is even a finer quality, hold back more than they give; and I feel sure she will only increase our friendship.

I have been reading a lot and working a little. My fancy was caught the other day by a young woman in the buss holding a baby in her arms, but thoroughly detached from him and looking far away (which is the only decent attitude for a mother). I came home full of thoughts on the beauty of silence[3] and put them in with my old ones. Sturge Moore[4] has very kindly asked me to join a little society "of a few who love poetry".[5] I will go to morrow.

My little Cat[6] is away at the country and I can't remember the date of her birth but I will get it from May: Thank you so much for doing her Horoscope. I am so worried about her future and not knowing exactly what is best for her, never know what to advise.

Good bye until Thursday[7]

Yrs affectionately

Maurice

*Iseult's 'little Cat' was the petite, pretty, flirtatious Thora. Kathleen was in Switzerland with her youngest son Pat who had contracted tuberculosis. Thora was enjoying getting to know her father, Major General Pilcher, whom she met regularly for a chat; he suggested she should do something towards the war effort and so she had become a land girl. He was in England because he disobeyed orders, doing what he was told but not in the prescribed manner; though his way worked he was sent home to train people. When off duty from hoeing turnips and milking, Thora sometimes visited the family in Chelsea, meeting their callers, including the ubiquitous Captain Jack White, of whom Maud advised her to be careful as he was a lady killer, and Ezra Pound, who was tutoring Sean.*

*Yeats's anxiety about Iseult still weighed on him, but he was greatly relieved, when, shortly after his marriage, he secured a post for her which would enable her to stay on in London on her own, which he still thought very important – 'from sheer happiness I burst into tears'. The post was as assistant librarian in the School of Oriental Language. 'The pay will be small but with what she has and with some help from relatives she will be all right.'*

**Fig. 10** Thora Pilcher in Laragh, c. 1930s – 'my little Cat' © Christina Bridgwater

**22**
265 King's Road
Chelsea
26–10–17

My dear Willy,

I am sending you back the essay[1] as you asked, with thanks for all your kindness in taking the trouble to correct it. The little bit about cubism was especially dear to me, but of course you are quite right to cut it out; it is'nt ripe at all.

The Oriental School[2] where I have been working now for a week is a delightful place, and every body is most kind. I am still wondering though weither I will be able to do the work properly. I am so awkward and impractical, I almost feel as if I was stealing the money they pay me, and I come in in the evening filled with shame and despair. Don't laugh; it's quite serious.

I burnt your first letter;[3] it made a very ghostly little flame in the chimney. All our thoughts about the immediate moment were then such rubbish after all, since memories are so much more important. I felt your trouble as if it was mine, and it is just as well I did not write you at once, for it mends no ill, if someone says: "life is wicked", for someone else to answer: "it is."

I happened this afternoon to enter into a little protestant church quite bare but welcoming. I spoke to God there (for it was in the spirit of the place) as if he was a simple old friend, a kind of outlaw like ourselves yet with some influence on the authorities. "Why should Willy of all people, not be happy;[4] why should I who have always loved him in all affection have had any share in causing him sorrow; and how could it all be arranged?"

And the same rush of emotion came to me as in Havre:[5] I could almost read and hear the answer: "Go back to Christ." And Alas is it true? Hermas and Cypris[6] lead to knowledge, but is peace only in Christ? I have not thought this out further, I am very sad and tired.

If only as one more kindness to me, try to be happy. It is too late and it is too early just now to look into yourself. An abruptly new condition is bound to have a little of the fearfulness of a birth, though it may be for the better. Though it may feel dreary to you, would it not be better to renounce for a time the life of emotion, and live on a few maxims of the early Patricians.[7]

But here am I speaking as if I knew when really all I know is that I share your sadness and will share your joy when you will tell me: "All is well."[8]

Give my love to Georgie; she has a sweet nature, and her kindness is no doubt the best wisdom.

Yours most helplessly
Maurice.


**23**
Thursday evening
[Oct/Nov] 1917

My dear Willie,

Your last letters brought me great happiness, the first with this good message which I was waiting for anxiously yet with confidence; the second saying that you will soon be coming.

Yes of course, come and lunch with us on Sunday. Don't bother to wire, we shall be in anyhow, and we can manage to have a quiet talk.

I am doing my best to be very happy at the School, and I ought to succeed, for everything there is as nice as it can be. Both the Sanskrit and Bengali[1] professors are charming; Dr Ross[2] is what you said, a most kind and enthousiastic person, and Miss Barry[3] with whom I am working has all the makings of a friend. The office work is very mild and everybody (safe myself) seems most indulgent over my stupidity. Only I feel mentaly very tired and powerless to adaptation or understanding. I keep thinking of the little house where I shall end my days in the Pyrénées and I wish I were already in my spinsterhood; this last is a lie, I don't. Country life, it is true, seems to me the only life I am fitted for, but I dare say I will get over this fatigue, and take life as it comes honestly and bravely; at any rate I am trying to.

I am longing to hear your last poem. There are two things which occur to me several times every day. One is a martial tune from Ivan the Terrible,[4] and the other that line of yours.[5]

When her soul flies to the predestined dancing place.

They are to me like those big smoothe waves that are such a solace to the swimmer.

I lunched to day with Miss Barry in White-Chapel; it's a gorgeous mixture of France and Palestine; we mean to go there often and get our clothes there; it feels quite homely. Talking about Miss Barry; she is a very brilliant and promising little person if only she could be saved from Eliot and Lewis;[6] some of her poems are both abominable and exquisite.

It's time for bed now. The condition of sleep is the nearest to Heaven I can picture.

Yrs affectionatly
Maurice

*After the first unhappy letter from Yeats, which Iseult had burned, his letters must have been telling her 'all is well'. In the first days of their honeymoon, seeing her husband so despondent feeling that he had betrayed three people, George attempted some automatic writing to interest him. (Yeats thought of George as a medium through whose automatic writing various spirits communicated. He then asked these spirits many questions.) On this occasion they got the words 'with the bird all is well', the bird being Iseult. Yeats immediately started to feel much better, his pains and aches were gone and he became intensely interested in his wife's special ability, which seemed to clarify his ideas and his thoughts on his relationships. Fascinated, Yeats urged her to continue the automatic writing on a daily basis and it had a great influence on his subsequent work.*

*Iseult's comment to Thora was that 'Georgie is really very clever'.*

24
Sunday
[Late November 1917]

My dear Willy,

Do forgive me for having been so long without writing. Activity is so new to me that I live in confusion and have not yet learned how to create leisure hours.

I am much more contented now than I have been for a long time. Here at last is the discipline I was craving for. I am not quite sure that it is of much practical utility, but it gives the mind a certain wholesome repose which after all is the great thing; and I am deeply grateful to you.

There is both too much and too little to write about; too much in the way of events, too little in the way of thoughts as either of these must exist at the detriment of the other. I had the great joy the other day of meeting Arthur Symons.[1] We went to an an exhibition of John's pictures[2] together; and I am dining with him on Tuesday. I was first very disappointed by him. He seemed vague and disconected, but as we talked more I realised that his illness had really more affected his manner I mean his power of persuasion than his actual jugement; for his appreciations were not only accurate but remarquable. His wife[3] is an appaling creature, as selfish and tactless as the heroïn of an American novel I have just been reading. I am writing you all this about him because I have been touched by him.[4] He seems very self-conscious and sensitive. When you are in London do spare an evening to go and see him, I am sure it would mean much more to him than you think.

I am very sad not to be with you to day, there is so much I want to tell you and so much I want to hear about those wonderful revelations. I dreamt a few nights ago that I was in a big room quite empty. It was very dark. I knew something was coming, I wanted to run away yet I had to wait. The door opened and the room was filled with a vague green light. But still nothing came and I was getting frightened. I kept thinking: "If only I had my watch on me it would be alright." At last I heard a sound of sighs outside and an old woman came in she said: "don't be cruel to her other wise she might go mad." and then, a young woman came in all dressed in pale yellow and carrying a big wooden box which I took to be a coffen. She was very beautiful. She came close to me and put the box at my feet and she said "The women weep for Adonis"[5] (I had been reading again Shelleys Adonis a few days before) and then she added: "There's no more wood for the fire." And she wanted me to open the coffin. All the time I was strugling very hard with thoughts. It seemed to me that it would be wrong to open the coffin and I said "no let me light the fire first" and I went upstairs to get some wood, but then as I was coming down with the wood I saw by the door that the three of them (the young woman, the coffin and the old woman) had turned into tigers, and I ran away, and awoke. I do not understand this dream at all, but it was very intense and strained.

I am afraid it may be difficult for me to come at Xmas, as it appears I have to undergo all sorts of formality about an identy[6] book. The question of time is a difficulty and I see also, that very exact particulars about father and mother are required. It is a somewhat uncomfortable situation.

When are you coming back? I should be glad to get a line from you if you have the time. I suppose you shall have finished your new play by the time we see you again.

Alexis[7] and I are doing our best to keep Moura[8] here as long as possible. She is well but bored poor dear.

My love to all those beautiful trees I cannot see.

Yours affectionatly

Maurice

*Arthur Symons, a very old friend of Yeats, found Iseult shared many of his intellectual and literary interests. Both recognising each other's vulnerability, the friendship quickly grew into a gentle romantic attachment, in which they met for meals, exchanged some letters and worked together. He inscribed one of the books he gave her 'To Iseult of Ireland from Arthur of Cornwall'.*

*Yeats happily reported to Lady Gregory that Iseult and George were becoming great friends and Iseult had stayed with them a few times at Stone Cottage and later in Oxford. But his efforts to prevent Maud from 'wild political plans' had not worked as she had met old friends and made new ones among socialists and suffragettes, including Charlotte Despard, a new friend and a socialist. She gave two lectures on Ireland for Sylvia Pankhurst, spellbinding her audience, and then she finally managed to escape her watchers. Jackie or Alexis (as Iseult, with her fondness for nicknames, now called her brother) had taken careful note of her watchers as they retired to the nearby pub while Maud went for her regular Turkish bath. So, as planned, one day, when they were safely inside the nearby pub in the warmth, he gave Maud the all clear. She came out unobserved and went to Eva Gore Booth's flat (she was an old friend and a suffragette), while Sean hastened off to gather their luggage and catch the train on his way to Dublin. Helen Molony, released with the rest of the prisoners before the end of 1917, went to meet Maud's boat, but not finding her hastened back to Dr Kathleen Lynn's to find Maud had already arrived.*

*From her answer to Yeats it was obvious Iseult was exploring and enjoying the rather liberal side of social and literary life and had probably begun her affair with Ezra Pound.*

**25**
265 King's Road
Chelsea
[January 1918]

My dear Willie,

Your letter which I have just received saying "I have not seen Moura's[1] name in the paper, and that is a good sign while it lasts." Alas!, sounds like irony. She has gone to Ireland; she got Sylvia Pankhurst,[2] to announce a meeting in which she was suppose to speak last Sunday, so that the thoughts of the detectives should be centered on that. Then she wrote to all her friends in Ireland knowing that the letters would be opened by the censor, that she, though broken hearted, had to send Jacky[3] to Ireland all alone to be put to school there as she could'nt come too. Jacky effectively left on Friday with the luggage, and she left on Saturday. She had dinner with Eva Gore boothe[4] first; they dressed her up as a midleclassish respectable stoggy[5] woman. Her hair powdered white with a little blue hat that stood on the top of her head, a man's stiff coller, a dowdy grey coat, and a worn grey fur muff and collar. She apparently was not noticed at the station, and I got a telegramme from her yesterday saying that she had arrived safely in Dublin. The question is, will they let her stay?

Meanwhile I feel very miserable and anxious, and don't know what to do. For the present I have kept this house as the lease still lasts 3 months. Iris Barry[6] is coming to live with me, and Sophia[7] is staying with us and so are all the beasts[8] until Moura has found a house for them to go into. I mean at any rate, that is to say if nothing goes wrong, to stay another 3 months in London; and then....I don't know.

Do give my love to Georgie.[9] I have been wanting to write to you both; but felt too scattered and worried. I had a heavenly time in the country with you;[10] I can still see how the grass was peeping through the snow. How dismal London is!

I am sorry to hear that you have been ill. Do you feel quite well now? I hope you are enjoying Oxford[11] and your beautiful old house.

I am once more caught in the network of Sanskrit and Bengali; and going out a great deal. It is all very interesting, but too crammed up. I have not thought a thought for weeks. It is very lonely here without Moura and Alexis.

I must stop now for it is late.

Yours affectionatly

Maurice

PS.  Isn't uncle nicer than father?[12]

**26**
Sunday

My dear Willie,

At last a whole day of solitude![1] I am reading again your essays[2] in the book you sent me; and that, and some Wagner's music[3] which I heard last night, makes me dream of some sea wind blowing upon serious, happy faces. The mental air here is in movement as if motionned by a ventilator, but there is no breze, no wind: Machinery has invaded the arts, and the mind itself is seeking a kind of precision not so much mathematical as mecanical.

Why write to me as to a bad child in danger of perdition? Perdition ... perhaps, but not that kind. They have spots on their faces you say.[4] Yes, Adonis[5] is not among them; nor is the God of Wisdom, for they have no hesitation, but dogmas without faith.

Yet I want to know them for a time, and try to understand; after all a movement[6] must have something good in it, even if only in its intentions.

Have you found a house yet? Do tell me all about it. Talking about houses, Moura seems to have discovered a charming place,[7] with a garden and a field, rather as Temple Hill[8] was, I suppose. I hope she will take it.

I am feeling much better now. This week end with you both did me a lot of good, and also I have not been sitting up so late.

I found that learning both Bengali and Sanskrit took too much time, and it ended by my doing neither properly; so I asked Dr Ross[9] if I might drop Bengali for a time; so now I can really take some interest in Sanskrit. It isn't very wicked, is it?

Barry wears a ring on her left hand, is engaged, in love, and away for the week end. He seems an honest, simple young man;[10] and on the whole it is a wise choice. Oh, do find me a pale faced student for Thora! And then I shall not have anymore responsabilities; and will you ask Georgie, if it isn't giving her too much trouble, weither she would be so kind as to send me Thora's Horoscope;[11] and give her my best love and thank her again, and yourself from me for those two lovely days spent in Oxford.[12]

Yours affectionatly
Maurice

P.S.   Also can you ask Georgie to give me the address of the little dressmaker she spoke to me about.


*Iseult herself had been busy finding young men for Thora. One especially, whom Iseult had known in France, Thora thought she was 'rather in love' with. He had been in the Foreign Legion and spoke fluent French, 'but he wore a bowler hat wrong', a sign he was not presentable enough for the family. Flirt and all as she was, Thora also thought that since the war morals had become perhaps too easy.*

**27**
265 King's Road
Chelsea
Friday [February 1918]

My dear Willy,

I have been thinking over those passeport difficulties.[1] For my part I do not intend to go to Ireland before the summer holidays; but Moura wants Joséphine to come and join her in March. She wanted me to write to some

Irish M.P.s to get them to arrange things; but, as you know, my papers are not pleasant to show and I would rather not let strangers know my private affairs. So, if really it isn't giving you too much trouble, I should be extremely grateful to you if you could get this Defence of the Realm order revised both for Josephine's passeeport and mine; but don't let this interfere with your other occupations; it isn't worth it, and besides there is no great hurry.

Moura's letters sadden me. I think she is very tired, and running round looking for houses[2] is not good for her; she is all the time asking me to come; I shall not do it; nevertheless I do not think I am quite justified, and I feel a little remorseful.

Thankyou for the little poem;[3] it might almost be used as an exorcism.

I have not been seing many people lately; Ezra and Symons[4] occasionally, but most evenings we come in and read or I work at my Sans Krit. I am growing fatter and feeling altogether stronger, Iris[5] is very busy with her novels. We have twisted and stretched every possible hypothesis and theory so far that there is very little more to talk about, and we can afford she and I to be silent now and not sit up to all hours of the night talking.

Have you found your house now? And how are you? Indeed I should love to hear more about the system.[6]

Give my love to Georgy.[7] Will you never be coming to London for a few days?

Yours affectionatly
Maurice

*Yeats felt that the Authorities would do nothing about permits for Josephine and Iseult to travel to Ireland as this would be tacitly to recognise Maud's right to be there. But, still worried about her, and in an effort 'to keep her Orthodox', he was proposing to send her the Encyclicals of Leo X111 and Pius X and suggesting she should study Catholic economics. Maud bought a Georgian town house in St Stephen's Green in March and was becoming politically active, primarily in public relations work with visiting journalists and politicians as the political situation was becoming more heated, with Sinn Fein contesting by-elections and conscription for Ireland threatened. Sean, now fourteen, had joined the nationalist boy scouts, Fianna Eireann.*

*It would seem that Iseult's affair with Ezra was in full swing by this time and Iseult was doing her best at dissembling. But sadness struck in the midst of her new and happy social life. Her father died. She wrote to her mother in French about this. Here is the relevant part of the letter translated:*

My dear,

Have you read any French or English newspapers recently? If so I have nothing to tell you and you will have already read the heartbreaking news. The Wolf is dead. I have not got the details. I only know of it from the newspapers, or really from May who has read them. My eyes are sore from crying. One never knows just how much affection one has for somebody until they are lost, then one remembers all the things one could have done for them but neglected to do and above all of all the hard things one thought about them and this seems so unjust and cruel.

Oh! May God have his soul! I am having a mass said for him but I do not know how to pray any more; you will pray, won't you? After all we are in Christ's Kingdom where the symbol of justice is not a weighing scale, but a heart, and however misguided a person is, the further he has to return, the better he is welcome; it is what I hope for him.

At least I have the poor, small satisfaction of telling myself that the last letter I received from him three weeks ago, was very affectionate and I answered almost immediately. We had really become friends again. My poor darling, if you have not yet learnt of his death, I fear my letter will give you a lot of pain. For you it is all the past which must be put aside for ever, it is all the memories which re-awaken and I feel with you all that you must be aware of that is tiresome and almost ironic for there is always much irony to wring the heart when one looks back on things past. If you have much grief, write of it to your old Rat.

**28**
54 Beaufort Mansions
Beaufort Street
Chelsea
24–3–18

My dear Willie,

I was thinking over your letter yesterday when Ezra came with the news that the Little Review[1] could now take me on full time. I am yet undecided; because I can hardly imagine that I am fit for the work, still if I could do it, it would be more intelligent than card indexing.

As you know perhaps Iris has had measles, so for fear of infection not only she, but I also have had to keep away from the School for the past fortnight and have another 12 days before we return; so anyhow I could not for mere decency's sake, having been paid a month for doing nothing, leave them at once after; I must at least stay another month.[2] This, Ezra quite understands; and I suggested to him that during this month he should give me some samples of the sort of work I would have to do, which I could do in the evenings so that he may judge weither I am fit for it or not; but I do not wish anybody to know about this yet (especially not Ross)[3] as it is still so vague in my mind.

The address on the other page is the flat we are going to move into tomorrow. It is very small and rather expensive for us, but eminently respectable which I feel you will approve of. We have been committing wild extravagances in the way of furniture buying, but we are so tired of a sordid frame! We have decided to arrange the sitting-room in a way that will not offend either of our contradictory tastes so there shall not be a single picture in it, luckily about furniture and stuffs we quite agree; but we are ... [MS incomplete].


**29**
54 Beaufort Mansion
Beaufort Street
Chelsea
28–3–18

My dear Willy,

I am really at a loss[1] to answer your letter. Ezra tried to kiss me?!![2] My first impulse was to summons the good lady of Normandy so as to get a little light, but then I thought it would mean tears and a row and a reproachful letter from her to Moura which would not help matters, so I decided not to say anything to her. The only thing I can possibly imagine is that the poor old thing fresh from her village must have been horrified at the way people call on us in the evenings, and as Ezra comes in rather often, must have drawn fantastic conclusions. But what I cannot account for are the circumstantial details she seems to have given; it would all be very laughable if it wasn't at the same time rather distressing and humiliating. Really life seems made of one beastly thing after another. Between mental and household complications I feel my poor brain shall give way; I almost am tempted to go to Dublin and there take to bed for a month.

Forgive this, it's only child's talk, really I am upset about my father's death;[3] it has been a great blow to me I don't quite know why.

I want to thank you and Georgie[4] ever so much for your kind offer about Woburn Buildings,[5] but we have taken this little flat on for a year, and we think we shall be able to manage quite alright; it is really not bad, and we can make it quite livable. Do thank Georgie about the typewriter; it will be a great comfort and joy to us; as a matter of fact I had already been thinking over again the job Ezra[6] offers me, and I had come to your conclusion (not as regard shades of affection); but it had occured to me that possibly both Ezra and Dorothy[7] out of kindness to me were offering a thing they might not be able to comfortably afford. I think I shall go on with the School work, which after all I do not dislike any more than any other work (as you know I do not love work.) Every body there is very charming, and in the monotony of card-indexing, there is even something rather restful. So don't worry to look for something else, you have already both been too kind and taken too much trouble about me.

I am so glad you are having a joyful time in the country Give my love to your Cat,[8] which if he is worthy of his name, must be a very remarquable person

Yours affectionatly

Maurice

**Fig. 11** Frontispiece photo of 'Ezra Pound' by Alvin Langdon Coburn, from *Lustra* (poems) by Ezra Loomis Pound, 1916. Reference (Shelfmark) 28001 e.1557, reproduced with kind permission of Bodleian Library, Oxford

30
54 Beaufort Mansions
Beaufort Street
Chelsea
[Late March 1918]

My dear Willy,

Your letter and what you said about my father[1] did me good to read. Thankyou for having understood that his death was a great grief to me, for during his life I had spoken and felt so unkindly about him! But then I suppose, as long as one's father or mother are alive one has to like them in spite of the fact that they are one's parents and if they have a few failings such as might bring one closer to a friend one does not forgive them. Then they die; and the link that was compulsory and a little shameful dies also because beyond this life no such links exist. They are only little children yet unborn to which much tenderness and some pity can be given. One thinks that after all the choice may have been a free one and then not only does one forgive them everything because they have been one's parents, but because of that also one wishes for their forgiveness.

We are going back to the School tomorrow. This holiday has done us good, but we both feel that returning to regular work will do us even more good. We have spent some of our time arranging the flat, going out for walks and seing a few people. We have found that since we cannot possibly agree on most things there is at least a way of disagreeing harmoniously, and we get on quite well together; the monkey has been put in pension, Minoulouche[2] has rather forsaken me for Iris preferring the curves of her knees to the angles of mine. I feel rather hurt, as to the parrot he is merely bent on disturbing the peace of the Curate below. Poor Sophia[3] is the only pathetic figure. She sits in her kitchen with red eyes longing to get away. I have been several times to the Home Office, but they tell me that they have sent my application to the Secretary of State and I must wait till he answers; there doesn't seem to be much hope and all I am doing seems rather a waste of time, but I do feel sorry for the poor old thing,[4] and also it would be much more convenient if I had an authorisation to go to Ireland next summer than go without which I will probably have to do.

Tell Georgie, giving her my love, that I have got myself a black and very monastic garment which is a real joy. I tried to type your father's letters[5] but found the writing so difficult to read and my handling of the typing machine so slow that I would have been centuries at it. I should have loved to do it if I hadn't had to return to the School, but as it is I really would not have time; So am sending them on to Miss Jacobs.[6]

Have you read the last Joyce in the "Little Revue"?[7] It really is splendid, more violent and as subdued as the Portrait[8] and the same queer treatment of beauty; beautiful thoughts, beautiful images must be blighted before or directly they take any definite form so as to keep their distance from life.

It is as if he used to scare his ideal beauty from earth a terrifying and distorted mask of a kind of Medusa's Head. I cannot help seing in him, though not quite mature all the sombre side of greatness, too tragic to be bitter, not under any delusions but perhaps mad; but perhaps also I am exaggerating, I should like to know what you think of it.

Now, alas, I must dive into Sanskrit, or I should not dare face the Chiken of the Valey[9] tomorrow.

Yours affectionatly

Maurice

*Because of an alleged conspiracy with Germany, there was a general round up of Sinn Fein leaders. The Chief Secretary for Ireland signed an order for Maud's arrest on 17 May. She was arrested on 19 May, brought first to a police station followed by Joseph King MP and Sean. From there, followed by Sean in order to bring her food and clothing, she was taken to the Bridewell where she sat up all night as the beds were verminous. The following day she was brought to Arbour Hill Military Barracks, unsuited to housing women, and at one in the morning was brought under military escort to the Mail Boat, presented with the detention order under the Defence of the Realm Act and told she was going to Frongagh in Wales but instead was brought to Holloway Prison in London. After two weeks there she was eventually allowed contact with the outside world in the form of three letters of half a sheet each a week and one business letter by special permission. All her frequent requests for a solicitor to advise her about signing the undertaking, which was required for her release under the Act, were ignored. She was kept in solitary confinement and only met her fellow republican prisoners Constance Markiewicz and Kathleen Clark in the exercise yard.*

31

25–5–18

54 Beaufort Mansions

Beaufort Street

Chelsea

My dear Willy,

I was thankful for your telegramme[1] and letters, for imagine, the anxiety I was in,[2] with no news but the papers!

Visits ar't [aren't] yet allowed, I have been twice to Holloway but was not even permitted to leave a note; I have now applied for a permit to the Secretary of State, and wait for the answer. Alexis[3] arrived here early this morning, he told me you had very kindly invited him to stay with you and wishes me to thank you for him, but he feels that now he must be near his mother to be of what help he can.

As the family, even the saintly Chotie,[4] is undergoing an acute crisis of uncompromising jingoism, there is no question of his going there, and somehow I can manage to put him up here. By what I gather from various people, Lynch,[5] Nevinson[6] and Eva Gore-Boothe,[7] all that story of a German plot[8] is a pure make up and no evidence can possibly be produced against her. I am taking a week's holiday from the School, giving fatigue as a pretext, to have some time to see people and what can be done to get her out as soon as possible. They are most likely to keep her in for a month or two, and then release her but forbid her return to Ireland until the end of the war. In which case I would try and decide her to come and live in Oxford, a quiet safe place which she would love for its beauties and where the boy's education[9] would at last get a chance. I myself would give up the School, and this flat and resume a quiet family life which I now long for more than any thing else. But these are hazy dreams; yet meanwhile the situation is really too precarious and uncertain to enable me to think of a secretaryship to the "Little Review"[10] or any other mental activity; besides I am gradually getting more stupid and helpless every day; in fact the mask of the Idiot[11] threatens to fit altogether too closely. However of what interest or importance are the wanderings of my mind just now? Hard facts are beating at the door, and these, if not any more real, seem at least more urgent.

You tell me but little in your letters what you are doing just now? It must be hard to work in the turmoil of present events, but you are in a beautiful country place, far away, where no doubt you draw the only wisdom and strength available in our days, that which is to be found only in the connections with vegetal life; for in the human relations (at least over here) one seems to be faced with nothing but mechanical problems: locomotion, the War, Wyndham Lewis[12] and his increasing disciples, and above all that which seems to pervade the arts and friendship itself, the theory of: "what use can be made out of this or that." Thank heavens, a few people and a few thoughts are free from this and one lives for those.

Thank Georgie for her sweet letter to me: I do wish indeed I could come to you next summer, but if Moura remains in Holloway, I cannot think of leaving London.

When are you thinking of coming, it will be a blessing to see you both again!

Yours affectionatly

Maurice.

for the censor Iseult Gonne.

*Mrs Yeats, having already sent Iseult a loan of five pounds, and being fully aware that Iseult's income would now be inadequate for the needs of the little household without Maud's allowance arriving, wrote to Ezra Pound on 24 May sending some more money for him to dispense to Iseult as needed 'for work' or some other quibble his 'ingenious' mind could invent so that Iseult would not suspect a gift or loan.*

*The Yeatses were also proposing to come over from Ireland in order to provide*
*Iseult with a country holiday with them.*

*Thora tells of Josephine's strict economies and ability in making nourishing*
*meals, so that when Iseult would say 'We shall have Pomme de terre a la Matelot*
*for lunch to-day' Josephine would put her Normandy sabot-clad foot down and say*
*'You are having eggs'.*

32
54 Beaufort Mansions
Beaufort Street
Chelsea
[late May/early June 1917]

My dear Willy,

Everything is so confused, and our situation such a perfect mess that I can
hardly write you a clear answer.

About Bichon.[1] Your plan of sending him to a kind of homely School in
the country certainly seems the best. Unfortunatly the child has come back
his head packed with rubish and will hear of nothing for the present but
resuming his former life in Dublin. I will do all I can to prevent that, but
I don't quite know how. I went to see Law[2] Yesterday, he is going to ask
Short[3] to day if, at least, I may be allowed to communicate with Moura[4] as
to her intentions about Bichon, and will give me an answer this evening.

About myself. I have delayed accepting Ezra's offer[5] as long as I could because
really I felt scruples about accepting payment for a work I may not be fit to
do. I am alone to know that full extent of my incapacity for any intellectual
form of activity. Only now I really feel so tired and run down that I can't go
on with the School.

So I have spoken to Ross[6] and will probably leave in a week or a fortnight.
I have given Ezra a fair warning of my inaptitude and if after a month I find
that really I can't do the work properly I shall try and get some translation work
which, with the money I get from France[7] will be sufficient to keep us going.

I am so glad that you are coming soon.

Excuse this dull scrible

I have to rush home now

Yours affectionatly

<u>Maurice</u>

*As was to be expected, Iseult did not feel she could leave London, but at last the*
*silence from the prison was broken and they could communicate by occasional*
*letter, but if Maud put in a request for Iseult to get her a solicitor the letter was*
*confiscated. Sean was allowed one visit to his mother to discuss his education.*
*When Sean or Iseult took the long journey to Holloway or Iseult was working,*

*Thora described going shopping with Josephine to translate for her. Josephine 'always wore her peasant costume, a voluminous skirt pleated at the waist, a black woollen shawl, clogs and thick black hairnet....In the greengrocers she would ask for one parsnip, half a cabbage, two potatoes, a leaf of this or that. The shopkeepers were charmed with her and gave her what she what asked for'.*

33
54 Beaufort Mansions
Beaufort Street
Chelsea
15–6–18

My dear Willy,

How I long for that wild rose at the top branch of the tree, just out of reach; that is your invitation to come to the country. For Alas it is for me out of reach. I have thought it over, and really do not see my way to leaving London for the present.

We have to bring food to the prison[1] every day. I tried to make some arrangement with a little restaurant near by to have the food sent in, but it was so bad, that even the prison regime was better, and Holloway is such a distance that it is impossible to get other shops to send things there; so either Bichon[2] or I have to go every day. Besides poor Josephine[3] is depressed and lonely and has taken a violent dislike to Barry[4] so it would be uncharitable to leave her for a long time. This is a great disapointement, it would have been heavenly; still I can manage to come to you for week ends, since you are both so kind as to ask me.

We have at last received letters from Moura.[5] She is in good health and hopeful to come out soon. This is heartbreaking as I fear they mean to keep her in till the end of the war.

Could you write me a line when you are coming, because I have still got the keys of W. Buildings[6] and can bring them to you directly you arrive.

Yours affectionatly
Maurice

34
Beaufort Mansions
Beaufort Street
Chelsea
2–7–18

My dear Willy,

Here are the typed copies of your poems.[1] Gorgeous stuff! and it was great fun to do. I have kept the originals in case you want more copies; but if you need them write me and I will send them.

Alexis[2] and I dined with Mrs Tucker[3] the other evening. She told us your house had been damaged. What a nuisance! When will the repairs be over; and when will you come back?

About Moura, nothing new. Useless endeavours. A wall of silence and stupidity.

I am delighted with my new work. Have been mostly copying and typing fragments from translations of the Illiad[4] and been reminded of my fourteen years old heroic dreams and plans of a life which would be nothing but a great epic.

My love to Georgie

Yours affectionatly

Maurice

I love most of all the song of Solomon to Sheba[5] and the Beggar's dream.[6] A wise man that beggar!


35
Beaufort Mansions
Chelsea
23–7–18

My dear Willy,

Alexis is I hope by now with you;[1] it is most kind and gracious of you and Georgie to have him and you mustn't either of you let him interfere with your occupations, he will find plenty of amusement in the woods and the lake.

I am glad to think he is with you; he could be no where better; but I did feel a little anxious and worried in letting him go to Ireland; Russell[2] has written me that later on there is likely to be trouble; he is both too intelligent, too active and too young to be in the midst of it. If, when you leave Galway Miss Barten[3] isn't ready for him do send him back to me weither he wills or not. I dread to think of him in Dublin alone.

About Father Sweetman's School,[4] Moura had already thought of it for him; but there is one objection. Among the teachers is a man called Collins,[5] he used to be a great friend of MacBride and did more to lead him to drink and mischief than anyone else, altogether an undesirable person, and she wouldn't wish Bichon[6] under his wing. Of course he may not be there anymore. Do you think you could inquire?

If school arrangement in Ireland fails, he must come back here and work with a tutor.[7] I feel very disheartened about Moura. No chance, I fear, of an open trial or release during war and they seem determined as well to refuse visits.

I enjoy my work at the museum,[8] we are reading through now all the translations of Sapho;[9] the pain-taking labours of the Victorian era would be amusing weren't they so boresome, but some of the 16th and 17th century stuff is really pleasurable. For my private delectation I am reading Voltaire's letters[10] and feel each day for him a greater respect.

The coakrooch[11] now has taken to playing at being a cameleon; the old circle of obsessions is somewhat broken but new ones spring up to prove the truth of the old saying: there is no rest under the sun.

Do, if you have anything to type send it to me, I enjoy it so; and let me know if there are any researches I could do for you at the museum.

Your country life[12] sounds peaceful and beautiful, I hope you are enjoying it.

Give my love to Georgie

Yours affectionatly

Maurice

*Sean was with the Yeatses in Galway, all his illnesses, aches and pains long forgotten, and now the young man Yeats had described in Colleville in 1917 who, to Yeats's 'amusement has begun to criticize his mothers politics. He has a confident analytic intelligence & is more like a boy of 17 than 13.' So now, apart from fishing and swimming, he was writing from Ballinamantane House to the authorities, to the papers, and to his mother on various matters; one subject in particular came up regularly, his education. He fended off unwelcome suggestions concerning his education from all quarters; for him it was to be in Ireland and 'I already told you I could not work with' Ezra Pound. Pound's own comment later was that Sean probably 'has never forgiven me for trying to lam some Ovid into his very allergic head'.*

*Many of Maud's friends had been working to get her released, including her old American friend, John Quinn, Yeats and Stephen Gwynn, also Joseph King, who besides repeatedly asking questions in the House of Commons on the prisoners' conditions, also paid frequent visits to the Chief Secretary, Shortt.*

**36**
18 Woburn buildings
W.C.
26–8–18

My dear Willy,

I have thought over your letters a long time, and our last talk. I had not ment that the link of our friendship could ever be weakened. It was a certain spiritual connection to which I was alluding to, of the kind one might say: "we have seen together that the yellow of the sunlight is made of Gold and white." There are times when the atheistic tendancies of my childhood come back so strongly that all but the revelations of the senses seems a myth and then I cannot hope to participate in discoveries of a world which may not be, yet may be Maïa.[1]

This is a case more of instinct than of reason, and I know that my instinct in most things is wrong but in a life of small turmoils irrelevant to the mind, one is apt, when not strong, to lose power for serene thoughts and give in to instinct. I am so much the prey to environment!

And now I can never thank you and Georgie[2] enough; I have found in this house,[3] with the old world feeling and the quiet, that my mind is ready to awake again. I am writing a little; when I shall have done something I am not too ashamed of, will send it to you.

Your poem is a beautiful and clear synthesis. And how I love:

> The soul remembering its loneliness
> Shudders in many cradles;[4] ...

and all this sober clear cut definition which yet curves and wanders like an incantation! Are you going to use it as a preface to your book?[5]

I am glad my little Alexis[6] is coming back to me. It has been so kind of you to keep him with you all this time; it will have been a valuable contrast with the Sylvia group[7] and the editors!![8] I went to see again Father Kelly,[9] walked in, looked listened, shuddered, walked out, the most loathsome typical type of Irish priest. For all Moura's wishes I cannot bear to think of him in the clutches of bigottry and stupidity.

I am going this afternoon to see an other priest who, I hear, is wise in such matters, and a man of some intelligence. A day school would be the best.

Give my love to Georgie,[10] and thankyou both so much for everything you have done for us.

Yours ever

Maurice

P.S.  Mrs Old[11] has just dropped in. Tears and sighs in profusion. I have consoled her as best I could with a dark blue sweater, a pair of nickers, and the assurance that she took almost as large a room in your thoughts as you do in hers, and that etc. etc.

*While leaving Sean in the care of their neighbour, Edward Martyn, the Yeatses had come over to England to look after Iseult, taking advantage of her visit to Joseph King's Somerset home to rescue her from that 'scandalous person' Iris Barry, 'who seems to have kept her [Iseult] in submission with tears and temper.' They 'kidnapped her maid, her cat & birds & all her furniture & transferred them to Woburn Buildings.' Yeats added in his letter to Lady Gregory that Iseult 'is afraid of the young woman, of Ezra, of me, of everybody and that the very devil.'*

*Later, on 18 August, Yeats had written to Iseult saying 'we must not let the old link be broken. . . . nothing endeed can break this link – never up to this broken in my thoughts – but the unhappiness of another.' He finished by asking her to be friends with George who 'has become happy only very lately.'*

**37**
18 Woburn buildings
W.C.
28–8–18

My dear Willy,

Immediatley on receiving your letter I went to the prison, and asked the matron[1] if she couldn't as a special favour ask Moura weither in the case an interview was granted she was ready to give her parole not to speak of any political or public matters; the matron refused to convey this message and so did the Governor[1] saying it was against the rules, all they could say was that when the interview was granted, they would see to the restrictions. I am writing to Moura on the subject, but letters are so slow, it means a week's delay at least. However I am almost sure that Bichon is talking rubbish and that she *will* give her parole; and I think you can let Stephen Gwynn[2] take that for granted and act as soon as possible.

I long so much to see her again!

Yours affectionatly
<u>Maurice</u>

*It is not clear what parole was expected of Maud. She would not have given an undertaking not to partake in politics if released, but she might have undertaken to refrain from talking politics to Sean if he were allowed to visit, or to see a specialist concerning her health, which might have been the case in this instance.*

*Back in London in late August, Sean wrote to the authorities continually about the state of his mother's health – he said she had lost two stone – and was threatening to go on hunger strike, asking did they want another scandal like the death of Thomas Ashe, who died on hunger strike in September 1917. Sean's state of hyperactivity must have been very trying for Iseult; according to Arthur Symons's account she threw him down the stairs in Woburn Buildings in a great temper. Allowing for Symons's exaggeration the story would still indicate the stress they were under, which does not show in her gentle letters, as her trouble with Barry had not shown.*

*Yeats interviewed Shortt, the Chief Secretary, in Dublin and gained permission for a doctor to be allowed to see Maud. On the advice of Dr Tunicliffe, a visit from whom it appears King managed to arrange, Maud was eventually released on 29 October to a nursing home. Dr Tunicliffe saw her again there and finding her somewhat improved, recommended that, failing some high altitude resort, she be allowed to go to Ireland and be treated by her own doctor, Dr Crofton, a chest specialist. This was expressly against Shortt's wishes, for he wanted her to be kept*

*in England. Maud only stayed a week in the nursing home and was able to leave*
*for Woburn Buildings without hindrance.*

38
18 Woburn buildings
Upper Woburn Place
W.C.
18–10–18

My dear Willy,

I was overjoyed getting your last letter. What good news! And how many candles[1] we should burn for you at every shrine-corner!

King yesterday had just had a private talk with Short[2] and told us that Moura's release was only now a matter of a few days; it is however, he said, doubtful whether she will be let go back at once to Ireland. Still I suppose that may soon be settled also, and meanwhile we can all three live very comfortably here. Yet I should so like to see you again and it would be so much more pleasant to be all together!

I enclose the "Orpheus."[3] I am not really very pleased with it, something is wrong and I don't quite know what.

Apart from buseness visits about Moura, I have seen very few people of late; chief occupations: typing, scrubbing Bichon[4] in his bath and combing Minoulouche,[5] and an occasional visit to the School[6] where Barry[7] and the Chicken of the Valley[8] feed me with chocolates and confidances. I spent last sunday a delightful afternoon with Mrs Tucker,[9] she was most charming and kind.

Do write me more about Yourself and what you are thinking, and if you have anything you want typed to send it me.

Give my best love to Georgie[10]

Yours affectionatly

<u>Maurice</u>

39
18 Woburn buildings
[Last week in October, 1918]

My dear Willy,

I was waiting before writing to you for the situation to be somewhat more definite, but it hasn't cleared up. Moura was released on tuesday[1] evening and accompanied by a prison wardress in a taxi to a nursing-home which King[2] had advised. The official letter from the Home-Office which both we and Ezra received says she is "temporaly released to be nursed in a nursing-home" and it adds that this arrangement is for a week.

King does not seem to know what their plans are after the week, nor if she is really free.

I have been to the Home Office but they won't say anymore.

Meanwhile the price of this nursing-home is an impossible one: 10 guineas a week, and it is not very congenial, she can only see us from three to six, and of course she would much rather come to Woburn buildings. I think this may be obtained in time, only I am rather nervous that Bichon's present state of agitation and drastic plans may endanger matters.

Moura is writing you herself, and will tell you more. Thank you so much for your last letter and your kind criticism. I quite agree with you, but I have got to feel so shy of myself that I shrink from the old form. I will write you more about this some day. The war may be coming to an end, if so we shall meet shortly in Ireland. Yet is it really coming to an end??

Thank Georgie for me for sending Mrs Old,[3] the room is now quite ready for Moura if only she could come. Give Georgie my love, I hope she is feeling quite well again.

Yours very affectionatly

Maurice

**40**

18 Woburn buildings

Friday

[November 1918]

My dear Willy,

This is not really an answer to your last letter to me. I shall say no more of Moura's affairs but thank you again for all your kind help; now that she is out,[1] I don't think we can do much more, and I agree with you that there isn't much chance of her getting to Ireland at least until peace is signed and the general elections are over. Meanwhile we can live quite happily here. It makes all the difference to be in a charming house like this with the right kind of atmosphere for rest and quiet thinking.

I have just been reading over your poem,[2] the one about the cat and the hare. It is beautiful and pathetic with the pathos I admire most – destiny. I was thinking to myself after reading it: "All, even hysteria becomes respectable when set spinning by the thumb of fate, and it is part of the fate of hares to run wild and to be hunted." Then I began to think of it as applied to myself and my speculations became more dreamy, less precise. Why did you feel anxious about me,[3] I mean anxious in that way? The hare seems to me a symbol of a personality – as helpless – but more active than mine, of one that both fears yet has to encounter danger, altogether a more dramatic personality. I don't really think I belong to that order of things. Sometimes I wish I did ("enforced love of the world",[4] I suppose), but I doubt that it is in my destiny ever to meet directly with drama, unless it be the obscure drama of the mind in the hard process of sheding illusions. Why should that be so hard? I wonder, But it is. For instance the other day it suddenly dawned upon me that really Huysmans[5] is only secondary; I could have wept. It feels as painful to extract an admiration as a tooth.

I was very depressed when I wrote to you last, but am feeling a little more lucid now. I do wish I could see you again, there are so many things I would like to ask you about. Life realisation for me seems to proceed by an accumulation of question marks.

Moura tells me that you propose I should come to Dublin at Christmas, I should love to, but it depends on circumstances and chiefly on Moura's health. For the present she is not really bitter, but very tired and needs a lot of looking after.

I have for a long time been wanting to read some Wordsworth,[6] I opened a book at hazard and found it deadly dull, do tell me what is the best of his works; for Ezra[7] has such an unmitigated loathing of him that he will not advise any, and I do not feel the courage to venture upon it again at hazard.

And chiefly, it if is not too much trouble, do send me a carbon copy of any poem you write.

Now it is very late, my eyes are blinking with sleep

Yours affectionatly

Maurice

*Saturday morning*

Have just heard your last letter to Moura.[8] How alarming! And what confounded brutes these officials are! She is just beginning to feel a little better and to get some sleep; if they drag her away now, it would realy be a bad shock to her nerves. Let's hope it is partly bluff on their part.

**41**
18 Woburn buildings
2–11–18

My dear Willy,

Moura has just read me your letter; I feel very alarmed. Do you think the Government really means internment for her? In her present condition it would be very bad. Any sanatorium with the best medical care and attention even, is not what she requires. Her nerves chiefly are very shattered and what she needs is quiet home life with us to look after her and no more fuss of official regulations.

I really cannot see why she shouldn't be allowed back to Dublin, for she would be happiest there and more likely to recover quickly under the care of Dr Crofton[1] whom she trusts than in the uncongenial atmosphere of a sanatorium in England; at least she ought to be let come to Woburn buildings; but as regards that we do not yet know how the situation stands: no open prohibition, but disquieting hints. I also think the visit of Dr Haze,[2] a friend of Short not very advisable, he might not feel altogether friendly to us, and his advice would hardly be the best in the circumstances.

The whole thing is a dilemma. The taro cards frighten me; whenever I pick them up, they always tell me the same yarn and it's a bad one; also I am feeling tired this evening; even the bright bunch of marigold I bought this afternoon assumes to my eyes an ominous meaning; I could only talk gloomy rubbish so had better stop.

Yours ever affectionatly
Maurice.

P.S.   If by chance you see Short again, *do* convince him of the necessity for Moura in her present state of health to be left at peace with us to look after her; after having caused her health to be ruined, it is the least he can do.

*When Maud came out of prison she found Iseult terribly thin; she had only got out of bed to greet Maud. The possibility that Maud might be interned again when she became stronger, coupled with the fact that the war was over and passports and documents were not needed for travel, induced her once more to escape to Ireland. All the family went this time including Iseult, but there is little detail of this escape, except that Arthur Symons visited them a few days before they left and when seeing him off Iseult made him promise to absolute secrecy as she told him that they were all leaving in a day or so.*

*It is not clear on what terms Iseult parted with Ezra. He said much later that the last he heard of her was when he left her at a bus stop in Kensington High Street, but in actual fact she wrote regularly to him on her arrival in Ireland. Apart from telling him how much she loved him and missed him, she gave Pound details of the first few months of her life in Dublin. Among these was the outrageous row between Maud and Yeats, who had rented her house on a monthly basis, not only for convenience but as a kind act. On arriving in Dublin Maud had naturally gone to her house expecting to be welcomed, looking forward to peace and comfort in the care of Josephine. But George was pregnant and very ill so when Yeats saw Maud on the doorstep he panicked, fearing police raids and all the trouble Maud's presence could generate. So, like waifs, Maud, Iseult, Sean and Josephine had to find lodgings with other friends until, by the terms of the agreement, the month was up and George sufficiently recovered to move. Maud and Yeats become reconciled and were to share a common worry over Iseult's marriage.*

*In the post-war general election at the end of 1918 Sinn Fein had won a resounding victory over the old Irish Parliamentary Party. Refusing to take their places in Parliament, they followed their pacifist policy of forming their own government, of necessity in hiding, in Ireland.*

*In January Pat Pilcher wrote to Maud saying his mother had not much longer to live. Thora and Toby, then working in Paris in Intelligence, travelled to Switzerland to be with her. Toby was married by this time but Katheen had never met his wife. When she was dead, they wrapped her in a 'length of white satin brocade embroidered with lilies', wearing her pearl necklace. She was buried in Switzerland.*

*Though far from well, always believing in work to drown sorrow, Maud launched herself into political activity. Her experience of the journalistic world of Paris came in useful for the Minister of Propaganda in helping produce the Sinn Fein paper* The Bulletin. *None of her activities, which became more intense as the year progressed, suited Iseult, who was almost totally apolitical, though remaining loyal and helpful to her mother. George Yeats, kind as ever, seeing Iseult pale and in need of fresh air, suggested that she should take a few weeks in the spring in their castle in Galway, as a respite from politics and living in the city, so she could enjoy the countryside in peace on her own before they went there. Iseult's letters for the rest of the year speak for themselves, except for the mention of 'Ann'. Yeats, very proud of his Butler lineage, had called his new baby daughter Anne Butler Yeats, after a Butler Countess of Ossory. When George Yeats was doing the automatic writing an Ann Hyde, also married to a Butler, and a Countess of Ossory, had come through the automatic spirit, apparently looking for reincarnation. This was preoccupying Yeats's mind very much at the time.*

**42**

[20–5–1919, Co. Galway]

[MS incomplete]

... little lake near the Larkins[1] and the Kellys.[2] I often strain my eyes trying to find the inscription on the tombstone of the Lord of Ballylee[3] who was killed by the fairies, then climb to the fort wondering who will dare dive into those undergrounds and find the treasure. Then I kneel by the well. (There is something about that well...) then find a smile and peace in looking at the lake sailed by swans and all the may-trees in bloom around it. There is something more for the mind in that spot than admiration, there is delight and awe.

Coole and its woods[4] are lovely, but placid compared to that. Lady Gregory has been extremely amiable to me, and I have enjoyed reading in the library and playing with the children.[5]

Those lines you have added to your poem[6] are most beautiful. But if Ann lives up to her phase her life may be different to your wish, and as to me, such is the drifting that I have even stopped thinking of anchors. Possibly even I like drifting, I don't quite know.

Give my love to George, and again deep thanks to you both for this fortnight.[7]

Yours always affectionatly

Maurice

P.S.   I do hope you will at least spend a day in Dublin on your way back. There are one or two things I would like very much to have a talk with you about.


**43**
[Dublin]
[July 1919]

My dear Willy,

I am much afraid the enclosed will be but of small use to you. What between nicotine, patiences[1] and spiritual chaos my memory is gone to the dogs, and facts are always hard to remember.

I have been camping for 3 weeks in the Wicklow hills:[2] tell George[3] she is never again to say they are touristy and commonplace until she has seen Lough Nahanagan[4] and the Valley of witch Magnach.[5] I would live in a tent, scrub saucepans, shake braken for a bed, read Herodotus[6] and walk in the heather and paddle in the rivers if I had my choice of one kind of life to lead for ever.

It is a beautiful plan of yours, that of going to Japan,[7] but two years is a long time and we shall miss you dreadfully over here.

Give my love to George and do tell me what has happened about Ann.[8] I am so anxious to know

Yours
Maurice


**44**
73 Stephen's Green
Dublin
[3–8–19]

My dear Willy,

Unfortunatly I cannot remember the complete details of what you told me at Oxford in January 1918 concerning Ann Hyde.[1] I only remember your telling me then that you had got by automatic script a message from an Ann Hyde. You told me also when she lived and circumstances of her life, but I forget. She had a little boy, and I think you added that she died when the child was still a baby, and he did not survive. She was seeking reincarnation either for herself or for her child. You had just been at the time making researches on the subject at the Bodleian Library and found that indeed such a lady had existed at the time she mentioned and corroboration to others of her statements.

Yours affectionatly
Iseult Gonne

**45**
[Dublin]
23rd of Sepb.

My dear Willy,

I am so sorry to hear you have a cold, and hope it is nothing serious and you will be here soon; it is so long I haven't seen you and I am dying to hear of the psychic events which took place at Gogarty's.[1] We have just bought a cottage and some land[2] including a mountain in the very wildest and most beautiful part of the Wicklow hills, that is the head of Glenmalure Valley,[3] and our house is the last in civilization,[4] after that comes the Glen Imaal[5] of the songs. It's a perfect place, the house is too small and we shall have two or three rooms more built on it, then we mean to farm on a humble scale with a few sheep and poultry and play at forest growing. This seems at last the entire realisation of a dream, and life has become sweeter for that.

Colleville[6] is sold, and the furniture from Paris is coming over as we have given up the flat. I mean now to withdraw into greater solitude, and live as much as possible in the country, there to evolve some spiritual realisation, for the "wordly world" holds nothing for me but Neptune and waste. Moura has been ill[7] but is now getting much stronger than she was the whole winter, she also has centered her longings on Glenmalure.

I was much puzzled with your analysis of Titian,[8] I can only see the primary aspect of 14 in him in his serene felicity of vision, for the rest he seems too lacking in subjective discernment to belong to such an advanced phase. He expresses a state of being which he has not yet begun to analyse. Is he not more like an Antinoiis[9] of a very advanced cycle?

I must be going to Mrs Salkeld[10] now.

Yours affectionatly

Maurice

**46**
17–11–19
73 St. Stephen's Green
Dublin.

My dear Willy,

I was greatly interested in what you wrote me about Titian;[1] and greatly amused (if my uncle does not find this disrespectful) by your concern in match-making.[2]

Robinson[3] is a nice young man, but ... A man. How can you seriously think that I could marry him? And *do* you seriously think it?

I am glad your house is so beautiful, the selection of place and objects is perhaps even more vital to the soul than the right choice in people.

Our hut in Glenmalure[4] has been cleaned and whitewashed, and when the furniture from France which is on its way arrives, we can send some of it there, and I will often go during the winter to get a week's peace.

I have made great friends lately with a youth called Stuart.[5] He is not 19 and has written such poems that even you would like them. He has an adoration which amounts to religion for you, but he is very shy and I cannot get him to send you any of his work.

Could you sometime write to me again what Gogarty[6] said about laughter and the soldier on the battle-field. I remember it was quite a beautiful saying, and it would be useful to me as a quotation for something I am writing.

Yours affectionatly

Maurice

I dined with your sisters[7] about a week ago. They were very nice and I spent a very pleasant-evening, but I am afraid your sister Lily's handling of the Taro cards is rather coercive!!

**47**

Monday

73 St. Stephen's Green

Dublin.

[December 1919]

My dear Willy,

I had never partaken in such impassioned conversations as since your play.[1]

The fury of the pro and the anti-Drefusards[2] of my childhood was no worse that that of the pro and the anti-Unicornians[3] among certain people I know. Mrs Salkeld[4] (anti-Unicornian) says she will never be the same person again!

I was greatly delighted myself with it, and even Moura who beleived the first tragic version[5] was finer had to change her mind after she had seen it. The acting was good and the little Ulster girl[6] who played the part of the holy queen and Arthur Shields[7] as Septimus were quite splendid.

The only unconvincing part was the acting of the prophetic old man.[8] He spoke in a distant toneless voice, and I remembered that when you had read us the play at Colleville you had put a kind of grotesque tremulous intensity in his speech which sounded far more effective. But that is only a detail and on the whole the performance was very good.

I am thinking of going to England for a month after Xmas. I am also thinking (this is quite between ourselves) of getting married[9] at Easter, but I cannot tell you about himself until our plans are surer. There is such a hard fight to be made against the world and the mind, we are like knights in

quest of the graal, and we may fail, really I hardly dare hope. Do write me
sometime soon, and give my love to George.
　　Yours very affectionatly
　　Maurice

When are you going to America?[10]


**48**

73 St. Stephen's Green
Dublin.
14–1–20

My dear Willy,
　　I have not written you all this time because of too much chaos and uncer-
tainties and a fear that having described you my hopes, I might have had to
write after: "It was only an idle dream."[1] Now he and I have made up our
minds and our souls that nothing can separate us. His name is Francis Stuart
and he is 18 years old.
　　You have often told me that I am your spiritual child, perhaps he is even
more that than I; there are times when I wonder even if you might be his real
father. Many young people have imitated your manner and your style as he
does from the things they knew about you and from your books, but when
I see in him a reflexion of things in you which only I know, then I am amazed.
　　I cannot quite make out yet wheither he belongs to 14 or 17,[2] he seems to
be a mixture of both. He is becoming Catholic because he loves the ritual
and also it makes things easier[3] for our marriage. We shall be married in
3 weeks, then we shall go to Glenmalure[4] and stay there until we can decide
where we want to live; probably it will be Dublin, unless we decide to go to
Paris. I told Lady Gregory the other day, she had met him, and told me she
thought it was a wise choice, but apart from her people do not give us much
encouragement. I told Lennox;[5] perhaps he has written you himself; he is
showing great generosity in taking Francis to live with him until we can get
married. I will write you more soon. Do let me hear from you. Lecturing in
America must be so tiring and unpeaceful! When will you come back?[6]
　　Yours very affectionately
　　Maurice


*Things did not turn out as Iseult planned. Francis was duly received into the Cath-
olic Church, but then things went awry. Maud, in her first existing letter to Yeats
after their row over the St Stephen's Green house, wrote in June 1920 deploring*

*Iseult's marriage. Apparently having tried to reason with Iseult about its inadvis-
ability she wrote 'they bolted to London before the marriage', adding bitterly 'she
certainly took your advice of taking no notice of what I might think or advise'. The
couple were not happy in London, where Francis would often go off on his own.
It was only after Iseult had told him that she had had an affair with Pound that he
was able to consummate the relationship in anger and pain, having forgotten she
had already told him of this affair before.*

In April on their return to Dublin they were married. They were still in deep
trouble, both in the isolated worlds which each had inhabited since childhood;
he adolescently angry, self-centred, self-regarding and jealous, she patiently passive,
dreamy, cool and vague with sudden outbursts of anger, all tempered by her old
desire of attaining perfection in life and love. Was it a dissociation both had from
others around them because of their difficult, yet so different, childhoods, that in
some way drew them together? Or did she feel less threatened by someone so much
younger, she who had the subtle intelligence and beauty to attract writers and
poets such as Yeats, Symons, Pound and Lennox Robinson, all of whom were also
aware of her fragility, and Pound in some ways a precursor to Francis. In marrying
Francis it was as if she was courting danger. Later she said she thought he had
genius, so was it that, feeling herself unable to write to her own high standards,
she thought she could guide him to attain his promise, that she could be of help to
him and mould him? But as it transpired he was not mouldable. It would seem her
cool mysteriousness and the air of foreign places and people that hung around her
was attractive and yet a challenge to him, an attraction which he then needed to
shatter.

Maud, in a desperate mood of anxiety and worry over Iseult and with an intense
dislike of Francis, described the continuing drama of the marriage in a series of
letters to Yeats in June and July 1920. She told him how Francis had deprived
Iseult of food, of money, and had kept her from sleeping, of the noise of their rows,
and of how in one terrible climax in Glenmalure he had burned all Iseult's clothes.
In some exasperation, she had deliberately broken a valued object of his, and he
had locked her out of the house in her dressing gown, piled up all her clothes,
thrown kerosene over them and set them alight, and then had gone out and started
burning the gorse on the mountain. Later he described how Iseult brought him in
and they lovingly made it up.

At Maud's request, Yeats came hurriedly and quietly to Ireland, finding Iseult
pale, ill and pregnant. He listened to Maud's and Iseult's stories and corroboration
from witnesses. Iseult agreed to go into a nursing home for rest and care and not to
see Francis, who seemed to show no anxiety to see her, until a proper marriage
settlement was drawn up, the arrangement of which required the inclusion of his
mother and aunt, Janet Montgomery, the business woman of the family. Neither of the
Stuarts had any money of their own, though Maud had given Iseult an allowance,
but not large enough to keep them both. Iseult, forever forgiving and objective in
her own way, tried to explain her husband's need to have power over her, and that

*after giving in to him they could be happy for days, but agreed, now she was preg-
nant, she had to take care of herself and her child. Yeats wrote to George that
Iseult was still in love with Francis and defended him, which made him think of
his prophetic line in his poem 'Two Songs of a Fool' – 'the horn's sweet note and
the tooth of the hound'. He added that 'with her fine brain for all literary
and ethical subtlety she is credulous in all practical things beyond belief'. One of
the truest things Maud said of this affair is that 'Iseult will only see the beauty
of the geste & not the consequences & will not bring her mind to the practical
details of life'.*

*Things calmed down somewhat but no agreement was ever made. Maud was
very busy with Dr Lynn caring for the wounded, in relief work and concerned for
Sean as the house raids and activities of the Black and Tans had escalated. It was
against this background that Iseult's little daughter was born in March in Maud's
house a few days after an extensive raid by the military.*

*In April Iseult went with her baby to Bettystown where her mother-in-law, Lily
Clements, and Francis were staying. In July, worried that the baby was not doing
well, Iseult took her up to Dr Lynn in her hospital in Dublin, St Ultan's. Francis
did not go with her as he was engrossed in his new motorbike, which he could only
admire or sit on in the living room, as he had as yet no permit to ride it.*

**49**
Thursday

Baravore[1]
Glenmalure
Near Rathdrum
Co Wicklow

My dear Willy,

Many many thanks for your letters and those beautiful books; I knew
a little of Landor[2] from a little book of selections you had given me before,
and that had always made me long to know him better; so this will be
a great joy.

You must forgive me for having been so long without writing to you;
I have been spending a few strenuous and troubled months from which
perhaps I have learned a good deal or will have learned in a few years but
which for the time being make me feel like a walnut tree that is being
shaken.[3] Often I have thought of writing to you, but then thinking of myself
in terms of a walnut tree I thought: "soon I will cease being shaken, then
I will have a steadier hand."

But that time never comes. Moura[4] may have written to you saying some
very hard things about Francis, they are mostly true, but as she hates him
she probably never tells you of the good things. He is a wilful spoiled child
with a half unconscious but fierce longing for power and he would do
almost anything to attain what he wants. If he had more knowledge or

instinct of abstract and practical values that would be excellent, but so far he wants mostly only mad or second-rate things; I began by giving in to him in everything but found this sheer stupidity; so now I have to put up a hard fight and it is harder for me than for most because I find it so difficult to cope with circumstance. But then it is worth it, because I really beleive he has not only charm but genius and a great asceticism and beauty of nature in some things.

I am sorry you will not be able to come to Ireland for so long; there is so much to talk about.

For the moment Francis is paying a visit to his mother in the North[5] and I am staying with Moura in Glenmalure.

We shall meet again in Dublin in a fortnight and stay in our new flat awhile,[6] then go over perhaps to England or to Belgium, but these plans are vague. Give my love to George.

Yours very affectionatly

Maurice

*A truce was called around the time Dolores died. Later to help Iseult over her loss, Maud took her, Francis and Sean abroad for a holiday. Iseult and Francis stayed on their own, with Francis disappearing now and then alone, once to see Karsavina dance and take her out. He had met the famous ballerina in London and fallen in love with her before, when he had gone to London alone to sell Iseult's necklace in 1920, as he had run into debt before the crisis in their marriage came to a head. They did not return from this trip, telegraphing for money, until the Civil War was breaking out over the Treaty. In spite of the fact that his aunt Janet and her first cousin, Captain Jack White, were confirmed nationalists, Francis, who apparently had no interest in the upheavals around him up to this, and apparently despising idealistic nationalism, now decided to join the anti-Treaty forces. He felt, as a poet, he could 'now breathe more easily'. He was sent abroad to buy guns and then was involved in action at home until he was arrested. He was not released until over a year and a half later, at the general release of 1923 when the Civil War was over.*

*The ground floor of the house in St Stephen's Green was full of wounded for whom Maud was helping to care. After one weekend in Glenmalure Iseult and she came back to find the house had been raided by the Free State forces, with graffiti on the walls, rooms ransacked, and all their papers and letters taken out and burned, including Yeats's letters, and Iseult's journals and writings. Charred scraps of paper floated around the Green for days. Maud's friend Mrs Despard, whom she had first met in London in 1917, then urged her to join her in the purchase of a house just outside Dublin. They signed the agreement to buy Roebuck House in August, 1922.*

*At the end of the year Maud was looking for compensation from the government for a car, bought with money from what Maud had put aside for Iseult, possibly from the sale of Colleville; the car had been taken by the Black and Tans. At Iseult's request Yeats had asked Ernest Blythe, a member of the government, for help, which was refused. Yeats wrote asking for a reason for the refusal, writing on 29 December that 'Mrs. Stuart can recognise the justice of an action even if it be one by which she herself must suffer'.*

**50**
Loch Dan[1]
Co Wicklow
Friday, [End of July, 1921]

My dear Willy,

I should have written you sooner but I hadn't the heart; each time I say it, or write it, it seems as if I made it happen again. My little one[2] died 5 days ago. She had been very strong until she was three months and then she began not to digest well, we were staying in Bettystown;[3] the doctor there was rather incompetent so I became anxious and took her back to Dublin where Dr Lynn[4] said it was not serious but she would take her into hospital until she had found exactly what kind of [food] suited her, I went to see her there every day, she was getting better and increasing in weight, she had become most adorably pretty and *really* more advanced in mind than babies a year old, sometimes though I felt frightened and so did the matron because she was so unnaturally gentle and had a way of sleeping with her hands folded as in prayer. I was going to take her back to the country in a few days when suddenly one day I went there and hardly recognized her, she had so changed; it was meningites, I spent those last 5 days with her day and night, I don't think after the first convulsions she suffered much, she was mostly in a kind of coma, sometimes she regained consciousness and would look at me with the most pathetic eyes and tighten her hand round my finger. Sunday morning at 7 she had a final collapse, there was no reaction to the brandy and injections, she was nearly cold, her heart hardly beat [corner of page torn?] apparently quite unconscious, I held one lifeless little hand in mine, then the matron took a little crucifix which she put in her other hand, and then to our amazement she gripped it strongly and pressed it against her chest, the next minute her heart had ceased to beat. She is buried at Dean Grange,[5] a really beautiful graveyard near Black Rock. Francis is feeling this terribly, we feel he and I that we have lost on earth the companionship of the most blessed thing.

Please give my love to Georgie. I hope that you are both well, and would like to hear from you soon. I cannot write anymore now.

Yours affectionately
Maurice

We are only staying here till tomorrow then going back to Dublin for 3 weeks.

*Early in 1923 both Maud and Iseult were interned, Iseult for only a short time thanks to Yeats's efforts. While in prison, Iseult, worried about the effect of the poor diet, decided to make some nettle soup for her fellow inmates, nettles being obviously plentiful in the prison yard. One prisoner, dreading the thought of having to drink the soup, found not having to do so the best part of her timely release.*

*It was to Roebuck House, standing in its own grounds with large trees and a walled garden, that Francis returned at the end of 1923. He found that Iseult had collected his poems into a little green book,* We have kept the Faith, *which later won an award from the Irish Academy, and in 1924 at the Tailtearn Games Francis was crowned with laurel leaves.*

*Roebuck House was a much busier place than St Stephen's Green, full of the comings and goings of people and the activities of Maud and Mrs Despard. The Stuarts were still being subsidised by their mothers but Francis had received a small legacy, bought a car and told Iseult he wanted to go racing. Because of having the car the Stuarts were now able to rent a cottage in Glencree near Enniskerry. Though Francis has written that he considered his marriage hopeless at this time he still continued to live within it on his terms. He had erected a prefabricated hut outside the cottage where he retired to live the life of a hermit and started to read all Iseult's books on mysticism. In their first year there they decided to produce a literary monthly jointly with Cecil Salkeld and a few other friends, and went to Yeats for advice. Yeats's dream was of 'a wild paper of the young' which would make enemies everywhere but his suggestions were suppressed by the printer. When it did come out it ran into trouble because of a story by Lennox Robinson and only survived for two months.*

**51**
[Roebuck House]
[Early January, 1923]

My dear Willy,

Thank you so much for your letter and your kind attempt on our behalf.[1] I hadn't really much hope of success as I thought it was probably spite on the part of Blythe[2] which his letter to you confirms.

I was in the last war a very obscure but fervent partisan of what he would term "destruction"; but really Moura, though far more emotional always consistently stood out against destruction of any kind in this last war both in private talk and in her speeches. But she met Blythe in the tram some months after the reprisal murders and said to him "I suppose you are thinking of Liam Mellowes"[3] and this is the answer. The plebeian mind when it is not lit up by idealism is always spiteful and vulgar. We must be ruled either by idealists or aristocrats.

But I don't want to worry you; and indeed I shouldn't write like this when you are not well and perhaps still anxious over your little girl.[4] I do hope she is quite out of danger now. I have just been goodmother to Cecil's daughter;[5] it makes me feel like a fairy.

Yours always affectionately
Iseult

*Thora came to visit and she and Francis flirted, as her Bill had flirted with and kissed Iseult on their visit to their farm in June 1921. Thora asked if she could kiss Francis but Iseult said she would rather she did not. It was because of these visits Thora was able to say later that the light went out of Iseult after the death of Dolores.*

*In 1925 before going to America to lecture, Ella Young, accompanied by Maud and Delany, made a farewell visit to the Stuarts. They sat around the fire and chatted while two wild rabbits that Iseult had tamed played around their feet. Ella Young admired the 'tawny beauty' of Francis and Iseult's 'passionate changes of mood of tragic exaltation, her dreamfast silences'. As Iseult gathered armfuls of carnations from the garden for her, saying they were too red and needed some rue, Ella remembered her eloping 'against the wishes of her people' with him who had little to offer but his 'tawney beauty' and wondered how much rue Iseult had gathered for herself.*

*It was this year that Francis indulged in his passion for racing by buying a racehorse. Where the funds came from is not clear, for as yet he was earning no money.*

**52**
Ballycoyle
Sunday [1924?]

My dear Willy,

I am returning you the translations.[1] The best that can be said for them is that they are doggedly faithful to the litteral meaning; but the language is lifeless and either too archaïc or painfully commonplace; this applies to the prose as well as to the verse. Yet as I am writing this I feel a mean brute, yet it would be worse to let them pass; yet also perhaps I am over critical. You might send them to André Gide,[2] I think he has a fine judgement of such things and you could rely on his advice.

I am writing this in case you are not in. I am also enclosing the two things of mine[3] I told you about, the only things I have written for ever so long, I would be grateful if you would read them and let me know if they are any good.

Yours affectionately
Iseult

**53**
Ballycoyle
Enniskerry
Co Wicklow
Wednesday [September/October 1924]

My dear Willy,

I am ever so sorry to hear of your illness.[1] From your letters I gather it is the same thing that a stupid doctor told Moura lately that she suffered from,

**Fig. 12** Francis Stuart – 'his tawny beauty' © Christina Bridgwater

but when we went to a specialist he told her on the contrary she was afflicted with abnormally low blood pressure. But before knowing this I had been making inquiries about treatments for arterio-sclerosis and heard there is a famous doctor in Paris who has found a new cure; it consists of an operation on some gland,[2] and every one he has performed has been successful and the patient entirely cured. Unfortunately I have a bad memory and cannot remember the doctor's name, but it could easily be found out and it might be worth your while to inquire about it.

Lennox wrote to me lately but never told me anything about his trouble with the Carnegie people.[3] It is distressing as I think he has much of his heart in the library work; I told Francis and Cecil, they are having a meeting of "To Morrow"[4] today and will probably compose the letter to the Holy Office.[5] Georgie is to write to me what day you can come, but if it is too tiring for you let me know when and where we can see you.

Yours affectionately
Iseult

*In May of 1925 Iseult had had an operation, 'appendicitis & something else, what I was not told' according to Yeats. She was curetted, which had needed to be done since the birth of Dolores and had been continually put off. In October 1926 a healthy boy was born who thrived, his mother having had a more peaceful pregnancy.*

**54**
Ballycoyle
Enniskerry
Co. Wicklow.
28th [early 1926]

My dear Willy,

I was thrilled to get your book,[1] thank you every so much for it. I have not yet been able to read it very far because unfortunately for me Francis is equally interested and as we neither care to read aloud to each other, since the book has come we are living on terms of a dangerous chilly politeness!

Who made the picture of Geraldus?[2] It has a quaint resemblance to you. It is almost a miracle to have embodied the exposition of a difficult system in such a clear beautiful poem[3] as that dialogue between Aherne and Robartes.

We are going down to Meath[4] shortly and when we come back which I expect will be about the middle of the month I hope you and Georgie will come to dinner with us in Dublin; we can arrange the day later.

Here is a fact may amuse you if you do not know it already: Krishnamurti[5] has declared himself as Christ at a huge meeting held at the Theosophical H.G. in India. Some friends of Mrs Despard[6] who were present wrote to her that there was a white light above his head and such a feeling of divinity that most of those present who were not sobbing went into ecstasy. He said "I have come to bring joy to the world." Could he be Antichrist?

I do hope your little Ann is quite well now.

Yours affectionately

Iseult

**55**

29th [? Spring 1926]

My dear Willy,

Perhaps you are in Ballillee,[1] but if not when could we see you? Could you and George come to dinner with us at the Moira[2] one evening after next week.

Moura has been very ill, the doctor says she must have complete rest which is impossible in Dublin, so we are taking her to the cottage in the hills[3] for a week and then she is going to France. I am very anxious about her; it is worse than an ordinary nervous break down.

But we shall be back[4] on Tuesday week, let me know what day would suit you after that.

Yours affectionately

Iseult

**56**

Ballycoyle
Enniskerry
Co Wicklow
Thursday [Early October 1926]

My dear Willy,

Please forgive me for not having written sooner to thank you for your kind invitation[1] and for your book.[2] The baby is in rags and I am in rags, not really out of penury but lazyness, and our car is out of order, so it is difficult to get away. But I am going to stay with Moura for 3 weeks on the 10th Oct. and I am getting a nurse for that time to take the baby off my hands so I hope to be able to see you then if you are in Dublin.

I liked your book very much...all but some things. I wish I was years older than you instead of it being the reverse. It is cruel for me to have a tyranical mind which thinks itself wise and to have neither the age nor the standing nor the grace sufficient to give it a free rein. I think you are trying to make shadows substantial, or rather to imagine there is substance in shadows; but I love all the verse about old age.[3] My hair is beginning to get grey and when I run down the hill it hurts my knees, let that be my excuse for any criticism. I wish so much you were out of this Free State Senate.[4] Since you won't resign I think I'll ask the boys[5] to kidnap you!!
Always yours affectionately
Iseult

**57**
Ballycoyle
Enniskerry
Co Wicklow
6th [October 1926]

My dear Willy,
Thank you so much for your letter and forgive me for not writing sooner, but I am demoralised with house-work; I have been whitewashing my room and painting all my furniture cream and making crimson and gold curtains, it will look very sumpteous and austere but meanwhile I am getting sick of honest work and wish Moura had bought that black negro baby who would be doing it all for me. I would so much like to see you but I have nobody to leave the baby with, I do wish you and Georgie could manage to come up if you are in Dublin.

The baby's name is Ian[1] and in case he does not grow up lean and wiry enough for that name his second name is Nicholas.

Thank you ever so much for correcting Francis' essay,[2] he is very grateful and longing to have it back with your notes. He lives now in a hut in the garden like a hermit, he is very happy but writes little, I am hoping the MSS with your annotations may give him the stimulus he needs.

Are you quite well and strong. Give my love to Georgie. Do write to me again.
Yours always affectionately
Iseult

I have been reading: "Revelations of Divine Love"[3] by Julian of Norwich. It is obscure, but filled with the beauty of happiness – a rare thing. Although she does not deny evil nor explains it in any way, still she seems to do away with it. She was shown the depths of the sea and the crucifixion and I feel she really saw them.

*It was probably in 1927 that Maud bought Iseult a small barracks converted to a 'castle' in Laragh near Glendalough as the little cottage in Glencree had got too small to hold the baby and Lily Clements who had come to help. Francis, using a legacy left to Iseult, set up a poultry farm and virtually gave up writing poetry for writing novels, coupled with wine, women, and horses in Dublin or London.*

*Yeats visited Glendalough twice, in 1929 and 1932, where he saw the Stuarts frequently. As when they had stayed with him in Dublin in 1926, his fondness and enjoyment of Iseult's company was tempered by Francis's silences unless the conversation turned to St John of the Cross. In a letter to Iseult in 1932 Yeats, having read Francis's fourth novel* The Coloured Dome *and pleased to acknowledge the book's value for her sake, wrote effusively to Iseult that Francis 'had the most noble & passionate style of anybody writing in English at this moment' and to Olivia Shakespear he marvelled at the mystery of 'sexual selection' saying that Francis was now Iseult's 'very self made active and visible'.*

**58**
Laragh
Glendalough
March 16th [1929]

My dear Willy,

Thank you so much for your letter. I cannot tell you how grateful I am for your great kindness, I feel rather guilty taking up so much of your time for these poems of Francis'.[1]

I know they are full of imperfections, but is there not enough loveliness about them to make them worth while? You see, unless you really think they are not good enough, the reason why I am so anxious for them to be published is chiefly to counteract on Francis the influence of O'Flaherty[2] and such people. He must remain cold and lyrical. If he becomes all hot and cynical like them his mind will lose virtue in the old Roman sense.

What a desperate prig[3] I sound!

Thank you so much for giving me your book[4] it was such happy reading.

Yours very affectionately
Iseult

P.S.   Francis is away. I sent him on your letter.

**59**
Laragh
Glendalough
Co Wicklow
March 12th [1930]

My dear Willy,

I was suffering from tooth ache when I got your letter and the shock caused by the horrible news in it nearly drove it away, but really I almost prefer tooth ache to the mental contemplation of you with a beard.[1]

Even being a senator isn't as bad as that.

Moura has just had the flu, so I haven't forwarded your letter to her yet, although she must read it because it is better she should be prepared before she meets you again, and yet as there is no absolute standard of aesthetics, she might think it was very becoming; but there is in the divine mind (which is mine also) an absolute standard and I do not like to think of what your chin will suffer in the fires of purgatory.

And I too will have to suffer for the unbecomingness of writing this way to someone who has been very ill and should have nothing but nice things said to them. Gogarty[2] told me that this kind of malaria is what you have been suffering from these last few years and not high blood pressure at all. I think that is ever so much better because you can get completely cured; but isn't high fever a very dreadful thing while it lasts; besides writing to George Moore,[3] did you not get into the heart of metaphysical horror? It's the only way to name it, that is the way it takes me.

Francis has a poultry farm and an assistant[4] and is on his way to becoming prosperous unless something happens. I try to think what could be made to happen because I have been reading over some old poems of his and felt quite annoyed to find he really had genius because it gives me a guilty feeling, I am sure Georgie would never have allowed you to keep a poultry farm, but then I put it to her, which is worse a poultry farm or a beard? Give her my love.

And thank you so much for writing to me when you were still feeling so weak; I hope you will have got so well and beardless when you get this letter that all the upbraiding and sympathy will be quite out of date.

Yours very affectionately
Iseult

**60**
Laragh
Glendalough
Jan 18th [1934]

My dear Willy,

I am sending you to day Flory Salkeld's[1] poems. If you are too busy or not in the mood just read only the two I have underlined and crossed in the table of contents. I have crossed some others but they have imperfections, so have most of them. Yet they nearly all have some beauty of sincere intellectual passion. (She would hate to hear that!) She beleives the mind is the devil.

It is so long since I have seen you, I was so much hoping you would be able to come and see us at Roebuck,[2] while I was there. But you were in London.

Please give my love to Georgy.

Yours very affectionately
Iseult

*Yeats's health was deteriorating and he spent much time abroad in warmer climates but he still enjoyed the company of new and interesting women. Lady Gregory was dead and he had not gone to Ballylee since 1929. In July 1936, Iseult invited him to stay in Laragh after a severe illness. Answering her he wrote, 'I wish I could go to you but I cannot just now, I am too bothered. A little while ago I was longing that you would ask me, but recovery is slow'. The last time she visited him he said to her 'My dear, my dear, you should have married me.' And she answered 'We would not have lasted a year.' He died on 28 January 1939 in France.*

# 3
# Iseult Gonne and Ezra Pound

*A. Norman Jeffares*

Ezra Pound, aged 23, arrived in Europe in March 1908. From Venice he wrote to his father, Homer Pound, in Hailey, Idaho, to tell him that he wanted 'to have a month up the Thames somewhere & meet Bill Yeats & one or two other humans if convenient.' Once in London he began to meet some writers and publishers and 'the most charming woman in London', Mrs Olivia Shakespear, at whose Kensington House in Brunswick Gardens he was made welcome on increasingly frequent visits. Olivia's brief affair with Yeats in 1895 and 1896 had given him his first experience of sex; the affair ended when she realised he was still obsessed with Maud Gonne. For several years they were out of touch, but by 1904 they were establishing the close friendship that was to last till her death in 1938. Through her Pound met Yeats, the main reason for his being in London; he had wanted to sit at his feet 'and learn what he knew'.

Olivia and her 23-year-old daughter Dorothy took Pound to one of Yeats's Monday Evenings at Woburn Buildings. Dorothy had fallen for Pound and they became friends, meeting clandestinely in the British Museum. In 1911 Ezra had told Dorothy's father, Henry Hope Shakespear, that he had £200 a year apart from his literary earnings. Mr Shakespear replied to a letter from Homer Pound saying that he and Olivia did not think Ezra was in a position to marry until he had 'some regular income in addition to a permanently secured £200 a year'. However, when Ezra reached an arrangement with Swift & Co. early in 1912 that they would pay him an advance on royalties of £100 a year as his sole British publisher, he informed Dorothy's father that he now had a total income of about £400 a year. Mr Shakespear was still not impressed; this was not an adequate amount to justify marriage, and Dorothy told Ezra that her father wouldn't recognise their engagement.

Swift & Co. only published Pound's *Ripostes* in October 1912 before going into receivership, its managing director, Charles Granville, who had fled to Tangier, serving a prison sentence. Even though their engagement was unofficial Ezra and Dorothy had to break it off; their friendship continued with, as Ezra put it, 'due placidity and decorum'. The relationship caused Olivia no little anxiety, expressed very clearly indeed in a letter to Ezra, telling him that Englishmen didn't understand his American ways and 'any man who wanted to marry her wd be put off by the fact of your friendship (or whatever you call it) with her'. If he had £500 a year, she continued, she would have been delighted if he married Dorothy but as he hadn't she felt obliged to tell him she wouldn't mind him coming to see Dorothy once a week. Ezra and Dorothy, now 26, disregarded Olivia's pronouncements and, despite several disagreements, were finally – a reluctant consent having been given by the Shakespear parents in February – married on 20 April 1914.

When Pound first met Iseult, on the visit she made to her aunt Kathleen in London in 1913, he wrote to Dorothy describing her as 'a scioness of the house of Gonne to whom the Eagle is burning tapers.' 'The Eagle' was the name they had given to Yeats, who introduced Iseult to several of his London friends – they included Sturge Moore and Arthur Symons as well as Tagore, who was impressed by her and later wrote to Yeats on 31 August 1915 saying he had 'often thought of the beautiful girl I had the happiness to meet in Chelsea and I shall try to induce and, if possible, to help her to resume her Bengali studies and do some more translations, when I meet her.' Yeats first met Tagore in June 1912, had written part of his Introduction to Tagore's *Gitanjali* when he was staying in Colleville in Normandy in August that year: his enthusiasm for Tagore's writings (and political views) infected Iseult, who began learning Bengali from Devabrata Mukerjee, Tagore's nephew, then living in Paris. Many of Maud's letters to Yeats from March 1914 on urge him to get Tagore's permission for Iseult and her friend Christiane Cherfils to translate *The Gardener* or *The Crescent Moon* into French. Iseult and Mukerjee fell in love, but when he returned to India in 1914 the translation project was abandoned.

Iseult met Ezra in London again; this time he was accompanied by his wife Dorothy, when they all came to dinner with Yeats at Woburn Buildings on 22 May 1916. Iseult, then aged 21, had travelled to London on this occasion to tell Yeats that Maud was unwell, lonely and unhappy. He had enjoyed introducing Iseult to more of his friends before accompanying her back to France, having written to Lady Gregory describing Iseult as very distinguished, beautifully dressed and self-possessed. At Colleville he proposed to Maud (now a widow after MacBride's execution for the part he had played in the Easter Rising) yet again, and then, a week later, to Iseult, returning there in August 1917 and proposing to Iseult again. He helped the family in their removal to London in mid-September, issued an ultimatum to Iseult on the boat demanding she make up her mind, and received a refusal from her a week after their arrival there. He married Georgie Hyde Lees on 20 October 1917, Ezra Pound acting as his best man. She was related to Dorothy Shakespear, and both young women were related to Lionel Johnson.

Iseult had been given a post in the School of Oriental Studies by Yeats's friend Sir Denison Ross, and she began work there in late October 1917. After Maud's successfully disguising herself and getting to Dublin despite the prohibition of the authorities, Iseult stayed on in 285 King's Road, Chelsea, where the lease Maud had taken had another three months to run. She invited Iris Barry, who was also working at the School of Oriental Studies (having been encouraged to come to London by Pound), to stay there with her and Josephine Pillon, the cook who had accompanied the Gonnes from Normandy. Somewhat lonely without Maud and Sean, Iseult went out a good deal in January 1918, somewhat less so in February. She saw Ezra and Arthur Symons occasionally. Symons had a romantic view of her, to which she probably played up with gusto. He thought the blend of three races in her gave her an exotic quality – she told him Millevoye's mother was Spanish. His poem 'Deirdre', celebrates a dinner with her in the Café Royal; he wrote her a poem, 'Song for Iseult', and dedicated his *Colour Studies in Paris* (1918) to her. She helped him with his translation of Baudelaire and impressed him with her strength (later telling him how she had thrown Sean downstairs at Woburn Buildings when he annoyed her). He and she shared, Symons thought, a common fear of death.

At first Iseult got on relatively well with Iris Barry and in March the two girls moved to 54 Beaufort Mansions in Chelsea. Shortly before the move Ezra had asked her if she would work full time – which meant three days a week – on the *Little Review* for which he would pay her £5 a month. She wrote to Yeats on 24 March 1918 saying that she was undecided about this, imagining she was hardly fit for the work. She must have been getting bored with her work at the School for she added that if she could do it, it would be more intelligent than card indexing. But four days later she wrote again, this time thinking she would continue at the School where everybody was very charming and where even in the monotony of card indexing there was something restful. She was worried that both Ezra and Dorothy might be offering her something they might not be able to afford comfortably.

This letter to Yeats, of 28 March 1918, told him 'Ezra tried to kiss me' (see p. 99). Apparently Ezra's coming in often and staying late had horrified Josephine Pillon, who had written to Maud giving circumstantial details for which Iseult could not account. Something that would all be very laughable, she added, 'if it wasn't at the same time rather distressing and humiliating'. Was her letter to forestall any repetition of all this?

Yeats had been disturbed by the bohemian company (which included Iris Barry and her lover Wyndham Lewis) that Iseult had been keeping in London, about which she had been talking when she visited the Yeatses at 45 Broad Street, Oxford for a weekend in January 1918. This had provoked 'To a Young Beauty'.

> Dear fellow-artist, why so free
> With every sort of company,
> With every Jack and Jill?

When relations between Iseult and Iris Barry became strained – as they had been for some time between Iris and Josephine Pillon – the Yeatses promptly came over from Galway to London in August and moved Iseult out of Beaufort Mansions to Woburn Buildings (which he had earlier offered her, an offer she had refused) where, he told Maud, Iseult could live rent-free as he and his wife would be living in Oxford. He gave a graphic account of the event to Lady Gregory in a letter of 14 August:

I cannot yet return though we had shifted Iseult two days after our arrival. She was going into the country for two or three days & with the understanding that she was to seem to know nothing about it we kidnapped her maid, her cat & birds & all her furniture & transferred them to Woburn Buildings. The young woman [Iris Barry] turned up too late (warned it seems by Aleck Sheppeler[1] of our arrival – Chelsea clings together). She is a scandalous person & seems to have kept Iseult in submission with tears & temper. Iseult was of great practical use to her, especially as she had frequently omitted to pay her half of the rent or for the meals she eat whenever she quarrelled with [Wyndham] Lewis her lover. The trouble is that Iseult after gratitude for delivery has seen her again & is full of remorse for having got rid of her. Maud Gonne has brought Iseult up in such a strange world that she is not shocked at what other girls are shocked at. As long as she herself lives & thinks rightly, she thinks nothing else matters. I am playing the stern uncle sent by her mother to carry off a foolish neice. The neice says that she must obey. It is an absurd comedy but I think there will be no talk as both Lewis & the young woman have been warned that if anything reaches Ross (head of school where young woman works) & he questions me I will tell all. Of course nothing to anybody least of all to Aleck Sheppeller who can hardly be expected to sympathize with ones dislike for Comus & his rout. (John & his troup to translate it). . . . Iseult is afraid of the young woman, of Ezra, of me, of everybody & that the very devil. It was George who got the furniture van & seized the furniture glad to exercise her hatred of Chelsea.

Earlier Mrs Yeats had been eager that Iseult should leave the School: she had written to Ezra on 24 May telling him that she was urging Yeats to make Iseult take the plunge of leaving at the end of June. Her urging led Yeats to write to Ezra on 6 June to tell him that he had suggested to Iseult that she might give notice at the School 'on the eve of her holiday so that the month's notice & month's holiday should run concurrently as they say of criminal sentences' and he added cautiously, the commercial genes of his merchant relatives, the Pollexfens, no doubt guiding him: 'Having first made an arrangement with you.' His letter was business-like:

> I understand that your plan is to pay her £5 a month for 3 days a week & to pay her apart from this for such work as she may do in her own time. I mean that having worked her 3 days for you for her £5 you would purchase from her what you cared for in work done during the rest of the week, & on my side wish me to promise you £20 of work the £20 to be used to increase what payment you would otherwise make for this work done in her own part of the week. I agree on the condition that she is quite free to send her work elsewhere. I look on this as entirely essential, as I don't want to limit her development, or her power of making friends, for herself with other people & papers. Of course I don't know if she will accept any of these suggestions. You may find that she will be upset too much for another month to come to a definite decision. By that time however we shall probably have seen her.
>
> Now another point. The exact name of Maurice's activities is important. For obvious reasons she cannot be your secretary, & I don't think it desirable, for less obvious reasons, that she should be called say assistant editor of the Little Review. She is a young girl & must like the rest of us live in a world of fools. She should not seem responsible for let us say the audacities of Joyce or Wyndham Lewis. Call her french or foreign correspondent. When she speaks of it she can call herself that & it need not limit her activities.
>
> Now to sum up. I want Iseult to get £5 a month as I think that is the sum you named, for 3 days work a week, & have no responsibilities to you beyond those three days. If she wishes she can publish other work with you & I can make that easy to you by giving you £20 of work free. But she must always be at liberty to send her work elsewhere. I may say that I have given up the idea of getting her a job to fill up the other 3 days a week, so she will have time to write.

Pound accordingly announced that he had taken Iseult on as his typist, not altogether liking to call her his secretary. His poems were, he said, 'much too ithyphallic for any secretary of her years to be officially in my possession'. She began work for him in July. Was it Pound whom Yeats had cast in the role of the hound in the second of 'Two Songs of a Fool', a pair of poems begun in July 1918 in the first week that the Yeatses were occupying the cottage beside the tower at Ballylee? The first poem emphasised his responsibilities, looking after a cat (the pregnant Mrs Yeats) and a tame hare (Iseult); in the first poem he awakens out of his sleep, anxious that some day he may forget their food and drink.

Or, the house door left unshut,
The hare may run till it's found
The horn's sweet note and the tooth of the hound.

The second poem depicts a cat asleep on the sleeping poet's knee, neither of them thinking to enquire where the hare might be 'And whether the door were shut.' Had he awakened from sleep and called her name

...she had heard,
It may be, and had not stirred,
That, now, it maybe, has found
The horn's sweet note and the tooth of the hound.

It was the hound that had found the hare; Iseult, Pound's 'great love', and he became lovers. He wanted to leave his wife for Iseult, but there was no question of his parting from Dorothy (who said it wasn't Iseult who broke up their marriage) for he depended upon her income. Later (in 1925), when he had a daughter by the American violinist, Olga Rudge, who 'charmed one by the delicate firmness of her playing', he wanted to christen their child Iseult, something her mother firmly vetoed.

Iseult was on her own in Woburn Buildings when Maud was arrested in Dublin on 15 May 1918, moved to England and incarcerated in Holloway prison. Sean then joined Iseult in Woburn Buildings; he had been briefly tutored earlier by Ezra, who remembered in September 1954 that 'Shawn (Sewan or however he spells it Sua Eccelenza McB /has never forgiven me for trying to lam some Ovid into his VERY allergic head/ and probably never approved of art and letters ANYhow)', so he now had two other tutors.

Once Maud emerged from Holloway at the end of October, had her week in the expensive London nursing home, and stayed briefly in Woburn Buildings she then evaded the watch kept on her, to arrive, successfully disguised again, in Dublin in late November 1918. Yeats had been trying to get them all passports to get to Ireland after Maud had first eluded surveillance in 1917 but Iseult, Sean and Josephine Pillon seem to have had no difficulty in getting to Dublin at the same time, passport restrictions having been, presumably, lifted after the end of the war.

In Dublin Iseult continued to worry about her mother's health, for the recurrence of Maud's tubercular condition meant that she now looked gaunt and frail, though she was soon characteristically busy in Dublin working for the Sinn Fein government.

The brief love affair of Ezra Pound and Iseult Gonne was over. It had been conducted in complete secrecy. Iseult's letters to Ezra from Dublin convey her sense of desolation; being away from him made the first year in Ireland a desert to her. She realised starkly that she had lost him. Her letters break into French telling him how she loves him and misses him. Ezra's discretion about their affair – apart from telling Olga Rudge about it, and their daughter Mary de Rachewiltz (in 1943) – extended to denying even in a letter to Eva Hesse written as late as 14 September 1954, that he had not heard from Iseult since they had parted at a bus-stop in Kensington High Street:

> Yunnerstan I ain't heard word nor hide of 'em (Gonne-McBride clan) since Iseult misunderstood my reason for leaving her at bus-stop in Kensington High Street 35 or 37 years ago. If you will realise that I left Iseult in Keng/High St in front of Barkers at the bus-stop 35 years ago, and have not had a word since and have NO idea whatbloddygodam who begat which. All I kno is that 'all of 'em' were reported in jug at one time or another. Sigan never much liked me. Iris [Barry] once saw Iseult at a distance by, or on the other side of a lake. And No on, meaning when the li'l red box goes by it's all (Pennslvania Deitch dialect for na poo).

This was despite Iseult's thanking him for letters written to her in Ireland. He reverted to this in another letter of 5 November 1954, also written to his translator Eva Hesse. In this letter he settles on this parting occurring 35 years before, which might mean that they had met in 1919, as two of her letters to him suggested they might (see pp. 140, 145 and 147). Was his memory at fault or was he still continuing to be discreet about their affair? He went on to describe Iseult as 'a great dear with a sense of humour, 6ft 2 I think. And no one else so appreciated the spectacle of Unc Wm/ as we two from the Non-prix Nobel angles'.

Both Iseult and Ezra realised their short spell of great happiness was over. Her letters express an awareness of finality, an acceptance of their both being unable to break out of their situations, he out of marriage, she out of her family life. Yeats put it to her directly: she must become a writer or marry. She did not like his suggestion of Lennox Robinson nor that of Sarah Purser, but she did marry Francis Stuart on 6 April 1920. She continued to write, in her own way, while encouraging Stuart; but once her not great supply of energy was absorbed in domesticity, she expressed herself largely through her letters to her friends.

# 4

# Letters to Ezra Pound

Saturday morning [? June/July 1918]

My dear Ezra,

I meant to speak to Dr Ross[1] yesterday afternoon but he was away. I am not going to the School this morning so I shall only see him on Monday, and he might be a little offended if I gave him such a short notice. If it is not too inconvenient for you,[2] it might be wiser that I should stay at the School as now for another week.

This in haste as Sophia required an escorte[3] to the Butcher's and the dairy, and there is a house to be seen, and the cat to be combed, and a train to be caught, and its all very distressing.

Yours
Maurice

2
16–10–18

My dear Ezra,

I have lost Mrs Patmore's[1] letter and cannot remember her address, will you please forward this to her.

There isn't a place in the house now I have left unsearched for the Theocritus. I am beginning honestly to think you must have it.

Yours
Maurice

**3**

c/o Dr Lynn

9 Belgrave Rd

Rathmines

Dublin

Tuesday [? late Nov 1918]

First of all Yourself, you will find all your books and some typescript in the library in the [? corner] where my furniture is on the top of a table (2 books a Conrad and a Street belong to Mrs Mucker[1])

That's that I had to begin with it or I would have forgotten.

Now for the journey: it was tame enough, the sea was not; but thanks to Mothersills all went well,[2] and we arrived in Dublin at 11am. Moura wanted to stay at Stephens Green but George is too ill so she is staying ... elsewhere.

Sophia Bichon the Cat and I descended at the Russel Hotel[3] but the atmosphere of the place being too uncongenial I have come to stay in Dr Lynn's house[4] where Helen Molony is also staying until we can all go to Stephen's Green.[5]

So far safe but at any moment anything may happen. I went to the Lord Mayor[6] yesterday to explain him the situation, he was very kind and said he would do all he could and speak to the authorities for us, but he isn't sure himself how it will end.

I am afraid George[7] is seriously ill; she had a bad cold, which turned to flu[8] and yesterday the doctor who is attending her felt more anxious and had another doctor brought in who declared inflammation of the lungs; she has now a night nurse and a day nurse, to look after her. Poor uncle William[9] is beside himself with anxiety (of course all this is 'entre nous').

I am staying in a filthy rickety old house but the manner of living in it is pleasing. There's Dr Lynn and Helen Molony[10] and another girl and myself, and everybody does their own room (or not as they care) and nobody is expected in for meals but bring in what they like and when they like, and there are 5 cats and my room looks onto the hills. This is quite amusing ... for a short time. I have been walking a great deal, the air is much cleaner to breathe here; I can't yet say whether I hate this place or like it, I don't feel quite awake and when I shake myself to think it is only to realise que c'est bien bete d'etre si loin de toi.[11] Only as you say 3 months is really a cheap price for independence and I shall come back at the end of February unless ... I come back in a week.

Write to me here for the present.

Yours

Maurice

**4**

30 Upper Fizwilliam St
Dublin Saturday
[? late Nov 1918]

My dear Ezra,

I have sent you the keys of W. Buildings,[1] but will you ever receive them?!

I had tied the label to them and addressed it, and told Dr Lynn's charlady[2] to post them but she tells me she just put an ordinary stamp on it and threw it in the letter box so it is rather in the hands of the Gods.

Thank you for your letter. As to the James,[3] I have left it among the other books. Give it to de Boschère.[4]

Strange rumours may soon reach you about Uncle W. and Moura's fight.[5] The truth is that they have both behaved as badly as they could, so badly that I greatly fear they have this time quarrelled for good; and it is from an impartial point of view impossible to say which is most in the wrong or which has been most tactless, or rather, thinking it over, I should say Moura has been more tactless and Willy more in the wrong.

I have spent 3 days running from one to the other trying to soothe matters; but with little effect, and as profit have only been enforced in my conviction that there should be a law by which after 50 people should be placed under the tutelage of their juniors.

However, the cheering points are that Georgie is now in [a] good way of recovery; the crisis is over. Also thanks to the Lord Mayor's intervention[6] Moura is going to be left in peace. She has gone to rest for a week in Wicklow.[7]

Meanwhile I had begun to find the Dr's house[8] really too mad, even for my taste only, and poor Sophia[9] was in a worse condition still. She was staying in Delany's room.[10] Delany slept on the bed, Sophia on a mattress on the floor, there were 15 [? Gascon] canaries and the parrot screaming [? at] the top of their voices; and for cooking Delany had a cauldron which she never empties but in which she flings an occasional leak or potatoe and adds water.

This couldn't last so we have found some fairly decent lodgings for her and me until we can go to Stephen's Green. Jacky[11] is settled with a friend and busy doing canvassing for Countess Markiewitz election;[12] he comes here for meals. It is just as well you should write to me c/o Dr Lynn, 9 Belgrave Rd, Rathmines, Dublin. I have found Helen[13] in a very sad condition, and it breaks my heart to be able to do so little for her; always that d...question of L.S.D.

Uncle W has faced me sternly with this alternative.

'Are you going to write?'

Probably not.

'Then you must marry'. And the same evening asked me to dine with Lennox Robinson.[14] The poor young man quite unaware of William's murderous scheme seemed to me fairly sane and innocuous, and after he had gone I said to our Uncle 'No that won't do' – 'Very well then, we shall find somebody else.'

So in short what with hideous wranglings, shifting from place to place, meeting one crank after another and Uncle W's matrimonial scheme, I am beginning to wonder whether if I broke a shop window I wouldn't find prison more comfortable.

And do I expect him to read all this rubbish?

There's enough of it; but really one has to talk at times, and I can be 6 years old with you.

Et je t'aime et je t'embrasse de tout mon coeur.[15]

              Maurice

Raconte moi ce que tu fais;[16] and don't [? freeze] me up with business letters.


                                               5

[First portion of letter missing]                      [? early December 1918]
'Is pity or terror[1] the chief element of tragedy; the difference between the tragic mind and the epic Napoleon and Julian the Apostate, the ethics of lives etc etc.'

It may sound an apalling programme of the type dear to the Cambridge undergraduate but really they delt with it in a remarquable way; I was both impressed and delighted and felt I had found some real friends.

Imagine my horror when yesterday morning two young men came to ask me if I could canvass in this quarter. I told them that I was a much too timorous person, and the unionist old ladies would reduce me to abject terror. At which they showed polite scorn and went. You needn't be afraid that your beast will get into political scraps; she is much more in danger over here of becoming a tea-swilling aesthete shaping honeyed sentences *about* beauty, which perhaps is nearly as detrimental.

More beastliness between M. and W.[2] The mission of peacemaker between those two is not easy. M. calls me a coward, W. a martyr, and I am merely bored; may the Gods, *our* gods rescue their faithful from melodrama. Poor George is better,[3] but still very weak cannot get up yet; luckily she knows nothing of the fuss.

Meanwhile the noble Alexis in the midst of electioneering[4] seems to show sound sense and perhaps this complete immersion in political life may be his salvation, but this may be a eutopian hope.

Et puis je deviens timide pour te dire que je t'aime – parceque c'est vrai.[5]
Maurice.

6

[? 8/9 December 1918]

Tuesday evening

You have seen someone like me, but I, strive as I may, cannot remember the look of you; only pictorial details that are not pictures; that your eyes seem even greener[1] than they are, that the way you walk is half like an ostritch half, like a tiger, and qui sourit comme toi? Mais purement litteraire tout ça;[2] I have lost you.

I have not, since the last [? 4 or 11] days gone to sleep much before 5, and been out for most of the day. At last a quiet evening! And I am falling asleep.

Wednesday [? 9 December 1918]

Helen[3] has just brought me your last letter. Is America not so far as the East?[4] To me it seems further, and I am beginning to think seriously, more perilous. I watch the papers and listen to quite sensible people's opinion, and it really looks as if Moura's prophecy may not have been so rash after all. Danger not immediate of course, perhaps a matter of a few months, perhaps not at all; still...And I do not want you trapped in any idiotic national mess. Let's go to Spain!

No I won't get into riots. To begin with the atmosphere is not riotous for the present. I went to one or two election meetings at which M. [Maud Gonne] spoke fearing there might be trouble, but all went off peacefully; quite enter-taining in a way. Patriotism over here more absurd in its manifestations but less absurd in its essence than elsewhere; a sensuous element at least. I have been in the hills, the soil speaks. Only I wish Moura would rest; she has lost more weight and looks quite ill.

Thank god, we are moving into our house[5] tomorrow,[6] she will be better there than in these wretched lodgings. Meanwhile M. and W.[7] are becoming the gossip of the city; they each go to their friends confiding their wrongs so that there is now the W. clan and the M. clan. Russel[8] and I are the only two who refuse to take sides with this only difference that Russel says there [they are] both right and I maintain they are both wrong. The climax came the day before yesterday. They met in the Green, and there, among the nurses and perambulators proceeded to have it out finally.

M: If only you would stop lying!

W. (gesture of arms): I have never lied, my father never told a lie, my grandfather never told a lie.

M. You are lying now.

Delightful family! And for all my dislike of frost I earnestly wished myself at the North Pole. Perhaps I shouldn't be writing you all this rubbish and of course it is strictly entre nous, Uncle William's vagaries chiefly being somehow our special property.

The O'Neills[9] and I have undertaken each other's soul; they are reading the Propertius[10] and starting me in Plowman.[11] Uncle W. is disappointed at my lack of appreciation of his suitor[12] and rather dispises my choice of sweethearts for I am cultivating two young men – the one aged 15 the another 16. With the latter I play drafts and chess, exchange cigarettes and chocolates and kiss him solemnly on both cheeks at the door. The other is immersed in a terrific psychich chaos: cynicism throughout life the proper tendancy, but death the only real issue. I like those 2 babies; they are really my contemporaries.

In fact the only person I have taken a dislike to since I am here is Lily Yeats,[13] and it is mutual.

She is the French bourgeoise under her worst aspects.

Mais qu est-ce que ça te fait tout ça? Et à moi, après tout, si peu ! Mais est-ce que je sais ce qui t'amuse ? Je ne t'ai jamais vraiment [connu] et maintenant j'ai même oublié l'air que tu as. Je sais seulement que tu as quelquechose de trés beau. Tout de même je t'embrasse 'because it is a custom this care for one living man'[14] et je t'aime tout.[15]

Maurice

7
73 St Stephen's Green
[postmark on envelope: 16 Oct 1918, but this
letter must have been written between 16 and
18 December, as the Yeatses left the house
on 10 December.]

I have not seen Helen[1] for a few days nor been able to go to the Dr's house,[2] so do not know if there are any letters from you there and this is an answer to yours of the 'pantherine' poem.[3] We have been in this house now for about a week; it is a pleasing house, but almost too big for use, and it's been hard work to get it into shape. My brain is paralysed with the cold and moreover an attack of cockrooch;[4] I cannot pick up the energy to 'tell you things' yet life is quite eventful and cheerful here.

Ezra chaque jour je t'aime un peu plus que la veille malgré que j'ai oublié la façon dont tu ris, et Dieux que c'est bête que tu sois si loin et de penser que plus ou moins ce sera toujours comme ça !

Sans courage
je t'embrasse[5]
Maurice.

**8**

23.12.18

My sunny head

I shall come to you in a fortnight. Scheme not altogether satisfactory (carting here of my furniture) still the only official motif I could find, and I may be able to stay 10 or 12 days.

It becomes less and less easy as days pass to live without you, and yet there is some peace in being away from you, but I can't cope with that peace, i.e. life is contradictious.

I had always thought of Mme [? Champion][1] as an elderly matron more important in breadth than hight; suggestion of name probably. And she marries a fool, it is one place less for you to go, and it is not decreed by the Gods that you should come here now, for which, for reasons not even wholly personal, I am grieved. Uncle Theseus[2] is wrong about Dublin, in fact, we must suspect our relative to be tainted in his appreciations by slightly unfair... but perhaps this also is unfair.

There is not much of the 'first rate' (but is there much anywhere?) but an entertaining variety and quite a decent percentage of intelligence. It's a better zoo than London. But apart from the O'Neills and Helen[3] I have been seeing very few people lately. Most of my time spent running round auction rooms or nursing the cockrooch[4] by the fire. Bitter cold and only one fire in the house – no intelligent leisure possible for the present, but this only a pretexte for usual incapacity. A great country for match-making evidently. Sara Purser[5] now is trying it on. She has produced a young [? Kaki],[6] a most harmless little specimen with a certain amount of intelligent appreciation of 16th cent. art and tendencies towards sentimental flirtation; Alexis[7] has immediately labelled him a spy of the darkest kind; the spy madness in the south of France during the first year of the war was nothing compared to here, but then there seems to be some reason for it, for what an army of detectives! Et tout ça ne t'interesse[8] guère ni moi non plus. Je lis les très mauvais poèmes de mes nouveaux amis, et aussi des pièces de theatre pires encore que les poèmes. Inclus une copie de seul poème qui vaille quelque-chose, c'est par Mme O'Neill.[9] Qu'en penses-tu ? Mais je ne lis rien, je ne pense rien. J'ai connu des jours plus tristes (comme dans la chanson)... Lorsq'on 'soit qu' on etait tout seul.' Moura et Willy ont terminé leur querelle en s'écrivant chacun une lettre définitive style 'Noble Vyking' de la part de Moura style 'Noble Bayard mourant'[10] de W. et tous les deux disent qu' ils ne se parleront plus jamais à moin d'excuses plates. Dis moi, si nous nous querellions aussi ? Veux-tu ? Nous nous dirions des choses horribles et nous prendrons tous amis à temoins et puis nous deviendrons très nobles et froids et puis nous nous attendrions des excuses. Non la vie est trop courte, et bien que ca manque de dignité, je t'embrasse dans l'oreille.

Maurice.

Excuse notepaper. Et si tôt ne m'aimeras plus.

**9**

Friday[1]

Am I to console with you about failure of American tour scheme?[2] I might as well since it IS a failure; but thank God it is!

Lectures over here of course would have a wild success but barren alas as to cash getting.

Did I mention to you Mr and Mrs O'Neill;[3] I went to see them yesterday evening and staid till 4 a.m. a perfect orgy of talk.

**10**

10 Stephen's Green

Dublin

11-8-19

My dear Ezra,

I was much delighted by the plenitude of monsieur [? Jamier's][1] virulent imbecility. I should have written you some ages ago, but virulence or any activity whatsoever is not as you know the form of *my* imbecility, and God knows I have been feeling and am still imbecile enough.

Desert waste but for one brilliant oasis: 3 week's camping in the Wicklow hills,[2] mode of life altogether congenial.

Dove lei?[3] And will you also be going to Japan?[4]

The heat is flat without a throb, the town smells bad, people of the north are uglier in summer than in winter, there is nothing to say.

Yours

Maurice

**11**

67 Fitzwilliam Square[1]

Dublin

[after the summer of 1920]

Ezra, je suis une brute! Et c'est vraiment gentil à toi de m'ecrire, encore ainsi. Je prends ma plus belle plume[2]; this is not figurative, a gorgeous flame coloured quill, I paid 2.6 for it yesterday; and I wish I had words to write worthy of it and of your highness. But one becomes very illiterate in this country; it's a case of the soul killing the mind!! All the same stylishly or not I want to tell you que je reste ton amie jusqu'à la mort malgré ma paresse.[3] There is no faithfuller beast in a way than me. I think you are the same. After those mawkish but sincere protestations what can I say. News…I don't care a damn about what happens. You wrote me some weeks ago had Russell[4] anything worth? I really don't know. I haven't seen him for ages. But Francis (that's the name of my blessed angel)[5] has written poems which beat by far anything I have heard here of lately. For the moment he and I are sulking. But when that blows over I'll make him send you a few. If you don't think they would do for the dial[6] tell me at least what you think of them. Oh? As you would put it la vita strania![7] And the further I go the less I understand it. I am expecting an heir or rather I hope an heiress in February.[8] I think it ought to be rather a nice person, but if it isn't I will dump it in the Assistance Publique tout comme Jean Jacques.[9] And you, apart from work; comment va la vie, comment vont les amours?[10] I may hop over to London next Wednesday and stay with May for a bit.[11] If so really we must arrange to see something of each other.

Affectionately.

Maurice

My name is Stuart.

# 5
# Epilogue

*Anna MacBride White*

Before entering Laragh village from Dublin by the gaunt old mill where two rivers meet, as the road turns left to go over the humpback bridge one turns right directly up a hill, past the little Church of Ireland chapel, to reach Laragh Castle. In the old days the car would struggle haltingly up in first gear. Through the open iron gates the rain-rutted drive, lined by rhododendrons and tall pines with a field on either side, runs straight to end at the hall door of the house. Behind what must have been an old coach house and out offices, but before that had had darker usages, was an enclosure, still called 'the prison yard', denoting the original use of all the buildings, which was to suppress the unruly Wicklow clans after the rising of 1798, a time of bloody revolution with bloody retribution. Like so many places in Ireland it was still haunted by memories of that time. It was the second last barracks on a military road that cut through the bare high mountain bogs to end in the Wicklow fastnesses of Glenmalure. Behind the house, within the barrack wall, Iseult created her garden. There she spent as many daylight hours as she could, surrounded by her beloved mountains, with the smells and sounds reminiscent of Arrens – the trickle of endless rivulets running down off the mountainside, the wind in the pines, and the smell of sweet-scented gorse. A friendly farmer, coming once a week, kept their vegetable patch. His pleasant and cheerful daughter, Bridie, helped with the housework until she got married.

Iseult now had her 'wild and beautiful bit of earth', the old barracks was 'her little thatched house', and sunflowers were in her garden. It was the earthly paradise of her dreams, except that in life dreams are never perfect, and 'the flaming spear' was always present. Yeats had been upset at her 'poor ambition', but it was her wisdom to recognise her limitations. The period in London had taught her that.

From 1929 to 1939 Francis wrote 13 novels and a few plays. Many of these were failures. Mostly he wrote at home in a disciplined manner then took off to visit friends, see publishers in London, watch his horse racing, learn to fly, play golf and fish, and have affairs with women, some of whom he considered seriously in order to get out of his marriage with Iseult. He spent long spells in London and Paris annually, but said he always aimed to be at home for Christmas with the children, Ian and Kay. A great inventor of games and stories, he entertained them with droll stories coloured by his dry humour. But he was also a strict disciplinarian with a very short temper who ruled the household with a rod of iron and with strict economy, constantly blaming and scolding Iseult. There could be no noise when he was writing, and meal times were fraught with fear. Bridie helped to keep him quiet and as happy as possible. Iseult was interested in his work, did much typing for him, as she did for many others, including her mother, through the years. She socialised with their mutual friends and went with him when his horse was running. She encouraged his interest in the children, but did not like many of his associates. There was much autobiographical content in his work and Iseult appeared in his women characters, sometimes lovely and mysterious and sometimes doom laden. In his heroine Anne, in *Women and God*, (1931), there are snatches of the real Iseult as she continued to be through the rest of her life:

> In the face of difficulty she had chosen him; and a child and a place to live. Not that she was always happy, but she didn't want other things. Or what she wanted was something out of her power to get for herself.

Of her reveries he wrote:

> she lived much in her own mind, especially when left alone with Baby, surrounding with invented glamour the things she saw and did. There were certain paths through the bushes, certain parts of the garden that meant for her something that she could not have explained. They had become to her a symbol of an intangible heroic atmosphere, as though they were landscaped from the Iliad or the Morte d'Arthur.

By 1939 Francis's writing had come to a standstill and the family was in debt. Through Iseult's friendships, one with the German ambassador, Dr Eduard Hempel, he was offered the opportunity to lecture on English literature and to read from his own novels in Germany for a few months that year.

Francis going to Germany for a few months caused no great concern, for this would bring some badly needed money, but when the question of moving the family there when he was offered a university appointment as war was breaking out was another heart-searching matter. Francis wanted them to come to Germany, but having got a moralising letter from his aunt Janet Montgomery his more urgent need was to pay off his debt to her and the bank. Never mentioning the problem of what to do with the house, he kept writing that he missed them, and wanted them with him, that he would not have gone away if they were to be parted, but he finally decided not to come home and went off on holidays to the Tirol. In the meantime Iseult was agonising about what to do. Ian was in boarding school, Kay, just eight, was being taught at home, and what could be done about the house if she left? Would she lose it? She sought her mother's advice. Her mother's view, backed by her son's and daughter-in-law's views, was she should stay put, for she and Lily, living on Lily's income, could retrench and pay off some of the more pressing debts. Another reason for not going was that her mother was now 73 and Iseult did not want to leave her. None of them thought the war would last so long or cause such devastation. Bridie found Iseult weeping by the kitchen stove when she got the letter saying Francis was not coming home. This separation was virtually the end of their marriage which, against the odds, had lasted for 19 years. Iseult wrote of him, possibly at this time:

> You will come back in all your leafless grace, and I also unchanged. I will still be wishing that we were more happy and better, and you will still long for some distant land, for new friends and events.
>
> Yet if we ourselves are not our own distant land and our own ever new friends, there is no use in any land or in the company or absence of friends; under every different skies, you beloved, will get restless, I worn out as before. Every longing of the heart which is not love is symptomatic of disease.
>
> You long for places, for people and for events. I long for state of being, and that is even worse.
>
> My love, I grant you all the phantoms of the spheres, and as many Russian dancers as two arms can hold; (indeed this is not quite true) only I will not have you look up to impostors of nobility and think their brass is gold.
>
> Why was I not born your mother? – I would have brought you up so well! But I am only your unsatisfactory love.
>
> Luckily there are the phantoms.
>
> I am tired of crying, I am tired of not sleeping, I am tired of not being able to think well of you. I am tired of never seeing you anywhere any more.

Francis sent some of his salary home. He also wrote charming letters to the children, which as the years went by became repetitive, as he was not aware of the changes in them as they grew. When he started his radio broadcasts to Ireland they listened through the crackles of their old battery radio and waited for personal messages from him, particularly Kay whom he had made his special pet.

The ordinary events of Laragh continued. There were friends living near, Robert Barton and Roger Sweetman, who were her particular friends, both coming from the same political background, with whom she could have discussions that interested her. Lyle Donaghy, a minor poet, would come regularly to unburden his troubles; Iseult listened patiently to him for hours on end though it left her limp with exhaustion. Then there were the retired people residing in the area and 'tweedy gentry' who came for afternoon tea, in the summer in the garden under the apple trees, or in the winter in the pleasant drawing room – a simple tea of bread, butter and home-made jam. Or she went to tea with them. Though always polite and charming in her vague way she often found the conversation was of no great interest. She had, in ways, a man's intellect, an objective approach to people, never appearing as a victim wife, and, though finding some people, such as Francis and Cecil Salkeld, unpleasant, she liked them. She always got on well with the local people and was respected by them. Now, without a car or telephone, communication was by the once-a-day bus, and the post office. There were visitors from Dublin, and their children, in the summer especially, also biographers of Yeats. Visits to Dublin for shopping, especially at Christmas, included coffee and cakes in Roberts Café with her children, heedless of time strictures, taking them to the cinema in the middle of the show and waiting round again to get the start of the story, or, ignoring bus timetables and penury, getting a taxi back to Roebuck.

Occasionally Iseult would take a few days off, as her mother had, to visit the enclosed order of the Cistercians in Mount Melleray Abbey on the wind-blown bare slopes of the Knockmealdown Mountains, where, staying in the monastery guest house, she would endeavour to sort out her spiritual problems with the guest master, to find intimations of peace. Still constantly in a state of depression her great joy was her awareness of beauty for its own sake in everything as she had said to Yeats in 1916. She would admire, say, the photograph of a perfect cabbage for its sense of wholesomeness. Her personal perception of the divine came to her through nature. One of her special moments was to go out after a sleepless night into the freshness of the early morning before it was touched by the new day. And literature and art continued to inform her life.

Always retaining something of the child, she enjoyed the company of children and treated young people as near equals, prepared to discuss with them the big imponderables of life, or to admire and discuss a card or a popular novel. In such ways she was a charming companion for all ages.

On 5 May, 1940 an event shook the Stuart household, one apparently half expected. Kay, then just nine, gives her account which includes the memories of Bridie, who many years later still considered the story a top secret. Bridie, glancing out of the window saw a great tall man with a military air, wearing riding boots, a pullover and beret, dishevelled and in need of a shave, coming up the hill. She rushed into Iseult saying 'He is here' and Iseult turned pale. This obviously expected guest, Herman Goertz, had just landed by parachute from Germany to make contact with the IRA and Francis had supplied his address as a safe house. 'Uncle', as Iseult now called her half-brother, was later heard to mutter darkly and disapprovingly that it was 'Helen Moloney's doing'. The visitor slept the night in the house, but before he could move on he badly needed some more acceptable form of clothing. He had spent four days walking the 70 miles from Co. Meath to Laragh in his uniform and had swum the Boyne river, discarding or losing as he went his parachute, his radio, and his heavy uniform jacket. So the following day Iseult took the bus to Dublin, contacted her mother and they went to Switzers, one of the best and most expensive shops in town, where they were both known, to buy the clothes; then possibly they made contact with the IRA, maybe through Helen Molony. A night or two later a local, also in the know, came, throwing pebbles in a conspiratorial manner at the wrong windows by mistake, to fetch Goertz and take him to his IRA contacts.

Goertz's discarded paraphernalia was found around the countryside, the house he was staying in outside Dublin was raided, and though he managed to get out in time he left maps, codes, a wireless receiver, a tie with Berlin written on it and his clothes from Switzers which were later identified by Switzers' sales staff. The clothes naturally led to Iseult.

Kay gives her account of the result:

> The local Gardaí, ordered to search the house, were embarrassed as they liked and respected my mother, one in particular being very friend-ily disposed to her on account of some kindness of hers to his family. Luckily it was he who opened the drawer of a little table, saw a gun and quickly shut it again. My mother, desperate to know what to do with the dollars which Goertz had also left behind, stuck them inside a book on St. Bernadette, to whom she had a special devotion. Neither dollars or gun were found. Early next morning Bridie realised the house was surrounded by police and detectives. They had come with a warrant for my mother's arrest.

Iseult was interrogated, charged, tried and given three months in prison. Her simple defence from which she did not stray was that she had bought the clothes for an old literary friend of hers and her husband's whom she had known for years, but regularly refused to give his name. The authorities only knew there was a spy at large and the only possible connection with Iseult was the clothes they found in the house in which he had been staying.

While Iseult was in prison, Goertz, having escaped the raid on the house, wandering around at a loose end, made his way back to Laragh, where apparently Maud had asked Helen Moloney to take charge. According to Kay he arrived

> bleeding, having torn himself crawling on the mountain side through the furze bushes. He had a bath but went out to sleep on the mountain in a thicket of gorse bushes. I remember the excitement of going out with Ian carrying a hot lunch, creeping and crawling through the furze and

him impressing upon us in his German accent that we must be 'cotious'. We had all been sworn to secrecy. In the drawing room I remember his formal manners – clicking his heels and bowing over my hand when introduced, distinguished and with charm of manner.

Goertz was caught and imprisoned with other German spies. This episode strained Iseult's relationship with her great friends, the Hempels, causing the ambassador huge diplomatic problems, but for Iseult it was an obligation required of her by Francis. It also differs in some parts from Goertz's official and self-censored account. At the end of the war he was released along with the other prisoners and allowed to stay in Ireland. By this time he was an unhappy and unbalanced man. A question arose about returning him to Germany; he was imprisoned again then let out on parole. On 20 May, 1947, disillusioned in every way he wrote to Iseult: '... it is not the prison nor the uncertainty of whether I would succeed in committing suicide at the last moment when everything was lost. It was the feeling of shame.' Three days later, on 23 May, he succeeded in swallowing cyanide while waiting in custody to be deported.

Kay thought his arrival and their friendship had a profound effect on her mother. He had seemed an incarnation of some hero figure of her imaginings with whom she could discuss not only Nazism in an idealistic 'cosmic' way, but share a deep interest in Eastern philosophies. As untutored in the practicalities of ordinary life as she, he provided her with a dramatic involvement in what she believed. Also probably not since her friendship with Yeats had she been able to discuss so well the spiritual dimensions of ideas and philosophies.

It must be remembered that at that time very many people in Ireland were pro-German on the old principle that England's enemy was Ireland's friend. Also, like Yeats, Iseult believed in the aristocracy of thought and what she saw as the promise Germany had to offer the world. Her friendship with the Hempels recovered gradually from the diplomatic debacle of Goertz's arrival and deepened, becoming one of the most crucial things in her life. As with Goertz Iseult shared with them a common cultural European background with a shared vision of Germany as a power destined to ennoble and purify the world. The Hempels were the only Germans Iseult knew well, and Kay wondered how her mother, so sure in her assessment of people and, nearly always, right, would have had such an idealistic concept of Germany if the Hempels, and indeed Goertz too, had been very different representatives of their race. With the Hempels she shared the disappointment of defeat, the end of their dreams of a better world turning to disillusion and regret – 'There seems to be no "becoming" in anything. What disenchanted days we live in.'

Eduard, a career diplomat and not a member of the Nazi party, had served in India and the far east and had an interest in eastern religions, which he shared with his wife Eva and Iseult. This was a cause for their daydreaming that one day they would all go and visit that rare and distant land of Tibet, in the meantime reading and discussing religion and philosophy. In the long hours in the winter which Iseult spent alone with Lily while the children were away at school she read many of the scriptures and spiritual writings of the world, typing up passages which had special meanings for her; also, of course, she played endless games of patience, read novels and thrillers, all with equal pleasure. Though lonely at times, she enjoyed her solitude.

The Hempels came for visits, the basic amenities of the house providing a sharp contrast to Embassy life; oil lamps, water pumped from the underground well once a day to supply the bathroom and kitchen, lack of fuel in a damp house and Iseult's helplessness and bewilderment when faced with practical affairs. When they were expected Bridie went into a whirl of tidying, cleaning, polishing and bed-making. Finally all was done: two beds with sagging mattresses made up in their room, the kitchen, where they would have their meals, as ready as could be – with its cracked floor, old range and flaking whitewash. But the drawing room, with its fire burning, bookshelves and dilapidated antiques, and the old brass vases full of flowers had a more gracious atmosphere.

Other visitors came. Before the war, Thora arrived, looking glamorous. She was concerned about Iseult's lack of clothes, but more practically paid for her to have her teeth attended to. Toby and his family also paid a fleeting visit. Now, for old friendship sake's, Helen Molony came, causing frequent alarms and excitements, escaping from watchful eyes, getting lost and being found by the neighbours in a drunken stupor. Aunt Janet, stumpy in tweeds, square shoes, and a man's felt hat with a feather, came from her successful farm in County Meath to see how they were doing. Fond of them and looking upon them as her family, she considered it her right to lecture them, but was also helpful with money. By this time Kay was in a boarding school in Bray and Ian was studying carving and woodworking in Glenstal Abbey in County Limerick, but the summers were busy with the visiting children of her friends, the Hempels, the Salkelds, the children from Roebuck and others, so days were full of activities devised by Iseult to add to the fun: camping, walking, picnicking and swimming in the river pools, and searching for the treasures nature provided; learning the secret places where the river pearls could best be found, where the fraughans (bilberries) grew best, gathering the blackberries and later the hazel-nuts for Halloween, and saving the turf. Along with these things came the stories and legends of the countryside, the banshee that Bridie saw, fairy rings, the Devil's Corner where the horses shied, and looking for the leprechauns' footmarks that their father had told them could be found in the mud in the hazel wood. Going to the bog to save the turf was an essential activity; already cut for them, fine days with a picnic were spent turning and footing it, and, with a loan of a donkey and cart, taking it home when dry to store for the winter. In 1943 the children were riding the donkey and Ian, a true practical joker, to tease Kay, gave the donkey a whack. She fell off and broke her elbow, which never set properly and gave her great misery in her new school. When Maud visited she was taken on expeditions in the donkey and cart. Twice while staying there she also had accidents, once breaking her arm and another time her hip.

Life was very sparse and hard during the war and money perennially scarce. But after the war came to an end new worries, anxieties and disillusions set in. Francis, caught in the aftermath, along with Gertrud Meissner who eventually became his wife, had a very difficult time, in prison, in camps and in wandering around occupied Germany and France. Iseult, constantly in debt, did all she possibly could to help him; with the assistance of her brother and the Hempels, they managed to send him a monthly allowance as well as clothes and food parcels. She wrote 'You know if I had the money I would give it to you.' The Hempels sold a few antiques for her and Sean went with her to the authorities for permission to send £25 a month and he, also, sent Francis an overcoat.

Then Janet died leaving all her money to Ian and Kay, with her will carefully supervised by executors. When the opportunity arose they both went to see their father, a visit which was not an unmitigated success. Ian was studying in the School of Art while living with the Hempels and Kay, while living in Roebuck House, was going to school and university. Then with the help of the Hempels Ian went to Garmisch to study woodcarving, staying with the Hempels' friends. He fell in love and later married their daughter, Imogen Werner.

Francis, now living in London with Gertrud who was working, was again having books published, but was still writing for help and complaining bitterly that the family now had Janet's money as well as Lily's, and he wanted £500 from Lily, his share of Laragh and so on, deaf to the fact that executors ruled over a very debt-ridden situation. He was considerably annoyed to discover that his brother-in-law had replaced Janet as one of Lily's trustees. Iseult, with her sense of sharing all, had put his name on the deeds of the house long before, and he had taken out a mortgage on it, which he had never repaid, so that Ian had not been able to raise money on the house for badly needed repairs. He proposed that he and Gertrud would come to live with them and share the house. Gertrud wrote fond letters to Iseult, more as a prospective daughter-in-law than a supplanting wife. In his novels Francis had written as the outsider or victim, searching for spiritual meaning by seeking out adversity. In all this he was now playing the role of the bitter victim suffering adversity.

While all this was going on Iseult had a heart attack in 1950. Severely restricted, she was no longer able to garden or do anything physical. Kay, with special pleading, was able to get a car with the consent of her trustees to allow her to go home at the weekends to be with her mother and to relieve Ian and his wife Imogen with their growing family, now both endeavouring to earn a living with woodcarving. Lily, who, had supported Iseult and her children from her meagre income since Ian was born, a quiet and uncomplaining woman, enjoying the simple pleasures of life, had a stroke. It was thought she would not survive. Francis made a flying visit to see his mother. She recovered, though she was left paralysed and confined to a wheelchair.

One of the few joys left to Iseult was her correspondence with her mother and the Hempels, now living in Freiberg. When she heard they were going to Italy and sent her a book on Giotto, in a letter she remembered her visits to Assisi, 'the pagan temple, and St Francis marrying Lady Poverty and all that happy efflorescence of pure Christianity'. Shortly before her death they sent her a book of Chinese art, 'quite the loveliest I have ever seen...all art goes back to nature for some purpose or another...but they of the Far East went to nature for nothing but her own sake.'

When Iseult visited her mother, she would sit in an old rocking chair in her mother's bedroom, which filled with blue cigarette smoke as they talked and reminisced, sharing memories only they could share with each other, as everyone else was too young to remember. After such a visit to her mother in 1952 Iseult wrote to her.

My Lady-Heart,

These days, it seems to me, you live so much in the past and close to the people that you knew in the old days, that it is important to help you to retain a clear image of them and I have been worrying about a wrong impression I may have given you, the other day when we were talking about May Bertie Clay. It is quite true she was politically fanatical (a family failing, Darling) that she did try to undermine you with me, but not out of mean jealousy, only to get me on the English side, and she did say nasty catty things. At the same time she was deeply fond of you. She said to me: 'I don't know anybody with as much generosity and power for love as Maud has.' She really loved you very much, and but for this political complex, I truly think would have gone through fire for you; so I should hate to think that anything I said should spoil her image for you.

Even John MacBride, I am able to see now as someone rather pathetic because you were so much the wrong person for him and his whole life became cast in the wrong mould for him. He was physically brave but in other ways a very weak character. He wasn't a good man, but in different circumstances and with different people he might have been.

Of those we were talking about, the only one I still can't see any good to be said of is Eileen Wilson; she still appears to me an incredibly nasty little piece of goods and I can still laugh with unrepentant amusement when I rushed at her and rubbed half a pound of butter in her hair saying: 'Now you can get me punished without having to tell a lie about me!'. But since I firmly believe, as you do, that nobody is ever all bad, the fact that I can see no good in her, only goes to show she is someone I have not understood.

There is something I can never understand and that is all the brutish pain and suffering, such for instance as what you and I have to endure. Doubtless, as you say, there's a meaning in it, but it's one that one can only see from a distance safe in the heart of wellbeing. O my poor Darlingest, I so wish you hadn't to endure so much misery! My thoughts are always with you.

Kisses and kisses and hugs

Your old Rat.

Iseult's mother died in May 1953. Sometime shortly after that I had to go into Peamount sanatorium for a major operation. I was there six months.

**Fig. 13** Iseult, 1952 – 'I firmly believe nobody is all bad' © Imogen Stuart

While I was there Iseult came to see me because the family were too busy to come themselves. She travelled in winter from Laragh by bus to the city, and then had another hour's journey. She brought books to me and stayed awhile talking with me, her Minnie Ring, as she called me, looking more ill than I had ever felt. Then she decided to go. Characteristically, she would not bother to find the times of the infrequent buses but wandered off walking the empty country road. Long after she had gone my thoughts stayed with her, wondering had she managed to get home without collapsing. She seemed nearer death than I had ever been to whom she was paying a sick call.

Iseult died on 22 March, 1954, shortly before her sixtieth birthday. Ian wrote to the Hempels:

> I think in the end she was not so terrified of Death as she used to be and she never realised in the end that she was dying. Kay was sleeping beside her and did not know. . . . We buried her in a lovely spot at the foot of the round tower in Glendalough.

# 6
# Iseult as Writer

*A. Norman Jeffares*

Not much of Iseult's writing was published but she wrote a lot in French and English from her teens, keeping various journals, writing poems, stories and essays as well as recording her religio-philosophical thoughts. In this volume we have published her letters to Yeats and Pound. In an article in *Yeats Annual* No 16, forthcoming 2004, a kind of prolegomena, a sketch for a life, I have dwelt on her letters to others as well, notably to her cousin Thora and to her friends in later life, the Hempels. Some of her letters to Maud Gonne convey the close friendship between mother and daughter, and some of her letters to her husband Francis Stuart illustrate the difficulties of her marriage as well as her concern for their children. Here I have quoted from some of her *Journals* because I think these give something of the essence of her personality. She could be profoundly serious in her comments on a wide variety of subjects and yet delightfully humorous in her self-deprecation.

Maud's comment to Yeats that Iseult knew the *Iliad* and the *Odyssey* better than her prayer book (*GYL*, p. 255) is borne out by some of her earlier MSS. She had a codified form of the Greek alphabet which she used to describe various drawings of episodes in the *Iliad*. For a time she wrote on the backs of pages, which contained these drawings with their code beneath them. There are several pages giving a key to the code with its idiosyncratic versions of the letters of the Greek alphabet.

The drawings are of somewhat elongated figures, who appear as if on tiptoe, the women in long flowing robes, the men usually in tunics occasionally carrying shields or spears. Iseult also drew some of the artefacts she saw in Italy; occasional drawings appear elsewhere in her journals or the copybooks in which she wrote; sometimes these are somewhat abstract versions of animals.

Iseult wrote a *Journal* in French which began in 1911, amounting to 142 pages in all, these sometimes decorated with her drawings of somewhat heraldic, stylised birds and animals. She recorded her reactions to the family's holidays in Italy in 1912 where she described a storm vividly, and recorded her reactions to the beauty of the landscape and to architecture in the cities, the latter triggering off reflections on Christianity and Paganism.

The *Journal* also contains various stories, some recourse to Marcus Aurelius as well as an account of how when she visited London in 1913 – the occasion when Yeats introduced her to Tagore – she and her cousin Toby Pilcher went in for a fair amount of kissing (a repetition of earlier encounters with him in Colleville and in Florence) when Toby's character pleased her very much: 'very brave...very companionable...but'. She commented on the English part of the family's involvement in the suffragette movement as well as giving descriptions of the family holiday at Arrens in the Pyrenees, in September 1913, but first she briefly mentions how her half brother Sean, whom she called Bichon,

was at Colleville [in June 1913] with Delaney probably filling himself with the filth of devotion and grand airs. Towards the 17th August Kathleen and her family locked up their trunks for Dissard. May brought me once [from Alexandra Court, 171 Queen's Gate] to Bognor to see Charly [May's brother], Chotie and Pompon [Charley Gonne's son]. Their house was visible from afar because a flag violet white and green was flying from the top of the roof against the eternal grey of the English sky. All the windows were obscured by large and impressive posters 'Votes for Women'. One of them showed the Hunger Strike of Mrs Pankhurst and this phrase in large letters beneath 'Can one endure such things any longer?' Charly is charming with a good happy face and his rather baroque ideas. He is an unalterable optimist and for him humanity will become good again on the day the women will have the same rights as men. He has been stuck in bed this month because of a kick he got from a policeman in a scuffle of suffragettes. He doesn't care, he's all ready to do it again. I admire that.

Now to whether things would be better if women were concerned in the matter, that's another thing. I don't think women are worth much more than men; but neither are they worse and it would in any case be more fair to give them the vote and political equality since that would please them.

Now Moura Bichon and I are together at Arrens in a lost corner of the Pyrenees in the company of Marinette and Granié who has a little albumen and in consequence of this he thinks he's not far off the end; which depresses him horribly and makes him see everything in black.

'I have a horror of the Midi', he said to me, 'the light is bad, the inhabitants are brutes, the tones of the greenery are hard, no harmony, horrible country.'

Yet we are in an adorable corner at 800 metres up, surrounded by high mountains. It has a grandiose aspect, the flora is robust and perfumed as in Switzerland without the tiresome banality of [? Chromo] and without at every corner bumping against ignoble tourists who pronounce in front of a cascade or a chalet which would condemn for ever the most beautiful corner in the world 'Oh how picturesque it is'. No, this country is beautiful and escapes the worst picturesque with its funicular railways, its boarding houses, its countless little wooden chalets, its pine trees and above all the Swiss themselves.

While at 800 metres one has the impression of being in a valley because of the surrounding mountains being so close to us and the great dry rocks which throw their violent shadows over the village I have an impression of security and rest; sometimes their presence persists like an idée fixe and we feel within ourselves the revolt of the infinite being which accentuates the immobility of the masses [? of rock]...Then we climb by tiny paths picking bunches of pink from the grey rock where they are growing, picking uselessly the rocky ground with our irontipped sticks and when succumbing to fatigue, we finally heave ourselves on to the highest point of the rock, we thought we could see in the free space above our heads more paths which went on up to the heavy white clouds which seemed to us the summit of a glacier which emerged from a sea of blue sky and from there, we imagine other narrower paths; steeper still, rising through the air towards invisible heights. It is like this – that in our dreams the destroyed Titans gave up the conquest of the skies and it already seemed to our wide opened eyes that the door of Paradise opened on the highest peak.

But all of a sudden from below in the valley timid or distant there comes up to us the sound of bells from the village. And the shaded light of our houses shines vaguely from the bottom of the abyss. Then still shaken by the *frisson* of our great dream we came back down with bowed heads a bunch of rose coloured pinks in our hands while behind us the first stars trembled in the obscure heavens.

To a certain extent this touch of *O Altitudo* is offset by frequent descriptions of fits of depression – they seem to have recurred throughout her life – and these are in turn offset by her indulgence in engaging self-mockery. Here is an example of this written in Dublin in October 1913 at the time of the Strike and Lockout:

Well good! Here am I once more setting out on a silly story and all because of the fortune of a little forethought. How can I be so silly! Here is how it began. I meet the other evening at Russell's a young man who had come back from China. We spoke a little of the Far East and of the French romantic writers.

He admitted to me that philanthropy and good works bored him. It was a great point in his favour. Then he told me that his two favourite writers were Huysmans and Anatole France and to this effect he quoted a phrase from *The Gods are Thirsty* [Anatole France, *Des Dieux ont Soif* (1912)] and this was the moment when the old [? Brottean] is conducted to the scaffold with the daughter [? Athenais]. 'He looked at her white throat and regretted the light of day.'

Well, well! This young man is interesting I said to myself and worth cultivating. It is true that he is small, that his complexion is brick coloured and his eyes like a lobster's. Nevertheless he seemed amusing. Also in my most pleasing accent [I said] in leaving, 'I hope to see you again monsieur, we receive every Saturday evening'. Well right enough he turned up on Saturday and we once again began to speak of literature which led me to say that I spent nearly all my afternoons here [in Dublin] in the National Library. He caught the implication and answered that he too spent nearly all his time there. Good! I said to myself laughingly, we cannot be more expeditious! Yesterday I was too busy all day to go to the Library but I ran there after lunch to-day and I was thoroughly absorbed in *Le Rouge & Le Noir* of Stendhal (which begins to annoy me) when somebody came and sat down opposite me. It was my young man. I wasn't expecting it at all so that I blushed like a poppy and saluted him in a really stupid manner. I fully realised this and made myself this observation. If I blush like this this decent fellow will think that I am in love with him. This disagreeable reflection made me blush even more and after a while my only recourse was to get out my handkerchief and blow my nose violently. He seemed deeply absorbed in a book on law and then towards half-past four, I got up. He too naturally [got up] and we went out together. Once we were in the street he asked me where I was going and I said I was going home. Then he asked me to have tea with him in Fuller's [a Dublin tea-shop]. I made one or two objections saying that I mustn't be back too late because we were expecting a visit but naturally I finally accepted and there I was disillusioned: I realised that when talking to him I had mistaken him, and that he was one of these weaklings always of the same opinion as the person they are talking to and don't have the courage of their opinions!

He asked me 'Do you like Dublin very much?' I answered 'No, not very much' and that all these northern countries depressed me so that I who had heard him chez Russell say that it was the most beautiful country in the world, that the Irish people were the most admirable, the most heroic, [found that he] changed direction all of a sudden and assured me that he too found Dublin splenetic and that the people here were lazy. Upon hearing that I thought to myself (my good Fellow you're not worth much but I'd like to see how far your hypocrisy goes). Then I said to him 'Have you read the *Temptations of St Antony*?' 'In my opinion its the most beautiful book that has ever been written.'

'Oh,' he cried, 'how happy I am that you think like that. It's my opinion as well.'

But the other day I had heard him say that he couldn't understand how a genius like Flaubert could have produced such a poor book.

Hearing that, I had thought 'I wonder if it's true that Thora is correct that there is a sort of hypocrisy which reduces people; yes, stupid hypocrisy doubtless.'

Before leaving he said to me 'I know somewhere where they make coffee like they do in France. Would you come with me tomorrow?' Stupidly I said 'Oui' and now that I am reflecting quietly by the side of the fire I realise that it is a mistake.

We have fifteen more days here, so as his feeling for me doesn't seem specially Platonic he will ask me sooner or later to kiss him. Well there are two categories of men: those with a beautiful mouth and those with an ugly mouth. My Jacob belongs to the second class and I know that if he ever asks me to kiss him I will refuse and that by refusing I would give myself a perfectly absurd air of a young person priggish and virtuous. That is something to be avoided so I will go tomorrow since I have promised and after that I will use engagements as a pretext to space out our meetings.

This grave question having been resolved let us speak of other things – the strike, the present political situation which bothers poor Moura so much? Basically that's not very interesting seeing a great statue of Liberty with mad enthusiasm, having listened to vibrant discourse on the conviction and hopes and having had for a moment this magnificent triumph of the poor people and [? dreading] ferocious and stupid capitalism, and then seeing all of a sudden this hope crumbling miserably because its representatives only have the energy to make great speeches, and when it comes to action they hang back stupidly; all this is not amusing! And I understand that Moura gets distressed, all the more so because there will be ten thousand poor idiots without work who will come and join the list of the starving who end up by emigrating to America where they forget the land of their birth. It's very sad! And yet... Come on now, a little courage! It is a confession which is reprehensible but it is the truth. *I don't care!* I am saddened when I see small children go by asking for a few pence to buy a bit of bread. But the minute I no longer have them in my sight I no longer think of the fact that a few thousand metres away a sordid misery and distress rumbles away in their ignoble tenement houses. And I say to myself 'Life is a dirty trick' much more for me than for them. Oh, there's nothing to be conceited about in oneself when one knows the egoistical mediocrity which hides beneath the exterior of a young lady with enormous compassionate eyes. Here's a piece of daily elucidation as [Jean] Malya would say which I prefer to call philosophic study.

Perhaps the conclusion of this entry was what prompted Iseult into writing 'The Desire', a diffuse, rambling meditation typical of much of her writing before the war. In it she had wanted to distinguish between desire and free will.

I include it here to illustrate her wrestling with often abstract ideas and trying to put them clearly.

### The Desire

The Greeks said of old: 'Men are under the Gods and Gods are under Zeus. His power is enormous; the universe shakes if he frowns and when he shakes his immortal head the earth is shaken in its mysterious depths. But above him rules Fate [Moira], the sombre veiled Fate which makes even the Master of the skies bend and the joyful procession of Immortals who celebrate their eternal youth while drinking ambrosia in golden goblets. When she passes in the midst of them they bow, their hands shake, and the divine nectar spills on the earth with the roses from their heads, because they all know that one day this blind goddess will turn them upside down and that they will go with the Titans bemoaning their lost divinity in the heart of chaos. It is she too who holds in her powers, both the tumultuous waves which roll their eternal flood over the great bosom of the sea, and the peaceful lakes where there come to rest all the clouds of the setting suns, and the oaks of the forests which cling to the earth with their great powerful roots to lift to the sun their giant trunks, and all the little winged divin- ities who animate their cheerful souls, the flowers and the crickets, and the hard-working insects, great constructors of cities and even including feeble mortals who wander the earth, a prey to the nostalgia of blue skies.

The Greeks didn't then see in us anything but feeble [? creatures], menaced, oppressed and finally vanquished by a triple evil force: divine jealousy, death and destiny. Later the Christians arrived with their new sayings, with laws just as terrible for the pride of humanity but a little more hope. They said Oh man who are you? A body of dust and an immortal soul into which God [in] his infinite mercy lends one life with its short days and its limited joys. What would you be if he withdrew his support? You would just be a homage to the nothing from which you came and to which you will return. You are more [? lowly and] abject than the worm which you squash beneath your foot because it at least goes humbly to earth throughout the tiny space that divine clemency has awarded it in the immense universe; he is thankful and thanks God whereas you the only creature in creation with whom there have been shared intelligence and hope of a better life; you are also the only one who lifts towards the sky a disgusted head and in your presumption finds that God did too little for you. Oh man don't you see that you're [on] a hiding to nothing? So that instead of audaciously lifting your head towards the sky you should bend it & see the abyss which is opening before you if you don't go back to him [God]. But there is still time. Recognise your vanity and your stupidity, fall on your knees before this god, that you don't recognise when you say Lord I am nothing but you can do everything to defend me against Hell and against my enemies and save me from myself. Take pity on my frailty because I have confidence in you who are the unique truth.

And the centuries passed. Men prayed in order to avoid the Eternal Damnation that waited for heretics and the vain.

Then all of a sudden a revolutionary wind blew over old Europe & new men rose with a sarcastic smile on their lips and much bitterness in their spirits.

'People,' they shouted, 'Look at yourselves and look at the kings: you work from morning till night building them palaces where they eat off golden plate. You weave them brocade while your children sleep on the stones of the street. But your wives have not even one miserable rag to cover themselves and you break your teeth eating bread that their dogs would refuse. Is this living?

We who suffer in this life will have better times in the next life. God promised this.

But do you believe that if there was a God that he would permit such injustices, that he would permit his ministers the horrors committed in his name and that he would have died on earth only to see men mutually detesting each other and the strongest making martyrs of the feeblest? No, people, you have been abused. There is neither God, nor heaven, nor hell. All that is only an invention of tyrants and the only survival of the body after death is the life of young plants who are born from its corruption. Throw these false beliefs far away. We bring you a new ideal, more beautiful because it is not based on superstition but in truth and in reason which has been too long unknown.'

So people walk about round him regarding him with the astonishment of a man who waking up in the morning doesn't recognise his bedroom and a crowd of questions rush to his lips.

This generation was stupid and ferocious. It killed its kings, devoured the priests and the rich and then when they were all massacred or exiled, it [this generation] leant on its bloody axe and shouted aloud that it was free and happy in order to silence the voice which murmured very quietly 'No, you are not free. Children, share the Universe, Chance and Nothingness! "Chance" shouts the man which for a moment gives him a joy then when the game is over throws it again into the Nothingness. That's your liberty.'

In our time men who speak of reason and of human liberty are only listened by a few old groups, who still read Voltaire in their old age. We know that the Nothing is our master but we have got tired of deifying it, we know that there is only one life and that it is short, but one doesn't even want to rejoice about it. One invents electricity, one perfects mechanical things, one does a hundred kilometres an hour, and one consumes frenetic energies not to leave one minute of the day unused. Sometimes, however, in the middle of this race one stops, looking at other people passing in a whirlwind of sterile activity one asks oneself all of a sudden 'What's the good of all that? We have lost the two single things that put joy in life: the art of wasting time and the cult of the beautiful.' But as the English poet says 'Each age is a dream that is dying or one that is coming to birth.'

Science and philanthropy are not enough to quench the thirst of violent emotions of a purely intellectual sort which is in you, a new ideal rises from the ruin of the ancients; we begin to listen more seriously to those who are called Christian scientists, they teach that everyman holds within him his God and that God is his free will. It is a force which sleeps in us and should be woken; then there will no longer be sorrow, nor illnesses and one would even end up by having vanquished death.

They are almost right and yet they make a mistake on one point: free will is not the primordial principle, it can go backwards indefinitely to the limits of the possible. This principle is the *desire* and free will is only the regulator.

One must put one's free will at the service of one's desires and by it one can keep up their intensity and their duration but there are only Utopians who will go and seek a drunkard at the café and say to him: My friend why you are here saturating yourself with alcohol, your wife and your children are dying of hunger, you are ruining your health, you are the ruin of your family. Come on, good fellow, a little will power, get rid of this disgusting habit.

The drunkard thus sermonised will promise to abstain from alcohol and our Utopians will go off full of gentle illusions, but the following day what will not be their horror on passing the café to see their new convert sitting at the same table conscientiously getting drunk. What, they will say to themselves, this man who only yesterday promised not to return to the café, how it is that he is back already?

O my dear people, try to understand one thing which is that you have tried to kill in this man a violent desire, a creative force of emotion by the will which is an active force, but only [indecipherable] in so much as the regulation of creative force is desire.

My Utopians would look at me lightly, astonished, would end up saying: 'Probably what you say is very deep but we [don't] understand anything of it'. Then I would give them an example.

Imagine a cartdriver sitting on his cart which is attached to a very bad horse which leads him to the edge of ditches, only just misses crushing passers-by and finally takes the bit between his teeth. An unhappy cart-driver lets go of the reins in his distress and the tangled up horse would certainly bring him to his loss. If at that moment you are not there to stop him, you then say to the cart-driver: 'You shouldn't keep this horse, it will certainly make you have an accident.' The grateful cart-driver lets you unbridle his horse and wanders further off then you can add. 'Moreover my friend, you can't drive, you must always hold onto your reins; now goodbye and be of good courage.'

And you go away while the cart-driver remains sitting in his cart, the reins in his hands. In your haste you have forgotten to offer him another horse; and our good fellow stays in the fresh air in the middle of the road and resolves never to let go the reins again, but after a while seeing that the cart doesn't advance at all he goes back to his bad horse and continues with him. And, what the hell, I would have done the same in his place.

Have you now understood that to tell a man to cure himself of a bad desire with the only resource of his free will it is as if one said to a cart-driver to drive his cart with the reins but without a [? Period]? It is by a different (better) desire but with the same intensity that one gets rids of a bad desire and the will then does not help to maintain or fortify a new desire.

I fear that this dissertation may have taken us a little away from the nub of my story, but, I wanted to mark the deep difference that there is between desire and free will. The real reason in this study is to prove that of all the religions since paganism[,] Christianity up to atheism, which, whatever you say, is also a religion, have committed the grave errors of squashing man under the sentiment of his inferiority and his eternal dependence.

However, at first sight everything makes them seem sensible. We see the child being born, an unformed and monstrous thing, which during the first six months of his life will only be a repulsive and malodorant creature; then he will grow and, like the first tentative flame which rises from a wood fire, intelligence gradually illuminates him and when his surprised eyes let their naïve admiration wander over everything that shines, everything that makes a noise, his parents will lean over him to explain to him that these things are hostile to him and that he is surrounded by danger. Don't go near the fire, fear deep water, don't stay out in the cold, beware of the large animals in the fields and of those that play amongst the flowers, they could prick you, take care of the flowers too, even they can be poisonous; and then he learns that he must also fear his parents because he owes his life to them and that they are towards their children as it were a distant image of him who created everybody and who must be feared over and all above every thing else.

Which is how fear which is not an instinctive sentiment of our early days first enters into the heart of men.

It is evident that if [we] consider human destiny from that point of view, if one places our physical feebleness against the formidable strength of the elements [3 illegible lines crossed out] controlled by a god who is more or less conscientious but always inexorable and omnipotent and the only thing we are given as a protection is the humility or doubtful reason; it is evident then that we are nothing in ourselves and that all the most courageous and the most useless [several illegible lines written over text here] we can serve as their image in the fable of 'The Oak and the Willow'. These of the oak are broken those of the other bend but all of them submit to the action of the storm.

In fact this terrible and omnipotent god, does he exist far away above the etheric regions in an inaccessible heaven, I'm not sure, but there is one thing sure, he doesn't exist in the centre of our being, he is the most profound of our being.

The sky was blue when the air is too heavy with unknown scents. When the sky is coloured with a too deep blue the infant joy is lovely but its anatomy is horrible, aghast and deadly.

There are 126 pages of manuscript which Iseult wrote, mainly in 1916; they are headed *De Torente in via bibet Propterea exaltabit caput*. In these pages are some poems; there are passages copied from various authors as well as passages in which she was drawing on ideas she found in various authors, Nietzsche and Steiner largely, but she referred to Sénancour and Swinburne as well, while also recording her reactions to Aleister Crowley, MacGregor Mathers and Eliphas Levi. The opening pages have some sound advice about writing: she would be preserved from the fascination of words that sound well and are used for the sake of their beautiful appearance, and from the silly pedantries of method and classification as well as from fear of the obvious. She would not want, she wrote, to mistake the obvious for the easy or the commonplace.

There are meditations on various elements in the spiritual life, which should have no ultimates, no 'now or never' attitudes. The spiritual life is like a tide rising or retiring, a movement which does not continue onwards flowingly, though effort must be made, to attempt to keep moving onwards.

Iseult throws out such opinions freely: Vice, she thought, is the invasion of physical instincts into the domain of the intellect; sentimentality is but the timidity or the affectation of the body. At intervals she is self-critical: 'in two years' time', she thought, she would find, on rereading, much remaining 'which is needless and much which is nearer the truth.' She had been reading *The Equinox*, dismissing the journal as 'a queer rag'. But while it gave her thoughts a new turn she described its sentences as 'coming from elsewhere than the sex obsessed brain of Aleister Crowley'. She had reflected that it was silly and dangerous for her to use the 'mine of truthful exploration' she found in Crowley's writings; she meditated trying MacGregor Mathers, but decided she could be no more sure of his tradition than Crowley's. It could be better, then, to remain an idle, free wanderer than to fall into any systematic psychic delusions. In this mood she dismissed Eliphas Levi's magic after reading a few chapters; it was superficial, more, she thought, a book of reference. She moved on, with, one imagines, a sense of relief, to the earlier Greek philosophers and wrote down a series of quotations from them translated into French.

Two particular passages are of biographical interest. One written in November 1916 was triggered off by a fragment of a letter she had just received from Willie Yeats:

> Certainly I think that only life matters. If by sacrifice we enrich the life (and that is enrich the love) of the soul it is right, but if we sacrifice the love for an idea, we may for all our sacrifice become no more spiritual than a gambler at Monte Carlo who neglects his meals in his excitement. The strength of will is to be able every day to give a little time to that mystic meditation that all the East practices with so perfect a regularity that it may view its neared end and open the inner pathway to God.
>
> Dear, there is but one sacrifice: the winning of quiet. When one has found it, one can, I think, be kind and thoughtful as easily as a bird can fly or sing.

Her comment was that Willie was right. Quiet is the thing:

> I used to name it Equilibrium of mesure, but these names appeal merely to the intellect. Quiet is better, it is a word of the soul. I know little of meditation though no doubt that is the higher form of life, I but know outside emotions reasoning and action, therefore it is in the right management of action through reasoning that I can fight for that winning of quiet.
>
> I think the secret is this: make duty a game and game a duty, bring fancy into work and seriousness into play; think both play and work are good for they hold each other company and are no longer lonely in their tasks.

These reflections may have made it easier for Iseult to look back on her love for Devabrata Mukerjee in December 1916. He had spent some time with the Gonnes at Arrens in the Pyrenees in the later part of July 1914. He went to Lourdes for some days with them, and then when back at Arrens was continuing to work on the translations of Tagore with Iseult in a somewhat desultory way. 'They prefer reading Plato or Pater or talking metaphysics,' Maud wrote to Yeats on 25 September, 'All very good in their way if they could only work as well.' And then she added 'Of course Mukerjee has fallen in love with Iseult which has complicated things a bit.' She didn't realise that Iseult had fallen in love with Mukerjee, who was to leave for India the following week if he could get a passage. Maud made no further mention of him in France (see *GYL*, p. 352). There was a later, vague rumour that he had committed suicide in India but he became Reader in English in Jadavpur University, Calcutta and was still alive in 1982. In December Iseult opened the copy of Plato he had given her which had remained closed since the days of Arrens; and between the leaves there were still blades of grass and moss and the odour of the hay. Sad, sad sweetness of memory! My little brother we spent too casually together the gifts of the Gods; I often think on it with remorse; a sinner to whom his sins have brought success is unrepentful; remorse, you know, comes with failure; that is why we have right to remorse, you and I, my little brother. We have failed. Nostra Culpa, nostra maxima culpa.

Two years have passed now. Of strength I know no more than I did then but I have learned the wisdom of weakness. I know why one failed and that doubtless if we were to be together now, we should fail again.

Dear, it is better we should not meet again. Oh! But these are hard words to write. Is it for ever really that you are gone?

Yet that stupid woman I went to last spring told me that I should see you in years to come. Maybe then I will have learned the wisdom of strength. Your hair will be turning grey, and there will be the beginning of a wrinkle round my mouth. I often picture our meeting. I come to you with open hands and say as in some Irish peasant play: 'My little brother, this is a good day'. And you look at me in the eyes and answer: 'Indeed, a very good day, my sister.' Then we laugh together a merry frank laughter, and you sit down to smoke your pipe by the fireside while I light my cigarette.

But that's all rubbish, isn't it? We shall never meet again. We have passed each other by and said the wrong pass word – and now its all over. Well God bless you! May life be kind to you!

In memory of him she then wrote down the passages of Plato's *Symposium* that they had marked together.

The contents of this MS, written mainly in an elegant convent-style hand, are diverse. At the end of November 1914 she had recorded an infallible way of cheering herself up; reading her old copybooks and realising 'how silly I was then.' She decided to tear up the copybooks but there were two or three things worth preserving: 'The Field' and 'Venus and the Moon', atmospheric pieces, and 'Resignation' echoing the praise of Quiet. Then there is an attempt at vers libre, 'Lassitude', 'Chanson sur un air lithurgique', 'Chanson sur un air agreste' and 'March', an evocation of the spring. An Essay, 'On D'Annunzio', rather generalised, was followed by one on 'Youth' and, in December, a somewhat introspective piece on the force of inaction. She copied some extracts from Senancourt and wrote critically on some lines of Swinburne; later she recognised some parallels between Nietzsche's and Steiner's writings and her own. After some memories of Arrens and the thoughts the scenery had provoked in her there in June 1914, she copied passages from Steiner in February 1917, and then between the following April and May she wrote 'To the Sea. A Hymn', a somewhat banal piece, followed by 'The Lovers', romantic but not effective. 'Sunday Morning' is a curious mixture of description and whimsy, the Sea Fairy seen as the mother of the snake of Eden, the Venus-bearer. Only sinners and cats can roam on the shingle because they understand her, and coastguards because they don't understand her at all. 'Thoughts of Love and Hate' is a not very effective plea for escape echoing Wilde. On 27 May 1917 she wrote about sleep and repetitive patterns in life, the whole of this entry an extravagance of melancholia.

After the move to London in September 1917 there cannot have been much time for Iseult's writing: there was the unaccustomed need to work regularly at the School of Oriental Studies, then came the exhausting time-consuming and worrying period of getting food to Maud Gonne in Holloway prison, and all the while there was the passionate, secret affair with Ezra. John Harwood has commented (in 'Secret Communion', *Yeats and Women* ed. Deirdre Toomey (1997), p. 258) that while Yeats was constantly trying from 1914 onwards to get her to work on various literary projects, when he asked the spirits in November 1917 how he could help her the reply was 'lazy now – no solid work indolence stopped her obstinate as a mule'. And yet by April 1919 she had had four items published. There had always been an expectation that she would become a writer, on the part of Maud, of Yeats, of Pound. But Maud, even in her unbounded enthusiasm for Iseult's potentiality, had often written to Yeats about her daughter's laziness. She lacked the drive and most probably the intellectual and physical energy needed for a successful career as an author. She could be overwhelmed by depression, painfully aware of her lack of legitimate status. And yet, and yet, there was always the expectation. She was more than a very attractive, even beautiful young woman, she was well-read and in a wide variety of authors, highly intelligent, intellectually curious, amusing and possessed of that indefinable quality of charm. It existed throughout her life. Though she told Yeats English was her second language, not only did she write it evocatively, she always spoke it with the hint of a French accent which seemed to make it unusually interesting, and, even when seeming casual or irresponsible, significant. Not for nothing did Yeats and Pound and Arthur Symons as well as some French intellectuals write poems to her; they responded to more than her beauty: she was deeply involved in literary life and concepts, and they responded to this involvement, to her thoughtful individuality and her complex personality.

# Appendix: Some of Iseult's Writings

## Published writings

### The Shadow of Noon

I thought this book in my hand
When walking by the water
On the sun-delighted strand,
This grey pictureless book,
This book of weighty thought,
This so elaborate book
That some slow mind has wrought,
A strangely useless thing.

The hours of noon are done,
My shadow is twice my length
This violet afternoon
As I in my indolence
Tread on the delighted strand.
And yet when all is said,
The beauty of the place
Seems like the words I read,
A strangely useless thing.

But even the sun-flecked blue
And this elaborate book
Have got a work to do:
Not to be out of place,
To be eager, solemn and gay,
Solemn to run their race.

I neither rule nor obey
A strangely useless thing.

## Landscape

The other morning I was walking back from the cliffs along the shore skirting the fringe of foam on the wet sands. It was already dusk. Clouds of blue and mauve lay amid greyness. The breeze was gently hesitating, as if a little tired. I walked fast, looking downwards. The foaming waves were advancing, retreating, over and again, with always the same inbreathing and outbreathing sound. This sent me into a kind of trance, and my mind was blank of thoughts.

It was stopped abruptly by a pool and [I] had to look up and turn aside. What had happened of a sudden? What straying spirit had crept over the shore while I walked unawares? Why was every pulse in the air, every quiver in the water, throbbing with meaning?

And this odour, the odour of the sea, that salt scent that is incorporated with the wind and almost of the same nature; why was it now no longer a strong caress? Why was it that it had something more, something in it of the nature of speech? It was not like the cry of the blue hills in the distance that sigh faintly: 'Come! In our distance, in our vagueness, a God is hidden!' but a close encircling cry; and in myself a yearning came in answer – a yearning for a wilderness of fierce virginity, wind-swept, untrodden.

It was a scene of rocks and rolling clouds. The dangerous grey seemed to intimate to me that this was a land on which the sun must never shine. There was no growth of flowers or trees, no beasts, only white seagulls carried disconsolately on the winds under the clouds; and sometimes also, like an icy, burning flame, a seagull alighted on a peak, sat there motionless, and with radiant eyes gazed beyond the regions of space. It was not the gentle purity of lambs and daisies, but the awful whiteness which is to be found nowhere but in the heart of night.

And I thought fervidly, 'To wash from oneself the sweat of this earth, and its bad honey, this is the sight to dwell on.' Then in my mind the vision obscured itself. And on my way back I thought, 'I have been dreaming of one of the real gods.'

## The Poplar Road

Now at last it was morning!

I had risen in the night and opened wide the door when none was astir but the wind and a stream. The wind was blowing black upon dark – a companion only to the night; but the stream, intimately brilliant, beckoned me, and I followed, knowing the waters' travels to be wise.

Thus following, I had passed the hills and seen there first the coming of age upon the night in a dim paleness on her face, then I had entered the rocky woods where she was yet a stark, smooth matron, but in the openings, where the branches thinned, I had seen her wrinkle and stumble, and she had grown so old among the hazel trees that she could only crawl like a wandering lunatic haggled by children, for the younglings of day were upon her through all the meagre twigs, and as I emerged into the crops of juniper and stones, her last attribute, decrepitude even, left the ancient witch; she had melted away in the grey youth of dawn. I had reached the pastoral regions, and now was walking between a screen of poplars, first lit by the sun, through a land of jewelled grass. It was morning!

What gave to my lungs such delight in their breath? Why so companionable the stream? All the glum days of stingy dreams were effaced now by this one adventure of having walked through the change of night, ahead of the whitening hours, and of now being immersed in the morning – myself the morning.

Who is at one with any one thing in Nature is at one with all things; this I did not think, but rather underwent in an ecstacy where all boundaries receded into infinity, and I communed with the whole past of the earth and with the earth itself, they being part also of the dawn foster-mother of this terrestrial life. I looked on the stream at my side, and from there my roving eyes wandered up the poplar trunks to the clouds, and a vast song opened my mouth:

> To the dawn and to the dew
> Foremost of all,
> Salve!
> And then to noon and to the night,
> And the failing of day;
> To all the years of life
> In a man,
> And to his death;
> To all the years of life
> In the world,
> World without end,
> Salve!
> For although all, as I
> Now, wandering,
> Know not why,
> They owe their birth
> And will return
> To the dawn and to the dew,
> And the cry of all is still
> Our cry,
> Being mingled
> To the dew and to the dawn.

Then I fell into silence, but it seemed as if the stream, and the birds, and the high rustling leaves, with more amplitude of speech and of sound, had caught up the song, and no other song could ever intrude upon the morning.

But presently I encountered a donkey tied to the gate of a meadow; something in the sad homely beast recalled me to humble facts, and I was aware of a slight fatigue; so I leaned to the gate for a rest and looked into the meadow.

Sheltered at the far end by the elderly kindness of a wood, and displaying to the sun its tingling variety of tones and quivers, it was indeed a fine meadow. Cows grazed in it, and a farm girl was milking; she seemed staid and unimportant among all the treasures of the grass. 'I'd give the whole of her,' I thought, 'for a blade of grass,' and I was about to resume my walk. But she began to sing.

She began to sing, and all of a sudden the grass, for all its varied perfection, vanished – so docile is sight to sound – and I remained where I was, my cheek to the nose of the patient donkey.

It was such a voice as Dawn might have if she were to sing her own coming on the hills, candid as a cuckoo's, irresponsible as death or the breeze, and it seemed strange to me that such a voice should be proclaiming human cares, and love especially, and stranger still that I should stand there listening, not so much to the voice as to the tune, and still more to the words, tune and words of an Eighteenth Century Pastoral. Therein some Daphnis or other tenderly reproved his shepherdess for inconstancy, yet seemingly most in love himself with all the accessories of his grief: Cupids whose darts were no more deadly than mosquito-bites, wolves that would not have found cream unpleasing, lambs ... Oh, false innocence!

The words seemed to waver an instant, and then to alight on the thorns of the hedge in half withered garlands; I could discern a scent of dried blossoms, and in the air the throbbing of that subtle gloom exhaled by morrowless frolics. Then I laughed and sighed to think how swiftly moods can change, and changing, call each other liar. I had thought a moment ago that the rhythm of nature was all embracing – a belt round eternity. But a little girl singing of Daphnis had opened my heart into a world which has known nothing of the sun, nor has shaken to the great winds; and I, fickle as the shepherdess, had forgotten the song of the blended times for this frail, disconnected fragment.

I looked into the little donkey's eyes; they were quite resigned, and I felt we would never understand each other.

He was just thinking; 'Another dull noise, but then everything is dull; God's will be done.'

I was thinking: 'This is something which has gone away, and can never come back; this is something irreparable. O charm almost funereal of images that once, and once only, had a passionate meaning! They stand now isolated in their final attitudes to which no other age can give life again, for they are not in nature. Some, touched by the pathos of their futility, would wish perhaps to do something for them, but how? The lover of to-day may still complain to his Galatea in the same words as the Cyclope used some thousands of years ago; but who, from the sincerity of his heart and body, could now repeat a madrigal to Chloe? We can hardly even understand how Chloe could have been convinced.'

Yet is it not an unjust irony that this least platonic of ages should henceforth be the prey of our unsubstantial minds only, and receive a purely ethereal homage? And again I turned to my furry companion, yet his eyes only said: 'The will of God be done.'

The girl was still singing, but I went my way. It was no longer the same morning on the poplar road.

## Unpublished writings

Various unpublished pieces probably written between 1920 and 1921, are 'Footprints in Hades', 'L'Ombre Embarbe' (translated as 'The Beardless Shadow'), 'The Creed of the very Poor,' 'Dans un cimetière' (translated as 'In a Graveyard') and 'Words and Hours'.

### Au chat Minet
*[This was written in French by Iseult as a child]*

Oh hump, plus le temps passe, plus les jours m'eloignent de toi, plus je t'aime, plus ta perte reste graveé dans mon cœur, tu ne fut pas qu'un chat, tu fus une âme qu'il est impossible que j'ai pleuré tant un chat. Vois-tu, ce n'est pas assez d'avoir crie ma douleur en vers, je veux que tout ce que m'environne retentisse de mon désespoir, je veux que si jamais j'arrive à quelque chose, on dise, ses premières penseés furent pour sa petite bète, je te dis donc adieu, adieu à tout jamais, on dit que la mors romp les plus grands bonheurs oui mais elle romp aussi les plus grandes douleurs, je conserve donc un derniér espoir c'est que quand je serai morte, je te retrouverai au parade des ames.

### To Minet the Cat

Oh hump, the more time passes, the more the days distance me from you, the more I love you, the more your loss remains engraved in my heart; you were not just a cat, you were a soul; it is impossible that I should have cried so much for a cat. You see, it is not enough to have proclaimed my grief in verse, I want everything that surrounds me to echo my despair, I wish that, if ever I achieve anything, that people should say, her first thoughts were for her little beast. Therefore I bid you adieu, adieu for evermore. They say that death breaks up the greatest joys, yes, but it also breaks up the greatest sadnesses, so I retain one last hope, which is that when I am dead, I shall find you again in the paradise of souls.

# Notes to the Letters

## Abbreviations

ASQ      Maud Gonne MacBride, *A Servant of the Queen. Reminiscences* (1938; 1994, ed. A. Norman Jeffares and Anna MacBride White)

GYL      *The Gonne–Yeats Letters 1893–1938. Always Your Friend*, ed. Anna MacBride White and A. Norman Jeffares (1992)

WYANB    A. Norman Jeffares, *W.B. Yeats. A New Biography* (rev. edn 2001)

YANC     A. Norman Jeffares, *A New Commentary on the Poems of W.B. Yeats* (rev. edn 1984)

YP       *Yeats's Poems*, edited and annotated by A. Norman Jeffares with an appendix by Warwick Gould (1989; third edn 1996)

## (I) The Letters to Yeats

### 1

1. **your sisters**: either Susan Mary ('Lily') Yeats (1866–1949) or Elizabeth Corbet ('Lolly') Yeats (1866–1940). For Maud Gonne's comments on the fan see *GYL*, pp. 284–5.

2. **wild gutter cat**: a name given in reproof by May (Mary Kemble) Gonne (1862–1929), Maud Gonne's cousin, who married N.S. Bertie-Clay, to Iseult and her cousin Thora, the daughter of Kathleen Gonne, who married Captain (later Major General) Thomas David Pilcher. Thora Pilcher (1892–1983) married William Forrester in 1919; they had two sons. After their marriage they bought a small farm, moving to France after five years and then settling in Sussex.

3. **Bichon**: a pet name given by Iseult to her half-brother Jean Seagan (later known as Sean) MacBride (1904–88) from French *bichon frise*, a lap-dog with curly hair. According to Thora Pilcher it meant a curly-haired puppy, a French endearment, 'little dear'. This type of dog originated in the Mediterranean and was popular with French and Spanish nobility in the eighteenth century.

4. **to Paris**: where Maud Gonne occupied 13 Rue de Passy (see photograph of it, *GYL*, facing p. 177); she vacated it in 1912 (see p. 31), thinking (erroneously, as it turned out) that it was to be demolished. She then moved to a second-floor apartment at 17 Rue de l'Annonciation, which she described as 'comfortable and modern and in a quiet street just opposite the Passy Church.' It had electricity, central heating, a bathroom and lifts. Maud Gonne had written to Yeats, also on 26 December 1909, to tell him that the fan was 'quite lovely.' She also told him that the family was going to Laval for the New Year, but that she would only stay a day or two, leaving Iseult with her godmother for the holidays, something she often did on other occasions when she was away herself. Iseult's godmother was Madame Suzanne Foccart, a Carmelite nun at Laval, who, when the nuns there were being secularised in 1901, founded the Association de Dames de Sainte Thérèse, which specialised in embroidery. Later she and the nuns had to leave the convent after a dispute with the Bishop, by whom Madame Foccart was reputed to have had a son, who became one of General de Gaulle's entourage. She died in poverty in Brittany in 1921.

**2**

1. **Arrens:** a village in the Hautes Pyrénées, near Argelès-Gazost, 32 kilometres from Lourdes. Maud, Iseult and Sean first went there in the summer of 1913 to recuperate from the previous winter's illnesses. Maud was painting there, and the family was joined by Joseph Granié (1866–1915) and his wife Marinette, artist friends from Paris who lived in an apartment in 17 Rue de l'Annonciation (where Maud had also had an apartment since 1912). On this occasion in 1914 they were accompanied by their friends the Cherfils (whose daughter Christianne was a friend of Iseult); by Helen Molony (1884–1967), known as Helena by her family and as Emer in Inghinidhe na hEireann, which she joined in 1903, a member of the Abbey Theatre Players from 1909 (see note 1, Letter 9); and by Devabrata Mukerjee, an Indian student, Tagore's nephew, who had translated Tagore's *The Post Office*. Maud Gonne and Iseult had met him in Paris in 1913; he was probably introduced to them by Madame Bhikaji Cama, Editor of *Band Mataram* who was then living in Paris. See further note on him, p. 179. The party went on to Lourdes on 12 September. See *GYL*, pp. 339, 340, 344 and 346.

2. **The 'Gardener' and the 'Crescent Moon':** the English titles of prose poems by the Indian poet Rabindranath Tagore (1861–1941).

3. **The translations:** they were not completed.

4. **Mr Tagore:** he was knighted in 1915 but resigned this honour in protest against British policy in the Punjab. In addition to poetry and philosophy he wrote a novel and several plays and was awarded the Nobel Prize for Literature in 1913. He founded a school to combine Eastern and Western systems. Iseult had met him in 1913, a meeting arranged by Yeats, who had read Tagore's *Gitanjali* (1912) with her in Normandy the previous summer (he had written an Introduction to the book). Iseult shared his enthusiasm for Tagore's poems and Yeats advised her to learn Bengali so that she could translate them into French. She and Mukerjee spent their time in Arrens translating some of them; he had been teaching Iseult and Christianne Cherfils Bengali in Paris. Maud wrote to Yeats on several occasions, asking him to recommend Iseult to Tagore as a translator.

**3**

1. **the hospital at Paris Plage:** This was the Infirmière Hopital, Militaire 72, 1 Village Suisse, Paris Plage, Pas de Calais. It was near Etaples. Maud, her cousin May Bertie-Clay (1863–1929), who had trained as a nurse before her marriage (see *ASQ*, pp. 59–61. She had married in 1902, but left her husband, an Englishman working in the Indian Civil Service, the following year. She spent much time in France at the time of Maud Gonne's divorce and subsequently lived in London during the war and later intermittently in Italy where she died) and Iseult were working in two French military hospitals at Paris Plage. Maud and Iseult were given the rank of lieutenant; this enabled them to travel with the French army and move where required.

2. **now we are back in Paris:** This was after six months' nursing, when Maud Gonne had asked for six weeks' leave for Iseult and herself; they returned to Paris at the end of September, but went back to nursing in Paris when the new French offensive meant that the hospitals were crowded with wounded soldiers.

3. **Moura:** what Iseult called Maud Gonne; the name began as Amour, and was altered to Moura for public use; she could not call Maud mother and was officially Maud's adopted niece and sometimes 'adopted daughter'.

4. **an aviation comity of which I am secretary:** a position probably arranged for Iseult by her father, Lucien Millevoye (1850–1918), a member of the House of

Deputies from 1889 and Political Editor of *La Patrie* to his death. He was chairman of the French Army's committee on Aviation. Maud Gonne was pleased about it, for it meant Iseult met many interesting people, engineers, aviators and politicians, and it brought her in £100 a year. Later she commented that the £6 a month enabled Iseult to dress well and the work occupied only a few hours in the afternoons (see *GYL*, pp. 360 and 367).

5. **My knowledge of Bengali is very misty**: Earlier, in March 1915, Maud Gonne had written despairingly to Yeats that Iseult could not be got to think of Bengali at all.

6. **Mukerjea is gone**: Mukerjee (Mukhopadhyaya) Devabrata was an Indian who had studied at Calcutta, Exeter and Cambridge. He gave up the idea of a career at the Bar and applied for a professorship in India. He went back to India in the autumn of 1914. He was thought to have committed suicide there but in fact lived to a ripe old age, still alive in 1982. He held the position of Reader in English at Jadavpur University, Calcutta. Iseult and he fell in love (see *GYL*, p. 350). Iseult's *Journal* confirms this, but writes of the failure of the affair; no reason is given for this. See pp. 45 and 48.

# 4

1. **Colleville**: The letter was written from Les Mouettes (French, the seagulls or sea-mews), a large house on the edge of the sea, its garden just above high water mark, overlooking the English Channel (see photograph on p. 12 and one facing p. 320, *GYL*). It was situated at Colleville-sur-Mer, near Vierville, Calvados, Normandy. It was reached by train from Bayeux to St Laurent, and then on foot or by cart over the fields. Maud Gonne had bought it with part of a legacy from her great-aunt Augusta before her marriage, when she gave up the house in Samois-sur-Seine, a place associated with Millevoye, with whom she had broken in 1900 on discovering he had a new mistress, a café singer who shared his desire to regain Alsace-Lorraine for France (see Maud Gonne MacBride, *ASQ*, p. 279.) She did not visit Les Mouettes until 1903; the purchase was officially registered in Caen in 1904. An elderly friend, Adrienne de Grandfort, had suggested its purchase and Maud Gonne wrote an enthusiastic description of it in the second unpublished, and unfinished, volume of her *Autobiography*. For Iseult's delight in the place, see her letter of 29 March 1917 to Yeats (p. 79).

2. **Madame Péguy**: the widow of the poet and essayist Charles Pierre Péguy (1873–1914) who, initially a socialist with anti-clerical convictions, became a neo-Catholic (remaining outside the Church) and patriot. He died leading his company at the Battle of the Marne. He was born at Orléans, educated at the Ecole Normale and the Sorbonne, and opened a bookshop. He founded the *Cahiers de la Quinzaine* in 1900, in which he published his own works and those of Romain Rolland (1868–1944), the dramatist, author of many biographies and a ten-volume novel, *Jean-Christophe* (1904–1912); professor of the History of Music at the Sorbonne, he was awarded the Nobel Prize for Literature in 1915. Péguy had an intense admiration for Joan of Arc, exemplified in his *Le Mystère de la Charité de Jeanne D'Arc* (1909). His other works included *Victor Marie, Comte Hugo* (1990), *L'Argent* (1912), *La Tapisserie de Notre Dame* (1913) and *Eve* (1914).

3. **my intentions**: Iseult wanted to translate Péguy's poems into English, an idea that may have been suggested by her reading Péguy and translating him for Yeats. He thought that she might write a book about the new French Catholic poets, as he wrote in a letter to T. Sturge Moore, saying 'I am starting Iseult on

what I hope will grow to be a book about the new French poets. What do you think of Péguy (whom we are both reading) Claudel, Jammes ? Which is the most admirable? Péguy I find impressive but monotonous.' See *W.B. Yeats and T. Sturge Moore. Their Correspondence 1901–1937*, ed. Ursula Bridge (1953), p. 25.

4.  **Mac Millan:** Yeats had been published by the firm of Macmillan since 1916.

5.  **'wise delirium':** This may be a reflection of a line in Yeats's poem 'September 1913' (*YP*, p. 210). 'All that delirium of the brave' where Yeats praises the 'delirium' of past Irish heroes. For the Swinburnian source of the image see *YANC* (1989), (rev. edn 1984), p. 111.

6.  **a convent near Caen:** Colleville was about 40 kilometres from Caen.

7.  **Pater:** Walter Horatio Pater (1839–94), born in London, educated at King's School, Canterbury and Queen's College, Oxford, became a Fellow of Brasenose College, Oxford, and gained the reputation of being something of a recluse. He reflected the influence of the pre-Raphaelites in his *Studies in the History of the Renaissance* (1873). *Marius the Epicurean* (1885), a philosophical romance, dealt with the spread of Christianity during the period of the catacombs. His *Imaginary Portraits* (1887) and *Appreciations* (1889) were followed by *Plato and Platonism* (1893). He advocated a cultivated hedonism, and is best known for passages in his *Studies in the History of the Renaissance* concerning the Mona Lisa, and for two often quoted passages: 'To burn always with this hard, gemlike flame, to maintain this ecstasy, is success in life' and 'The love of art for art's sake.' Pater's involuted style affected Yeats's prose in the 1890s, especially in *The Secret Rose* (1897).

8.  **Landor:** Walter Savage Landor (1775–1864), a polished minor poet and prose writer, raised a volunteer force at his own expense to fight Napoleon in the Spanish Peninsula in 1808. He travelled in Europe for several years, finally settling in Florence. His best-known works are *Poems* (1795), *Imaginary Conversations* (1824–29) and *Pericles and Aspasia* (1836). Yeats read him between 1914 and 1916. His poem 'To a Young Beauty' (*YP*, p. 242) written to Iseult, probably in autumn 1918, ended with the lines

> And I may dine at journey's end
> With Landor and with Donne

These lines recall one of Landor's *Imaginary Conversations* (XXXV, Archdeacon Hare and Walter Landor). See Landor, *Works* (1876): 'I shall dine late: but the dining-room will be well lighted, the guests few and select.'

9.  **Marius:** Yeats, re-reading Pater's *Marius the Epicurean*, found it still seemed to him 'the only great prose in modern English.' See his *Autobiographies* (1955), p. 302. He gave a copy of Pater's romance to Iseult.

10. **Anima Vagula:** Yeats referred to this, the eighth chapter of *Marius the Epicurean* ('the New Cyrenianism' was the ninth), in *Memoirs*, ed. Denis Donaghue (1972), p. 36. In 'The Phases of the Moon' (*YP*, p. 268) he mentions 'that extravagant style' that 'he' [Yeats] had learned from Pater.

11. **Maurice:** a name used by Iseult; it arose originally out of her friendship with her cousin Thora who was addressed as Victor by Iseult. The girls regarded themselves as brothers and also addressed each other as cat. St Maurice, whose feast day is 22 September, was an officer in the Theban legion, composed of Christians from Upper Egypt, serving in the army of the Emperor Maximian Herculius. The Emperor ordered the legionaries to sacrifice to the gods to ensure victory over the Bagaudae, who were in rebellion. When the legion, encouraged by Maurice

and two of his fellow officers, Exuperius and Candidus, repeatedly refused to obey these orders, withdrawing from the army, which was encamped at Martigny (Octodurum) near Lake Geneva, to St Maurice-en-Valais (Agaunum), the entire legion was put to death by order of the Emperor. This is the account given by St Eucherius, who became Bishop of Lyons about 434. Whether an entire legion was massacred is uncertain, but Maurice and other Christians were certainly put to death. Saint Victor (his feast day is 10 October) was one of these; he had refused to accept any of the dead soldiers' belongings. Others who were martyred during September and October were Ursus and another Victor at Solothurin, Alexander at Bergamo, Octavius, Innocent, Advento and Soluton at Turin and Gireon at Cologne.

12. **not exactly easy to read**: Yeats's handwriting, no doubt affected by his bad sight, is notoriously difficult to read.

## 5

1. **Aunt Kathleen**: Kathleen Pilcher (1868–1919), Maud Gonne's sister, 'That beautiful mild woman, your close friend' of 'Adam's Curse'. (*YP*, p. 132)

2. **Donne**: Yeats introduced Iseult to the poetry of John Donne (1571/72–1631), the metaphysical poet and Dean of St Paul's Cathedral, London, whom he had read in Professor H.J.C. Grierson's edition of 1912. He wrote to Grierson that 'the more precise and learned the thought the greater the beauty, the passion; the intricacy and subtleties of his imagination are the length and depth of the furrow made by his passion. His pedantry and his obscenity – the rock and the loam of his Eden – but make me the more certain that one who is but a man like us all has seen God.' (Letter of 14 November 1912 in *Letters*, ed. Wade (1954), p. 570.) He commented on Donne not being tempted to linger or pretend we can linger between spirit and sense, and contrasted Donne with Shelley to the latter's disadvantage – 'unhuman and hysterical' a part of the reassessment of Keats and Shelley about which he remarked to Iseult (see note, p. 190) in his *Autobiographies* (1980 edn), p. 326.

3. **the state of filth and disorder and the stupid fatigue**: This probably refers to the family's moving to the attic apartment on the seventh floor from the more spacious one on the second floor, in anticipation of moving to Ireland (see *GYL*, p. 385), a journey which had to be abandoned as the British authorities would allow Maud Gonne to go to England only, not to Ireland. Maud described the 'confusion and wearyness' of this move, this 'déménagement' to Yeats in a letter of 8 November 1916.

4. **Marius**: Pater's *Marius the Epicurean*, see note, p. 180.

5. **renunciations**: They echo resolutions in her earlier French *Journal* where she records vain attempts to make her life more religious; but, on the other hand, she may be reflecting more mundane aspirations, such as cutting down her smoking.

6. **the Dyonisiac months**: They began in September when the grapes and wheat were ripe and reached a climax in December when the Dionysiac festivals were held.

7. **sacred delyrium**: The followers of Dionysus experienced religious frenzy, induced with the aid of wine, music and dancing at his rites, which celebrated orgiastically the earth's fertility as well as the idea of mortals achieving union with the god.

8. **the Order**: probably the Order of the Silver Star. See note on p. 183.

9. **a daimon**: Socrates thought a daimon was a power influencing a person's fate. Yeats altered the meaning he gave the term. He used it in the accepted sense of an evil spirit (see his *Mythologies* (1959), pp. 284–6), but later, influenced by

reading Heraclitus, Plutarch, Plato, Henry More, Blake and other authors, indicated either the self beyond time and change, the permanent ghostly self, or the spirit of a dead person who would ally himself or herself to an incarnate spirit as nearly as possible his or her opposite. Iseult alludes to a daimon as some spirit advising her rather like an eternal conscience.

10. **Madame Péguy:** See note, p. 179.
11. **Burns and Oats:** Burns and Oates, a London firm of publishers, who published many books focused upon a Catholic audience.
12. **Methuen:** A London publishing firm established by Sir Algernon Methuen Marshall (1856–1924) in 1889. He taught classics and French from 1880 to 1895. His success began with Kipling's *Barrack Room Ballads*, and his authors included Belloc, Chesterton, Conrad, Masefield, Stevenson and Wilde. He was created a baronet in 1916.
13. **Madame Mielvarque:** Described as 'a nice sunny little thing' or 'a pretty little widow', she also lived in 17 Rue de L'Annonciation. She was at Colleville when Yeats proposed to Iseult and stayed on there after he left. See Iseult's letter to Thora quoted in note to letter 21, p. 197–8.
14. **Christiane Cherfils:** Christianne Cherfils, Iseult's school friend, was the daughter of Christian Cherfils, a French author whose works included *Un Essai de religion scientifique* (1898), *Canon de Turner. Essai de Synthèse Critique de theories picturales de Ruskin. Thesès neo-ruskiniennes* (1906) and *Mimes et Ballets Grecs* (1908).
15. **Claudel's poems:** Paul Claudel (1868–1955), a diplomat, dramatist and poet, was influenced by symbolism. His plays include *L'Otage* (1909) and *Le Soulier de Satin* (1921). His poems include *Corona benignitatis Anni Dei* (1913) and *Cinq Grandes Odes* (1922).
16. **The book on Péguy:** Felix Andre Yves Scantrel Suares, *Péguy* (1915).

**6**

1. **my cousin May:** see note, p. 177.
2. **Sir Maurice:** See note, p. 180. Yeats addressed the Prologue of his *Per Amica Silentia Lunae* (1917) to her, dated 11 May 1917:

> My dear 'Maurice' – You will remember that afternoon in Calvados last summer when your black Persian 'Minnaloushe,' who had walked behind us for a good mile, heard a wing flutter in a bramble-bush? For a long time we called him endearing names in vain. He seemed resolute to spend his night among the brambles. He had interrupted a conversation, often interrupted before, upon certain thoughts so long habitual that I may be permitted to call them my convictions. When I came back to London my mind ran again and again to those conversations and I could not rest till I had written out in this little book all that I had said or would have said. Read it some day when 'Minnaloushe' is asleep.

The Epilogue, with the same date, alludes directly in its last two paragraphs to Yeats's conversations with Iseult on the French Catholic poets and Catholicism in Colleville in the summer of 1916:

> Last summer you, who were at the age I was when first I heard of Mallarmé and of Verlaine, spoke much of the French poets young men and women read to-day. Claudel I already somewhat knew, but you read to me for the first time

from Jammes a dialogue between a poet and a bird, that made us cry, and a whole volume of Péguy's *Mystère de la Charité de Jeanne d'Arc*. Nothing remained the same but the preoccupation with religion, for these poets submitted everything to the Pope, and all, even Claudel, a proud oratorical man, affirmed that they saw the world with the eyes of vine-dressers and charcoal-burners. It was no longer the soul, self-moving and self-teaching – the magical soul – but Mother France and Mother Church.

Have not my thoughts run through a like round, though I have not found my tradition in the Catholic Church, which was not the Church of my childhood, but where the tradition is, as I believe, more universal and more ancient?

3. **Saladin:** Salah-ed-din Yussuf Ibn Ayub (1137–93) was the Sultan of Egypt and Syria, who, after the death of Nur-eddin, Emir of Syria, in 1174, reduced Mesopotamia, received the homage of the Seljuk princes of Asia Minor and spent his remaining years in warfare against the Christians. He was defeated by Richard Coeur de Lion, who obtained a three year treaty from him. Saladin was regarded as pious, just, reliable and chivalrous as well as an efficient administrator.

4. **the Jew:** An unidentified person, probably a lawyer or financier, who was dealing with the family's finances, as Maud was arranging money for a move to Ireland.

5. **to pay off on the 10th October:** Maud Gonne's letter to Yeats of 3 November tells him that their money affairs are still unsettled 'though promising' (*GYL*, p. 383).

6. **Moura's health:** Maud Gonne did go to Dax on the Adour in the Landes (its baths were known for the alleviation of rheumatism) in November. She stayed at the Etablissement Thermal et Grand Hotel des Baignots, paying for her stay by doing a couple of sketch portraits. The treatment was beneficial.

7. **the cockrooch:** cockroach, from French *le cafard* (*avoir le cafard*: to be depressed) gloomy.

8. **your castle:** Yeats had told Iseult of his plan, one encouraged by Lady Gregory's son Robert, to buy Ballylee Castle near Gort in County Galway. He finally acquired it for £35 in 1917 and it was used after his marriage as a summer residence until 1929.

9. **the fool or the saint:** This idea may have been discussed between Yeats and Iseult. Cf. Robartes in Yeats's poem 'The Phases of the Moon' (*YP*, p. 115), who remarks 'Hunchback and Saint and Fool are the last crescents' and see Phases Twenty-Six, Twenty-Seven and Twenty-Eight in Yeats's *The Great Wheel*, in *A Vision and Related Writings*, ed. A. Norman Jeffares (1990), pp. 196–200.

10. **the new flat:** The attic flat on the 7th floor of 17 Rue de l'Annonciation, Paris.

11. **'Thy will be done':** an echo of the Lord's Prayer; but in her 1916 Notebook Iseult recorded that she got great help from a very simple saying of Willie Yeats: 'In distress or in difficulty, bow to God and say "Thy will be done"'.

12. **the Equinox:** a serial publication appearing twice a year, at the Spring and the Autumn equinoxes, the official organ of the AA (The Argentinum Astrum, the Order of the Silver Star.). It was mostly written by Aleister Crowley (Edward Alexander Crowley (1875–1947) who was also known as Count Swanoff, the Laird of Boleskine and Aleister MacGregor. A magician and writer who claimed he was the Beast from the Book of Revelations (see John Symonds, *The Great Beast. The Life of Aleister Crowley* (1959)), Yeats described him as 'a fiend in human form, a man who was well known to be an expert in Black Magic, a man who hung up naked women in cupboards by hooks which pierced the flesh of

their arms'. (*The Collected Letters of W.B. Yeats*, Vol. II, 1997, p. 524, fn.) Crowley claimed *The Equinox* was the first serious attempt to give the public the facts of Occult Science since Madame Blavatsky's *Isis Unveiled* (1877), which he called 'an unscholarly hotch-potch of facts and fable'. Iseult described *The Equinox* as 'a queer rag'.

13. **the Kaballa:** Or cabbala; it was a Jewish mystical tradition based upon esoteric interpretations of the Old Testament.

14. **Péguy:** See note, p. 179.

15. **Your poem on the Easter Week:** This was 'Easter 1916' (*YP*, p. 287). The poem is dated 25 September 1916 and was first printed in an edition of 25 copies in 1917. Yeats wrote it while staying at Colleville. It records his reaction to the Easter Rising when the centre of Dublin was occupied by about 700 republican members of the Irish Volunteers and the Citizen Army who held out against British troops until 29 April. The centre of the city was heavily shelled. After a series of courts martial held from 3–12 May 15 of the leaders were shot. Yeats names some of them in the poem. Maud wrote him a letter on 8 November, telling him why she didn't like the poem, commenting in relation to the line 'A terrible beauty is born' that even Iseult didn't understand his thought until Maud had explained his theory of 'constant change & becoming in the flux of things' (*GYL*, p. 384).

16. **poor old Delaney:** Mary Barry Delaney, Delany, or O'Delan(e)y (1862–1947), a devout Catholic who lived as a journalist in Paris, residing in the Avenue Kleber, wrote under several pseudonyms. She met Maud Gonne there and became her devoted assistant, acting as Secretary of the Paris Young Ireland Society. In 1918 she followed the family back to Ireland, looking after Maud Gonne's affairs there while Maud was in Holloway prison. Her knee was shattered by a bullet in the Black and Tan war and she eventually went to live with the Gonne household at Roebuck House, Clonskeagh, Co. Dublin.

7

1. **Her Knighthood:** See previous letter where Sir Maurice is an aspect of Iseult's personality, and see p. 50 and note, p. 180.

2. **Madame Péguy:** Maud Gonne gave Yeats an account of the second equally unsatisfactory visit in a letter of 3 November 1916 (*GYL*, p. 363):

   She [Madame Péguy] said the French editor was publishing a collected edition of this work, & was afraid an English translation of part of it would prevent English readers from buying it – She also spoke vaguely of some young man in the trenches who had known her husband & was writing on him who might want to translate him into English . . . Iseult was very disappointed at not getting an answer as she likes the idea of translating Péguy very much.

3. **the editor:** Macmillan, the London publisher. Iseult is using the French word for publisher here.

4. **Dax:** see note, p. 183.

5. **Samois:** When Iseult was a year old Maud Gonne rented a house in Samois-sur-Seine (about 6 kilometres from Fontainbleu on the right bank of the Seine, bordered on either side by the river and the forest) in the Rue de Barbeau, a house which opened on to the street and had at the rear a courtyard with a well, and a walled garden beyond it. Maud's first child, Georges Sylvère, was buried in Samois and Iseult was conceived on his grave in the mausoleum Maud had built in the cemetery.

6. **we shall be starting now in a very short while**: Maud Gonne hoped to take the family to Ireland.
7. **Initiation by Steiner**: Rudolph Steiner (1861–1925), born at Kraljevec, an Austrian social philosopher, studied mathematics and science and edited Goethe's scientific papers at Weimar before coming under the influence of Mrs Annie Besant (1847–1933) and the Theosophists. He founded his own 'science' of spirituality, inventing 'Anthroposophy'. He established at Dornach near Basel a centre called the Gotheanium where he applied his theories, claiming that contemporary life had isolated artistic myth-making activity from practical activity; he aimed to reunite them for educational purposes. Steiner schools have been established very successfully in Europe and North America. His writings include *Philosophy of Spirituality, Knowledge of the Higher World* and *Outline of Occult Science*.
8. **Horton**: William Thomas Horton (1864–1919), born in Brussels, where he spent his early years, was an Irvingite, who lived in Brighton. He was a painter, an illustrator who had trained as an architect, whose mystical drawings appeared in *The Savoy* and in his *Book of Images* (1898) to which Yeats wrote an *Introduction*. He appears in Yeats's poem *All Souls' Night* (*YP*, p. 341) with reference to his Platonic relationship with Amy Audrey Locke (1881–1916). Maud Gonne and Iseult met him at lunch with Yeats at 18 Woburn Place (Yeats's London residence from 1895 to 1919) on 20 September 1917. See G.M. Harper, *W.B. Yeats and W.T. Horton* (1980). He was knocked down by a car in 1918 and died the following year, having become a convert to Catholicism.
9. **last summer... your biography**: In the summer of 1916 Yeats dictated a further instalment of his memoirs to Iseult when he was staying at Colleville. These were to succeed *Reveries over Childhood and Youth* (1916) and were entitled *The Trembling of the Veil*, Book I's title and subject being 'Four Years 1887–1891'.
10. **the winning of Quiet**: Cf. Yeats's early poem 'Maid Quiet' (*YP*, p. 105). He had written a letter to Iseult in November 1916 which is the subject of an entry, dated November, in her *Notebook*:

> Certainly I think that only Life matters. If by sacrifice we enrich the life (and that is enrich the love) of the soul it is right; but if we sacrifice the love for an idea we may for all our sacrifice become no more spiritual than a gambler at Monte Carlo who neglects his meals in his excitement.'

He continued that a little time given to that mystic meditation that all the East practises with perfect regularity may open the inner pathway to God, and added:

> Dear, there is but one sacrifice: the winning of Quiet. When one has found it, one can, I think, be kind and thoughtful as easily as a bird can fly or sing.'

11. **M. Cherfils... book of English poems... the best**: He was Christianne Cherfils' father. See note, p. 182. She quoted the poem 'The City of the Soul' by Lord Alfred Douglas, included in his volume of that name which was published in 1899. This was the book of English poems M. Cherfils had discovered on the Quays.
12. **Marcel Schwob**: A French scholar (1867–1905) who was also a poet, essayist and novelist, an early contributor to the *Mercure de France* (see note below on Samain).
13. **Jammes**: Francis Jammes (1868–1938) born at Tournay in the Pyrenees wrote poems of nature and religion, including *De l'angélus de l'aube a l'angélus du soir*

(1898), *Deuil des primivères* (1901), *Triomphe de la vie* (1904) and *Géorgiques Chrétiennes* (1911–12). His prose romances included *Le Roman du Lièvre* (1903).

14. **La Lampe de Psyche**: Published in Paris in 1903, it contained *Le Livre de Mouelle, Mimes, La Croisade des Enfants* and *L'Etoile de Bois*. It was Schwob's most perplexing book, striking but mentally anarchic, virtually incoherent at times.

15. **The poems of Samain**: Albert Samain (1858–1900), a French poet and dramatist born in Lille, a clerk in the Prefecture of the Seine, was one of the founders of the symbolist review *Mercure de France*, a fortnightly review which took its name from the periodical founded by Donneau de Visé in 1672 which lasted until 1825. Samain's collections of poems include *Au Jardin de l'Infante* (1893), *Aux Flancs de la Vase* (1898) and the posthumously published *Le Chariot d'Or*. His early poems were elegiac, their yearning note typical of much contemporary symbolist poetry. His later poems dealt with Greek antiquity in a dreamy way.

16. **two thoughts of Heraclitus**: 'The Harmony of the world comes back in itself like the lyre and the bow' (ό'u ξυνιασιν ὅπως διαφερομενον ἐωαυτῳ ὁμολογέιν παλιντροπος ἀρμόνη ὅκωσπερ τόξον καὶ λυρῃς). This dictum is numbered 51 in Hermann Diels Berlin edition of 1901; see also his *Die Fragmente der Vorsokratiker* (3 vols, 1903) and is numbered 45 in Bywater's edition, *Heracliti Ephesi Reliquae* (1877). 'The Daimon of Man is his destiny': this dictum was originally attributed to Xenophanes but transferred to Heraclitus by somebody who lived before Clement (who died before 215 A.D.) and Epiphanes (who died 403 A.D.). It is numbered 119 in Diel's edition of 1901 and 121 in Bywater's. Heraclitus (*fl.* 5th century B.C.), a pre-Socratic Greek philosopher, was born at Ephesus and founded his school there. He was known as the weeping philosopher because of his pessimistic outlook. His monistic theories were opposed by Parmenides. He believed that the first principle of the universe is change (becoming and perishing: flowing) but Parmenides, a native of Elea, a Greek settlement in Southern Italy (*fl.* 5th century B.C.) held that nothing changes. Heraclitus is best known 0for his statement πάντα ρεὶ, οὐδεν μένει (All is flux; nothing remains stationary).

## 8

1. **Major Lampton**: He was Head of the British Control Bureau in Paris and had received orders from London that he was to inform Maud Gonne that she could travel to England, but would not be allowed to proceed to Ireland. He was probably a friend of Maud's father, whom she remembered meeting as a child. (See *GYL*, p. 391.)

2. **us three and the cook Josephine**: Maud, Iseult, Sean and Josephine Pillon (1865–1927), who came from Normandy. She accompanied the family when they left France, lived with them in London, in 73 St Stephen's Green, Dublin and at Roebuck House, Clonskeagh, Co. Dublin, where she died.

3. **the editor of Madame Péguy**: the French publisher, who had agreed that Iseult could proceed with the translation of Péguy's poems into English if she could reach an arrangement with an English publisher (*GYL*, p. 385) *The Oevres Complètes de Charles Péguy 1873–1914* were published between 1916 and 1932 by Editions de la Nouvelle revue française.

4. **the English editor**: Maud Gonne told Yeats in a letter of 20 January 1917 that Iseult was waiting to hear from Meynell (*GYL*, p. 388). This was Sir Francis Meredith Wilfrid Meynell (1891–1973), the publisher, typographer and poet, educated at Downside and Trinity College, Dublin, who entered the firm of Burns & Oates (see note, p. 182). He founded the Nonesuch Press in 1923. His *Poems and Plays 1911–1961* appeared in 1961, and he was knighted in 1946.

5. **I haven't the heart to write anymore**: This may mean that she didn't want to write any more of this letter to Yeats, or, more likely, that she hadn't the energy to pursue her work on French Catholic writers and the Earth which she had begun. Maud Gonne wrote to Yeats on 20 January 1917 (*GYL*, p. 388) to suggest that he should ask Iseult to send him the article, as then she would have to finish it. Maud thought it 'VERY good.'

## 9

1. **Helen**: Helen ('Helena') Molony (1884–1967), known as 'Emer' in Inghinidhe na hEireann, which she joined in 1903. This was a women's organisation formed in 1900, of which Maud Gonne was elected President. It contributed to the nationalist movement by giving classes in Irish and History to children and developing an interest in drama which was one of the strands that led to the creation of the Abbey Theatre in Dublin. Helena Molony edited *Bean na hEireann* (*Woman of Ireland*), the paper of Inghindhe na hEireann, Ireland's first political women's paper which began publication in 1908. She joined the Abbey Players in 1909, the year she helped Constance, Countess Markiewicz to found the Fianna Eireann, a revolutionary scout movement for boys. She was arrested with the Countess in 1911 for taking part in anti-monarchical demonstrations. She stayed with Maud Gonne in France, recovering from breakdown before returning to Dublin in 1915. That year she was secretary of the Irish Women's Workers' Union, joined the Irish Citizen Army, and in 1916 took part in the attack on Dublin Castle, and was imprisoned. At the time of this letter she was in prison in Aylesbury. An opponent of the Treaty in 1922, she became President of the Irish Trades Union Congress in 1922–23 and continued to be active in political and trade union affairs. Though her interests and Iseult's were very different, she remained a close friend, frequently visiting Iseult when she lived at Laragh Castle (see note, p. 234). Her excessive drinking habits were a cause of concern to her friends.
2. **the poem I sent you**: This was 'The City of the Soul'. See pp. 69–71.
3. **the letter to the editor**: This was for the English publisher who was being offered Iseult's translations of Péguy's poems into English.

## 10

1. **Lane's pictures**: Sir Hugh Lane (1875–1915), Lady Gregory's nephew, was a successful picture dealer, who offered his collection of French Impressionist paintings to Dublin on condition they would be suitably housed. Disgusted by the reception of his gift, Lane placed the pictures in the National Gallery, London, leaving them to London in his will. However, he altered this bequest in an unwitnessed codicil, leaving them to Dublin instead. Yeats was involved in the controversy that ensued after Lane's death; he died when the *Lusitania* in which he was travelling was torpedoed by a German submarine in 1915. The pictures were retained in the Tate Gallery, London, until a compromise agreement was eventually reached in 1959 through which the pictures are now shared between London and Dublin.
2. **the theatre**: *At the Hawk's Well*, the first of Yeats's *Four Plays for Dancers* (1921); had been performed in Lady Cunard's drawing room in London in April 1916. It marked Yeats's interest in the Noh drama of Japan, to which Ezra Pound had introduced him, and demonstrated, as he put it in the *Preface* to the play when it was first published in *Harper's Bazaar* in March 1917, his disillusion with 'sending

my Muses where they are but half-welcomed'. He had no longer, he admitted, the appetite to carry him through 'the daily rehearsals.'

3. **Hugh Law:** Hugh Alexander Law (1872–1943) a barrister and MP for West Donegal, Assistant Secretary of the Irish Literary Society. (See a letter to him in this capacity from Yeats, dated 16 March 1907, *The Collected Letters of W.B. Yeats*, Vol III, ed. John Kelly and Ronald Schuchard (1994) p. 49.) In 1916, then a British Civil Servant, he had been helping Maud Gonne in her attempts to get back to Ireland. He wrote *Anglo-Irish Literature* (1926).

4. **Derfin:** unidentified; Develyn is crossed out in the text.

5. **Baily:** William Frederick Bailey (1847–1917), Irish Jurist and man of letters, was an Irish Land Commissioner and Governor of the National Gallery of Ireland. He aided Yeats's purchase of his tower in County Galway in 1917.

6. **old William Field:** (1848–1935) was a butcher by trade, who became an MP for the St Patrick's district of Dublin City from 1892–1918. A Parnellite, he followed John Redmond at the time of the split in the Irish Party. He appeared on many platforms with Maud Gonne, who was fond of him. He also helped in gaining a theatre licence for the Irish Literary Theatre, an issue Yeats discussed with him in 1898. Field did not introduce a specific Bill about the licence, but asked that the process of Private Bill legislation for Ireland should be simplified in order to make changes in the law easier to effect. See *Hansard*, 14 February 1898.

7. **Rummel the musician and his wife:** Walter Morse Rummel (1887–1953), an American composer and pianist, was the son of Franz Rummel (1853–1901), a distinguished German pianist, and the grandson of Samuel Morse, the inventor of the Morse code. Rummel, who had had an affair with the dancer Isadora Duncan, was Debussy's favourite pianist; he had a special interest in French and Provençal songs of the twelfth and thirteenth centuries. In 1911 he shared a house with Ezra Pound in London. See Ezra Pound, *Canto 104*, where he remembers Iseult Gonne, Walter Rummel and Ford Madox Ford: 'Iseult is dead, and Walter and Fordie'. Mrs Rummel, also interested in Provençal poetry, translated Yeats's *The Countess Cathleen* into French.

8. **Steiner's philosophy:** anthroposophy; see note on him, p. 185.

9. **Ella Young:** a mystic poet (1867/8–1956), a member of George Russell's Theosophist group, of Inghinidhe na hEireann and of Countess Markiewicz's Cumann na mBan, became Professor of Celtic Mythology in the University of California at Berkeley in 1925, moving to a theosophist community in Oceano in the Pacific ten years later. She wrote poetry and stories. Her *The Coming of Lug* (1909) and *Celtic Wonder Tales* (1910), as well as two other books of hers, were illustrated by Maud Gonne, who was a close friend. Iseult was translating some of Ella Young's Irish stories into French, but nothing seems to have come of this. Her autobiography, *Flowering Dusk*, was published in 1945, and contains some interesting vignettes of Maud Gonne and Iseult.

10. **Aylesbury:** Helena Molony (see note on her, p. 187) was in prison there.

11. **your castle:** Yeats called it Thoor (the Irish for tower, *tur*) Ballylee: it was called Ballylee Castle originally and was a medieval stone building, originally the property of the de Burgo family. It features in many of Yeats's poems, notably those of *The Tower* (1928) and *The Winding Stair* (1933). He had been interested in buying it from 1911 on, and finally completed the purchase, for £35, in 1917.

12. **Maurice:** See earlier note, p. 180.

**11**

1. **Minoulouche:** Iseult's black Persian cat, sometimes alluded to as he, sometimes as she. James Stephens (see note on him, p. 196) gave this cat to Maud Gonne in Paris and it became Iseult's pet: it was one of a pair of kittens produced by Stephen McKenna's cat (McKenna (1872–1934) was a translator, notably of the *Enneads* of Plotinus (5 vols, 1917–1930), a scholar and Gaelic revivalist. E.R. Dodds edited his *Journal and Letters* (1936)), which Stephens was looking after. He kept one kitten for himself which he called Noirro. Yeats refers to Minnaloushe (whose name was also spelled as Minoulouche, or Minoulooshe) in the *Prologue to Per Amica Silentia Lunae* (1917) and in the poem 'The Cat and the Moon' (*YP*, p. 273). Minou is used as an affectionate name for cats in France, or as a proper name for a cat.

2. **the possession of art treasures:** This refers to Yeats's involvement in the struggle to get Sir Hugh Lane's pictures back to Ireland. See note, p. 187.

3. **The Rummels:** See note p. 188.

4. **Annie Besant:** Annie Besant, neé Wood (1847–1933), born in London of Irish parents, was brought up in Harrow. At twenty she married the Rev. Frank Besant (brother of Sir Walter Besant, the novelist and advocate of social reform). She was separated from her husband in 1873, became a Theosophist in 1889 and its high priestess in 1891. She wrote her *Autobiography* in 1893.

5. **Michael Angelo:** Michelagniolo di Lodovico Buonarroti (1475–1564), the Italian sculptor, painter, poet, engineer and architect, was born in Tuscany. He was bound to Ghirlandaio for three years and then entered the School established by Lorenzo de' Medici, whose son did not treat him well, so he fled to Bologna, returned to Florence (where he completed his statue of David) and then moved to Rome for four years, summoned back there by Pope Julius II in 1503. He was ordered to paint the ceiling of the Sistine Chapel while hoping to complete the tomb of Julius (of which the statue of Moses remains.) He designed fortifications for Florence in 1529; his monuments to Giuliana and Lorenzo de' Medici were completed there and he became the architect of St Peter's at Rome.

6. **Leonardo da Vinci:** The Italian painter, sculptor, architect and engineer (1452–1519) who was born at Vinci, settled in Milan in 1482 where he attached himself to Lodovico Sforza, completing his painting *The Last Supper* there. He moved to Florence in 1503, entering the service of Cesare Borgia, Duke of Romagna. He completed the *Mona Lisa* in 1504 and was employed by Louis XII of France from 1505. In 1514 Francis I granted him the Chateau Cloux near Amboise, where he died.

7. **Villon:** François Villon (1431–?), the great French poet, born de Montcorbier or de Logos in Paris, took the name of his guardian Guillaume de Villon, a priest and close relative. He studied at the Sorbonne and graduated in 1449 and as an M.A. in 1542. He had to flee from Paris in 1455, having fatally wounded a priest in a street brawl. Pardoned in 1456, he returned to Paris and joined a criminal organisation, the Brotherhood of the Coquille, and wrote his *Petit Testament*. After taking part in an armed robbery he fled to Blois, where he was sentenced to death, but was released as an act of grace on a public holiday. The same thing happened at Meung-sur-Lovie in 1461, the year of his *Grand Testament*; he was again sentenced to death, but this time, in 1463, the sentence was commuted to banishment and he left Paris, nothing further being known about him. His poetry reflects the starkly ironic, dispassionate realism with which he infused medieval verse forms.

8. **Anacreon:** A late sixth century B.C. Greek lyric poet, born at Teos, an Ionian city in Asia Minor. He emigrated to Thrace, lived at the court of Polycrates of Samos, at Athens and elsewhere, finally dying at Teos at the age of 85, reputedly choked by a grape stone. He praised the Muses, love and wine: a few fragments of his five books survived; the majority of the *Odes* attributed to him probably are of later origin.

9. **Wagner:** Wilhelm Richard Wagner (1813–83), German composer born in Leipzig, was largely educated at Dresden. He became operatic conductor at Magdeburg, Königsberg and Riga. Owing to his revolutionary politics he was in exile for several years and experienced great poverty until Ludwig, King of Bavaria, provided him with a home at Munich. He later lived at Bayreuth where his festival of theatre was established in 1876. He wrote his own librettos, aiming at a central unity. His operas included *The Flying Dutchman, Tannhauser, Lohengrin, Tristan and Isolde, The Master Singers. Der Ring der Nibelungen* and *Parsifal* (1849–82).

10. **Steiner:** See note, p. 185.

11. **Nietzsche:** Friederich Wilhelm Nietzsche (1844–1900). A German philosopher, who studied at Bonn and Leipzig and, while still an undergraduate, was appointed Professor of Greek at Basle (1869–79). He became insane in 1889. His writings distinguished two ethical types, the weak and the strong (who had no need of utilitarian virtues.) Only by the morality of the strong can men, he argued, rise to the state of being supermen. His first work, *The Birth of Tragedy* (1871) was dedicated to his friend Wagner, whose operas he thought the successors to Greek tragedy. He broke with Wagner, however, regarding his *Parsival* as Christian-inspired, his *Frohliche Wissenschaft* [Joyous Wisdom] (1882) demonstrating this. His *Zarathustra* (1883–85) was his major work.

12. **Zarathustra:** *Also sprach Zarathustra* is the work in which Nietzsche developed his idea of the superman. His doctrines appealed to the Nazis, though he was himself neither a nationalist nor anti-Semitic. He greatly influenced existentialism.

13. **Science Occulte:** This appeared in English as *Outline of Occult Science.*

14. **Shelley and Keats:** Iseult told Richard Ellmann (see his *The Man and the Masks* (1988 edn, p. xiii) that Yeats had said to her that he had been rereading Shelley and Keats and thought it strange that he had ever seen anything in them. (This is recorded in his notes of an interview with Iseult in 1947; these are now in Tulsa). See the reference to Keats in Yeats's 'Ego Dominus Tuus' (*YP*, p. 266) and that to Shelley in 'The Phases of the Moon' (*YP*, p. 268). Both poems were written in 1918. See also the note on Donne, p. 181.

15. **The Dark night of the Soul:** This is a poem by St John of the Cross (Juan de Yepes y Alvarez, 1542–91), a Spanish mystic, founder with St Teresa of the Discalced Carmelites. He was born at Fontiveros, Avila. He accompanied St Teresa to Valladolid where he lived an ascetic life in a hovel; she appointed him to a convent in Avila. He was arrested and imprisoned in Toledo from 1576 to 1577 for following St Teresa's reformed movement. He escaped in 1578, lived at the monastery of Igbeda and was canonised in 1726. While imprisoned he wrote three linked poems, *The Dark Night of the Soul, The Living Flame of Love* and *The Spiritual Canticle.* These express religious feeling through sexual love. Yeats had a 1916 translation of St John of the Cross in his library, and may have owed his interest in this Spanish mystic's poems to Iseult.

**12**

1. **blocces:** French *blocage*, the blockade. Iseult is probably alluding to the presence of German U boats in the Channel.
2. **Mr Law:** see note on him, p. 188.
3. **Colleville:** See note, p. 179 and letter of 29 March, 1917, p. 79.
4. **quiet little icy attic:** The family was living on the seventh floor of 17 Rue de l'Annonciation at the time, having moved from the second floor in anticipation of going to Ireland.

**13**

1. **your order:** The Hermetic Order of the Golden Dawn, an occult society into which Yeats was initiated in 1890. See his *Autobiographies* (1980), note, p. 575, and text, p. 183 *ff.*, which give, inaccurately, the date of his initiation as May or June 1887. Maud Gonne was initiated into it on 2 November 1891 and left it in 1894, thinking its members 'the essence of British middleclass dullness'. Georgie Hyde Lees was initiated in 1914. Yeats had been initiated by Samuel Liddell Mathers (1854–1918), later MacGregor Mathers (see note, p. 192), who had composed the Order's elaborate rituals, drawing upon his knowledge of ancient Egyptian religions and of Freemasonry. He was formally expelled after he had involved Aleister Crowley (see note, p. 183) in seizing the vault of the Adepti in London in 1990, Yeats leading the opposition to him and reorganising the Order (see *WBYANB*, pp. 97–100). He remained a member himself, attaining the grade of Theoricus Adeptus Minor in 1912, but announcing, in the Notes to *The Trembling of the Veil* (*Autobiographies* (1980), p. 576), that he was not now a member of a Cabbalistic society. See R.A. Gilbert, 'Seeking that which was Lost: More Light on the Origins and Development of the Golden Dawn', *Yeats Annual*, no. 14, pp. 33–50, and Ellic Howe, *Magicians of the Golden Dawn* (1972).
2. **the Kabballa:** See note, p. 184.
3. **Steiner's theosophy:** See note, p. 185.
4. **a soothing chapter of Pater:** See note, pp. 180 and 181.
5. **George Dandin:** *George Dandin, ou le Mari confondu* (1668), a comedy in 3 acts by Molière (see note on him below) in which a husband has to put up patiently with his wife's extravagances.
6. **L'Etourdi:** *L'Etourdi, Le Depit Amoureux*, a five act comedy of intrigue in verse written by Molière, probably first played in Lyons in 1655, in Paris three years later.
7. **Mollière:** Molière was the stage name of Jean Baptiste Poquelin (1622–1773), the French dramatist who was born in Paris and studied in the Jesuit Collège de Clermont under the philosopher Gassendi and regular teachers of law. He inherited his share of his mother's property and began a theatrical venture, *L'Illustre Theatre*, with the Bejart family in 1643. The company failed after three years in Paris, but then survived by touring the provinces. Molière gained the patronage of the king's brother, Philippe d'Orléans, and organised a regular theatre in the petit Bourbon, later in the Palais Royal. He discovered his genius for comic writing, developing from a writer of successful farces to true comedy, writing a new play every year from 1659, the year his *Les Precieuses ridicules* was produced, to his best, and almost his last, *Les Femmes Savantes* (1672). In 1662 he married the nineteen-year-old Armande Bejart (according to some the daughter of Madeleine, reputedly Molière's lover); in 1665 the King (Louis XIV) adopted Molière's troupe as his own servants.

## 14

1. **your castle; that road**: Yeats sent Iseult a photograph of it and confirmed his purchase of it for £35 (see A. Norman Jeffares, *W.B. Yeats: Man and poet* (1996 edn), pp. 194–206). There was a road bridge beside the tower.
2. **Joyce's book**: *A Portrait of the Artist as a Young Man* (1916) by James Joyce (1882–1941). Maud Gonne, who had found the book 'deadly dull', passed it on to Iseult, but thought she would hardly have the courage to read it. She rallied Yeats about the novel: 'Tell me the truth – confess – you have not read the book yourself? Pound has perhaps read you extracts – isn't that so?' (*GYL*, p. 368, a letter of 16 March 1917).

## 15

1. **Madame Leroux**: Unidentified, probably a neighbour.
2. **Religio Medici...Urn Burial**: Works by Sir Thomas Browne (1605–82), a Londoner by birth, who was educated at Winchester and Broadgates Hall, Oxford before studying medicine at Montpellier, Padua and Leyden (where he graduated as a physician). He settled in Norwich in 1637, and was knighted in 1671. *Religio Medici*, written some years earlier at Shipden Hall, near Halifax, appeared without his permission in 1642, with it in 1643. It is a confession of Christian faith, modified by Brown's sceptical attitudes and accompanied by a collection of opinions on a large number of subjects. *Urn Burial*, or *Hydriotaphia* was published with *The Garden of Cyrus* in 1658. In a meditative fashion Browne considers various modes of disposing of the dead in Britain, this done in a rhetorical prose of the most evocative kind.
3. **Guabalastic**: Iseult's somewhat idiosyncratic spelling of Kabbalistic or Cabbalistic. See earlier note on the Kabbalah, p. 184.
4. **MacGregor**: See earlier note on **your order**, p. 191.
5. **very dark...His wife**: Moina, neé Bergson, sister of the philosopher Henri Bergson. In 1894 the Mathers moved to Paris and lived in a flat at 1 Avenue Duquesne, Champ de Mars, where Yeats stayed with them on various occasions. Mathers had previously been Curator of the Horniman Museum in London. They were financed in Paris by Annie Horniman (1860–1937) for some years, but she gave this up in 1896, being upset by Mathers' Jacobite politics (he styled himself the Comte de Glenstrae and went about in highland dress), by his excessive drinking and general extravagance. Monia, an artist, kept the household going while Mathers went downhill, and is reputed to have died as the result of a psychic duel with Aleister Crowley (see note, p. 183). Yeats and Mathers remained estranged after the quarrelling over the Order of the Golden Dawn in 1900, until his death. He is commemorated in Yeats's poem 'All Souls' Night' (*YP*, p. 340)
6. **Horton**: See earlier note, p. 185.
7. **Demeter**: An ancient goddess of corn or of the earth and its fertility whom the Romans called Ceres. Here Iseult is suggesting that Maud is something of an earth-mother presiding over agriculture, or, in her case, being content with a country life, accepting its seasonal rhythms and especially the harvest time of summer and early autumn.
8. **Minoulouche**: Iseult's cat. See earlier note, p. 189.

## 16

1. **books of Morris**: Yeats may have given Iseult those prose romances of William Morris (1834–96), the English craftsman and pre-Raphaelite author, which

greatly pleased him. He once wrote that *The Sundering Flood* and *News from Nowhere* were the only books he ever read slowly 'so that I might not come quickly to the end.' See J. Hone, *W.B. Yeats 1865–1939* (1942), p. 65.

2. **the delightful family of Morris:** Iseult is presumably here including May Morris, William's daughter.

3. **your castle:** See note, pp. 183 and 192.

4. **the cockrooch:** See note, p. 183.

5. **tobacco:** Iseult was a heavy smoker.

6. **A book of St Ignatius of Loyola:** One of the *Spiritual Exercises* written by Ignatius de Loyola (1491–1556), Inigo Lopez de Recalde, a Spanish soldier and ecclesiastic. Born at his ancestral castle of Loyola in the Basque province of Guipuzcoa, he became a page, then was badly wounded in the siege of Pamplona and renounced soldiering. He tended the sick in the hospital at Manresa, withdrew to practise austerity and became ill. He went to Rome, Venice and Cyprus and the Holy Land, returning to Venice and Barcelona in 1524. He founded the Society of Jesus with five associates in 1534, but instead of the intended pilgrimage to the Holy Land (which was cut off by the Turks) he went to Rome to submit the rules of his proposed Order, of which he became the first General in 1541. His *Spiritual Exercises*, finished in 1548, were intended for the training of Jesuits, who were bound by vows of chastity, poverty and obedience, and formed a spiritual army designed to support the Roman church against sixteenth century reformers, and to carry out missionary work among the heathen. He was beatified in 1609 and canonized in 1622.

Iseult is referring to *Exercise VII* here:

> If he who gives the Exercises sees that he who receives them is in desolation and temptation, let him not be severe with him but kind and gentle, encouraging and strengthening him for the future, pointing out to him the wiles of the enemy of human nature and exhorting him to prepare and dispose himself for future consolation.

*Exercise VI* has prepared for this:

> When he who gives the *Exercises* finds that the exercitant experiences no spiritual movements in his soul such as consolation or desolation nor is agitated by diverse spirits he ought to question him fully about the *Exercises* whether he makes them at the right times and how . . .

*Exercise VIII* is also germane:

> He who gives the *Exercises* according to what he perceives to be the need of the exercitant as regards desolation and the wiles of the enemy, and also as regards consolation, may explain the rules of the First and of the Second Week which are for discerning the various spirits.

The rules for the Discernment of Spirits include *III*, 'Of Spiritual Consolation':

> When there is excited in the soul some interior movement by which it begins to be inflamed with love of its Creator and Lord, and when, consequently, it cannot love any created on the face of the earth in itself but only the Creator of all.

And *IV* 'Of Spiritual Desolation':

> I call by the name of Desolation all that is contrary to what is described in the third Rule, such as darkness and confusion of soul, attraction towards base and earthly objects, disquietude caused by various agitations and temptations which makes the soul distrustful, without hope and love, so that it finds itself altogether slothful, tepid and as it were, separated from its Creator and Lord. For as consolation is contrary to desolation so the thoughts that spring from consolation are contrary to those that spring from desolation.

*V, VI,* and *VII* urge the need to stand firm in time of desolation, to be constant to resolutions made the day before the desolation, argue that it is helpful to make a change in his opposition to desolation, and urge the person in desolation to consider how the Lord, to prove him, has left him to his own natural powers with sufficient grace left to him to ensure his salvation.

*VIII* stresses the need for persevering in patience while *IX* gives three reasons for desolation. *X* suggests that in a state of confusion it is wise to lay up fresh strength to combat desolation and *XI* urges the man in a state of desolation to remember to humble himself and remember when in desolation that he can achieve much with the grace that he is given (which is sufficient enough for him to resist his enemies). These quotations have been taken from *The Spiritual Exercises of Saint Ignatius of Loyola,* translated from the Spanish with a commentary and translation of the *Directorium in exercitia* by W.B. Langridge (1919), pp. 12–13 and 184–8.

7.   **old Cherfils**: See note on him, p. 182.

## 17

1.   **These revelations**: Possibly from a séance with Geraldine Cummins, one of Yeats's favourite mediums (he attended a séance with her sometime in 1916) and found the plot of his play *The Dreaming of the Bones* (1919), (*Collected Plays* (1952), pp. 431–55) was being realised in her communications. See Katharine Worth, 'The Words upon the Window-Pane: A Female Tragedy', *Yeats Annual*, no. 10 (1993), p. 139 and notes, p. 156. Another medium, Hester Travers-Smith, recorded in *Voices from the Void: Six Years' Experience in Automatic Communication* (1919) how she contacted Sir Hugh Lane's spirit after he drowned in the U Boat's torpedoing of the *Lusitania* in 1915. It is possible that Yeats was consulting her in 1917 about the Lane bequest (see note, p. 187). He also used Elizabeth Radcliffe ('Miss X'), an English medium, in an attempt to find a second will made by Lane. See Lady Gregory, *Sir Hugh Lane: His Life and Legacy* (1973), pp. 209–15. It is, however, most likely that 'these revelations' came from some séance in Dublin.

2.   **your castle...The L shape**: There were two single-storied thatched cottages adjoining the tower, which was rectangular in shape and had three rooms one above the other, connected by a winding stair.

3.   **May's villa in Florence**: The Villa Castiglione (into which they moved from a hotel in 1911) on the Via Montughi. See note, p. 178. Iseult stayed there with her in 1912.

4.   **flowing water under your windows**: See Yeats's poem 'In Memory of Major Robert Gregory' (*YP*, p. 234) with its

> The tower set on the stream's edge
> The ford where drinking cattle make a stir

and 'Coole and Ballylee, 1931' (*YP*, p. 358) with its

> Under my window-ledge the water race.

5. **for a knight**. See note on Sir Maurice, p. 180.
6. **Minoulouche's ears**: A reference to her cat. See note, p. 189.
7. **translations from Péguy**: See earlier Letters, pp. 61 and 67.
8. **trouble for nothing**: Yeats had been trying to find an English publisher for Iseult's proposed translations of Péguy's poems into English.

**18**
1. **Minoulouche and I...in your book**: A reference to Yeats's *Prologue*, dated 11 May 1917, to his *Per Amica Silentia Lunae* (1917); this is quoted on p. 182.
2. **the Epilogue**: Here is the text of it minus the last two paragraphs included in note 2, Letter 6, p. 182 (from W.B. Yeats, *A Vision and Related Writings*, ed. A. Norman Jeffares (1990), pp. 63–4):

My dear 'Maurice' – I was often in France before you were born or when you were but a little child. When I went for the first or second time Mallarmé had just written: 'All our age is full of the trembling of the veil of the Temple.' One met everywhere young men of letters who talked of magic. A distinguished English man of letters asked me to call with him on Stanislas de Gaeta because he did not dare go alone to that mysterious house. I met from time to time, with the German poet Dauthendey, a grave Swede whom I only discovered after years to have been Strindberg, then looking for the philosophers' stone in a lodging near the Luxembourg ; and one day, in the chambers of Stuart Merrill the poet, I spoke with a young Arabic scholar who displayed a large, roughly-made gold ring which had grown to the shape of his finger. Its gold had no hardening alloy, he said, because it was made by his master, a Jewish Rabbi, of alchemical gold. My critical mind – was it friend or enemy? – mocked, and yet I was delighted. Paris was as legendary as Connacht. This new pride, that of the adept, was added to the pride of the artist. Villiers de l'Isle-Adam, the haughtiest of men, had but lately died. I had read his *Axel* slowly and laboriously as one reads a sacred book – my French was very bad – and had applauded it upon the stage. As I could not follow the spoken words, I was not bored even when Axel and the Commander discussed philosophy for a half-hour instead of beginning their duel. If I felt impatient it was only that they delayed the coming of the adept Janus, for I hoped to recognise the moment when Axel cries: 'I know that lamp, it was burning before Solomon'; or that other when he cries: 'As for living our servants with do that for us.'

The movement of letters had been haughty even before Magic had touched it. Rimbaud had sung: 'Am I an old maid that I should fear the embrace of death?' And everywhere in Paris and in London young men boasted of the garret, and claimed to have no need of what the crowd values.

For the conclusion see note 2, on Letter 6, p. 182.
3. **Where you write: 'Have I not too travelled through a like thought ?'**: Iseult is querying Yeats's claim in the last paragraph of the *Epilogue*: 'Have not my thoughts run through a like round...' with its comment that the Catholic church's tradition is more universal, more ancient.
4. **Péguy**: See note on Madame Péguy, p. 179.
5. **Villiers de l'Isle Adam**: Auguste, Comte de Villiers de l'Isle Adam (1838–89), French author, a pioneer of the symbolist movement, was born at St Brieuc. A Breton count, he claimed descent from the Knights of Malta. His *Premières*

*Poésies* (1856–58) were followed by the short stories of *Contes cruels* (1883) and *Nouveaux Contes cruels* (1888), reminiscent of Edgar Allen Poe. His novels and plays were didactic, the best of them *Axel* (1885), a performance of which Yeats attended in Paris with Maud Gonne in 1894. Yeats liked quoting his remark 'As for living our servants will do that for us.'

6.   **Huysmans:** Joris Karl Huysmans (1848–1907), born in Paris, was of Dutch extraction. A novelist and art critic, he moved from the realism of *Les Sœurs Vatard* (1879) and *A vau-l'eau* (1882) to the novel that became known as his most famous work, *A Rebours* (1884) with its hero Des Esseintes, who, disgusted by his times and his own personality, tries to find a reason for living in his search of art and literature. (His use of artifice as a specific for disgust influenced Oscar Wilde's writing of *The Picture of Dorian Gray* (1890)). He turned to mysticism and magic in *Là-Bas* (1891) and then, with *En Route* (1892), returned to Catholicism. (Iseult read this novel before she was 17, and it had a considerable effect on her – as on many others. Her sense of beauty was then blended with her religious feelings.) Huysmans said in it that he had tried to trace the progress of a soul surprised by the gift of grace and developing...'to the accompaniment of mystical literature, liturgy and plain chant'. Arthur Symons, in *The Symbolist Movement in Literature* (1899; 1919) thought it was perhaps the first novel that did not set out to amuse its readers. It could be considered, he said, on the same level as *Paradise Lost* or the *Confessions* of Saint Augustine. In his *Art Moderne* (1882), an autobiography, Huysmans wrote well of Impressionist painting.

7.   **Pater:** See note, p. 180.

8.   **Moura:** Maud Gonne, see note, p. 178.

9.   **the Daimon:** See note, p. 181.

10.   **Mowrer:** Paul Scott Mowrer (1887–?), a brother of Edgar Mowrer, was born in Bloomington, Indiana. Both brothers served on the *Chicago Daily News*, Paul as a foreign and war correspondent and an expert on foreign affairs. He won a Pulitzer Award in 1928 for his work as a foreign correspondent, his books including *Balkanised Europe* (1921) and *On Foreign Affairs* (1924). His autobiography, *The House of Europe*, appeared in 1945, and he published several books of poems which include *Hours of France* (1918), *Poems between Wars* (1941), *Twenty-one and Sixty-five* (1958) and *The Mothering Hand* (1960).

11.   **Stephens:** James Stephens (?1880/1882–1959), poet, novelist, short-story writer and conversationalist, was born in Dublin. In 1896 he worked as a clerk-typist in the office of a Dublin solicitor, Mecredy (Oliver St John Gogarty gives an amusing account of how Stephens sacked himself from this firm in *It isn't This Time of Year at All* (1954), p. 196). Stephens lived in Paris from 1912 to 1915 when he returned to Dublin as Registrar of the National Gallery of Ireland, a post he held till 1924, moving to England in 1925. His early poems, *Insurrections* (1909), and his novels *The Charwoman's Daughter* (1912), *The Crock of Gold* (1912), and *The Demi-Gods* (1914), blend realism and fantasy. He frequently undertook lecture tours in America, drawing, in part, on the interest he had developed in the Gaelic literary tradition; this had resulted in his *Irish Fairy Tales* (1920), *Deirdre* (1923) and *In the Land of Youth* (1924). His *Collected Poems* appeared in 1926, a revised edition in 1954. He gave more than 70 talks for the BBC, the best collected in *James, Seamus and Jacques, Unpublished Writings of James Stephens* (1964). His graphic account of the Easter Rising, *The Insurrection in Dublin*, was republished by Colin Smythe Ltd in 1992 with an *Introduction* and *Afterword* by John A. Murphy.

12.   **Minoulouche's thanks:** See note, p. 189.

**19**

1. **here**: at Les Mouettes.
2. **your castle**: see notes pp. 188 and 192.
3. **Maurice**: See note, p. 180.

**20**

1. **Dax**: See note, p. 183 Maud found the mineral baths there efficacious in the treatment of her rheumatism.
2. **that essay of yours**: Possibly *Per Amica Silentia Lunae* (1918).
3. **Seeger**: Alan Seeger (1888–1916), an American poet, born in New York, who graduated from Harvard University in 1910. Having gone to Paris in 1913, he enlisted in the French Foreign Legion at the outbreak of the First World War and was wounded on 4 July in the Battle of the Somme, where he committed suicide. His posthumous *Poems* (Paris, 1916), for which William Archer wrote an Introduction, contained the well-known 'I have a Rendezvous with Death'. T.S. Eliot, a former classmate at Harvard, reviewed the book favourably in *The Egoist* remarking that Seeger 'lived his life…with impeccable poetic dignity.' His *Letters and Diary* appeared in 1917. He was awarded a posthumous Croix de Guerre and Medaille Militaire.
4. **The Abbey Theatre…closed now for the duration of the war or not**: It was only closed for Easter Week, 1916.
5. **Helen Molony**: See note on her, p. 187.
6. **her old mania**: This may refer to Helena Molony's excessive drinking.

**21**

1. **Georgie**: Bertha Georgie Hyde Lees (1882–1968), then living with her mother Nellie and stepfather, Henry Tudor (Harry) Tucker, who was Olivia Shakespear's brother. Yeats called her George after their marriage. She was studying astrology, reading philosophy, and was interested in the Tarot cards. She was admitted to the to the Order of the Golden Dawn in 1914, and attended séances with Yeats, whom she met in 1911 and with whom she had become friendly. Her mother feared that he might propose to her in 1915, and he had already discussed marriage with her. She had confided to her cousin Grace that she intended to marry the poet. She became involved in war work as a hospital cook and nursing assistant. The fact that Maud Gonne had become a widow when John MacBride was executed in 1916 altered matters; Yeats then switched his attention to Maud and Iseult, proposing to Maud and being refused in the usual way, and then proposing to Iseult. Iseult recorded her reactions to Yeats's proposal in a letter to her cousin Thora Pilcher:

> Willie Yeats and I read a lot together, he is very interested just now in the movement of young Catholic literature in France, and I have to translate for him all the books of Péguy and Claudel and…but that's quite between us, he has proposed to me :
> Thirty years' difference is all the same a little too much, so, of course, I said *No* and it didn't seem to affect him much, he has lost no appetite through this; so I came to the conviction that he had merely done it to follow a mad code of politeness which he has made for himself: he often told me: 'I think that a proposal is the myrrh and the incense which every beautiful young woman has the right to expect from every man who comes near her'.
> I think, alas that the myrrh and the incense are not the compliments or the love that we receive but the love which we give. That alone would be happiness

and a real homage to oneself. I wish I could fall in love: But I am almost afraid I never will!

When the entire Gonne family entourage, with all its birds and animals, was moving to London in 1917 with the intention of proceeding to Dublin, something forbidden by the British authorities under the Defence of the Realm Act, Yeats, who had got them their passports and accompanied them to England, told Iseult on the boat that she must give him a definite answer within a week; they were to meet at an ABC teashop in London then. If she would not marry him, he said, he knew someone else who would, a friend who was 'strikingly beautiful in a barbaric way'.

2. **Moura tells me you are going to be married on the 20th**: Iseult had refused him and some confusion arose, as he sent a series of letters to Lady Gregory, having decided that he would ask Georgie Hyde Lees to marry him. In one letter he told Lady Gregory that Georgie might have become tired of the idea; he would, however, make it clear that he would 'still be friend and guardian to Iseult'.

3. **I came home full of thought on the beauty of silence**: 'The beauty of silence is a quotation from Alan Seeger's 'Broceliande':

Broceliande! in the perilous beauty of silence and menacing shade,
Thou art set on the shores of the sea down the haze
    of horizons untravelled, unscanned.
Untroubled, untouched with the woes of this world
 Are the moon-marshalled hosts that invade
                    Broceliande.
Only at dusk, when lavender clouds in the orient twilight disband,
Vanishing where all the blue afternoon they have drifted in solemn parade,
Sometimes a whisper comes down on the wind from the valleys of Fairyland ——
Sometimes an echo most mournful and faint like the horn of a huntsman strayed
Faint and forlorn, half drowned in the murmur of foliage fitfully fanned,
Breathes in a burden of nameless regret till I startle,
    disturbed and affrayed:
                    Broceliande –
                    Broceliande –
                    Broceliande . . . .

See note on Seeger on p. 197 and Iseult's comments on him in previous Letter 20.

4. **Sturge Moore**: Thomas Sturge Moore (1870–1944), elder brother of the philosopher George Edward Moore, was an English poet, dramatist, critic, designer and wood engraver, born in Hastings, Sussex. Laurence Binyon, the poet and art critic who was in charge of oriental prints and paintings in the British Museum (he wrote the first European treatise on *Painting in the Far East* (1908), followed by his *Japanese Art* (1909)) introduced him to Yeats in 1899; they became lifelong friends and collaborators. Their correspondence shows Yeats's developing stagecraft and his criticisms of Moore's impracticality as a stage designer. Sturge Moore designed beautiful covers for twelve of Yeats's books, these for *The Tower* (1928) and *Last Poems and Plays* (1940) being particularly effective. See *W.B. Yeats and T. Sturge Moore: Their Correspondence*, ed. Ursula Bridges (1953), F.L. Gwynn, *Sturge Moore and the Life of Art* (1951) and Moore's own article 'Yeats' *English*, 2:11, 1939, pp. 273–8.

5. **a little society ... 'who love poetry'**: There were several such coteries in London at the time. This one may have been Ezra Pound's circle, or it may have been the one which met at the Poetry Bookshop. See J. Grant, *Harold Monro and the Poetry Bookshop* (1967). Sturge Moore was in touch with both groups.

6. **My little Cat**: Thora Forrester (neé Pilcher, 1892–1983), Iseult's cousin, the daughter of Maud Gonne's sister Kathleen Pilcher (neé Gonne, 1868–1919).

7. **until Thursday**: Ezra Pound's group met at the Chinese Restaurant in Regent Street. The Poetry Bookshop group met at the Poetry Bookshop in Bloomsbury, on Thursdays also.

## 22

1. **the essay**: One of Iseult's essays on Beauty, probably the one beginning 'I went to see the pictures of a man who called himself a realist'. This had as starting point an exhibition of work by Wyndham Lewis. Born on a yacht in the Bay of Fundy, Percy Wyndham Lewis (1882–1957) was educated at Rugby School and the Slade School of Art, London. He travelled on the continent from 1902–08, then settled in London where he was a co-founder of the Camden Town group of artists in 1911, a founder of the Vorticist group in 1913, a member of Roger Fry's Omega Workshops in 1913, and a founder with T.S. Eliot and Ezra Pound of *Blast*, 1914–15. After a year with the Royal Artillery he became a war artist from 1917 to 1919. He founded X group in 1920 and travelled in France with T.S. Eliot in 1921. In 1929 he married Gladys Anne Joskins (see note on Iris Barry and his relationship with her, p. 201). His work included fiction, of which *Tarr* (1918) and *The Apes of God* (1930), a satire on Bloomsbury, are perhaps the best known. *Time and Western Man* (1927), the autobiographical *Blasting and Bombardiering* (1937) and *Rude Assignment* (1949) are still effective examples of his lively versatility.

2. **the Oriental School**: Yeats had got Iseult a post as assistant librarian at the School of Oriental Studies in the University of London through his friendship with the Director of the School, the distinguished orientalist Sir Edward Denison Ross (1871–1940). Educated at Marlborough School and University College, London, he studied Oriental languages on the continent, obtaining a Ph.D. at Strasbourg. Professor of Persian at University College, London (1896–1901), he was Principal of Calcutta Madrasah (1901–11), then worked in the British Museum before becoming Director of the School of Oriental Studies and Professor of Persian in London University (1916–37). He was knighted in 1918 and served as counsellor in the British Embassy, Istanbul (1939–40). He edited an Arabian manuscript history of Gujerat (3 vols, 1910–28.)

3. **your first letter**: This refers to Yeats's proposals to Iseult in the summer of 1917 (he had first proposed to her in 1916, a week after proposing to her mother). He had told her on the cross-channel ferry – he was accompanying the Gonne family to England – (see note, p. 198) that she must answer him a week after the family had reached London in 1917. She told me [A.N.J] that she had greatly enjoyed flirting with him in the summers of 1916 and 1917, but, as her letter to Thora confirms (see note, p. 197), she finally rejected him because of the difference in age between them, something to which his letter to her had referred. It had been written in a spirit of misery shortly after his marriage. See also his poem 'Owen Aherne and his Dancers' (*YP*, p. 328) which records some of his reactions to realising he was too old for her.

4. **Willy ... not be happy**: Yeats married Georgie Hyde Lees on 20 October 1917 and wrote 'Owen Aherne and his Dancers', the first section on 24 October and the second on 27 October. The poems were originally entitled 'The Lover Speaks' and 'The Heart Replies'; the first was a somewhat mythologised version of his courting Iseult in Normandy, the second introduced his wife into the poem as well as Iseult. They were first published in *The Dial*, June 1924, and in the Cuala Press volume of Yeats's poems, *The Cat and the Moon and Certain Poems* (1924). The title 'Owen Aherne and his Dancers' was first given to them in *The Tower* (1928) and subsequently (see *YP*, p. 328 and pp. 589–90). They record his emotional turmoil in the days immediately after his wedding; in this letter Iseult advises him to renounce for a time the life of emotion though it is very doubtful whether he could have adopted instead her suggestion of living on a few maxims of the early Patricians. Owen Aherne was an invented persona who appears elsewhere in Yeats's poems and prose, a disguise for aspects of Yeats's own personality. In this poem Aherne is worried about Iseult as well as being angry that he is too old for her. But 'the woman at my side', his wife, began the automatic writing which released his tension and unhappiness and was the basis of *A Vision* (1925).

5. **rush of emotion ... as in Havre**: See Yeats's letter (quoted by Joseph Hone, *W.B. Yeats 1885–1939* (1942), p. 306) which described how 'Poor Iseult was very depressed on the journey, and at Havre went off by herself and cried because she was so ashamed at being so selfish in not wanting me to marry and so break her friendship with me.'

6. **Hermas and Cypris**: Hermes, the herald and messenger of the gods and the guide and helper of travellers. He was passionately in love with Aphrodite who did not return his love. (In one version of the legend she gratified his desires in order to get one of her sandals back from him, it having been stolen for him by the eagle sent by Zeus, who had taken pity on the love-stricken herald.) Cypris was another name given to Aphrodite, as Cyprus was one of the chief centres of her cult. In one account she was said to have come ashore on the island after her birth in the sea (Greek *aphros* means foam). Here Hermes and Cypris represent respectively Wisdom and Beauty although Iseult may be referring to the Hermes Trismegistus of occult tradition rather than to the Hermes of classical legend. Aphrodite was the goddess of erotic love, so Iseult may be suggesting here that knowledge and love are not enough, that Christ is the true source of peace.

7. **the early Patricians**: This was a title borne by numerous princes in medieval Europe from the eighth to the twelfth centuries. Here, however, Iseult is alluding to the writers on Christian doctrine of the pre-Scholiastic period. She probably had Marcus Aurelius particularly in mind, his predilection for 'nobility' being one she shared with Yeats; both of them probably found it also in Nietzsche. It can be noticed in Yeats's plays *At the Hawk's Well* (1916) and *The Only Jealousy of Emer* (1918).

8. **When you tell me 'All is well'**: Yeats's marriage was saved by his wife's automatic writing, which told him 'with the bird [Iseult] all is well at heart' See *WBYANB*, pp. 222–6, and 'Iseult Gonne', *Yeats Annual*, No. 16, Palgrave Macmillan (forthcoming 2004).

## 23

1. **the Sanskrit and Bengali professors**: one of Iseult's teachers was Lionel David Barnett.

2. **Dr Ross:** Sir Denison Ross who seems to have advised Iseult on her Bengali Studies, which she continued for a time at the School, though she was soon studying Sanskrit as well.

3. **Miss Barry:** Iris Barry (1895–1969), born Frieda Crump in Birmingham, seems to have adopted the name Iris Barry. She began publishing poetry c. 1914 (four of her poems were published by Harold Monro in *Poetry and Drama*, December 1914) and was encouraged to come to London in 1916 by Ezra Pound, through whom she met Yeats and Wyndham Lewis. She worked as an Assistant Librarian at the School of Oriental Studies. Pound published eight of her lyrics in *The Little Review* in August 1917; these were very much in his style. Her 'Nishi Hongwanji' appeared in *The Little Review* in July 1918. She became Wyndham Lewis's mistress (see note on him, p. 199), living with him from 1918 to 1921. He drew and painted portraits of her, the best as 'Praxitella' in 1921. They had two children, in June 1919 and September 1920; the daughter was adopted and the son farmed out, Lewis taking no responsibility for her or the children. She wrote three novels: *Splashing into Society* (1923) – a parody of Daisy Ashford's *The Young Visiters* (1919) – *The Last Enemy* (1929) and *Here is Victory* (1930). Ezra Pound wrote to Margaret Anderson on 11 June 1917 that Iris Barry has done 'the draft of a novel (nearer Joyce *in spots* than any female established novelist has yet to come) and it has the chance of being literature'. She also wrote a biography of Lady Wortley Montagu in 1928, and edited the *Memoirs* of Laetitia Pilkington (1748–54), also in 1928. She became known for her work as the *Daily Mail's* film critic (1925–30), publishing *Let's go to the Pictures* (1926), by which time she had seen over 3000 films. She married Alan Porter (see note on her fiancé, p. 204) and later John Abbott, an American financier, having moved to the States in 1930, and, playing a significant role in the history of cinematography, developed the world's first film library at the Museum of Modern Art in New York. She was its Curator until she retired, in 1950, to Greece, where she lived with a smuggler 20 years her junior. She died in France. Particularly interesting in the present context is her 'The Ezra Pound Period' in *The Bookman*, LXXIV, October 1931, pp. 159–71. In this she refers to Iseult as 'the young woman who married – [Francis Stuart] and went to live in a ruined castle'.

4. **Ivan the Terrible:** Ivan the Terrible was Ivan IV (1533–84), Grand Duke of Muscovy, first Tsar of Russia (1547–84), who conquered Kazan, Astrakhan and Siberia but was defeated by Poland in the Livonian War (1558–82), after which his rule became increasingly oppressive and despotic. Iseult is referring to the opera by Nikolai Andreievich Rimsky-Korsakov (1844–1908) called *The Maid of Pskov* which he began in 1868, a revised version of which was staged by Diaghilev as *Ivan the Terrible* in 1908.

5. **that line of yours:** 'When her soul flies . . . dancing place.' This is the first line of 'Her Courage.' Section VI of Yeats's poem 'Upon a Dying Lady' (*YP*, p. 263) written about Aubrey Beardsley's sister Mabel (1871–1916), who was dying of cancer. It was first published in *The Little Review* under the title 'Seven Poems', August 1917; it was written between January 1912 and July 1914.

6. **Eliot and Lewis:** Iris Barry was evidently *au fait* with the latest contemporary poetry and with poets living in London. The first volume of poems by T.S. Eliot (1888–1965), *Prufrock and Other Observations*, was published in 1917. She would, obviously, have read the work of Wyndham Lewis, co-founder with Ezra Pound of *Blast*, the magazine of the Vorticist School. See note on Lewis, p. 199. Humphrey Carpenter, *A Serious Character. The Life of Ezra Pound* (1988), p. 263, writes

of Eliot 'being passionately but mutely adored by the three of four young females who had been allowed in [to Ezra Pound's Thursday evening gatherings] because of some crumb of promise in painting or verse.' Eliot, born in St Louis, Missouri, spent four years at Harvard and a year in Paris before returning to Harvard to study philosophy for three years. After that he had a year at Oxford. Ezra Pound persuaded him to stay on in England, where he became naturalised in 1927. At the time Iseult wrote this letter Iris Barry was very much under the influence of the modernism of Eliot and of Pound's poetic style as well as being impressed by Wyndham Lewis's work. See note on her, p. 201.

## 24

1. **Arthur Symons**: Born of Cornish stock in Wales (1865–1945) he translated d'Annunzio in 1902 and Baudelaire in 1925. His *The Symbolist Movement in Literature* (1899) was most influential. He and Yeats were close friends: he sub-let some of his rooms in Fountain Court in the Middle Temple to Yeats, who moved there, leaving the family home for the first time, in October 1895. Symons accompanied him on a visit to the Aran isles in the summer of 1896. A member of the Rhymers' Club, he edited *The Savoy* (1896). In 1908–10 he had a nervous collapse, from which he recovered, aided by various friends and helped by the Royal Literary Fund. His *Confessions: A Study in Pathology* (1930) give a horrifying account of his collapse in Italy when he was thrown into prison in Ferrara and his subsequent experience of mental hospitals in England, of his delusions and of the cruelty with which he was treated.

2. **John's pictures**: Augustus (Edwin) John (1878–1961), born at Tenby, was trained at the Slade School, London. His Autobiography *Chiaroscuro* (1952) contains anecdotes about the writers he knew, who included Wilde, Shaw, Yeats, Joyce, Gogarty and Wyndham Lewis. Among other authors he painted Shaw, Yeats, Joyce, Gogarty, T.E. Lawrence and Dylan Thomas. This particular exhibition was held in the Alpine Club on Mill Street off Conduit Street. See Michael Holroyd, *Augustus John. A Biography*, II, (1965), p. 64.

3. **His wife**: Rhoda Bowser (1874–1936), the daughter of a wealthy Newcastle ship-builder and shipowner, to whom Symons had proposed in May 1900 and whom he married on 19 January 1901. Iseult's characterisation of her as appalling was justifiable.

4. **I have been touched by him**: As he was by Iseult, of whom he saw a good deal in the latter part of 1917. (She dined with him on Tuesday 27 November 1917, a meeting he celebrated in his poem 'Deirdre'.) They also met fairly often in the summer of 1918. He gave her inscribed copies of *Knave of Hearts* (1913), *Tragedies* (1916), *Tristan and Iseult* (1917) and later *The Symbolist Movement in Literature* (the American edition of 1919). He dedicated his *Colour Studies in Paris* (1916) to her, inscribing her copy 'To Iseult of Ireland from Arthur of Cornwall' (although of Cornish stock, he was born in Milford Haven, Pembrokeshire). His 'Song for Iseult' was included in his *Lesbia and Other Poems* (1920). Iseult helped him with his translation of Baudelaire, on which he had been working intermittently for two years. Somewhat surprisingly, he did not acknowledge this help in his Baudelaire, *Les Fleurs du Mal, Petits Poemes En Prose, Les Paradis Artificiels*, published by the Casanova Society in 1925. He had translated Baudelaire's *Poems in Prose* in 1905, wrote a study of Baudelaire published in 1920 and after that published a translation of *The Letters of Baudelaire to his Mother, 1833–1886* in 1928. See further note on him, p. 206.

5. **Adonis**: In Greek mythology he was loved by Aphrodite, but, devoted to hunting, he was killed by a boar while still a stripling. Yeats was probably suggesting the Adonis legend in his poem 'Her Vision in the Wood' (*YP*, p. 388), written in August 1926, the eighth section of *A Woman Young and Old*. 'The women weep... Adonis'. Percy Bysshe Shelley (1792–1822) wrote *Adonais* in June 1821, the poem prompted by the death of John Keats earlier that year in Rome. Iseult has seized on the dominant note in the poem's opening line, the command 'Weep for Adonais – he is dead!' which sets the poem's elegiac tone, caught up again insistently in the third stanza, 'Oh, weep for Adonais – he is dead!' in the fourth, 'Most musical of mourners, weep again!' and in the fifth's echo, 'Most musical of mourners, weep anew!' This emphasis, this command to weep, occurs again in the sixth, ninth and thirty-eighth stanzas.

6. **all sorts of formality... identy book**: Iseult was very sensitive about giving details of her parentage, which had to be supplied in an application for a passport. Her birth certificate did not record the identity of her parents.

7. **Alexis**: Sean MacBride.

8. **Moura**: Maud Gonne.

## 25

1. **Moura's name... She has gone to Ireland**: Maud Gonne was in London, forbidden, under the provisions of the Defence of the Realm Act, to go to Ireland, but she disguised herself successfully and crossed to Dublin.

2. **Sylvia Pankhurst**: The second daughter of Emmeline Pankhurst (1857–1928), the English suffragette and pacifist who organized the Women's Social and Political Union in 1905 and fought for women's rights, using violent means. Sylvia (1882–1960) wrote a book about her mother's life, published in 1935. She herself became a pacifist and turned to Labour politics and Internationalism. See note, p. 213 on **the Sylvia group**.

3. **Jacky**: Sean MacBride.

4. **Eva Gore Booth**: Eva (1870–1926), a sister of Constance (1868–1927) Gore-Booth, who married Count Casimir Markiewicz, wrote poetry (her best known poem is 'The Little Waves of Breffny'), worked for the women's suffrage movement and went to Manchester to undertake social work. Yeats visited the Gore-Booths at Lissadell, a 'Big House' in Sligo in 1894–95. His fine poem 'in Memory of Eva Gore-Booth and Con Markiewicz' (*YP*, p. 347) is set at Lissadell, and was written between September and November 1927.

5. **stoggy**: stodgy.

6. **Iris Barry**: See note on her, p. 201.

7. **Sophia**: This was Joséphine Pillon (1865–1927) an illegitimate servant who had worked for the family in France. Born in Normandy, she accompanied them to London in 1917, then to Dublin. She acted as cook and general servant, was devoted to Sean whom she called 'Le Patron', and eventually died at Roebuck House, Clonskeagh, County Dublin in 1927.

8. **all the beasts**: At Colleville they had included dogs, large and small, singing birds, a parrot, a monkey and a goat. In London Iseult had the parrot, the monkey and her Persian cat Minoulouche.

9. **Georgie**: Yeats's wife. See note, p. 197.

10. **A heavenly time in the country with you**: She had been with the Yeatses at Stone Cottage, Coleman's Hatch, Sussex before Christmas, and may be referring to this rather than her later stay with them in Oxford in January.

11.   **Oxford:** The Yeatses had rented rooms at 45 Broad Street Oxford (now demolished), as Woburn Buildings had been let, and their plans to visit Connemara and Galway had to be postponed. They were to lease 4 Broad Street, Oxford in October 1919, on a six monthly lease. They stayed there with intervals when they sub-let it, until 1922 when they acquired 82 Merrion Square, a Georgian house in Dublin.

12.   **uncle nicer than father?:** Yeats had written to Lady Gregory from France telling her that 'as father, but as father only I have been a great success.' And he may have described himself in this role to Iseult later.

## 26

1.   **a whole day of solitude!:** Charles Rickett's statuette of Silence prompted Iseult to write, in an unpublished essay on this work, 'Silence is Solitude for the mental eye; solitude is silence for the mental eye'.

2.   **your essays:** Probably an advance copy of *Per Amica Silentia Lunae* (1918), the Prologue and Epilogue of which were addressed to Iseult as 'Maurice'.

3.   **Wagner's music:** See note on him, p. 190.

4.   **a bad child ... They have spots on their faces ... Adonis is not among them, nor is the God of Wisdom:** Yeats must have expressed concern at the Bohemian company Iseult was keeping.

5.   **Adonis:** See note on Adonis, p. 203.

6.   **A movement:** Perhaps the Vorticist group, launched by Ezra Pound and Wyndham Lewis.

7.   **a charming place:** Was this an early viewing of Roebuck House, Clonskeagh, Co. Dublin, which Maud and Mrs Despard bought later?

8.   **Temple Hill:** This was an old house standing in its own grounds, beyond Terenure, on Kimmage Road East which Ella Young rented and shared with its owner. (It had reminded Maud Gonne of Floraville, the house in Donnybrook, outside Dublin, where the Gonnes lived until Mrs Gonne's death on 21 June 1871. See note on her, p. 188.) The house belonged to (Olive Alise) Moireen Fox, the daughter of Henry Fox, of the Earl of Ranfurly's family. She was a clairvoyant who published some poetry, including *Liadain and Curithir* (1917). In 1917 she married Claude Albert Chavasse (1885–1971), whose family had French origins. He was born in Oxford, where his father was a don at Balliol College. He went to Waterford about 1912 after graduating, wore kilts and spoke only Irish or French while staying with a cousin Henry Chavasse.

9.   **Dr Ross:** See on pp. 199 and 201.

10.  **Barry ... is engaged ... an honest simple young man:** Alan Porter (1899–1942), whom Iris Barry eventually married as her first husband (see note on her, p. 201). She later referred to him as being as helpless as a child. He published two collections of poetry, *The Signature of Pain and Other Poems* (1930) being the better known. He edited the MSS of John Clare's poetry with Edmund Blunden in 1920, edited *Oxford Poetry* in 1920 and 1921, and was editor or sub-editor of *The Spectator*. Yeats wrote to Lady Dorothy Wellesley, on 26 July 1936, about him. The passage was suppressed but was later quoted by Richard Ellmann in 'Yeats's Second Puberty', *Four Dubliners* (1987), p. 35:

> We let our house in the Broad, Oxford to some American girl students. In the middle of the night Alan Porter climbed through the window. He was welcomed but found to be impotent. He explained that he had a great friend and when

the friend had tired of a girl [he] had always taken her for himself. If he found a girl for himself he was impotent. The student said fetch your friend. He did. And after that all went well ... I have worked it up into a charming fantasy of shyness. If the girl lay with the friend he felt she belonged to the family: once was enough.

The fantasy was part of *Stories of Michael Robartes and His Friends* in the 2nd (1937) edition of *A Vision*. See *A Vision and Related Writings* (1990), pp. 99–100, where, apart from the story based on Alan Porter, Yeats is giving a twist to the early reverence he accorded Villiers de l'Isle Adam's play *Axel* (see Ellmann, *op. cit.*, pp. 35–6). Denise has adopted the name de l'Isle Adam:

Denise began: 'I was reading Axel in bed. It was between twelve and one on the 2nd June last year. A date that I will never forget, because on that night I met the one man I shall always love. I was turning the pages of the Act where the lovers are in the vault under the castle. Axel and Sarah decide to die rather than possess one another. He talks of her hair as full of the odour of dead rose leaves – a pretty phrase – a phrase I would like somebody to say to me; and then comes the famous sentence: 'As for living, our servants will do that for us'. I was wondering what made them do anything so absurd, when the candle went out. I said, 'Duddon, I heard you open the window, creep over the floor on your toes, but I never guessed that you would blow the candle out.' 'Denise,' he said, 'I am a great coward. I am afraid of unfamiliar women in pyjamas.' I said: 'No, my dear, you are not a coward, you were just shy, but why should you call me unfamiliar? I thought I had put everything right when I told you that I slept on the ground floor, that there was nobody else on that floor, and that I left the window open.' Five minutes later I said: 'Duddon, you are impotent, stop trembling; go over there and sit by the fire. I will give you some wine.' When he had drunk half a tumbler of claret, he said; 'No, I am not really impotent, I am a coward, that is all. When Huddon tires of a girl, I make love to her, and there is no difficulty at all. He has always talked about her, but if he had not, it would not make much difference. He is my greatest friend, and when she and he have been in the same bed, it is as though she belonged to the house. Twice I have found somebody on my own account, and been a failure, just as I have to-night. I had not indeed much hope when I climbed through the window but I had a little; because you had made it plain that I would be welcome'. I said: 'Oh, my dear, how delightful; now I know all about Axel. He was just shy. If he had not killed the Commander in the Second Act – and it would have been much more dramatic at the end of the play – he could have sent for him and all would have come right. The Commander was not a friend, of course; Axel hated him; but he was a relation, and afterwards Axel could have thought of Sarah as a member of the family. I love you because you would not be shy if you had not so great respect for me. You feel about me what I feel about a Bishop in a surplice. I would not give you up now for anything'. Duddon said, wringing his hands: 'Oh, what am I to do?' I said: 'Fetch the Commander'. He said, getting cheerful again: 'I am to bring Huddon?'

11. **Thora**: Iseult's cousin; see note on her, p. 117.
12. **two lovely days spent in Oxford**: see note on Oxford in previous letter, p. 204.

27
1.  **those passeport difficulties...Joséphine...not pleased to show**: These difficulties related to the fact that both Iseult and the cook, Joséphine Pillon, were illegitimate and Iseult was sensitive about revealing the fact in any passport application as she had been when visiting London early in 1917.
2.  **running around looking for homes**: in Dublin; she had not yet purchased 73 St Stephen's Green.
3.  **the poem**: This might be 'To a young Beauty' (*YP*, p. 242), written in 1918 and first published in *Nine Poems* [Oct.] (1918) In this poem Yeats records his dislike of the Bohemian company Iseult was keeping :

> Dear fellow-artist, why so free
> With every sort of company,
> With every Jack and Jill?
> Chose your companions from the best;
> Who draws a bucket with the rest
> Soon topples down the hill.

4.  **Ezra and Symons**: Ezra Loomis Pound (1885–1972), born in Hailey, Idaho, graduated from Pennsylvania University in 1906, but, after four months as an Instructor at Wabash College, moved to Europe, travelling in Spain, Italy and France (largely in Provence). In London where he arrived in 1908 he co-edited *Blast* (1914–15), was London editor of the Chicago *Little Review* (1917–19) and became Paris correspondent for *The Dial* in 1920. The *Little Review* was an influential avant-garde magazine which began in 1914 and lasted till 1929. Pound's desire 'to make it new' probably had some influence on Yeats's changing style; they became friendly, Pound pontificating at Yeats's Monday Evenings, and they shared Stone Cottage, Coleman's Hatch in Sussex in the winter of 1913, Ezra acting as Yeats's secretary, teaching him to fence and introducing him to Noh drama. Yeats stayed there in 1915 and 1916 also, with Pound and his wife (see note on Dorothy, p. 208). In 1917 the Cuala Press published Pound's *Selection* of the *Letters* of John Butler Yeats, Yeats's father. From 1924 he lived in Italy, giving offence by anti-democratic broadcasts in the early stages of the war. He was indicted for treason in 1945, but was declared insane and confined in an asylum, from which he was released in 1958, pronounced sane. An imagist in his early career, his poetry contained much curious learning in his further experimental work. His *Cantos* first appeared in 1933 and continued up to the *Pisan Cantos* (1949).
    It is not clear when Iseult first met Pound. In 1913 he referred to her in a letter to Dorothy Shakespear (whom he married in 1914) as a 'scioness of the house of Gonne' to whom the Eagle (the name by which he and Dorothy alluded to Yeats) was 'burning tapers'. By 1917 she was seeing Ezra 'occasionally'.
    Symons appreciated Iseult's gifts and character greatly. (See earlier note on him, p. 202.) In an unpublished manuscript (now in Princeton University Library) entitled 'Iseult Gonne' he wrote of her 'purity, luxury, beauty, youth, womanhood, extravagance, perfect taste, sure instinct, discrimination, imagination, vision.' He recorded her passion for 'books, cats, travel, nature, change.' He admired her 'wonderfully pure French accent which made her so fascinating and so foreign'. Their friendship was aesthetic and literary and not a little flirtatious.
5.  **Iris...busy at her novels**: See note on her, p. 201.

6. **the system**: This was the material of *A Vision* on which Yeats and his wife were working; it was based on her automatic writing. Yeats described it to Lady Gregory as 'a very profound, very exciting mystical philosophy' in a letter of January 1918. A vast amount of work went into it. See *WBYANB*, pp. 222–6, and George Mills Harper *The Making of Yeats's A Vision* (1987) for an account of this.
7. **Georgy**: Mrs W.B. Yeats.

## 28

1. **Ezra ... The Little Review**: See earlier note on Ezra Pound, p. 206.
2. **I must stay at least another month**: Ezra Pound wanted her to work as his secretary but not officially, calling her his typist: 'my poems are much too ithyphallic for any secretary of her years to be officially in my possession.' For a more detailed account of this period see A. Norman Jeffares, 'Iseult Gonne', *Yeats Annual*, No. 16 (forthcoming 2004).
3. **Ross**: Sir Denison Ross, the Director of the School of Oriental Studies, see note, pp. 199 and 201.

## 29

1. **I am really at a loss**: Was this a reaction to Yeats's advising her against taking the post with the *Little Review*?
2. **Ezra tried to kiss me ?!!**: Perhaps an outcome to be expected from Ezra's coming in 'rather often'. Was this a remark designed to insure against any reproachful letter from 'the Good lady of Normandy', the cook, Joséphine Pillon, who does seem to have written a letter with 'circumstantial details' to Maud Gonne, as she was horrified at the way people called on Iseult and Iris Barry in the evenings.
3. **my father's death**: Lucien Millevoye (1850–1918), Iseult's father, the grandson of the poet Charles-Hubert Millevoye, was married; his only son Henri was killed in battle on 30 September or 1 October 1915. Millevoye became a member of the House of Deputies as a representative of the National Party in 1889. In 1893 he was trapped into making a fool of himself when he accused his friend Comte Henri Rochfort (then in exile in England) of corruption in what became known as the Norton and *Cocarde* forgery trials. See Maud Gonne MacBride, *A Servant of the Queen* (1994) pp. 194–6 and 279, and see also Joseph MacCabe, *Georges Clemenceau, France's Grand Old Man: his Life and Opinions* (1919), Ch.8. By 1895 Millevoye regained his seat, and Jules Jaluzot, the owner of the *Printemps* store, who had bought the ailing *La Patrie*, appointed Emile Massard as its editor, and Millevoye as its political editor in 1895. Maud Gonne persuaded him to take this post, to rebuild his own confidence and the influence of his party, using the then little-read Parisian evening paper as his instrument. See *Histoire Générale de la Presse Française*, Vol iii, (Paris, 1972). Millevoye did much to increase its circulation and remained on the staff as political editor until his death. Here is part of the letter Iseult wrote in French (There is an English version of it on p. 97) to MG about it:

Cherie,

As tu lu des journeaux Anglais ou Français ces jours-ci? Si oui je n'ai rien à t'apprendre et tu auras lu la nouvelle navrante. Le loup est mort. Je n'ai pas de details, je ne le sais que par les journaux ou plutot par May qui l'a lu. J'ai mal aux yeux a force d'avoir pleuré. On ne sait jamais aux juste la mesure d'affection qu'on porte aux étres avant de les perdre: et puis alors on se souvient atrocement de tout ce qu'on aurait pu faire pour eux et qu'on a négligé et surtout de toutes les choses dures qu'on a pensé d'eux, et cela semble si injuste et cruel!

O que Dieu ait son ame! Je fais dire une messe pour lui, mais je ne sais plus prier; tu prieras, toi, n'est ce-pas. Apres tout nous sommes sous le royaume du Christ où le symbole de la justice n'est pas une balance mais un cœur; et si errant qu'ait été une etre, de plus loin qui'il revienne, le mieux est-il acceuilli; c'est ce que j'éspère pour lui.

J'ai au moins la pauvre petite satisfaction de me dire que la derniere lettre que j'ai reçue de lui, il y a 3 semaines etait très affectueuse et moi je lui ai repondu presque immédiatement. Nous etions redevenus tout-a-fait amis. Ma pauvre Chérie si tu n'as pas déjà appris sa mort, je crains que cette lettre te donnes une grande peine. C'est tout le passé pour toi qui s'endort à jamais, c'est beaucoup de souvenirs qui se reveillent; et je suis avec toi tout se que tu peux y sentir de navrant et presque ironique, car il y a toujours beaucouop d'ironie qui serre le cœur quand on regarde dans les choses d'autrefois. Si tu as beaucoup de chagrin écris-le à ton vieux Rat . . .

4. **Georgie:** Mrs W.B. Yeats.
5. **Woburn Buildings:** 18 Woburn Buildings, Yeats's London home from 1896.
6. **the job Ezra offers me:** On the *Little Review*, see pp. 206 and 207.
7. **Ezra and Dorothy:** In 1914 Ezra Pound had married Dorothy Shakespear, the only child of Yeats's friend Mrs Olivia Shakespear (1863–1938), his first mistress. Dorothy was a close friend of Georgie Hyde Lees, to whom Olivia Shakespear introduced Yeats in 1911, having introduced him to Ezra Pound in 1909. See John Harwood, *Olivia Shakespear and W.B. Yeats. After Long Silence* (1989) *passim.*
8. **your Cat:** Pangur Ban, a white cat, named after the cat celebrated in the poem by a medieval Irish monk. See Robin Flower, *The Irish Tradition* (1947) and his *Poems and Translations* (1931). His translation is neater than that of Thomas Kinsella in his *The New Oxford Book of Irish Verse* (1989 edn), p. 31.

**30**
1. **my father:** See note, p. 207.
2. **Minnoulouche:** Iseult's cat.
3. **Poor Sophia:** Joséphine Pillon, the maid. See note on her, pp. 186, 203 and 206.
4. **I feel sorry for the poor old thing:** Presumably Iseult was trying to get permission for Joséphine Pillon to go to Ireland with her. As she did not speak English she would have to stay with the family.
5. **your father's letters:** There were three selections of these: the first, selected by Ezra Pound, entitled *Passages from the Letters of John Butler Yeats* (1917), the second *Further Letters of John Butler Yeats* (1920), selected by Lennox Robinson and the third Joseph Hone's *Letters to His Son W.B. Yeats and Others 1869–1922* (1946).
6. **Miss Jacobs:** Louise Jacobs was Yeats's favourite typist (the only one to be trusted with the MS of *A Vision*). She ran a typewriting agency from approximately 1915 onwards, first at 47 Great Russell Street and later from 1920 to 1930 (and perhaps for some time after that) at 47 Museum Street, London.
7. **the last Joyce . . . in the Little Review:** Episodes from James Joyce's *Ulysses* (1922) began to be published in the *Little Review* in March 1918. This letter probably refers to 'Ulysses II', included in the April issue. It was serialised until December 1920.

8. **The Portrait**: Joyce's *A Portrait of the Artist as A Young Man* (New York edition, 1917) was serialised in *The Egoist* and published by *The Egoist Ltd* in February 1917.
9. **Chicken of the Valley**: not identified, but probably a name Iseult used for Sir Denison Ross.

**31**

1. **your telegram**: Contents unknown but Yeats may have told Iseult in it that Maud Gonne had been arrested in Dublin.
2. **The anxiety I was in**: Maud Gonne was arrested on 19 May 1918 when returning from an evening at George Russell's house in Dublin, accompanied by her son Sean, Miss Barton and Joseph King, an English MP then in Ireland on a fact-finding mission. She was taken to the Bridewell and put on the boat for England the next day. There followed her first imprisonment, in Holloway prison where she was placed in the Criminal wing. Along with Constance Markiewicz and Mrs Kathleen Clarke she was moved to the VD wing. She wrote to Yeats that she was allowed no visits, no solicitor and no charge had been made. She was released in October 1918 after a Harley Street specialist had diagnosed a recurrence of her tuberculosis. After five days in a nursing home she went to Woburn Buildings and later travelled to Dublin again successfully disguised.
3. **Alexis**: Sean MacBride.
4. **the saintly Chotie**: Chotie (Katherine) Gonne (1861–1931), who was considered saintly by all the family as she never took sides in any arguments. She remained unmarried, was a sister of Maud Gonne's cousin May (née Mary Kemble Gonne, 1862–1929) who had married N.S. Bertie-Clay in London in 1902; he was then in the Indian Civil Service (see *GYL*, p. 227).
5. **Lynch**: Arthur Lynch (1861–1934), an Irish-Australian journalist, a long time member of the Paris Young Ireland Society, formed in 1897, and a friend of Maud Gonne over many years. He went to South Africa and founded the 2nd Irish Brigade there to fight the British; it did not take part in any major action. He was elected MP for Galway in 1901, retaining the seat until 1909. On arriving in England to take up his seat in Westminster he was arrested on charges of high treason and condemned to death but later reprieved. He was elected MP for West Clare (1910–18) and became a colonel in the British army in 1918.
6. **Nevinson**: This is probably Henry Wood Nevinson (1856–1941), the distinguished English journalist and war correspondent who was a friend and admirer of Yeats's writings and of Maud Gonne's oratory as well as her beauty. It is less likely to refer to his son Christopher Richard Wynne Nevinson (1889–1946), who studied at the Slade School in London and in Paris, painting a number of futurist paintings about 1912. He achieved fame as a war artist from 1914–15, his war pictures being exhibited in London in 1916.
7. **Eva Gore-Booth**: See note on her, p. 203.
8. **a German plot**: No evidence was produced by the authorities, who issued a proclamation alleging Sinn Fein had been engaged in a treasonable conspiracy with the Germans.
9. **the boy's education**: Sean's education. See p. 213, fn 9, for some of Iseult's anxiety about tutors for him in London in 1918.
10. **The Little Review**: See pp. 98–9, 103–4, 106.
11. **the mask of the Idiot**: This was a phrase used in the horoscope that Yeats had cast for Iseult.

12. **Wyndham Lewis...his increasing disciples**: See note on him, p. 199. Iseult prob-
    ably means such people as Lilian Roberts, Edward Wadsworth and Frederick Etchells,
    and, perhaps, David Bamberg (though he could hardly be classed as a disciple).

**32**
1. **Bichon**: Sean MacBride, Iseult's half-brother.
2. **Law**: See note on him, p. 188.
3. **Short**: The Rt Hon. Edward Shortt (1862–1935), MP for West Newcastle (1910–22).
   He was Chief Secretary for Ireland (1918–19) and Home Secretary (1919–22).
4. **Moura**: Maud Gonne.
5. **Ezra's offer**: this was to work as secretary to the *Little Review*. See pp. 206 and 207.
6. **Ross**: Sir Denison Ross, head of the School of Oriental Studies.
7. **the money I get from France**: Possibly from Millevoye's estate but the source is
   not known. For Mrs Yeats's view of Iseult's finances see her letters to Ezra Pound
   quoted in A. Norman Jeffares, 'Iseult' *Yeats Annual*, No. 16 (forthcoming 2004).

**33**
1. **the prison**: Holloway.
2. **Bichon**: Sean MacBride, Iseult's half-brother.
3. **Joséphine**: Joséphine Pillon, the cook, who had come to London from Normandy
   with the family. See note on her, p. 203.
4. **Barry**: Iris Barry who was sharing the flat with Iseult. See notes on her, pp. 201
   and 204.
5. **Moura**: Maud Gonne.
6. **keys of W. Buildings**: of Yeats's rooms, 18 Woburn Buildings. See note p. 208.

**34**
1. **typed copies of your poems**: Iseult had been typing part of Yeats's *The Wild
   Swans at Coole* (1919), probably those poems included in *Nine Poems* (1918).
   They included 'Under the Round Tower', 'Solomon to Sheba', 'A Song', 'To a
   Young Girl', 'Tom O'Roughley', 'A Prayer on going into my House', 'The Cat and
   the Moon'. All these poems (except 'To A Young Beauty', which first appeared in
   *Nine Poems* and 'The Cat and the Moon' which appeared in *The Dial*, July 1924)
   were published in the *Little Review*, October 1918. Of these 'The Living Beauty',
   'To a Young Beauty' and 'To a Young Girl' were written to Iseult, while 'The Cat
   and the Moon' is about her cat Minoulouche. Yeats, in his Introduction to *The
   Cat and the Moon*, a play of his produced in the Abbey Theatre, Dublin in 1926,
   wrote about this little poem 'where a cat is disturbed by the moon, and in the
   changing pupils of its eyes seems to repeat the movement of the moon's
   changes'. As he wrote the poem he had allowed himself to think of the cat as
   'the normal man and of the moon as the opposite he seeks perpetually or as having any meaning I have conferred on the moon elsewhere.'
2. **Alexis**: Sean MacBride, Iseult's half-brother.
3. **Mrs Tucker**: Nelly (Edith Ellen) Tucker, neé Woodmass (?1868–1942), who
   married Harry Tudor Tucker (1866–1943) in 1911. She had previously been
   married to William Gilbert Hyde Lees (1890–1909), by whom she had a son
   Harold (1890–1963) and a daughter Bertha Georgie Hyde Lees (1892–1968) who
   married Yeats in 1917.
4. **Translations of the Iliad...reminded of my fourteen years old heroic
   dreams**: Maud Gonne wrote to Yeats in April 1908 (*GYL*, p. 255) to say that Iseult was

mad on Greek stories and 'knows the *Iliad* and the *Odyssey* better than her prayer book.'

5. **Solomon to Sheba**: A poem by Yeats about his relationship with his wife (see *YP*, p. 240).

6. **the Beggar's dream**: This is the beggar Billy Byrne of 'Under the Round Tower' (see *YP*, p.239) who dreams of the sun and moon, 'golden king and silver lady'.

## 35

1. **Alexis...with you**: Sean MacBride was staying with Yeats and his wife in County Galway. The village schoolmaster at Gort was tutoring him and Claude Albert Chavasse was teaching him Irish (see note, p. 204). He wrote to his mother to say that he was working at Irish, Latin, arithmetic and algebra. The woods and the lake are those of Coole.

2. **Russell**: George (William) Russell (1867–1935), born in Lurgan, was educated at Rathmines School and the Metropolitan School of Art, Dublin, where he met and became friendly with Yeats. He began work as a clerk in Pims' drapery store in Dublin in 1890 and became a leading figure in the Irish Agricultural Organisation Society, editing the *Irish Homestead* (1905–23) and the *Irish Statesman* (1923–30). He wrote poetry and plays under the pseudonym AE (from Greek Aeon), painted visionary pictures, founding the Hermetic Society and writing articles for the *Irish Theosophist*. He tried to unite his mystical philosophy with social reality, remaining true to his vision despite disappointment at the way the world went. Iseult got to know him well on her visits to Dublin.

3. **Miss Barton**: Dulcibella Barton, of Glendalough House, Annamoe, County Wicklow, a sister of Robert Barton (1881–1975), a progressive landlord. A British army officer, he resigned in 1916 and joined the IRA. Sinn Fein MP for West Wicklow, 1916, he was a signatory of the 1921 Treaty, though he later repudiated it. He was an abstentionist TD (1922–27). He was Head of the Agricultural Credit Commission (1934–54) and of Bord na Mona (1946). He proved a friendly neighbour when Iseult was living nearby in Laragh Castle. Dulcibella Barton had been with Maud Gonne, Sean and King, the English MP, when Maud was arrested getting off the tram at the bottom of Harcourt Street as they were coming from spending the evening at George Russell's house in Coulson Avenue, Rathgar. It had been proposed that Sean, staying with the Yeatses, should go to Miss Barton in County Wicklow but because of her mother's illness she could not have him to stay there. A letter of hers, dated 3 August 1918, to Sean MacBride, when he was staying with the Yeatses, is about a dog Poppet, belonging to Countess Markiewicz which she was looking after for her, the Countess then being imprisoned for the second time in Holloway prison from May 1918 to March 1919 for being a Sinn Fein leader and for having made seditious speeches.

4. **Father Sweetman's school**: Mount Saint Benedict, a school near Gorey, County Wexford, founded by Father John Sweetman, a Benedictine, with a loan of £5000 from his cousin John Sweetman. Many of the sons of nationalists were educated there. It was closed in 1925 because of opposition from both church and state. Father Sweetman grew excellent tobacco from which he made eccentrically shaped cheroots.

5. **Collins**: Victor Collins, who was teaching in Mount Saint Benedict in 1918. A journalist, who had been correspondent in Paris of the *New York Sun*, he was a friend of John MacBride. He had been godfather at Maud Gonne's baptism into the Roman Catholic Church in February 1903 and subsequently arranged details of the

marriage between MacBride and Maud Gonne, also in February 1903. Collins stayed at Colleville in the summer of that year and his children were there too. During the divorce proceeding brought by Maud Gonne he wrote a sensational article in the *Daily Mirror*, biased in favour of MacBride. See *GYL*, pp. 190, 194, 203, 220 and 232, and A. Norman Jeffares, 'Iseult Gonne' *Yeats Annual*, No. 16 (forthcoming, 2004). He spoke disparagingly about Maud Gonne in Ireland. See *GYL*, p. 395.

6.  **Bichon:** Sean MacBride.

7.  **Work with a tutor [in London]:** Ezra Pound seems to have tutored him briefly in 1917, but he refused to be taught further by him. He had two other tutors in September, one for mathematics and algebra, the other for Latin and English, and wrote to Maud Gonne on 10 October to tell her he was working with them in the mornings.

8.  **work at the museum:** This was the British Museum, now the British Library; she was now working for Ezra Pound.

9.  **translations of Sappho:** Sappho (b. *c.* 650 B.C.), the Greek poetess, born in Lesbos, fled from Mitylene to Sicily about 596 B.C., but returned after some years. Only two of her *Odes* are extant, but fragments have been discovered in Egypt.

10. **Voltaire's letters:** François Marie Arouet de Voltaire (1694–1778), French author, was born in Paris, educated in the College Louis-le-Grand, the chief French seminary of the Jesuits. Disliking the law, he went to Holland in the suite of the French ambassador, but was sent home after an undiplomatic love affair. He was banished from Paris on suspicion of lampooning the Duc d'Orleans, later imprisoned for eleven months in the Bastille for a lampoon accusing the Regent of various crimes. There he adopted the name Voltaire. His *Oedipe* was successfully performed in 1718. His epic poem on Henri IV, refused publication by the authorities, was printed surreptitiously in Rouen. He circulated epigrams at Court on the Chevalier de Rohan-Chabot, who had him beaten. Thrown into the Bastille again, he was freed on condition that he went to England in 1726. There he had a considerable social success, making the acquaintance of many writers and grandees, returning to France in 1729, having written *The History of Charles XII* and collected material for his *Letters on the English*. He became very wealthy by buying shares in a lottery and speculating in corn. He had an affair with Madame du Chatelet and wrote several books while staying at her husband's château. He also had an affair with his niece, Madame Denis. He was appointed Historiographer Royal and was elected to the French Academy. On Madame du Chatelet's death he moved to Berlin as Frederick the Great's chamberlain in 1750; he offended Frederick and had to leave in 1753. In 1755 he settled near Geneva at Ferney. His masterly short story *Candide* appeared in 1759. His anti-religious writings began to be published in 1762, and the *Dictionaire philosophique* appeared in 1764. His last illness and death were caused by the excitement engendered by the production of his last tragedy *Irène* when he was 84.

11. **The cockroach:** See note, p. 183.

12. **your country life:** The Yeatses were staying at Ballinamantane House, near Gort, County Galway which Lady Gregory had lent them so that they could supervise the building work at the tower, in which they lived, virtually camping there, in September.

## 36

1.  **Maia:** In Greek mythology she was the eldest of the seven Pleiades, the mother of Hermes by Zeus. But Iseult used the word for an imaginary country, a place of escape from 'the very dreary and sordid things of daily life.' She wrote to her

cousin Thora from Colleville in the summer of 1916 to tell her how, when tired and lonely, she would lie on her bed and tell herself stories 'full of drama, of wild and passionate living.' In these stories Thora was always with her, she wrote, in the land she called Maia. They had 'wonderful, adventures there, did finer deeds than anyone else and were the objects of everyone's admiration (alas!!)'

2. **Georgie:** Mrs W.B. Yeats.

3. **this house:** The first and second floors of 18 Woburn Buildings, off Russell Square, Yeats's London residence from 1895 to 1919. On 18 August he had written to Maud Gonne that he and his wife had gone to London (from Galway) 'and separated Iseult and Barry. Iseult had feared to be unkind but was grateful to be rid of Barry by the act of others. She [Iseult] can stay at Woburn Buildings until March next without rent to pay as we are moving to Oxford.' (See *GYL*, p. 295.)

4. **The soul remembering its loneliness/Shudders in many cradles:** Lines from Yeats's poem 'The Phases of the Moon' (*YP*, pp. 267–73), written in 1918, a poem which presents one of the central ideas expressed in *A Vision* (as 'Ego Dominus Tuus', a poem written by 5 October 1915 (*YP*, pp. 264–6) develops another basic idea of *A Vision*, that of the anti-self, discussed in the prose *Per Amica Silentia Lunae*).

5. **a preface to your book:** Probably to *Per Amica Silentia Lunae*, published in December 1918.

6. **Alexis:** Sean MacBride.

7. **the Sylvia group:** Friends of Sylvia Pankhurst (1882–1960), the second daughter of Emmeline Pankhurst (1857–1928). See note on her, p. 203. The 'Group' may be the Workers' Suffrage Federation.

8. **The Editors:** Probably a reference to the group of people who were involved in the *Freeman's Journal*, a political journal founded in 1763 which ran until 1923. From 1892, under the editorship of William Brayden, it supported the reconstituted Irish Parliamentary party. It then supported the Treaty Party, and its premises were destroyed by the IRA in March 1922; it subsequently survived for a year in a roneoed format.

9. **Father Kelly:** Iseult was afraid of his influencing Sean in any way. He had apparently been taking an interest in Sean MacBride's education, for on 24 June [1918] Ambrose O'Gorman, of 48 Bow Road, London, had written to 'Mr Mac-Bride' at the Beaufort Mansions address, enquiring if Father Kelly had got him a tutor and asking him to call on him about a tutorship. 'Mr MacBride' (Sean, then aged 14) had not answered O'Gorman (he was probably then staying with the Yeatses in Galway) who wrote again on 8 July asking whether he had received the card (of 24 June). From Galway Sean wrote to his mother (then in Holloway Prison) telling her that Iseult and the family (May Bertie-Clay among others) wanted him to be tutored by Ezra Pound and then to go to an English public school in October. For various reasons, he told her, he did not want to be tutored by Pound (did he dislike him or did he not like Iseult's relationship with him?), but would prefer to be tutored by his 'ancient professor', George Irvine, and Mrs Plessents in Dublin and then to go to a Franciscan school in Ireland. After being taught by the Gort schoolmaster and given lessons in Irish by Claude Chavasse, he was briefly tutored by Pound when he was staying with Iseult in Woburn Buildings in 1918. He went to Mount Saint Benedict in Gorey, Co. Wexford, in 1919, possibly staying there till he passed his Matriculation examination and entered University College, Dublin, at the age of sixteen in 1920.

10. **Georgie:** Mrs W.B. Yeats.

11. **Mrs Old:** Sarah Martha Old, neé Durrant, (?1855–1939) who was Arthur Symons's housekeeper in Fountain Court. When Yeats moved to Woburn Buildings he paid her for providing five meals a week and for some basic housekeeping. She was sometimes helped by her daughter Martha Sarah Old (1881–1953), later Mrs Eggleton, who had affectionate memories of 'Yeaty'. Thomas Old, a builder, was Yeats's landlord. See the excellent account of the house and Yeats's tenancy of it given in Volume II of *The Collected Letters of W.B. Yeats*, ed. Warwick Gould, John Kelly and Deirdre Toomey (1997), pp. 725–31.

**37**
1. **the matron . . . the Governor:** Of Holloway prison.
2. **Stephen Gwynn:** Stephen (Lucius) Gwynn (1864–1950) was brought up in Donegal before going to Oxford and subsequently living in London as a man of letters. Secretary of the Irish Literary Society in 1904, he was Nationalist MP for Galway from 1906 to 1916, serving with distinction with the Connaught Rangers in the First World War. A friend of Maud Gonne for many years, he did not always approve of her politics. He wrote some biographies, notably of Swift and Goldsmith, and his *Irish Literature and Drama* (1920) remains very readable. He wrote many books dealing with Ireland from a touristic point of view as well as political studies, his *History of Ireland* and his life of *Grattan* (1939) being good examples of his balanced outlook. Gwynn helped Yeats, who was, with others including Joseph King, the MP for North Somerset, carrying on a campaign for Maud Gonne's release from Holloway prison on health grounds, by introducing him to the Rt Hon. Edward Shortt, Chief Secretary for Ireland at the time, see Yeats's letters to Maud Gonne (*GYL*, pp. 396–8).

**38**
1. **how many candles:** She is thanking Yeats for his work in bringing Maud Gonne's deteriorating health to the knowledge of the authorities.
2. **King. . .Shortt:** See previous notes on them, pp. 209 and 210.
3. **the 'Orpheus':** One of Iseult's writings.
4. **Bichon:** Sean MacBride.
5. **Minoulouche:** Iseult's black Persian cat.
6. **the School:** Of Oriental Studies, where Iseult had worked as an Assistant Librarian.
7. **Barry:** See note on Iris Barry, pp. 201 and 204.
8. **the Chicken of the Valley:** see note, p. 209.
9. **Mrs Tucker:** See note on her, p. 210.
10. **Georgie:** Mrs W.B. Yeats.

**39**
1. **released on Tuesday evening:** Maud Gonne was temporarily released from Holloway to go to a nursing home in the last week of October. Iseult and Sean were there to meet her. She left the Nursing Home ('too expensive for a pauper like myself, £10.10 a week') when Dr Tunnicliffe, who was to supervise her treatment, went down with influenza. He had examined her in Holloway prison on 21 October and reported that she was suffering from a recrudescence of her former pulmonary tuberculosis and required suitable medical treatment and climate without delay (see *GYL*, pp. 397–400 and notes, p. 519). On 6 November he reported that her condition had somewhat improved and recommended that she be looked after by Dr Crofton in Dublin. She was not, however, given permission

to leave England. Francis Whittaker Tunnicliffe was registered in January 1889. Resident in Harley Street, he had studied at St Bartholomew's, London, Vienna and Prague and was Physician of King's College Hospital and Professor of Pharmacology, King's College, University of London. He was also Physician in the North London Hospital, specialising in chest diseases, and was the author of several papers. He was last entered in the Medical Register in 1928.

2. **King had advised**: See note on previous letter, p. 214.
3. **Mrs Old**: See note on p. 214.

**40**

1. **Now that she is out**: See note 1 on letter 39, p. 214.
2. **your poem ... about the cat and the hare**: Yeats's poem 'Two Songs of a Fool' (*YP*, p. 242) where the 'speckled cat' is Mrs Yeats, the 'tame hare' is Iseult. This poem was written between July and September 1918. Cf. also his poem 'To a Young Beauty' (*YP*, p. 242).
3. **Why did you feel anxious about me?**: The poem conveys Yeats's sense of responsibility for Iseult.
4. **'enforced love of the world'**: This relates to the ideas in Yeats's *Per Amica Silentia Lunae* (1918). See, in particular, Sections V–XIII of *Anima Hominis*. The phrase also occurs in her horoscope. The ideas are the basis of Yeats's poem 'Ego Dominus Tuus' (*YP*, p. 264) and 'The Phases of the Moon' (*YP*, p. 267).
5. **Huysmans**: See note on him, p. 196. 'Secondary' is probably used in one of its French meanings, 'of minor importance'
6. **some Wordsworth**: As a result of his letter Yeats gave her a copy of *Poems of Wordsworth*, ed., Mathew Arnold (1915) and inscribed it 'Maurice from affectionate Uncle W.B. Yeats.' Iseult underlined in Arnold's Preface the statement that 'By nothing is England so glorious as by her poetry.'
7. **Ezra**: Ezra Pound. See note, p. 206. He regarded Wordsworth as 'a silly old sheep with a genius ... for imagisme for a presentation of natural detail, wildfowl bathing in a hole in the ice, etc., and this talent ... he tuned in a desert of bleatings'. See Pound, *Pavannes and Divisions* (1918), p. 139*ff*.
8. **your last letter to Moura**: This may have been related to Maud Gonne's being only 'temporarily' released from Holloway. See later remark in the letter about the shock it would be to Maud if the 'confounded brutes' of officials were to drag her away now. Yeats may have triggered off Maud's decision to escape to Ireland in disguise.

**41**

1. **Dr Crofton**: A Dublin doctor, a specialist in diseases of the lungs, who had earlier been treating Maud Gonne for rheumatism. His unorthodox ways prompted the medical staff to resign when he was appointed to the Sanatorium at Newcastle, County Wicklow. This was established in 1893 and is not to be confused with the earlier Sanatorium at Peamount, Newcastle, County Dublin, founded in 1912 by Lady Aberdeen, the wife of the Lord Lieutenant of Ireland who also founded the Women's National Health Association. See Caoimhghin S. Breathnach, 'Doughty Women in the War against Tuberculosis in Ireland', *Borderlands* eds Davis Coakley and Mary O'Doherty (2002) and Maureen Keane, *Ishbel, Lady Aberdeen in Ireland* (1999). The Peamount Sanatorium specialised in the treatment of tuberculosis, emphasising the need for good food, cleanliness and fresh air.

It had a series of wooden buildings with verandas to enable the patients to be out of doors as much as possible.

William Mervyn Crofton was registered on 13 May 1904. He was a graduate of the Royal University of Ireland (MB, BS, 1904) and of the National University of Ireland (MD, 1911). He lived at 32 Fitzwilliam Square, while practising in Dublin, where he was Pathologist at Steevens Hospital and a lecturer in Special Pathology at University College. He published various medical papers as well as writing several operas: *The Wooing of Emer, Deirdre of the Sorrows and Cuchullain,* all published by the Talbot Press, Dublin. He was a temporary captain in the RAMC in the First World War, and medical officer at Wisbech. He moved to London in 1934, living in 22 Park Square, Regents Park. In 1935 it was alleged he advertised to obtain clients, but the General Medical Council decided, in 1937, not to erase his name from the Register. He appeared 'rotund, bespectacled and somewhat untidily dressed' and had responded in 1935 to the President's final remarks that reports would be expected from some of his professional brethren as to his professional conduct:

> Dr Crofton flung his arms in the air in gesture.
> How many do you want? Twenty? Fifty?

To which the President replied 'we do not specify numbers. It is the weight which is more important.' When cleared, Crofton accused the President of bias, and later, in 1953, won a High Court libel action against a Dr Lawson for alleging he peddled quack remedies for tuberculosis. He waived his claim to the £2000 damages awarded him. The *Irish Times* remarked that Dr Crofton had published his unorthodox work on bacteriology, and added 'what is particularly annoying to his critics is that his unusual theories, when put into practice especially in connection with certain animal diseases such as "hard pad" seem to give successful results'.

2. **Dr Haze [?Hayes]**: A friend of the Chief Secretary for Ireland, Edward Shortt. (See note on him, p. 210.) This Hayes may have been Reginald Hewlett Hayes of 93 Cornwall Gardens, Queen's Gate, London. He was registered on 8 February 1895: MRCS Eng. 1895; LRCP, London 1895; and LSA, London 1895. House Surgeon at the Royal Free Hospital and Resident Obstetrician at Guy's Hospital, he wrote various medical papers. His last entry in the Medical Register is 1951.

    Another possibility, though less likely, is James George Hayes (1879–1938) of 4 St James's Place, London. He was registered on 9 November 1903. L., L.M., RCP Ireland, 1903; L., L.M., RCS, 1903. He was Surgeon to the Sydenham Dispensary and House Surgeon at All Saints Hospital for Genito-Urinary diseases, and was a Lieutenant in the RAMC, attached to the London Regiment in the First World War. In 1920 he moved from London to Hove and practised there till his death.

## 42

1. **Larkins**: Not identified.
2. **Kellys**: There were several families of Kellys around the Coole area. Among them were Dennis Kelly of Cloonagee, Brian and Andrew Kelly of Corker in the Barony of Kiltartan, Brigid Kelly of Ardrahan and Laurence Kelly of Kinvara.
3. **Lord of Ballylee killed by the fairies**: Presumably a local legend. Ballylee was close to Coole Park, so this legend may be related to the very last Burke of Ballylee,

Edmond Wick Burke, resident in the castle in 1585 where he died in 1597. After his death the castle and land were taken over by the Earl of Clanrickarde, see Rev. Jerome Fahey, *The History and Antiquities of the Diocese of Kilmacduagh* (Dublin: M.H. Gill, 1893) pp. 247–8).

4. **the lake... Coole and its woods:** The lake and the seven woods at Coole Park, Lady Gregory's home near Gort, County Galway. *Lady Gregory's Coole* (1931) gives a good description of them, but see, especially, Colin Smythe, *A Guide to Coole Park Co. Galway. Home of Lady Gregory* (1983). Many of Yeats's poems describe them, for instance 'The Wild Swans at Coole' (*YP*, p. 233), 'Coole Park 1929' (*YP*, p. 357) and 'Coole Park and Ballylee' (*YP*, p. 358).

5. **the children:** Lady Gregory's grandchildren, Richard Graham Gregory (b.1909), Anne Gregory (b.1911) and Catherine Frances Gregory (b.1913).

6. **your poem:** Yeats's poem 'A Prayer for my Daughter' (*YP*, p. 295), written between February and June 1919 and first published in *Poetry*, November 1919 and the *Irish Statesman*, 8 November 1919. Anne Butler Yeats was born in Dublin on 26 February 1919; the poem was begun shortly after her birth and finished at Yeats's tower, Thoor Ballylee, County Galway in June 1919.

7. **this fortnight:** When Iseult was staying in County Galway.

**43**

1. **nicotine, patiences:** Iseult was an addictive smoker and player of patience from adolescence on throughout her life.

2. **in the Wicklow hills:** She may have been staying near Lough Dan, possibly based on Ella Young's cottage there.

3. **George:** Mrs W.B. Yeats.

4. **Lough Nahangan:** In a dark corrie about 1400 feet up, below the south side of Wicklow Gap, on the road from Glendalough to Hollywood, it is a cirque formed in the Ice Age, drained by the Glendaran River. Sometimes known as the lake of Misfortune or of the Calamity. See R. Lloyd Praeger, *The Way that I Went* (1937), pp. 292–4. Professor Daithé O hOgain has suggested that the name is derived from Irish *Loch na hAnachan*. (Synge refers to an evil spirit associated with it in *In the Shadow of the Glen* (1903)). It is reputed to have a puca (pooka, a sprite, a bogey, a hobgoblin). The lake is now used by the Electricity Supply Board, water being pumped up at night into a reservoir at Turlough Hill on Camaderry Mountain, to rush downhill by day to generate electricity. It is also spelt Nahanagan.

5. **Valley of the witch Magnach:** She was associated in local tradition with the area around Glenmalure and Lough Nahangan. Professor OhOgain has suggested that a scholar was playing with the word *Maighneach* (Old Irish, Maigneach, meaning large or massive), and that a huge witch was called Maigneach. A tradition associated famous hags or witches with the landscape, many aspects of it explained aetiologically as the work of witches or giants.

6. **Herodotus:** A Greek historian of the fifth century called 'the Father of History' by Cicero, he was born at Halicarnassus, a Greek colony on the coast of Asia Minor, and travelled widely. Author of *The Persian Wars*, he traced the causes as well as the events of the wars between the Greeks and the Persians, supplying much mythological, archaeological, geographical and ethnological as well as historical material.

7. **Japan:** in July Yeats had been offered a two-year lectureship in Japan at the Keio Gajuken University, Tokyo. He had earlier discussed the idea in letters to John Quinn, Ezra Pound and his father, telling the latter in August that he had

accepted subject to the terms offered. Mrs Yeats's automatic writing, in the person of 'Ameritus', a 'control', however, forbade this. *The Automatic Script: 25 June 1918–29 March 1920* (eds Steve L. Adams, Barbara J. Freiling and Sandra L. Sprayberry). See Yeats's *Vision Papers* ed. George Mills Harper, 1992, II, p. 256: 'I said before no Japan next year.' The idea was dropped once the Yeatses were established in Oxford in the autumn of 1919.

8.  **Anne:** See note on Anne Hyde below, and letter 44, p. 115.


**44**

1.  **Ann Hyde:** In Mrs Yeats's automatic writing of 23 February 1918 a spirit wrote that her name was Anne Hyde, Duchess of Ormonde (she had the courtesy title of Countess of Ossory). She had married her husband James in July 1681 and had now come to give her 'dear love' to the Yeatses. After confusing her with another Anne Hyde, daughter of Edward Hyde (the Lord Chancellor and Earl of Clarendon) and the wife of James II, Yeats found that the wife of James Butler, who became Duke of Ormonde in 1680, was Anne who had died in 1677, having had a miscarriage. The automatic script's spirit suggested that she, and the child which had never lived, wished to reincarnate. In July 1918 Yeats queried why Anne Hyde had chosen them as her son's parents; later a script suggested that their child could be connected in some way with an avatar or avatars. (The word came from a vision experienced by George Russell in 1896, of a child rising above Ben Bulben, a mountain in Sligo, a vision linking the ancient gods of Ireland with magic forerunners and spiritual revelation). The avatar was to be 'fifth from the work' which Yeats took to mean that his child would be fifth in line from the Reverend John Yeats, the rector of Drumcliffe, who had lived there in the shadow of Ben Bulben (see George Mills Harper, *The Making of Yeats's A Vision* (2 vols, 1987), I, pp. 209–26. That a daughter, christened Anne Butler Yeats after the Countess of Ossory, rather than a son, was born to the Yeatses in February 1919 was excused in the script by a communicator, Thomas. Another communicator suggested that Yeats should study the Hyde papers and write Anne's history. In July 1919 the Yeatses went to Kilkenny, the Butler seat, in a vain attempt to discover Anne Hyde's burial place.


**45**

1.  **psychic events…at Gogarty's:** The Yeatses had been staying at Renvyle, Connemara, Oliver St John Gogarty's large H-shaped house. Gogarty (1878–1957), the Irish writer, Ear, Nose and Throat specialist and Senator of the Irish Free State, graduated in medicine at Trinity College, Dublin. To that period of his life some of his racier and bawdier poems can be attributed. He rented the Martello Tower at Sandycove (erroneously known as Joyce's Tower. Joyce, then friendly with Gogarty, who lent and gave him money and some clothes, stayed briefly in the Martello Tower having paid the initial rent for it) and in 1917 bought Renvyle as a remote country house, made accessible by possession of a Rolls-Royce and a Mercedes. He wrote elegant and witty lyrics, some plays (the first anticipates Sean O'Casey's use of Dublin speech and subject matter), novels and various autobiographical books, including a masterly portrayal of his Dublin life, *As I was going down Sackville Street* (1937). See Chapter XIII of it for an account of how Mrs Yeats laid the Renvyle ghost (this is treated more briefly in Gogarty's *It isn't This Time of Year at all!* (1954), pp. 146–8 and 208). But see also Seymour Leslie, *The*

*Jerome Connexion* (1964), pp. 142–5. Gogarty left Ireland and the practice of medicine in 1939 to live in America, where he supported himself and his family in Ireland by writing and lecturing. He was a good friend of Yeats (whose tonsils he removed in 1920). See J.B. Lyons, *Oliver St John Gogarty, The Man of Many Talents* (1990) and *The Poems and Plays of Oliver St John Gogarty*, ed. A. Norman Jeffares (2001).

2.  **a cottage and some land**: Ballinagoneen, a two-storied house that Maud Gonne bought in October 1919 from some of the proceeds of the sale of Les Mouettes in Colleville, Calvados. The property consisted of the house and fifteen acres of land with grazing rites over 11 800 acres. She sold it in 1928 to Dr Kathleen Lynn (see note, p. 226) who left it to the Youth Hostel Movement; it is now a Youth Hostel.

3.  **the head of Glenmalure Valley**: About 30 miles from Dublin, it was then very isolated. The house was approached by stepping stones over a little river. The nearest public transport was the railway station at Rathdrum on the Dublin–Rosslare line of the Dublin and South-Eastern Railway. It was about ten miles from the station to Ballinagoneen.

4.  **the last in civilisation**: This is an echo of Synge's stage directions in his play *The Shadow of the Glen* (1903) where the cottage, called Barravore (Barravore is the next townland to Ballinagoneen), is 'the last in the Glen'. See Joseph Hone, *W.B. Yeats 1865–1939* (1942), pp. 326–8. This gives an account of Yeats's visit to Ballinagoneen in September 1920 before Gogarty removed his tonsils in a Dublin nursing home.

5.  **Glen Imaal of the Songs**: In County Wicklow, it can be reached by walking up the Glenmalure Valley (in Irish, Maolura's Glen) and is a large natural amphitheatre. Its name means the Glen of the descendants of Mal, a second century king of Ireland. To the right are Mullacore (2179 feet) and Lugduff (2154 feet) and on the left Lugnacullia (3039 feet), while Table Mountain (2308 feet) lies ahead. The north-eastern slopes are used as an artillery range.

Glenmalure and the Glen of Imaal were long the centre of Irish resistance to English forces, largely owing to their remoteness. In 1580 Fiach MacHugh O'Byrne had his headquarters in Glenmalure, where he defeated the army of the Lord Deputy Grey de Wilton. Red Hugh O'Donnell, on escaping from Dublin Castle made for the region to hide and recuperate. At the time of the 1798 Rebellion a military road was built with various barracks and blockhouses constructed at intervals along its length. It ran north from four miles north of Tinahealy to Aughavanagh (where there was a large barracks) thence to Drumgoff, Laragh (where the barracks were subsequently to become the home of Iseult and Francis Stuart), Sallygap, Glencree, and thence, at a height of 1600–1700 feet it was carried over the Featherbed to Kilakee, ending at Rathfarnham, a few miles out of Dublin. One of the many blockhouses situated along the road was at Drumgoff (about three miles below Barravore Ford and Maud Gonne's house Ballinagoneen) which Michael Dwyer, leader of the Wicklow Insurgents in 1798, raided and burnt down. It was subsequently rebuilt. Dwyer joined the Wexford insurgents before returning to hide for several years in the Glen of Imaal, where he had been born in 1771 in Derrynamuck Cottage, five and a half miles south-east of Donard. (It has been restored as a national monument.) A song tells of how, when he and four companions were trapped by an English force, one of them, McAlister, who was already wounded, sacrificed himself by exposing himself to the soldiers' fire so that Dwyer could escape. Another 1798 leader, Joseph Holt, hid in the hills around Lough Dan, then surrendered and was transported, later returning to write his *Memoirs*, dying in Dun Laoghaire in 1820.

The whole area is steeped in savage history, memories of battles, ambushes, murders, reprisals, men on the run, and commemorated in many songs and ballads. 'The Marching Song of Fiach MacHugh', for instance, reputedly first performed by Fiach MacHugh O'Byrne's pipers in 1580, establishes Glenmalure and the Glen of Imaal as centres of resistance. See Yeats's poem 'Under the Round Tower' (*YP*, p. 239) where the beggar Billy Byrne is probably founded upon another Wicklow rebel leader, William Byrne of Ballymanus, a member of the Leinster Directory of the United Irishmen, captured and hanged in 1798.

6. **Colleville**: Les Mouettes, Maud Gonne's house in Normandy was near Colleville, Calvados, and bombed during WW2 by the Germans because it obstructed their view of Omaha Beach.

7. **Moura has been ill**: at the time Yeats thought Maud was suffering from neurasthenia. This term, first used in 1869, became a blanket description over the following 100 years to cover a wide variety of symptoms. These ranged from chronic fatigue and headaches to psychological and physical ailments such as epilepsy, paralysis and schizophrenia. The term is no longer used by the medical profession. See J. Fitzgibbon, *Feeling Tired all the Time* (2001) *passim*. Considering the emotional stresses Maud had suffered in the previous seven years in nursing the war wounded in France, losing her (estranged) husband and many close friends in the Easter Rising, the strain of trying to get from France to Ireland, imprisonment, the deaths of Lucien Millevoye and her sister Kathleen and then not being allowed into her own house by one of her oldest friends it is not surprising that, apart from the recurrence of her tubercular condition, she showed signs of shock, trauma, and nervous exhaustion, all added to her anxiety about Iseult's marriage.

8. **your analysis of Titian**: Yeats may have thought of putting him in *A Vision* in Phase Fourteen, which dealt with 'the obsessed man' whose true mask was serenity, whose false was distrust. His true creative mind was dominated by emotional will, his false by terror and his 'Body of fate' by an enforced love of the world. Yeats finally gave as examples of this phase Keats, Giorgione and 'many beautiful women.' Iseult he regarded as belonging to this phase. Titian – perhaps as a result of Iseult's reactions – is finally mentioned in 'Book V: Dove or Swan' where Yeats contemplates the period in Greek history after the Persian Wars: 'In Phidias Ionic and Doric influence unite – one remembers Titian – and all is transformed by the full moon and all abounds and flows' (W.B. Yeats, *A Vision and Related Writings* (1990), p. 261). Titian, Tiziano Vercelli (d. 1570), one of the greatest Venetian painters, whose range included mythological, historical and religious subjects as well as portraits.

9. **Antinoiis of a very advanced cycle**: Antinous was a young Ithacan noble in Homer's *Odyssey*. The most arrogant of Penelope's suitors, he was the first of them to be killed by Odysseus on his return to Ithaca.

10. **Mrs Salkeld**: Blanaid Salkeld neé Florence ffrench Mullen (1880–1958). Born in Chittagong (Bangladesh) to Irish parents, she married an English member of the Indian Civil Service. Widowed at 28 and the mother of two sons, she returned to Ireland and acted with the second Abbey Theatre Company as 'Nell Byrne'. She was a member of Cumann na mBan. One of her sons, Cecil ffrench Salkeld (1901–71), born in India, studied Art in Kassel in Germany and lived as an artist in Ireland from 1908. He painted the murals for Davy Byrne's pub, and was a friend of Iseult and Maud Gonne and her family. He was staying with them in

Glenmalure on the occasion of Yeats's visit there in September 1920. His daughter Beatrice, who was Iseult's goddaughter, married Brendan Behan.

**46**
1. **Titian:** See note on previous letter, p. 220.
2. **match-making:** Yeats said to Iseult that if she was not to make a career as a writer she should marry. He introduced her to Lennox Robinson, thinking him suitable, a view shared by Mrs Yeats. Robinson fell in love with her, to no avail.
3. **Robinson:** (Esme Stuart ) Lennox Robinson (1886–1958), playwright and theatre manager, was born in Douglas, County Cork. He attended Bandon Grammar School and wrote Ibsenite plays about life in Cork. In 1909 he became manager of the Abbey Theatre until 1914, when he took up a post as an organising librarian for the Carnegie Trust. He wrote his best comedy *The Whiteheaded Boy* (1916) and returned to the Abbey as Manager in 1918. His many plays include *The Big House* (1926) and *Drama at Inish* (1933). A protégé of Yeats, he was also a close friend of Mrs Yeats. See Letter 53, note 3, p. 228.
4. **our hut in Glenmalure:** See notes on Letter 45, p. 219.
5. **a youth called Stuart:** (Harry/Henry) Francis (Montgomery) Stuart (1902–2000), born in Townsville, Australia was the son of Henry Irwin Stuart of Ballyhivistock, Dervock, County Antrim, and his wife Elizabeth, known as Lily (neé Montgomery), whose father died of alcoholism. He returned to Ireland with his mother when his father committed suicide in Callan Park Asylum in Sydney in August 1902. (Henry Stuart had emigrated to Queensland in 1874 with his brother James; they bought a station called Rockwood in 1882 and developed it into a town. Ballyhivistock, the Stuart estate near Dervock, County Antrim was not particularly prosperous, but when it passed to Charles Stuart in 1898 Henry returned to Ireland. Ballyhivistock was two miles from Benvarden House, the home of the Montgomerys. In 1901 Henry, having married Lily, had returned to Australia with her.) Francis was educated at Rugby School between 1916 and 1918. At the period of this letter he was being tutored by H.M.O. White (later Professor of English at Trinity College, Dublin) with the idea of his entering Trinity College, Dublin. Stuart's mother had married a second time. Her new husband, a cousin, Henry Clements, a former cowboy in Texas and Mexico, was an alcoholic. He left her to live in a hotel near Victoria Station, London, with a maid from Portrush. He bequeathed his money to his sisters, not his wife. Francis disliked him and his efforts 'to make a man of him'.
6. **What Gogarty said:** It has not been possible to trace this saying in any of Gogarty's writings. Yeats admired Gogarty's heroic song and there was often a two-way traffic between their thoughts and poetic imagery. His conversational remark may well have emerged years later (as often happened with Yeats) in 'Under Ben Bulben' (*YP*, p. 450):

> . . . when all words are said
> And a man is fighting mad,
> Something drops from eyes long blind,
> He completes his partial mind,
> For an instant stands at ease,
> Laughs aloud, his heart at peace.

7. **your sisters:** See note on p. 177.

**47**

1. **your play**: *The Player Queen*, first performed by the Stage Society on 25 May at the King's Hall, Covent Garden. It was first performed in Dublin at the Abbey Theatre on 9 December 1919.

2. **pro and anti-Dreyfusards**: See *GYL*, p. 437, where Maud Gonne reminds Yeats of 'the old days' when he was a Dreyfusard and used to think the thesis 'Better France perish than one man suffer injustice' fine. (She sympathised with French nationalists and was anti-Dreyfusard.) Alfred Dreyfus (c.1859–1935), born at Mulhausen in Alsace, the son of a rich Jewish manufacturer, was a captain in the artillery, serving on the General Staff. In 1893–94 he was falsely charged and court-martialled. The verdict was reversed in 1906, though he had already been re-tried, found guilty and pardoned. He served in the First World War and was awarded the Legion d'Honneur. For a time France was in a turmoil of controversy, between supporters of Dreyfus and his attackers who were often motivated by anti-Semitism. The last of Emile Zola's (1840–1902) three novels in his final work, *Les Quatre Evangiles, Vérité* (1903) refers to the Dreyfus case, in which his letter to the newspaper *L'Aurore*, 'J'Accuse', had led to a sentence of imprisonment for libel, avoided by his self-exile in England for 11 months (1898–99).

3. **the pro and anti-Unicornians**: In Yeats's play *The Player Queen*, according to the Tapster, the Queen has been seen, by the boy Strolling Michael, coupling with a great white Unicorn. Septimus the poet, in a fine flow of drunken rhetoric, will allow no one to speak against the Unicorn, and subsequently proclaims 'the end of the Christian era, the coming of a New Dispensation, that of the New Adam, that of the Unicorn, but alas, he is chaste, he hesitates, he hesitates.' Later he attacks the Unicorn for his chastity. Critics have argued over the putative mating of Decima with the Unicorn; their varying views are recorded in A. Norman Jeffares and A.S. Knowland, *A Commentary on the Collected Plays of W.B. Yeats* (1975), pp. 144–6. There are obvious parallels here with Yeats's poem 'The Second Coming' (*YP*, p. 294).

4. **Mrs Salkeld**: See note, p. 220.

5. **Moura . . . first tragic version**: Yeats began the play in 1908. In *Plays in Prose and Verse* (1922) where he published the play after its first appearance in *The Dial*, November 1922, he wrote that he had begun a verse tragedy:

> I wasted the best working months of several years in an attempt to write a poetical play where every character became an example of the finding or not finding of what I have called The Antithetical Self [This thought was explored in *Per Amica Silentia Lunae* (1918)] and because passion and not thought makes tragedy, what I had made had neither simplicity nor life. I knew precisely what was wrong and yet could neither escape from thought nor give up my play. At last it came into my head all of a sudden that I could get rid of the play if I turned it into a farce; and never did I do anything so easily, for I think that I wrote the present play in about a month . . .

6. **the little Ulster girl**: The Queen was played by Shena Tyreconnell.

7. **Arthur Shields**: The cast for the Abbey production in 1909 was as follows: 1st Old Man, Barry Fitzgerald; 2nd Old Man, R.C. Murray; Old Woman, Maureen Delaney; Happy Tom, Peter Nolan; Peter of the Purple Pelican, T. Quinn; Citizens, Bryan Herbert, J.J. Lynch, R.C. Murray, Philip Guiry, etc.; Tapster, P.J. McCormick;

Countrymen, Hugh Nagle, J.G. St John, P.J. McDonnell, etc.; Big Countryman, Ambrose Power; Old Beggar, Michael J. Dolan; Prime Minister, Eric Gorman; Nona, May Craig; Players, Margaret Nicholls, Barry Fitzgerald, Bryan Herbert, J.J. Lynch, P.J. McDonnell, etc.; Queen, Sheena Tyreconnell; Decima, Christine Hayden; Stage Manager, Philip Guiry; Bishop, Peter Nolan.

8. **the prophetic old man**: The Old Beggar, who appears in Scene 1 looking for straw. Septimus the Poet regards him as inspired when he says

> When something comes inside me, my back itches. Then I must lie down and roll, and then I bray and the crown changes.

In Scene II the Old Beggar is still looking for straw. What rolls, he says, is the donkey that carried Christ into Jerusalem, 'and that is why he is so proud and is why he knows the hour when there is to be a new King or a new Queen. He goes off stage announcing his back is beginning to itch, just as Decima, betrayed by Septimus, is prevented from committing suicide by the Queen, with whom she changes place. The Prime Minister banishes Septimus after the donkey's bray is heard announcing a miracle. The crown is now on Decima's head for good.

9. **thinking of getting married**: To Francis Stuart. See note on him, p. 221.

10. **America?**: Yeats and his wife went to America, leaving Liverpool on the *Carmania* on 13 January 1920, staying there until May 1920. On this trip Mrs Yeats met Yeats's father, the artist John Butler Yeats and his friend and patron John Quinn, the Irish-American lawyer. Yeats lectured in Canada as well as in the States, where the couple travelled widely by train to the West and Midwest.

**48**

1. **'it was only an idle dream'**: Is this an echo of Longfellow's 'A psalm of life' (1838): 'Life is but an empty dream'?

2. **14 or 17**: Phases in Yeats's *A Vision*, where Iseult was placed in Phase 14 (see note, p. 220) and Yeats himself in Phase 17, though neither were attributed to these phases in the published version. In Phase 17 were Dante, Shelley and Landor, examples of the *Daimonic Man*. Their true masks were 'Simplification through Intensity', their false 'Dispersal'. Their *Creative Minds*, when true, were 'Creative imagination through *antithetical* emotion, when false, were 'Enforced self-realisation', their *Bodies of Fate* 'Enforced Loss', see W.B. Yeats, *A Vision and Related Writings* (1990), pp. 171–4:

> He is called the *Daimonic* man because Unity of Being, and consequent expression of *Daimonic* thought, is now more easy than at any other phase. As contrasted with Phase 13 and Phase 14, where mental images were separated from one another that they might be subject to knowledge, all now flow, change, flutter, cry out, or mix into something else; but without, as at Phase 16, breaking and bruising one another, for Phase 17, the central phase of its triad, is without frenzy. The *Will* is falling asunder, but without explosion and noise. The separated fragments seek images rather than ideas, and these the intellect, seated in Phase 13, must synthesise in vain, drawing with its compass-point a line that shall but respect the outline of a bursting pod. The being has for its supreme aim, as it had at Phase 16 (and as all subsequent *antithetical* phases shall have), to hide for himself and others this separation and disorder, and it conceals them under the emotional Image of Phase 3; as Phase 16 concealed its greater

violence under that of Phase 2. When true to phase the intellect must turn all its synthetic power to this task. It finds, not the impassioned myth that Phase 16 found, but a *Mask* of simplicity that is also intensity. This *Mask* may represent intellectual or sexual passion; seem some Ahasuerus or Athanase; be the gaunt Dante of the Divine Comedy; its corresponding Image may be Shelley's Venus Urania, Dante's Beatrice, or even the Great Yellow Rose of the *Paradiso*. The *Will*, when true to phase, assumes, in assuming the *Mask*, an intensity which is never dramatic but always lyrical and personal, and this intensity, though always a deliberate assumption, is to others but the charm of the being; and yet the *Will* is always aware of the *Body of Fate*, which perpetually destroys this intensity, thereby leaving the *Will* to its own 'dispersal'.

At Phase 3, not as *Mask* but as phase, there should be perfect physical well-being or balance, though not beauty or emotional intensity, but at Phase 27 are those who turn away from all that Phase 3 represents and seek all those things it is blind to. The *Body of Fate*, therefore, derived from a phase of renunciation, is 'loss', and works to make impossible 'simplification through intensity'. The being, through the intellect, selects some object of desire for a representation of the *Mask* as Image, some woman perhaps, and the *Body of Fate* snatches away the object. Then the intellect (*Creative Mind*), which in the most antithetical phases are better described as imagination, must substitute some new image of desire; and in the degree of its power and of its attainment of unity, relate that which is lost, that which has snatched it away, to the new image of desire, that which threatens the new image to the being's unity. If its unity be already past, or if unity be still to come, it may for all that be true to phase. It will then use its intellect merely to isolate *Mask* and Image, as chosen forms or as conceptions of the mind.

If it be out of phase it will avoid the subjective conflict, acquiesce, hope that the *Body of Fate* may die away; and then the *Mask* will cling to it and the Image lure it. It will feel itself betrayed, and persecuted till, entangled in *primary* conflict, it rages against all that destroys *Mask* and *Image*. It will be subject to nightmare, for its *Creative Mind* (deflected from the Image and *Mask* to the *Body of Fate*) gives an isolated mythological or abstract form to all that excites its hatred. It may even dream of escaping from ill-luck by possessing the impersonal *Body of Fate* of its opposite phase and of exchanging passion for desk and ledger. Because of the habit of synthesis, and of the growing complexity of the energy, which gives many interests, and the still faint perception of things in their weight and mass, men of this phase are almost always partisans, propagandists and gregarious; yet because of the *Mask* of simplification, which holds up before them the solitary life of hunters and of fishers and 'the groves pale passion loves', they hate parties, crowds, propaganda. Shelley out of phase writes pamphlets, and dreams of converting the world, or of turning man of affairs and upsetting governments, and yet returns again and again to these two images of solitude, a young man whose hair has grown white from the burden of his thought, an old man in some shell-strewn cave whom it is possible to call, when speaking to the Sultan, 'as inaccessible as God or thou'. On the other hand, how subject he is to nightmare! He sees the devil leaning against a tree, is attacked by imaginary assassins, and, in obedience to what he considers a supernatural voice, creates *The Cenci* that he may give to Beatrice Cenci her incredible father. His political enemies are monstrous, meaningless images. And unlike Byron, who is two phases later, he can never see anything that opposes him as it really is. Dante, who lamented his exile as of all possible things the worst for such as he, and sighed for his lost solitude, and yet could never keep from politics, was, according to a contemporary, such a partisan that if a child, or a woman, spoke against his party he would pelt this child or woman with stones. Yet Dante, having attained, as poet, to Unity of Being, as poet saw all things set in order, had an intellect that served the *Mask* alone, that compelled even those things that opposed it to serve, and was content to see both good and evil. Shelley, upon the other hand, in whom even as poet unity was but in part attained, found compensation for his 'loss', for the taking away of his children, for his quarrel with his first wife, for later sexual disappointment, for his exile, for his obloquy – there were but some three or four persons, he said, who did not consider him a monster of iniquity – in his hopes for the future of mankind. He lacked the Vision of Evil, could not conceive of the world as a continual conflict, so, though great poet he certainly was, he was not of the greatest kind. Dante suffering injustice and the loss of Beatrice, found divine justice and the heavenly Beatrice, but the justice of *Prometheus Unbound* is a vague propagandist emotion and the women that await its coming are but clouds. This is in part because the age in which Shelley lived was in itself so broken that true Unity of Being was almost impossible, but partly because, being out of phase so far as his practical reason was concerned, he was subject to an *automatonism* which he mistook for poetical invention, especially in his longer poems. *Antithetical* men (Phase 15 once passed) use this *automatonism* to evade hatred, or rather to hide it from their own eyes; perhaps all at some time or other, in moments of fatigue, give themselves up to fantastic, constructed images, or to an almost mechanical laughter.

Landor has been examined in *Per Amica Silentia Lunae*. The most violent of men, he uses his intellect to disengage a visionary image of perfect sanity (*Mask* at Phase 3) seen always in the most serene and classic art imaginable. He had perhaps as much Unity of Being as his age permitted, and possessed, though not in any full measure, the Vision of Evil.

3. **it makes things easier**: As Iseult was a Catholic.
4. **Glenmalure**: Maud Gonne's house there. See note, p. 219.
5. **Lennox**: Lennox Robinson. Robinson (see earlier note, p. 221) was 'showing great generosity' to Stuart, since he was himself in love with Iseult, and still seems to have been so in 1930. See R.F. Foster, *W.B. Yeats. A Life*, II (2003). p. 351.
6. **When will you come back?**: The Yeatses returned in May 1920.

**49**
1. **Baravore**: The address of the letter; Barravore is the townland next to Maud Gonne's house in Glenmalure.
2. **Landor**: Walter Savage Landor (1775–1864). Born at Warwick, he was expelled from Rugby School for insubordination and rusticated from Trinity College, Oxford. He lived on an allowance, then inherited a considerable income on his father's death in 1805. He spent several years in Italy, from 1815 to 1835, having spent a good deal of his inheritance equipping volunteers to fight Napoleon in Spain in 1808. He lived in Italy again from 1856 to 1864 as the result of a scandal and a libel action. His best-known prose work *Imaginary Conversations* (1824–29) was written in Italy. His highly elaborate and polished poetry contains the short and pleasing lyrics to Ianthe. Yeats appreciated in Landor the metaphysical paradox of 'the most violent of men' – Landor was notoriously irascible and quarrelsome – using his intellect to disengage a 'visionary image of perfect sanity.'

3. **a walnut tree being shaken:** Probably an echo of the old jingle:

   'A woman, a dog and a walnut tree/The more you beat them the better they be'.

4. **Moura . . . hard things about Francis:** See her letters to Yeats about Stuart. She thought 'his family are a queer lot from Antrim who, though well connected have drunk themselves into degeneracy. He has talent of a queer morbid kind but no education & no power or will to work' (*GYL*, p. 403). She told Yeats that Iseult 'says he does not drink, she says he is not mad, she says I don't see the good there is in him. She says he has charm & great will power & possibility for genius. I see the will power & Northern cunning & selfishness. He MAY have talent' (*GYL*, pp. 406–7).

5. **his mother in the North:** See note on Mrs Clements, p. 221 and see *GYL*, pp. 408–11, 414, 416, 420 and note p. 527. She had taken a house in Cushendall, a glen in County Antrim.

6. **our new flat:** They were initially in lodgings in 5 Ely Place and then rented a flat in 67 Fitzwilliam Square. See *GYL*, p. 404.

## 50

1. **Lough Dan:** in County Wicklow, it is about 25 miles south-west of Dublin. She may have been staying in Ella Young's cottage there.

2. **My little one:** Dolores Veronica Stuart, born on 9 March 1921 at 75 St Stephen's Green, died on 24 July 1921 at St Ultan's Children's Hospital, Charlemont Street, Dublin.

3. **Bettystown:** A coastal village in County Meath, about 20 miles north of Dublin, where Mrs Clements had rented a bungalow.

4. **Lynn:** Dr Kathleen Lynn (1874–1956) was born in County Mayo, where her father was a Church of Ireland rector, and educated at Alexandra College, Dublin, and in England and Germany. Part of the first generation of women doctors in Ireland, she took her primary degree in the Royal University of Ireland in 1899 (24 other women graduated with medical degrees from the RUI between 1880 and 1899). In 1909 she gained her Fellowship at the Royal College of Surgeons of Ireland. She found it difficult to find a position at first but was finally accepted by Sir Patrick Duns' Hospital and the Rotunda, and set up her private practice at her home, 9 Belgrave Road, Dublin. She worked for women's suffrage, and during the 1913 Lock-out in Dublin joined the women's section of the Citizen Army, where she was among other women who were suffragettes, nationalists and members of the Irish Women Worker's Union. They included such women as Constance Markiewicz, a distant cousin of hers, Hanna Sheehy Skeffington, Helena Molony, Helen Laird and Maud Gonne MacBride when she came from Paris to join them. These women took care of the strikers and their families, operating a soup kitchen and providing medical aid. Dr Lynn took charge of this and was later appointed Chief Medical Officer of the Citizen Army, serving in that capacity in the Easter Rising in 1916. As a captain she was the highest ranking officer on the death of the commander, Sean Connolly (not to be confused with the founder of the Citizen Army, James Connolly, military commander at the Post Office, who was shot after a court martial). Yeats alludes to this Connolly, in charge of the rebel forces attacking Dublin Castle, as 'the player Connolly' (he had been an Abbey actor and was a close friend of Helena Molony) in the third

of 'Three Songs to the One Burden' (*YP*, p. 545). Dr Lynn made the surrender for the forces, was arrested and imprisoned.

On her release she continued her practice, travelling by bicycle to visit patients. In 1917 she was one of the four women elected to the Sinn Fein executive (of 24 members). During the War of Independence she took care of many wounded men, her house regularly raided by British forces searching for them. When on the run herself, she abandoned her bicycle, disguising herself in fashionable clothes and sporting a feather boa . . . She was arrested again, but released on the intervention of the Lord Mayor so that she could work with the dying and gravely ill in the 1918 influenza epidemic. Her extensive knowledge of the poor of the city – where two children in five died in the slums – led her to think that she must set up a hospital. With the help of her friend Madeleine ffrench Mullen (sister of Florry Salkeld), a fellow member of the Citizen Army, she bought 37 Charlemont Street, a derelict run-down house; with the aid of her friends it was ready to open by Ascension Thursday 1919 and was named St Ultan's after the early Christian Bishop of Ardbraccan (a former bishopric near Navan) who rescued and cared for many orphans in the period of the yellow plague. (see Margaret O hOgartaigh, 'St Ultan and Ardbraccan', *Piocht na Midhe* (2003).) Originally intended as a hospital for the adult poor, children were soon included among its patients. Dr Lynn, who opposed the Treaty, found that her energies were now taken up by her work for the hospital. She introduced pioneering courses in hygiene and infant care for young mothers; she fought with the authorities about the dreadful conditions of the slums and the unsafe milk, St Ultan's being the first hospital in Ireland to introduce a BCG vaccine scheme through the initiative of Dr Dorothy Stopford Price (see *Ireland in the 1930s* ed. Joost Augusteijin). Many well-known women doctors (among them Dr Ella Webb and Dr Dorothy Stopford Price) worked with her over the years, and the hospital acquired land behind the house as it grew, even including a special BCG wing there. Dr Lynn attended her last clinic in April 1955 and died the following September. She had bought the Glenmalure house from the Whelan family who had purchased it from Maud Gonne and, believing strongly in the benefits of fresh air and exercise, left it to *An Oige* (the Irish Youth Hostel Association.)

5.  **Dean Grange**: Deansgrange, about six miles south of Dublin.

## 51

1.  **our behalf**: At Iseult's suggestion, Yeats had taken up with Blythe (see next note) the question of compensation being paid by the Free State government for a car owned by Maud Gonne which had been seized by the Black and Tans.

2.  **Blythe**: Ernest Blythe (Earnan de Blaghd). Born near Lisburn, County Antrim in 1889, he died in 1975. He joined the Gaelic League and the IRB when a clerk in the Department of Agriculture in Dublin. He was imprisoned during the 1916 Rising. From 1918 to 1936 he was a TD. He held ministerial posts for Commerce, Finance and Posts and Telegraphs, losing his seat in 1933 as a result of becoming unpopular from reducing old age pensions. From 1933 to 1936 he was a Senator. He made the first government grant to the Abbey Theatre and served as its managing director from 1941 to 1967 in a drearily dull period of the theatre's history, his policy of engaging only Irish-speaking actors and actresses losing it the services of some excellent talent. His zeal for the revival of Irish led him to support the Irish language theatre (*An Taibhearc*) and to found the government's Irish language publishing house (*An Gum*). Blythe was a bitter opponent of the

anti-treaty side in the Civil War and so there was strong animosity between him and Maud Gonne who had opposed the Free State government by protesting and organising public demonstrations when the reprisal shootings of prisoners were taking place. (See *GYL*, pp. 425 and 428.) Two members of the Dail had been shot at and one killed (see *GYL*, pp. 428 and 435).

3. **Liam Mellows**: He was one of the four leaders of the anti-treaty IRA (the others were Rory O'Connor, Frank McKelvey and Joe Barrett) imprisoned by the Free State government and subsequently shot as reprisals, the first of 77 (Sean Mac-Bride had been sharing a cell with Rory O'Connor when he was taken out to be shot without trial). This prompted Maud Gonne to found the Women Prisoners' Defence League. This organisation drew attention to the plight of prisoners, publicising injustices and ensuring the prisoners were looked after in matter of food and clothing as well as supporting their dependants. Maud continued this work well into the 1930s. Political divisions had deepened after the deaths of Arthur Griffith and Michael Collins.

4. **anxious over your little girl**: Anne Yeats had been seriously ill at the time.

5. **Cecil's daughter**: Beatrice Salkeld, who married Brendan Behan, was Cecil ffrench Salkeld's daughter (see note on him, p. 220) and Iseult's god-daughter.

## 52

1. **the translations**: Yeats had asked her opinion of some translations into French.

2. **André Gide**: André Paul Guillaume Gide (1869–1951), the influential French author, was born in Paris; he wrote over 50 volumes which included fiction, poetry, plays, biography, criticism, translations and belles-lettres. He was a co-founder of the *Nouvelle Revue française* in 1909. His *L'Immoraliste* (1902), *La Symphonie Pastorale* (1919), his autobiographical *Si le grain ne meurt* (1929), *Les Faux Monnayeurs* (1926) and his *Journal* are perhaps his best known works.

3. **two things of mine**: not identified, possibly contributions intended for *To-Morrow*.

## 53

1. **your illness**: Yeats was suffering from high blood pressure. One of his eyes had become virtually useless, he was growing deaf and his increasing weight bothered him. On his walks he found himself short of breath; the doctor he consulted asked him if he had been over-excited, to which he had replied that he had lived a life of excitement. He had been working hard on *A Vision* during 1924 and took a holiday from November 1924 to February 1925, he and his wife going to Sicily, Capri and Rome. He was about to become 'a sixty-year-old smiling public man': Senator, Nobel Prize winner and holder of honorary degrees from the Universities of Dublin and Aberdeen (Oxford was to confer one on him in 1931) and with his book *A Vision* about to emerge.

2. **an operation on some gland**: Was this a suggestion that eventually led to Yeats having the Steinach operation?

3. **Lennox ... trouble with the Carnegie people**: In 1924 Lennox Robinson was dismissed from his post as organising Librarian with the Carnegie Trust, which he had held since 1915. This was because of the adverse publicity that ensued when his story 'The Madonna of Slieve Dun' was published in *To-Morrow*. This was a story on the theme of the Immaculate Conception which was considered offensive. In it a girl raped by a tramp professes to be the mother of Christ.

4. **Francis...Cecil...To-Morrow:** Francis Stuart and Cecil Salkeld (see note on him, p. [ ]) launched *To-Morrow*, a literary magazine which ran for two issues (August and September 1924), the latter published from Roebuck House, the price 7/6 per annum. Apart from Lennox Robinson's story 'The Madonna of Slieve Dun', Liam O'Flaherty's story dealing with sexual relations between races also gave offence. Yeats wrote the first editorial, which attacked bad writers and bishops (of all denominations) as atheists (the magazine was dedicated to the immortality of the soul). Yeats also contributed 'Leda and the Swan' (*YP*, p. 351) to the magazine. (The poem had first been published in *The Dial*, June 1924, two months earlier. See J. Hone, *W.B. Yeats 1865–1939* (1942), pp. 361–2.) Arthur Symons contributed a long article on Honoré Daumier to the September issue. Iseult herself contributed to both issues, 'Thy Kingdom come' in August, and 'The Poplar Road' in September.

5. **the letter to the Holy Office:** presumably in defence of *To-Morrow*. Yeats suggested that they should refer Lennox Robinson's story to the Pope.

**54**

1. **your book:** *A Vision* dated 1925, published 1926.

2. **Geraldus:** 'Portrait of Giraldus' which appeared in *Stories of Michael Robartes and his Friends. An Extract from a Record made by his Pupils* (see *W.B. Yeats, A Vision and Related Writings*, ed. A. Norman Jeffares (1990), p. 97). Edmund Dulac (1882–1953), the French-born naturalised British artist and book designer drew 'a sketch in pencil of the portrait of Gyraldus by an unknown artist of the sixteenth century' for Yeats in 1923. See *Letters to W.B. Yeats*, eds Finneran, Harper and Murphy, II (1977) p. 439. The portrait suggests a somewhat sardonic-looking Yeats.

3. **a clear beautiful poem:** 'The Phases of the Moon' (*YP*, pp. 267–73, annotation, p. 565, and see notes in the 1990 edition of *A Vision*, pp. 388–93).

4. **Meath:** Either Bettystown, where Iseult's mother-in-law, Lily Clements, had a bungalow on the edge of the sea, or Bridesbush, Duleek, where Janet Montgomery, Lily's sister, had a farm.

5. **Krishnamurti:** Jiddu Krishnamurti (1895–1986). At the age of 14 he was taken under the guardianship of Annie Besant, the socialist, reformer and president of the International Theosophist Society at Adyar, near Madras. She and her associates believed Krishnamurti was the vehicle for the Messiah whose coming the theosophists predicted. When 16 he was taken to England to be privately educated and trained for his role as a world teacher. In 1929 he had a spiritual experience which changed his life: he dissolved the organisation built up around him and gave up the money and property that had accrued to him. He stated that the truth cannot be found in a sect and that his concern was to see men absolutely free. He became an internationally known spiritual teacher, thousands being attracted to the gatherings in India, California, England and Switzerland. He published over 25 books and was involved in many love affairs.

6. **Mrs Despard:** Mrs Charlotte Despard, neé French (1844–1939), sister of Sir John French, later Earl of Ypres (1852–1924), Lord Lieutenant of Ireland (1918–21). She was an advocate of women's rights, a social reformer and a pacifist. She met Maud Gonne in London in 1917 and moved to Ireland in 1921, living in 73 St Stephen's Green and then in Roebuck House, Clonskeagh, Co. Dublin which she bought jointly with Maud Gonne in August 1922. She was sometimes known (like Maud Gonne and the Countess Constance Markiewicz) as Madame (Yeats alluded to her thus, as Madame Despard, in a letter to Maud Gonne, who called

her Mrs Despard in letters to him). She established industries there to give employment to prisoners released at the end of the Civil War and to those who opposed the 1921 Treaty and found it difficult to get jobs in the Free State. The jam-making industry was set up in 1924; it was taken over by Sean MacBride and his wife Catalina in 1927 and was sold in 1932. (At the time Maud Gonne had established Roebuck Shell Flowers; she designed the flowers herself, the idea coming from an African shell necklace she had seen in the National Museum of Ireland; she sold the business in the mid-1930s, just about recovering her initial outlay.) In 1933 Mrs Despard moved to Eccles Street, Dublin where she founded a Workers' College – she supported the Workers Party of Ireland – and housed the Irish Friends of Soviet Russia with which organisation she had visited the USSR at the age of 86. She finally moved to Belfast in 1934.

**55**
1. **Ballilee**: Thoor Ballylee, near Gort, County Galway, Yeats's tower, used as a summer residence until 1929.
2. **The Moira**: A Dublin hotel and restaurant, situated at 15 Trinity Street.
3. **Moura . . . very ill . . . cottage in the hills**: Probably to Ballycoyle, the cottage near Glencree where the Stuarts were living since 1924. See p. 123.
4. **back**: presumably from Paris, where Sean MacBride and his wife were living, where Maud Gonne visited them in 1926.

**56**
1. **your kind invitation**: Possibly to visit the Yeatses at Thoor Ballylee, County Galway.
2. **your book**: Probably *October Blast*, a Cuala Press edition published in Dublin in 1927, the poems of which were included in *The Tower* (1928). They were 'Sailing to Byzantium', 'The Tower', 'Two Songs from a Play', 'Wisdom', 'Among School Children' and 'A Man Young and Old'.
3. **I love all the verse about old age**: Iseult may have been thinking of 'Sailing to Byzantium', 'The Tower', 'Wisdom', 'Among School Children' and some of the 11 poems of 'A Man Young and Old'.
4. **Free State Senate**: Yeats was made a Senator in 1922, the year he bought a Georgian house in Dublin, 82 Merrion Square.
5. **the boys**: Perhaps a jocular allusion to the IRA. She would have met many of them in the circles in which she moved.

**57**
1. **the baby's name**: Ian Nicholas Stuart, born 5 October 1926.
2. **Francis' essay**: Not identified.
3. **'Revelations of Divine Love'**: Julian of Norwich (1343–after 1416), an anchorite, wrote *XVI Revelations of Divine Love*, two manuscript copies of which are in the British Library.

**58**
1. **'these poems of Francis'**: Not identified. He published 'At the Races' in *Mo Motley: The Dublin Gate Theatre Magazine*, March 1932 and 'The Outcasts to the Smug and Respectable' in the October issue, 1932. He was mainly occupied with his novels, *Women and God* appearing in 1931, *Pigeon Irish* and *The Coloured Dome* in 1932.

2. **O'Flaherty:** Liam O'Flaherty (1896–1984), born on Inishmore, the largest of the Aran Isles, was educated at Outquarter National School there, and at Rockwell College, County Tipperary, where he became a postulant of the Holy Ghost Fathers. In 1915 he joined the Irish Guards, using his mother's name, Ganly; he was wounded in September 1917 and discharged after a year of treatment for acute melancholia. He spent two somewhat aimless years before demonstrating his radicalism by holding the Rotunda in Dublin as chairman of 'The Council of the Unemployed', flying the red flag over the building. He began to write novels with *Thy Neighbour's Wife* (1928), followed by *The Black Soul* (1924), *The Informer* (1925), *Mr Gilhooley* (1926) and *The Assassin* (1928). His short stories about peasant life were shrewd and realistic. In 1926 he married Margaret Curtis (previously the wife of the historian Professor Edmund Curtis) but left her and their daughter in 1932, suffering a series of nervous breakdowns but continuing to write, his regional novels, such as *The House of Gold* (1929) and *Skerett* (1932) now giving a sensitive portrayal of a wide range of regional life. His last novels – *Famine* (1937) in particular – portrayed the growth of contemporary Irish nationalism. He gained a late reputation for his short stories written in Irish, collected in one volume, *Duil*, in 1953.

3. **a desperate prig:** Iseult had resented O'Flaherty's making a pass at her, and disliked his influence on Francis, who stayed with him in London occasionally.

4. **your book ... happy reading:** Probably *Words for Music Perhaps and Other Poems* published by the Cuala Press, Dublin in 1932. Yeats described them as 'all praise of joyous life.'

**59**

1. **you with a beard:** Yeats had been seriously ill at Rapallo, and during the six weeks he spent in bed in the spring grew a white beard. In the summer Gogarty advised him to take it off, as it made him look old, and he did so before returning to Dublin in July 1930.

2. **someone who has been very ill ... Gogarty ... not high blood pressure at all:** See earlier note on Yeats's high blood pressure in 1924, p. 228. For note on Gogarty see p. 218.

3. **George Moore:** Was seeing George Moore part of Yeats's fever? George Moore (1852–1933) had not spared Yeats malice in his autobiographical *Hail and Farewell, Ave* (1911), *Salve* (1912) and *Vale* (1914). Yeats did not get his own back until, after Moore's death, he wrote *Dramatis Personæ* (1935). Moore, the son of a racehorse-owning landlord in County Mayo who was an MP, had intended to be a painter, but instead became a realistic novelist, his *Esther Waters* (1894), the last he wrote in this vein. He returned to Ireland in 1900 but his earlier *A Drama in Muslin* (1886) was a novel about social injustice, the hypocrisy of the landlord class and the difficulties imposed upon intelligent young women expected to enter the marriage market. Later the stories of *The Untilled Field* (1903) recorded his dislike of the Irish scene. *The Lake* (1905) with its melodic line, based upon oral speech, was a very successful study of religious belief. He left Ireland for Ebury Street in London and wrote *The Brook Kerith* (1916), an apocryphal story of Jesus among the Essenes, and a *tour de force*. *Heloise and Abelard* (1921) is a masterly, atmospheric retelling of the famous love story. Moore played a part in the early period of the Irish dramatic movement, and brought into English and Irish intellectual life a greater awareness of the French impressionist painters (about whom he wrote enthusiastically) as well as the French symbolist poets;

his early life in Paris as an art student and frequenter of cafés had given him a wide acquaintance with the artistic life of France.

4. **Francis has a poultry farm... and an assistant**: This was at Laragh Castle, formerly a military barracks or blockhouse, later castellated by a Victorian owner; it had been bought for the Stuarts by Maud Gonne in about 1927. The assistant was an Englishwoman, Hilda Burnett, who became responsible for managing the poultry farm (the hens were kept in the former prison yard), which proved successful and then was sold in 1931.

**60**

1. **Flory Salkeld's poems**: Blanaid Salkeld (1880–1959). Her volume *The Fox's Covert* (1935) probably contained these poems. See notes on her, p. 220, on her older son Cecil ffrench Salkeld, p. 220 and on his daughter Beatrice, p. 228.
2. **At Roebuck**: Roebuck House, Clonskeagh, Maud Gonne's residence in Dublin.

# (II) The Letters to Ezra Pound

## Chapter 3 Iseult Gonne and Ezra Pound

1. **Aleck Sheppler**: of Irish extraction, she worked as a typist for the *Illustrated London News*, then on *Vogue*. Various letters Yeats wrote to her (he knew her as 'Seraphita') between September 1914 and 9 November 1917 have survived. See R.F. Foster, *W.B. Yeats, A Life* II, 2003, p. 23, where she is described as Yeats's 'intermittent mistress', and p. 30 for her accompanying him to Coole. She was living in Chelsea, at 20 Cremorne Road and then, in 1917, at 266 Kings Road. In the *Diaries of Antonia White, 1926–1957* (1991) Susan Chitty described her as a 'beautiful, rather tragic woman who had been a model (and therefore mistress) of Augustus John'. Antonia White had found her 'crankish and vinegarish'. She died of cancer living in the country 'old, alone and poor.'

**1**

1. **Dr Ross**: Sir Denison Ross, Head of the School of Oriental Studies, University of London (see note on him, p. 199) where Iseult was employed.
2. **inconvenient for you**: as she was to be employed by Pound. See her letters to Yeats, pp. 98, 99, 103–5 and 110 and notes on them.
3. **Sophie ... an escorte**: Josephine Pillon, the cook, the Norman woman who had accompanied the Gonnes from France and did not speak English.

**2**

1. **Mrs Patmore's letter**: Brigit Patmore, unhappily married to Coventry Patmore's grandson, a successful insurance broker, was beautiful and rich. She frequented literary circles, notably that of the Imagistes. She met Pound through Violet Hunt with whom Ford Madox Hueffer (later Ford) was living at South Lodge, where Pound was a frequent visitor. He dedicated *Lustra* (1916) to Brigit, disguised under the troubadour name 'Vail de Lencour'. He gave her the page proofs of *Canzoni* (corrected in Paris in May 1911), probably in 1916. She introduced Richard Aldington to Pound in 1912, and when they were living together they visited the Pounds in Rapallo in 1928, and stayed there on a temporary basis, Pound finding

them hotel rooms. Humphrey Carpenter has suggested that Brigit Patmore was the Cynthia of Pound's *Homage to Sextus Propertius*, four of the 12 poems of which were published by Harriet Monroe in *Poetry*, March 1919; three of these and three other sections appeared in the *New Age* between 19 June 1919 and 28 April 1920.

**3**
1.  **Mrs Mucker**: not identified.
2.  **the journey ... Mothersills ... all went well**: Maud, who had been staying at Woburn Place with Iseult, Sean and Josephine Pillon after leaving the nursing home to which she had been transferred, had disguised herself as a nurse sufficiently successfully to evade detection. Mothersills, a patent medicine of the time, probably used to ward off travel sickness.
3.  **The Russell Hotel**: in St Stephen's Green.
4.  **Dr Lynn's house**: See note on her, p. 226.
5.  **Stephen's Green**: Maud's house, 73 St Stephen's Green, then rented by the Yeatses on a monthly basis.
6.  **the Lord Mayor**: Laurence O'Neill, Lord Mayor of Dublin (1916–23), organised an anti-conscription meeting on 18 April 1918, formed the White Cross executive on 1 February 1921, and with the Archbishop of Dublin summoned a peace conference in April 1922. After the shelling of the Four Courts in June 1922 he organised women's peace delegations to the opposing sides in the Civil War.
7.  **George**: Mrs W.B. Yeats.
8.  **flu**: the Spanish influenza epidemic which arrived in Dublin in November 1918; the virus continued its lethal course until the spring of 1919. A severe strain had developed, often fatal if pneumonia developed in the patient.
9.  **Uncle William**: Pound's name for W.B. Yeats.
10. **Helen Molony**: See note on her, p. 187.
11. **que c'est bien ... de toi**: the thing is it's just idiotic to be so far away from you.

**4**
1.  **W. Buildings**: 18 Woburn Buildings, Yeats's residence in London. Iseult had been living there after Yeats and his wife 'shifted her' in August 1918 from the flat she had been sharing with Iris Barry (see note, p. 201) in 25 Beaufort Mansions since 25 March 1918. See Yeats's letter to Lady Gregory of 14 August 1918, quoted p. 135.
2.  **Dr Lynn's charlady**: see note on Dr Lynn, p. 226. Iseult had been staying in her house, 9 Belgrave Road, Rathmines, during the period after Maud had returned in disguise to Dublin. Iseult, Sean and Joséphine Pillon, the maid, had also left London with her for Dublin on 23 November. They had all been staying in Woburn Buildings after Maud, released from Holloway prison, had stayed a short while – less than a week – in the nursing home to which she had been sent on account of the recurrence of her tuberculosis.
3.  **The James**: Iseult may have been typing some of the extended commentary on Henry James which appeared in the August 1918 edition of the *Little Review*.
4.  **de Boschère**: Jean de Bosschère, a French artist, illustrator and poet then living in London; he praised Pound as a poet and scholar in three articles published in the *Egoist* in 1917.
5.  **Uncle W and Moura's fight**: Moura was Iseult's name for her mother. The Yeatses had been renting Maud Gonne's house, 73 St Stephen's Green. He had written to her on 2 October 'George & I have taken your Dublin house at £2.10.0 a week ... for four months. Should you be released and allowed to live in Ireland

we will move out which strangers would not.' When Maud arrived wanting shelter Yeats refused to have her in the house because he was afraid police raids would have an adverse effect on his wife, pregnant and now seriously sick with pneumonia. The doctor had said Maud's presence might endanger George's life.

6. **The Lord Mayor's intervention:** with the authorities, persuading them to leave Maud Gonne free. See note on him above, p. 233.
7. **She has gone... a week in Wicklow:** to stay with Ella Young near Lough Dan.
8. **the doctor's house:** Dr Lynn's house, see note above.
9. **Sophia:** Joséphine Pillon, the maid from Normandy, who had travelled to Dublin with them.
10. **Delany's room:** Barry Delaney or O'Delaney who had acted as Maud's secretary in Paris and had arranged the lease of the St Stephen's Green house to the Yeatses.
11. **Jacky:** Sean MacBride.
12. **Countess Markiewicz:** See note, pp. 187, 203, 209, 211. She was the first woman to be elected an MP but did not take her seat at Westminster. She was a member of the Dail from 1923.
13. **Helen:** Helen Molony. See note on her, p. 187. She had been deeply upset by the death of her close friend Sean Connolly, an Abbey actor, who was killed in the attempt to take Dublin Castle in the Easter Rising. Yeats alludes to him as 'The player Connolly', in 'Three Songs to the one Burden' (*YP*, p. 454).
14. **Lennox Robinson:** See note on him, p. 221.
15. **Et je t'aime... mon cœur:** And I love you and I embrace you with all my heart.
16. **Raconte moi... tu fais:** Tell me what you're doing.

## 5

1. **pity or terror:** a reference to Aristotle's definition of tragedy in the *Poetics* as the imitation of an action that is serious and also complete in itself, having magnitude. It was written in poetic language, and in dramatic rather than narrative presentation, incorporating incidents arousing pity and fear through which it accomplished the catharsis of such emotions. (Here catharsis is difficult to translate; it means purgation or purification or both. It can be argued that this catharsis does not apply to the audience so much as to the purgation of the guilt attached to the hero's tragic act.)
2. **more beastliness between M&W:** a continuation of the quarrel over 73 St Stephen's Green.
3. **Poor George is better:** When she had recovered enough the Yeatses moved, as the lease had stipulated, on 10 December, to 96 St Stephen's Green. Maud went to stay with Ella Young (see note, p. 188) near Lough Dan in County Wicklow and from there wrote Yeats what he called venomous letters, accusing him of unpatriotic cowardice. Cumann na mBan, the women's organisation, went so far as to accuse him of conspiring with Shortt, the Chief Secretary for Ireland, to have Maud shut up in an English sanatorium so that he could retain her house. In turn he described her as suffering from neurasthenia (see note, p. 220). Eventually some semblance of peace ensued as Iseult recorded in a later letter to Pound (see pp. 145 and (translation) 237–8).
4. **the noble Alexis ... electioneering:** Sean MacBride, involved in canvassing for Countess Markiewicz in the election held on 14 December in which Sinn Fein achieved a notable victory over the Irish Parliamentary Party and the Unionists.
5. **Et puis je deviens... vrai:** and then I become shy to tell you that I love you – because it's true.

6

1. **even greener:** Here is Dorothy Shakespear's impression of him when he visited the Shakespears on 16 February 1909:

> He has a wonderful, beautiful face, a high forehead, prominent over the eyes; a long delicate nose, with little, red nostrils; a strange mouth, never still, & quite elusive; a square chin, slightly cleft in the middle – the whole face pale; the eyes gray-blue; the hair golden-brown, and curling in soft wavy crinkles. (Notebook quoted in Humphrey Carpenter, *A Serious Character. The Life of Ezra Pound* (1988), 8106.)

Iris Barry, however, concurred with Iseult about the colour of his eyes, describing him in 'The Ezra Pound period', *Bookman* (NY), Oct. 1931, 'with his exuberant hair, pale cat like face with the greenish cat-eyes, clearing his throat, making strange sounds and cries in his talking but otherwise always quite formal.'

2. **qui sourit...toi?...tout ça:** And who smiles like you? But this is purely literary.

3. **Helen:** probably Helen Molony.

4. **Is America not so far as the East?:** This suggests some discussions of the possibility of Pound returning to America. Humphrey Carpenter, *A Serious Character. The Life of Ezra Pound* (1988), p. 376, describes Pound's discontent with living in London in September 1920 and his speculation about returning to America and supporting himself there by lecturing: a choice of giving up 'every shred of comfort, every scrap of personal life'; yet to remain in London might be mere 'masochism'. Iseult's question suggests Pound may have been considering such a move earlier, in 1918, to, as he put it in a later letter of 8 November to John Quinn, 'in the face of all too damn tumultuous seas and boat-rates emigrate and on the quayed and basket-covered banks of bleak Manhattan, chase the trade of letters.' 'The East' may have been mentioned as a possibility of Pound's and Yeats's interest in Japanese drama, stimulated by Pound's meeting Ernest Fenollosa's widow Mary in 1913; she gave Pound permission to edit and publish Fenollosa's notebooks, on which he worked in the winter of 1913–14 at Stone Cottage in Sussex when acting as Yeats's secretary. The Noh plays influenced Yeats's own *Four Plays for Dancers* (1921), the first of which was played in London in 1916. Yeats was to receive an invitation in July 1919 to spend two years as a lecturer in English Literature at Keio Gijuken University in Tokyo: at first he thought of accepting it, and, despite the reservations of Pound, John Butler Yeats and Quinn, did so tentatively on 9 August. See Iseult's query to Pound in her letter of 11 August as to whether he would also be going to Japan, p. 146. Once the Yeatses settled in 4 Broad Street, Oxford in the autumn, however, the Japanese adventure seems to have receded. In November Mrs Yeats had her doubts (see Ann Saddlemyer, *Becoming George. The Life of Mrs W.B. Yeats* (2002), p. 234 and notes 23 and 24, p. 720. Yeats wrote to John Quinn on 31 December 1919 to say 'I think Japan has faded.'

5. **Our house:** 73 St Stephen's Green, Dublin.

6. **tomorrow:** They moved into 73 St Stephen's Green on 11 December, the Yeatses having left for 96 St Stephen's Green on the previous day.

7. **M. and W.:** Maud Gonne and Yeats.

8. **Russel:** George W. Russell. See note, p. 211.

9. **The O'Neills:** Joseph O'Neill (1886–1953), educated in Galway, Manchester and Germany, began work as an Inspector of primary schools in Ireland in 1907, and became Permanent Secretary to the Irish Department of Education in 1923. His

successful novels included *Wind from the North* (1934), which won the Harmsworth
Award of the Irish Academy of Letters, and *Land under England* (1935). His wife,
Mary Devenport O'Neill, also came from Galway; educated at the National
College of Art, Dublin, she wrote verse plays (among them *Blue Beard* (1933) and
*Cain* (1945). Her poetry included *Prometheus* (1929). They lived in Kenilworth
Square, Rathgar, Dublin, their house often a centre for literary discussion.

10. **Propertius**: Sextus Propertius (54–48 B.C.–d. before A.D. 2) was born at Assisi; his
poems idealised Cynthia (actually Hostia) who proved faithless and he broke
with her after five or six years of a stormy relationship. A protégé of Maecenas,
he wrote four books of *Elegies*, the second and third mainly concerned with his
troubled love, his quarrels with Cynthia; the fourth one contains two poems
about her. His style changed with his subject matter. Iseult may have been influenced in her reading of him by Pound who was writing his adaptations of
passages from the second and third *Elegies* of Propertius (*Homage to Sextus Propertius*
(dated 1917, published 1919 and finally in 1934) and see note on Mrs Patmore's
letter above, p. 232.) They probably stemmed from his writing a *Kompleat Kulture*
programme for Iris Barry in 1916. He had written to her that if she couldn't find
any decent translations of Catullus and Propertius he supposed he would 'have
to rig up something.' These poems mark a greater erotic content in Pound's
writing. It can only be a matter of speculation whether his love affair with Iseult
had this effect on him. He seems to have seen Propertius as a rebel like himself,
who preferred to write his feverishly passionate lyrics rather than accede to his
patron's request for praise for the Empire. Pound's poems were attacked for their
inaccuracy though sometimes some of the howlers were deliberate, as for
instance 'votes' for the Latin 'vates' and the introduction of 'a frigidaire parent.'
(See M.J. Alexander, *The Poetic Achievement of Ezra Pound* (1979), pp. 30–2, 108–14
and 201.)

11. **Plowman**: *The Vision concerning Piers Plowman*, an alliterative poem existing in
three versions, attributed to William Langland who lived near Malvern and is
supposed to have written the poem between 1360 and 1399. When wandering
on the Malvern Hills the poet sees a vision of Truth as a high tower, of Wrong
as a deep dungeon and the earth as a fair field full of folk, between. In a second
vision Piers Plowman offers to guide the pilgrims (who seek Truth, having been
preached to by Conscience and Repentance) if they help him to plough his
half-acre.

12. **my lack of appreciation of his suitor**: Lennox Robinson. See Iseult's letter to Yeats,
p. 116. Robinson fell deeply in love with Iseult and Yeats advised her to recon-
sider her rejection of him. See Ann Saddlemyer *Becoming George. The Life of Mrs W.B.
Yeats* (2002), p. 236, and see 'Uncle W.'s matrimonial scheme', p. 142.

13. **Lily Yeats . . . the feeling is now mutual**: The poet's sister Lily Yeats (see note,
p. 177). She and her sister Lolly (see note, p. 117) had invited Iseult to supper
(with Lennox Robinson) at Gurteen Dhas, their house at Churchtown, County
Dublin; and after this she wrote on 10 November to her father, John Butler Yeats,
then living in New York, describing Iseult as having 'very little self-confidence,
as indolent and something of a charming humbug – enormously tall and rather
gaunt – like Maud, says little but looks much – she hates politics and her mother's
political friends – so can't be very happy – her position is too uncomfortable'
(National Library of Ireland, MS 31, 112). See also Iseult's letter to Yeats, p. 117.

14. **'because it is a custom . . . one living man'**: a quotation from Pound's *Homage
to Sextus Propertius*.

15. **mais qu'est ce que ça... tout**: But how does all that affect you? And how does it affect me, after all, so little, but do I know what amuses you? I never really knew you and now I even forget what you look like. I only know you have something very fine about you. All the same I embrace you... and I love you so much.

**7**
1. **Helen**: Helen Molony.
2. **the Dr's house**: Dr Lynn's, see note, p. 226.
3. **pantherine poem**: This poem to Iseult has not been traced.
4. **cockrooch**: depression, French, *cafard*. See note, p. 183.
5. **Ezra chaque jour...t'embrrasse**: Ezra, every day I love you a little more than the day before in spite of the fact that I have forgotten how you laugh and my God how stupid it is that you are so far away and to think that more or less it will always be like that. Without courage. I embrace you. Maurice.

**8**
1. **Mme [? Champion]**: not identified.
2. **Uncle Theseus**: not identified.
3. **The O'Neills and Helen**: see notes p. 235 and p. 187.
4. **the cockrooch**: depression, see note, p. 183.
5. **Sara Purser**: Sarah Henrietta Purser (1848–1943), a portrait painter and socially influential in Dublin, was known for her wit (to which, Yeats thought, she fastened 'like a pair of wings, brutality', *Memoirs*, ed. Denis Donoghue, (1972), pp. 43–4). Her portrait of Maud Gonne, fashionably dressed and complete with monkey, dated about 1888, is in the National Gallery of Ireland, Dublin. It has been reproduced in various biographies of Maud Gonne, including those by Samuel Levenson (1975), Nancy Cardozo (1979) and Margaret Ward (1990). There is a more vigorous, dashing portrait of Maud Gonne by her which was reproduced in Joseph Hone, *W.B. Yeats 1865–1939* (1942), p. 96. She was a friend of the Yeats family and in 1907 organised an exhibition of works by Nathaniel Hone and John Butler Yeats; this ran from 2 October to 3 November and was very successful, greatly increasing Yeats's reputation. With Edward Martyn, the landlord and playwright, she founded in 1903 the Tower of Glass (*Au tur Gloire*), a cooperative situated in 24 Upper Pembroke Street, Dublin; one of its first commissions was to design the stained glass for the vestibule of the Abbey Theatre; its early work was mainly undertaken for St Brendan's, the new cathedral at Loughrea, County Galway, largely the creation of Father Jeremiah O'Donovan (1871–1942) who left Ireland and the church for a literary life in London where he married Beryl Verschoyle. George Moore's novel *The Lake* (1905) was based on him. An undervalued novelist, his *Father Ralph* (1913) is autobiographical; *Waiting* (1914) may reflect his marrying a Protestant; *Vocations* (1921) and *The Holy Tree* (1922) are worth reading. He became Rose Macaulay's lover.
6. **Kaki**: possibly some personal allusion, could it refer to some soldier (khaki)?
7. **Alexis**: Sean MacBride.
8. **Et tout ça ne t'interesse...**: And all this doesn't interest you, nor me either. I read the very bad poems of my new friends, and also plays worse again than the poems. I am enclosing a copy of the one poem which is worth anything by Madame O'Neill. What do you think of it. I don't read anything for a thought but I have known as it were sadder days (as in the song) 'soit qu'on etait tout seul' [although one was alone']. Moura and Willy have ended their quarrel by

writing a definitive letter to each other, in the Noble Viking Style in Moura's case, in the noble dying Bayard style in Willy's. And they both say that they will never speak to each other again apart from flat excuses. Tell me if we quarrel like that? [or, Tell me, should we not quarrel like that?] Do you want to? We would say horrible things to each other and we would call on all our friends to be witnesses and then we'd become very noble and cold and then we'd wait for the excuses. No, life's too short. And although it lacks dignity I kiss you in your ear. Maurice. Excuse the paper and soon you won't love me any more.

9. **Mme O'Neill:** Mary Devenport O'Neill, see note on the O'Neills, p. 235.
10. **Bayard:** There are two possible explanations of what Iseult may have been referring to. The more likely is Pierre du Terrail, Seigneur de Bayard, who was born near Grenoble *c.* 1473. He gained fame in the wars of Charles VIII, Louis XII and Francis I, distinguishing himself at Fornoue, Canossa, Agnadel and Brescia. His bravery and generosity earned him the nickname of *chevalier sans peur et sans reproche.* With a small garrison he defended Mézières against the army of Charles V, consisting of a hundred thousand men. (There is an impressive statue of him in Mézières.) He died in 1524, killed by a shot from an arquebus at Abbiategrasso. On the other hand, she may have had in mind Boiardo's *Orlando Innamorato* (1487) and Ariosto's sequel to it, *Orlando Furioso* (1532) where Bayard or Baiardo was a magic horse given by the Emperor Charlemagne to Renaud or Rinaldo, the eldest son of Aymon, Count of Dordogne. Aymon's four sons carried on his war against Charlemagne; beleaguered in Montaubon, they were pardoned on condition that Renaud would fight against the Saracens and surrender Bayard. The horse, however, refused to allow anyone else to mount him and when he was thrown into a river, weighted down with stones by order of the Emperor, he made his escape, Renaud going to Palestine where, after various knightly exploits he ended up as a hermit. The name Bayard became used as a type of extreme chivalry, even recklessness in a mock heroic allusive way.

**9**

1. **Friday:** this is probably a part of a letter written in early 1919.
2. **failure of American tour:** See note on Letter 6, p. 235.
3. **Mr and Mrs O'Neill:** See note, p. 235.

**10**

1. **Monsieur [? Jamier's] imbecility:** he has not been identified.
2. **3 weeks' camping in the Wicklow hills:** presumably in the neighbourhood of Lough Dan or Glenmalure. To Yeats she wrote that she would 'live in a tent, scrub saucepans, shake bracken for a bed, read Herodotus and walk in the heather and paddle in the rivers' if she had her choice of the kind of life to live for ever. See p. 115. But she may have been staying in a cottage near Lough Dan or in Barravore in Glenmalure.
3. **Dove lei?:** (*Italian*): where are you?
4. **also going to Japan:** Yeats had been offered a lectureship there in July 1919. See note 4 on Letter 6, p. 235.

**11**

1. **67 Fitzwilliam Square:** Iseult had rented a flat in this house.
2. **je suis une brute ... plume:** Ezra, I'm a brute! And its very nice of you to write to me again like that. I take up my most beautiful pen.

3. **que je reste...paresse**: That I remain your friend till death in spite of my laziness.
4. **Russell**: George W. Russell. See note, p. 211.
5. **Francis**: Francis (occasionally 'Harry') Stuart (1902–2000) whom Iseult married in Dublin on 6 April 1920. See note on him, p. 221.
6. **The Dial**: A literary journal founded in Chicago in 1880; it moved to New York in 1918 and ran till 1929. It championed the modern movement and published many distinguished authors. Pound found and recommended material for it in England.
7. **la vita strania**: (*Italian*) strange life.
8. **heiress in February**: Dolores Veronica Stuart was born at 73 St Stephen's Green on 9 March 1921; she died of meningitis on 24 July 1921.
9. **Jean Jacques...assistance publique**: Iseult is referring to Jean Jacques Rousseau (1712–78), the political philosopher who, when he arrived in Paris in 1741, began an association with a maid working in his hostelry, Thérèse le Vasseur. He had five children by her whom he dispatched to a foundling hospital (hence Iseult's phrase *assistance publique*, the poor law administration), something ironical in a writer whose educational theories, put forward in his novel *Emile* (1762), had such a strong influence in Europe, those swayed by them including Richard Lovell Edgeworth, Froebel and Pestalozzi. After success with his opera *Le Devin du Village* (1752) Rousseau had written his novel *La Nouvelle Héloise* (1761) and his most famous work *Contrat Social* (1762) which became, in effect, the Bible of the French Revolution. His *Confessions* (1781) were, for the time, unusually frank; he wrote them in England where he was the guest of David Hume from 1766 to 1767. His later work included the self-justificatory *Rousseau, juge de Jean Jacques* and the relatively calm *Rêveries*, a continuation of the more sensational *Confessions*.
10. **Comment va la vie... les amours**: How's life, how are the love affairs?
11. **London... with May**: Maud's cousin May Bertie-Clay had a house in London. See *GYL*, p. 227 for Maud's comment in 1906 on her cousin's unhappy marriage.

# Select Bibliography

Abbot, Evelyn. *Pericles and the Golden Age of Athens.* G.P. Putnam & Sons, 1892.

Alexander, Michael. *The Poetic Achievement of Ezra Pound.* Faber & Faber, 1979.

Alexander, Tania. *An Estonian Childhood.* Cape, 1987.

Cardozo, Nancy. *Maud Gonne. Lucky Eyes and a High Heart.* Victor Gollancz, Ltd, 1979.

Carpenter, Humphrey. *A Serious Character. The Life of Ezra Pound.* Faber and Faber, 1988.

Elborn, Geoffrey. *Francis Stuart: A Life.* Raven Arts Press, 1990.

Foster, Roy. *Modern Ireland 1600–1972.* Allen Lane, Penguin Press, 1988.

Foster, Roy. *W.B. Yeats: A Life. I. The Apprentice Mage; II. The Arch-poet.* Oxford University Press, 1997; 2003.

Harding, James. *The Astonishing Adventures of General Boulanger.* W.H. Allen, 1971.

Hone, Joseph. *W.B. Yeats 1865–1939.* Macmillan, 1942.

Hutchins, Patricia. *Ezra Pound's Kensington.* Faber & Faber, 1965.

Jeffares, A. Norman. *A New Commentary on the Poems of W.B. Yeats.* Macmillan (now Palgrave Macmillan), revised edn, 1984.

Jeffares, A. Norman. *W.B. Yeats: Man and Poet.* Gill and Macmillan, 3rd edn, 1996.

Jeffares, A. Norman. *W.B. Yeats: A New Biography.* Hutchinson, 1988; Continuum, revised edn, 2001.

Jeffares, A. Norman. 'Iseult', *Borderlands.* (eds Davis Coakley and Mary O'Doherty). Royal College of Surgeons in Ireland, 2002.

Jeffares, A. Norman. 'Iseult Gonne' *Yeats Annual,* No 16. Palgrave Macmillan, forthcoming 2004.

Kelly, John. *The Collected Letters of W.B. Yeats* (general editor). Oxford University Press, 1986–.

Kenner, Hugh. *The Pound Era.* University of California Press, 1974.

Levenson, Samuel. *Maud Gonne.* Cassell, 1997.

Londraville, Janis and Richard. *Too Long a Sacrifice. The Letters of Maud Gonne and John Quinn* (eds). Susquehanna University Press and Associated University Presses, 1999.

Lyons, F.S.L. *Ireland Since the Famine.* Fontana/Collins, 1975.

MacBride, Maud Gonne. *A Servant of the Queen. Reminiscences.* ed. A. Norman Jeffares and Anna MacBride White. Colin Smythe, 1994.

Mullins, Eustace. *This Difficult Individual, Ezra Pound.* Fleet Publishing Corporation, 1961.

Mulvihill, Margaret. *Charlotte Despard: A Biography.* Pandora, 1989.

Pound, Ezra. *The London Years 1908–1920* (ed. Philip Grover). AMS Press, 1978.

Praeger, R. Lloyd. *The Way that I Went.* Hodges Figges, 1937.

de Rachewiltz, Mary. *Discretions.* Faber & Faber, 1971.

Reid, B.L. *The Man from New York, John Quinn and His Friends.* Oxford University Press, New York, 1968.

Saddlemyer, Ann. *Becoming George. The Life of Mrs W.B. Yeats.* Oxford University Press, 2002.

Stock, Noel. *The Life of Ezra Pound.* Routledge & Kegan Paul, 1970.

Stuart, Francis. *Black List, Section H.* Southern Illinois University Press, 1971.

Stuart, Francis. *The Wartime Broadcasts of Francis Stuart. 1942–1944.* (ed. Brendan Barrington). Lilliput Press, 2000.

Stuart, Iseult Gonne. 'Five Letters from Iseult Gonne Stuart'. *Journal of Irish Literature,* V, 1 Jan. 1976.

Stuart, Madeleine. *Manna in the Morning: A Memoir* (ed. Dermot Bolger). Raven Arts Press, 1984.

Toomey, Deirdre. *Yeats and Women* (ed.) Macmillan Press and St Martin's Press (now Palgrave Macmillan), 2nd edn, 1997.

Wade, Allan. *The Letters of W.B. Yeats* (ed.). Rupert Hart-Davis, 1954.

White, Anna MacBride and A. Norman Jeffares. *The Gonne–Yeats Letters 1893–1938. Always Your Friend.* Hutchinson, 1992.

Yeats, W.B. *Autobiographies.* Macmillan, 1955.

Yeats, W.B. *Memoirs* (ed. Denis Donoghue). Macmillan, 1972.

Yeats, W.B. *A Vision and Related Writings* (ed. A. Norman Jeffares) Arena, 1990.

Yeats, W.B. *Yeats's Poems.* (ed. A. Norman Jeffares, with an Appendix by Warwick Gould). Macmillan (now Palgrave Macmillan), 3rd edn, 1996.

Young, Ella. *The Flowering Dusk.* Longmans, Green 1945. Her other work includes *The Coming of Lug,* 1909; *Celtic Wonder Tales,* 1910; and *The Rose of Heaven,* 1920.

## Primary sources

MacBride family papers (including Maud Gonne MacBride's second unpublished volume of autobiography); l' Évêche de Laval Archives; Thora Forrester (née Pilcher) family papers, letters to Anna MacBride White and her unpublished *Memoirs of A Quiet Lady*; Kay Bridgwater (née Stuart) family papers and notes; Crime Branch Special papers (CBS), State Paper Office, Dublin; Military Archives, Dublin (transcripts and summaries of foreign wireless broadcasts and personal file on Francis and Iseult Stuart); National Archives, Dublin (file on Francis Stuart: German Broadcasts to Ireland); Francis Stuart Collection, University of Coleraine; New York Public Library (Berg Collection); Public Record Office, London (WO 76/10–13 00 2894); National Library of Ireland (*Visions Notebooks*), Ethel Mannin papers.

# Index